FIVE GREAT PLAYS
FROM THE RUSSIAN THEATRE

THE STONE GUEST   The tale of Don Juan, transformed by Pushkin's unique stamp and a distinctly Russian flavor

THE INSPECTOR GENERAL   Gogol's richly humorous, devastatingly satiric attack on official corruption and bureaucracy

A MONTH IN THE COUNTRY   Psychological penetration and sensitivity reveal the unhappiness beneath a calm surface in Turgenev's drama of frustrated loves

THE THUNDERSTORM   Ostrovsky's tragedy of the ruin of a dreamy young wife, misunderstood, persecuted and driven to desperation

THE POWER OF DARKNESS   Sin and expiation are the themes of Tolstoy's piercing drama of murder and brutality among Russian peasants

The Library of World Drama presents these outstanding dramatic works in vivid new translations.

THE LIBRARY OF WORLD DRAMA

JOHN GASSNER

Sterling Professor of
Dramatic Literature
Yale University

GENERAL EDITOR

19th CENTURY
RUSSIAN DRAMA

TRANSLATED BY
ANDREW MacANDREW

WITH AN INTRODUCTION
AND PREFACES BY
MARC SLONIM

BANTAM BOOKS / NEW YORK

19TH CENTURY RUSSIAN DRAMA

A Bantam Book / published January 1963

Library of Congress Catalog Card Number: 63-8351

Bantam Books are published by Bantam Books, Inc. Its trade-mark, consisting of the words "Bantam Books" and the portrayal of a bantam, is registered in the United States Patent Office and in other countries. Marca Registrada. Printed in the United States of America. Bantam Books, Inc., 271 Madison Ave., New York 16, N. Y.

CONTENTS

19th Century Russian Drama

"Before Chekhov" in World Drama

BY

JOHN GASSNER

It is not at all amazing that the Russian drama for most American readers starts (and frequently also *ends*) with Chekhov. "Before Chekhov" there is a void so far as they know that has not even been filled by two good but short-lived professional productions of a Turgenev masterpiece, *A Month in the Country,* and by a successful presentation of Tolstoy's *The Living Corpse* staged in 1918 under the title of *Redemption* with John Barrymore in the main role of Fedya.

The American public continues to have a remote impression of Gogol's great political satire of the year 1836, *The Inspector General,* an impression apparently compounded of a Danny Kaye harlequinade and a Hollywood "screen treatment." The most famous names on the roster of Russian playwrights before Chekhov fall into two categories: either the playwright is remembered for his nondramatic writing or he is simply unknown. Turgenev and Tolstoy owe their reputations to their novels rather than their plays, even though Turgenev's study of frustration, *A Month in the Country,* excels most European realistic plays and Tolstoy's peasant tragedy, *The Power of Darkness* (1886), is probably the most powerful "naturalistic" drama except Hauptmann's *The Weavers,* which followed six years later. Indeed, even more experienced playwrights than Turgenev and Tolstoy would have had considerable difficulty achieving dramatic equivalents for the former's *Fathers and Sons* and the latter's *War and Peace* and *Anna Karenina.* Gogol's dramatic masterpiece, *The Inspector General,* has also been overshadowed by a nondramatic one, his memorable picaresque novel *Dead Souls* (1842); and Pushkin, who wrote several brilliant one-act plays as well as the quasi-Shakespearian chronicle play *Boris Godunov,* is justifiably best remembered as a poet. It is worth noting that the Russian drama continued to derive much sustenance from short story writers, novelists, and poets who turned to playwriting.

The American public has had little acquaintance with writers whose chief work was dramatic, such as Fonvizin, whose comedies

1

The Brigadier General and *The Minor* made him the first important writer of comedy in the Russian language, and Griboyedov, who is famous for the Molièresque comedy *Wit from Woe*. This comedy (also translated as *Wit Works Woe* and *The Trouble with Reason*) was written in 1825, although printed eight years later and then only in strongly censored form. Other gifted Russian playwrights, such as Kobylin, Pisemsky, and Saltykov, are not even "names" to the English-speaking public. Only Ostrovsky, playwright-laureate of the Russian middle-class, has had some réclame, although he made an impression outside the Slavic theater only with the merchant-class tragedy *The Thunderstorm* (or *The Storm*) produced in 1859.

That the plays in the present volume provide welcome preparation for appreciating Chekhov's major works for the stage will be apparent. Only Pushkin's miniature Don Juan tragedy *The Stone Guest* stands outside the nineteenth-century Russian tradition of a type of realism that is enlivened with humor and spiced with satire but blended with a genuine feeling for human character. And even *The Stone Guest* partakes of one quality present in many a pre-Chekhovian and Chekhovian play in reflecting a critical and rebellious spirit—the spirit of Pushkin's Don Juan. The plays in this collection, nevertheless, claim our attention in their own right rather than as works ancillary to a study of Chekhov's dramaturgy. The qualities they foreshadow in Chekhov's work are qualities cherishable for their own sake, and they may be found here and there in sharper focus than in Chekhov's plays.

The Inspector General possesses a vivacity and breadth of observation distinctly Gogol's; only in Dickens is one likely to encounter as free and imaginative a talent in nineteenth-century European writing, and Gogol transferred this talent to the stage with what appears to have been instinctive ease and rightness. The mastery of nuance in Turgenev's *A Month in the Country*, a play written in 1849 nearly forty years before the Moscow Art Theater's first triumphant production of *The Sea Gull,* is as complete as Chekhov's. The sense of isolation and frustration is as pervasive, the restiveness as keen, and the rebellion as hesitant yet irrepressible as it is in *Uncle Vanya.* Only the rich, uniquely Chekhovian texture of humor is absent in *A Month in the Country,* and this merely makes Turgenev's play more distinctive.

Tolstoy's vehemence in drama, his didacticism, and his angry compassionateness are the distinctive qualities of his latter-day style when he developed an exacting personal morality with which he alienated the Czar, the Greek Orthodox hierarchy, and his long-suffering wife with approximately equal success. Tolstoy succeeded in doing the impossible in *The Power of Darkness* when he made didacticism, normally a stumbling block to dramatic power, a basis for tragic art. In 1886, six decades before the appearance of Arthur Miller's *Death of a Salesman,* Tolstoy created tragedy with patently "low," rather than exalted, characters; and what Miller aimed at, Tolstoy achieved with that naturalness, that easy authoritativeness, which is the mark of nearly all his non-polemical writing. Rebellion against the tyranny of the family, the narrow "bourgeois" family that has been the cause of intramural rebellion in plays since the eighteenth century, attains vivid reality in Ostrovsky's *The Thunderstorm*. Rebellion in this work is accompanied by as much compassion as realism and materializes in a form of drama to which the Russian theater appears to have been singularly attuned— namely, "middle-class tragedy," a genre developed in Europe since the times of Diderot, George Lillo, and Lessing, and peculiarly suited to the nineteenth- and twentieth-century stage.

As in the other arts, we are apt to encounter in the drama a felicitous combination of individual and representative qualities. In the Russian drama of the nineteenth century we find this combination especially noteworthy. In the present volume, for example, Pushkin's little work, *The Stone Guest,* represents the perennial *rapprochement* with poetry which is naturally most pronounced when the subject is tragic, the literary climate romantic, and the author a poet. The drama, it may be said, aspires toward the estate of poetry. But there are times and occasions when the theater calls for an anti-heroic, therefore often anti-poetic, approach to reality, and such is the case when there are strong incitements to satire. *The Inspector General* is one of world drama's outstanding satires. Gogol's shafts of laughter are directed at a target of some consequence, specifically the political and social corruption that was widespread in nineteenth-century Russia and most marked in the provinces. And in this respect *The Inspector General* is an especially representative work, for the play constitutes "social drama" and provides the kind of theater that appealed to the democratic tendencies of the nineteenth century. Its culmination was in the "critical realism" of Ibsen, Björnson, and Shaw. Gogol's satire, at the same time that it is realistic, also recovers some lost ground for poetry with its power of extravaganza or imaginative exaggeration, so that humdrum matter acquires originality, drab manners acquire color, and depressing subjects gain vivacity. It is worth noting that the transmuting, if not exactly transcending, power of realistic satire has continued to enliven the theater well into our own times. At least the satires, and *The Inspector General* was by far the best of the non-musical ones until the advent of George Bernard Shaw in the 1890's, provided some *poésie de théâtre* in exchange for the verbal poetry that went out with the arrival of realism in the theater.

Turgenev's play reflects the development of realism that began to affect significantly the novel decades before it impinged upon the nineteenth-century drama. The realistic novels of Stendhal and Balzac came some decades before Turgenev wrote *A Month in the Country,* and his own early ventures in fiction, notably *A Sportman's Sketches,* also preceded the play. Even so, however, *A Month in the Country* is one of the very earliest works for the stage that is realistic in the best sense of the term. It is not a "problem play" contrived by an author to support some thesis but rather an unfolding of life and a sensitive response to those manifestations of failure that are seemingly undramatic and those behavioral turbulences that explode into "dramatic action."

Tolstoy's play, by contrast, is "melodramatic" with its swirl of lust, bestiality, and murder. Yet the force of reality is ever present in the work and it permeates both the details of the environment and the peasant characters. In other words, the action possesses a high degree of credibility along with its high voltage. This is the "big naturalism" Strindberg had in mind in one of his famous critical essays. From this elevated "realism," there was a general decline in the theater and it is on a lower plane, on some *plateau* of realism, that most modern playwrights have erected their plays. At their best, they have provided more pathos than tragedy and more private drama than drama pyramided on commanding passions, crimes, and purgations. Ostrovsky's *The Thunderstorm* graces this plateau of realistic playwriting even while representing it, for its emotional force rises as high as the characters and the environment will permit. In Russia, as elsewhere in the Western theater, the theatrical landscape generally sank below Ostrovsky's plateau.

In the last analysis, however, it is the individuality of each representative achievement that must be the most immediate and valuable experience for the reader, the playgoer, and the producer of these plays. Ultimately this experience is subjective, although it cannot be effectively subjective without an objective reading of the play. It is necessary to stress the fact that *The Stone Guest* is *poetry,* as well as drama, and, like most poetry, is not easily translatable; even Russian actors as expert as Stanislavsky had difficulty in doing justice to Pushkin's verse.

In the case of *The Inspector General,* the variety of the

characterizations is matched by the exactitude of the portrayal of the rogues and dupes; there is exactitude even in caricature when it is successful, although Gogol's characters are not so much caricatured as "theatricalized." The light-minded protagonist of the comedy, Khlestakov, has been called "one of the great characters of Russian literature." He was incisively described by D. S. Mirsky in his *History of Russian Literature* as "the most alive of all the characters of Russian fiction [an exaggeration, I believe]—meaningless movement and meaningless fermentation incarnate, on a foundation of placidly ambitious inferiority." And perhaps Gogol's greatest feat in writing this play is that it should be so attractive despite "the absence of all love interest and of sympathetic characters," as Prince Mirsky put it.

The autobiographical element in *A Month in the Country*— Turgenev was Rakitin in his relationship with the famous opera singer Madame Viardot whom he followed slavishly all over Europe—seems largely responsible for the intimate reality and the rueful tone of the work. Its authenticity is such that it seems to have poured out of Turgenev, who apparently wrote the play more for himself than for the stage. At the same time it is important to realize that Turgenev was not wallowing in sentiment or seeking "morbid gain" from his playwriting. Like other great artists, he could be subjective and objective at the same time; he could be both inside and outside his own character. It might be well to heed Michael Redgrave, who played Rakitin in London in 1943, when he declares (in an introduction to Emlyn Williams' British adaptation) that "The essence of the play is, I am persuaded, comic and anti-romantic."

As for the *The Power of Darkness*, which has been criticized for Tolstoy's ultra-realistic use of superfluous details and allegedly strained peasant dialect, it is important to observe how poetic Tolstoy's naturalism becomes as a result of his ability to evoke atmosphere and mood, and this not by poetic but by dramatic means. It is the characters that produce the effect, sustaining in their passion and remorse the very didacticism of this mainly undisguised morality play, the subtitle of which calls attention to the power of one initial error or crime to multiply or compound itself. As for *The Thunderstorm*, we cannot afford to allow the individuality of the play to be obscured by its typicality as one of a number of studies of the merchant class by Ostrovsky. Its localization is poetic as well as "real" and the literary historian Mirsky was not altogether excessive in defining it as "a purely atmospheric" work or a "poem of love and death, of freedom and thralldom." It would appear that Ostrovsky, whose other plays have aroused less enthusiasm, managed for once to live beyond his artistic income in writing *The Thunderstorm.*

Readers, assisted by Professor Slonim in the present volume, will have no difficulty in arriving at the conclusion that the Russian drama deserves to be considered an important segment of modern drama. This was the case even before Chekhov removed all possibility of doubt with his turn-of-the-century masterpieces.

Introduction

BY

MARC SLONIM

The roots of the Russian theater can be easily traced to ancient pagan rituals, medieval morality plays and school and court representations of the seventeenth century, but the formal history of the national stage and its repertory does not begin until the eighteenth century. It was then that the Empire hammered out by Peter I finally reached the status of a great European power, and its military victories and diplomatic successes abroad were matched by spectacular achievements in the arts and sciences at home. Peter I, a revolutionary tsar, pushed his country along the road of Western development; under the impact of both his violence and his reforms, literature and theater followed European models. In their beginnings, drama, opera and ballet were led by the French, Italian and German and were patronized by the Empresses. The first Russian dramatic theater was established by Elizabeth I, Peter's daughter, at her court in 1752; she also subsidized theatrical schools and the public stage. In the following decade, and particularly under Catherine II, the number of theatrical ventures in Moscow, St. Petersburg and even in the provinces increased considerably; these included dozens of private companies, mainly recruited from the serfs, on the estates of rich aristocrats. The leading theaters were provided with funds from the treasury and were controlled by a special Imperial Administration. By the middle of the eighteenth century they became a public service and their actors were considered state employees. Thus until the 1917 revolution the Imperial Theaters in St. Petersburg and Moscow were in a privileged position.

The repertory of the Imperial and private theaters during the era of Elizabeth and Catherine was dominated by translations from various European languages, but the multiplication of playhouses served as an incentive to native dramatists. They started by imitating the pseudo-classical drama of the West, and Alexander Sumarokov (1718–1777), called "the Russian Racine," wrote tragedies glorifying mythical heroes and sublime

7

emotions. His poetic style inspired an entire school, and tragedies by such popular authors as Kheraskov, Kniazhnin, Ozerov
and others, moulded on French patterns, were greatly appreciated
by the nobility and the court. It is significant, however, that this
imitative tragedy could never take deep roots in the national
repertory. The Russians have always fared much better with
realistic comedy, and this continues to be true of current Soviet
productions. In the eighteenth century, especially under Catherine
II, the satirical tendency became widespread in literature (the
Empress herself wrote in this vein), and dozens of Russian playwrights followed it. Between 1780 and 1805 Russian comedies
constituted 44% of the billboards of Moscow theaters. In 1782
the actors of the St. Petersburg Imperial company presented *The
Minor* by Denis Fonvizin (1745–1792) on a private stage, and
this memorable date marked the passage from the imitative to
the national phase in the history of Russian drama. Within the
conventional forms of contemporary European comedy, including the unity of place, time and action, Fonvizin depicted real
home-grown provincial squires and ridiculed their backwardness
and ignorance. The bold exposé of social ills, the realistic portrayal of characters, the racy dialogue and biting humor of
The Minor assured its success with audiences. It is not unlike
Molière's *Le Bourgeois Gentilhomme* and has remained a classic
in Russia until the present time.

Satirical comedy in prose was the dominant genre in the second half of the eighteenth century, and *The Minor*, which denounced serfdom and conservative landlords, was followed by
other exposés, among them the excellent *The Slanderer*
(1798) by Vassily Kapnist, which hit at bribery and abuse in the
courts.

The flowering of Russian letters in the nineteenth century was
accompanied by a great intensification of theatrical life. Poetic
schools and esthetic theories clashed in the press, in literary
societies and on the stage. Traditionalists and innovators opposed
each other in prose and verse, and various currents of Romanticism and Classicism fought for dominance in novels, short
stories and plays. The struggle for a "truly national Russian art"
was combined with a satirical indictment of gallo- or anglo-
mania. The Napoleonic wars strengthened this anti-imitative
trend and Russian literature, including drama, acquired more in-
dependence and originality, discovering its own path of development in Pushkin and Gogol.

In the first quarter of the nineteenth century, sentimental
drama, often called lachrymose, competed with the productions
of the "national school." The latter comprised satirical come-

dies by Ivan Krylov (1768–1844), the great writer of popular fables, and by Prince Alexander Shakhovskoy (1777–1846) who wrote exclusively for the stage and laughed at the German-inspired sentimental drama and the French "noble drawing room comedy." In this field the decisive battle was won by Alexander Griboyedov (1795–1829), the author of *Wit Works Woe,* a comedy in brilliant verse with an extraordinary impact. It denounced the high society of Moscow and brought forth a gallery of idle parasites, rabid reactionaries and stupid obscurantists, contrasting them all with Chatsky, a young liberal. When his comedy was finished in 1823, Griboyedov wrote: "In my play there are twenty-five fools to one reasonable man, and this man stands, of course, in conflict with his surroundings." Chatsky, who kept making impassioned speeches, represented a new type of patriotic idealist, a precursor of the radical and revolutionary intelligentsia. The censors detected the subversive spirit of the comedy, and *Wit Works Woe* could not be produced until 1831, two years after Griboyedov's death. An unexpurgated text of the play was not published until 1862, and an unabridged version did not appear in the theaters until seven years later. Despite all this chicanery Griboyedov's masterpiece took the Russian stage by storm. For over a century the part of Chatsky, this "ardent dreamer in the land of eternal snow," has been played by all the great actors, from Karatyghin to Kachalov, while the grotesque characters have been impersonated by the leading comedians of the realistic school.

The romantic drama of the forties was for the most part French or English. The native defenders of Romanticism, such as the rhetorical Kukolnik or Polevoy, although they were successful with the audiences, did not contribute much to Russian dramatic literature. As a matter of fact, romantic plays of literary value, such as Pushkin's little tragedies (see the Preface to *The Stone Guest*), or Lermontov's *Men and Passions, Strange Man* and *Masquerade,* were hardly ever produced. In his *Boris Godunov,* a romantic historical chronicle in a Shakespearian vein, Pushkin expressed the very essence of the Russian spirit and he did it in perfect form. "Truth of passions, likelihood of feelings in imaginary circumstances," as he himself worded it, as well as the impetuous movement of action, made *Boris Godunov* an artistic masterpiece. But except for a couple of casual performances it did not see the footlights until Moussorgsky used it as a book for his famous opera in the seventies. Lermontov, the great Byronic poet of Russia, portrayed in his *Masquerade* (1835) a romantic hero who despises the vices and lies of society but kills his beautiful wife on a mistaken suspicion of unfaithfulness. It took more than eighty years before this drama of passion and jealousy was successfully presented by Meyerhold on the eve of the 1917 revolution.

Instead of true romantic drama the Russians were shown some "pseudo-majestic pieces," as Turgenev put it, or false melodramas in "grand" style filled with incredible coincidences and empty rhetoric. And next to these second-rate productions, which generally originated in Europe, there were dozens of vaudeville plays by domestic scribblers. Some of them had a long life: *Lev Gurych Sinichkin* (1840) by D. Lensky was a smashing hit in the forties and fifties and continued to be a box office success for almost one hundred years. The French farce occupied a large part of the repertory.

On the whole between the beginning and the middle of the century the situation in the Russian theater was rather paradoxical: its spectacular development was not matched by an adequate supply of Russian plays. At the same time the Imperial theaters, particularly the Maly in Moscow and the Alexandrinsky in St. Petersburg, became training grounds for generations of excellent actors, and while the number of playhouses increased throughout the country, audiences underwent a considerable change. Theater ceased to be an exclusive institution for the aristocracy and the nobility (except for the flourishing ballet and, to some degree, the opera), and spectators came now from the intellectuals, the white-collar workers, the middle class and the university students. They applauded frantically the great tragic actor Pavel Mochalov (1800–1848) who held Moscow under his spell and reached his height in *Othello, Hamlet, King Lear* and in Schiller's dramas. But the new audiences also admired and supported another great actor, Mikhail Shchepkin (1788–1863), the leader of the "natural school" (not to be confused with "naturalism"). Many actors became his pupils; he established the tradition of realistic acting in Russia, breaking away from the declamatory pathos and exaggerations of his predecessors, and his influence was felt for several decades, mostly in directing and acting plays by Gogol and Ostrovsky.

The Inspector General by Gogol was produced the same year the censors banned Lermontov's *Masquerade*. Its clamorous success marked the triumph of the natural school. The first performance of *The Inspector General* in 1836 (see the Preface to this comedy), stunned the public with its daring condemnation of the bureaucratic regime and its mockery of the governing officials. But it was also acclaimed by the critics as a continuation and a fresh affirmation of the traditional satirical trend. Belinsky, the great reviewer of the period, wrote that *The*

Minor, Wit Works Woe, and Gogol's *The Inspector General* and *Marriage* stand isolated in Russian dramatic literature—because all the rest is insipid trash. In his opinion Gogol's chief merit was in bringing contemporary reality to the stage. Gogol himself was very critical of the current repertory and exclaimed in one of his articles: "Where is our life, and ourselves with all contemporary passions and particularities? Do we see any reflection of them in the melodrama or the vaudeville?" He was proclaimed the head of the realistic school and had many followers, among them the young Turgenev whose first plays bore a distinct Gogolian imprint. But Gogol's influence on literature in general and on the theater in particular proved to be rather complex. While he affirmed the realistic, true-to-life approach and spoke of small people and trivial incidents in opposition to the cult of the heroic and strange in romantic drama, he also initiated his own cult of the grotesque, of distortions and exaggerations of the comical and the banal. The vast majority of Russian comedies of later years continued in the Gogal tradition.

It was in the fifties, sixties and seventies that the final victory of realism produced a rich flowering of Russian dramatic literature. The leading figure of this period was the great playwright Alexander Ostrovsky (1823–1886), the creator of a truly national repertory and a man whose influence on the Russian stage remains unparalleled. Ostrovsky wrote over fifty original plays, and their scope and range are amazingly wide. He began in 1847 with comedies about a particular social group, the old brand of paternalistic merchants, ignorant and wilful men who were petty tyrants at home and in the shop. He gave vivid portraits of all the variations of the species, and followed with a gallery of their victims. Traditional and stagnant Russia with all its national characteristics came to life in these highly realistic, well-structured plays which reproduced the spoken popular idiom and were meant not for individual reading but for public performance. With the same humor and gusto he wrote his comedies about bureaucrats (*The Profitable Job*), decadent landowners (*Wild Money*), corrupted noblewomen (*Without Dowry, The Ward*), and provincial actors (*The Forest, Talents and Suitors*). In all these works, which provided a wide panorama of Russian society, he combined precise observation with human warmth and enlightened national feeling. He also wrote historical chronicles and poetic legends which inspired many Russian composers (*The Snow Maiden,* for example, became the book for Rimsky-Korsakov's opera). Although he had to wage a bitter fight with the censors and with highly placed snobs who found his plays "too vulgar, smelling of barns and grocery shops," his comedies and dramas had a tremendous success with the public and with the actors. The plays created a whole school of acting, that of "national realism," and the Maly Theater in Moscow with its well-trained performers became "the house of Ostrovsky." Many actors and actresses specialized in the impersonation of despotic heads of families and their simple-hearted victims. Ostrovsky's plays reigned supreme on the Russian stage from the sixties on, and the communist regime did not change this situation. Under the Soviets Ostrovsky remained the most widely and frequently performed Russian playwright.

In contrast to Ostrovsky's productiveness, the second prominent playwright of the period, Alexander Sukhovo-Kobylin (1817–1903), wrote only one trilogy: *Krechinsky Wedding* (1854), a satirical picaresque comedy, *The Case* (1861), a satirical ironical drama, and *Tarelkin's Death* (1869), a satirical fantastic farce. Kobylin's humor, which ranges from light to grim and from realistic to symbolic, his inventiveness, the impelling force of his plots and the emotional intensity of his protagonists make these plays unique in Russian dramatic literature. Next to them in literary merit stands *A Hard Lot* (1859) by Alexey Pisemsky, a drama of peasant life with tragic scenes of crime and repentance, distinguished by stark realism, strong portraiture and religious accents. Two years earlier the prominent Russian satirist Mikhail Saltykov wrote *Death of Pazukhin*, which revolves around the struggle for money at the deathbed of a millionaire. It is a bitter comedy in the grotesque manner of Gogol, but with such accuracy of detail that it was immediately classified as a new achievement of the realistic school.

Historical drama also developed at this time. Already Lev Mey had excelled in this genre as the author of *The Tsar's Bride* (1849) and *Woman of Pskov* (1860), turned later into operas by Rimsky-Korsakov. But a more important contribution was made by Alexey Tolstoy. His trilogy on the "era of troubles" (toward the end of the sixteenth and beginning of the seventeenth centuries), *The Death of Ivan the Terrible* (1866), *Tsar Feodor Ivanovich* (1868) and *Tsar Boris* (1870) followed in part the tradition of Pushkin's *Boris Godunov*. But Alexey Tolstoy, a patrician poet and an esthete, was interested more in psychological than in historical material, and his anti-bureaucratic jibes and national aspirations were pervaded by philosophical, often pessimistic overtones. His heroes always search for a moral justification of their actions and are represented more as human basic types than as products of a given period. The trilogy exerted a considerable influence, however, and gave rise to a number of historical plays. Some of them, such as *The Old Days of Kashir* by Dimitry Averkiev, were box office successes for many years. *Tsar Feodor Ivanovich* became widely popular after its production in 1898 by Stanislavsky who had chosen Tolstoy's drama for the opening of the Moscow Art Theater.

In the eighties and nineties, with the double censorship of the State and the Church, the reactionary administration of the Imperial theaters and the money-centered policy of directors of private institutions, a great number of insignificant though well-made plays were produced by able craftsmen, some of them "dramatists in residence" of large theaters. They had dexterity in concocting stage effects and adapting parts for male and female stars but their dramas and comedies seldom had any literary distinction. Plays by Shpazhinsky, Krylov, Ryzhkov, Potekhin (perhaps the best of the group) were constantly on the boards. This situation provoked a reaction in the nineties: educated society began to yearn for a "literary theater" and audiences welcomed original works. This explains the enthusiastic response to *The Power of Darkness* by Leo Tolstoy (see the preface to this play) and to new European dramas and comedies by so-called "modernists." It was in this atmosphere of criticism and expectation that the first plays by Chekhov, after difficult trials, were finally offered to the public in a new and fitting scenic manner by the Moscow Art Theater at the very end of the nineties. They marked a new turn in the repertory and started a movement in Russian dramatic literature the full impact of which became completely evident only in the twentieth century.

The Stone Guest

by
ALEXANDER PUSHKIN

Leporello: *O statua gentilissima*
Del gran Commendatore! ...
Ah, Padrone!

DON GIOVANNI

Alexander Pushkin (1799–1837), the great Russian poet, wrote in 1830 "four little tragedies," probably suggested by "dramatic scenes" by Barry Cornwall (Bryan Waller Procter). The plot and the characters of these short plays were borrowed from Western history and literature: *The Avaricious Knight* had medieval settings and was allegedly inspired by Shenstone's tragi-comic *The Covetous Knight* (which we do not find in his works); *Mozart and Salieri* was based on the eighteenth-century belief that the great musical genius had been poisoned by his mediocre rival; *The Feast during the Plague* was a greatly changed version of *The City of Plague* (1816) by John Wilson (the pen name of the Scottish writer Christopher North); and *The Stone Guest* used one of the most popular and traditional subjects of world literature. It is doubtful whether Pushkin knew the seventeenth-century play by Tirso de Molina (*El Burlador de Sevilla y Convidado de Piedra*), which gave birth to a whole series of plays about the legendary seducer of women. But the Russian certainly was acquainted with Molière's *Don Juan ou le Festin de Pierre,* and with Mozart's opera *Don Giovanni* the book of which was written by Lorenzo Da Ponte. Pushkin's epigraph for his drama is taken from Da Ponte's Italian text.

The Stone Guest is an admirable example of Pushkin's faculty to feel and to render the spirit of various periods and countries. He never went out of Russia but he had an extraordinary understanding of Western civilization and a vision of European landscapes. The breath of a summer night in Madrid pervades the scene with Laura, and Don Juan is portrayed as a true Spanish nobleman. But the poetic merit of Pushkin's "little tragedy" goes beyond a simple reproduction of seventeenth-century Spain and its romantic hero. Pushkin transforms the material he had borrowed from European models and gives it his own individual, and often typically Russian, stamp. His Don Juan is not only represented as a man obsessed with women, but as a positive man of action. It is in the name of this principle that he challenges the frail old husband of Donna Anna and the gloomy Don Carlos whom he kills in front of his mistress. When, in a monk's disguise, he makes his declaration to the commander's widow at the cemetery, the great lover becomes a poet. There is no doubt that Pushkin stresses not only the sensual but also the perverse in the man who makes love to Laura next to a corpse, and to Donna Anna at the tomb of her husband. Because of the threat of censorship Pushkin could not dwell on the anti-religious, almost blasphemous traits of Don Juan, but he made him challenge the supernatural with unbending strength until the last moment. As some Russian critics pointed out, Don Juan struggles against death, and gloom and mourning, and although death finally overcomes him, he goes down fighting.

Perhaps all the implications of *The Stone Guest* are expressed in this memorable sentence of the play: "Of all life's pleasures, music is surpassed only by love, itself a melody." Don Juan, the flighty, crazy Sevillian, the chaser of girls, is the bearer of the spirit of music. Many years after Pushkin's death Nietzsche will call this spirit "Dionysian."

The Stone Guest was never performed during its author's lifetime. It was produced in occasional performances in 1847 and in 1862, but its true revival did not come until 1915 when "little tragedies" were staged by the Moscow Art Theater under the direction of Vladimir Nemirovich-Danchenko, with beautiful settings by Alexander Benois. The great actor Kachalov interpreted Pushkin's Don Juan as a man who in his striving to dare, to transgress, challenges the human as well as the divine law. He created an impressive highly romantic image and thus set a tradition for a whole generation of actors who have continued to interpret *The Stone Guest* under the Soviets.

The Stone Guest

CHARACTERS

DON JUAN, a Grandee of Spain
LEPORELLO, his squire
A MONK
DONNA ANNA, widow of Commodore Alvaro de Solva
LAURA, an actress
DON CARLOS, a Grandee of Spain
THE STATUE OF THE COMMODORE
GUESTS AT LAURA'S

SCENE 1. *Don Juan, Leporello.*

DON JUAN. We stand before Madrid's great gates at last!
Here will we wait for night to come. And, soon
I'll dart along the old, familiar streets
Whiskers in cloak concealed, hat over eyes.
Well, tell me, will they recognize me now?

LEPORELLO (*sarcastically*). How could they recognize a man
  like you?
In any crowd, who could pick out Don Juan?

DON JUAN. Come now, who'll know me?

LEPORELLO.   The first watchman met,
Or anybody, any Gypsy girl,
A drunken fiddler or someone like you,
Arrogant cavalier, wrapped in his cloak
His sword beneath his arm.

DON JUAN.   Why should we care?
As long as we don't meet the King himself.
And even so, I fear none in Madrid.

LEPORELLO. But by tomorrow news will reach the King
That Don Juan without the royal leave
Is back from exile. So, I ask you, what

19

Will happen then to you?

DON JUAN.   He'll send me back;
I'm sure he'd never have my head cut off—
I'm guilty of no crime; 'twas loving me
He sent me off. I think he simply wished
The dead man's kin to let me live in peace
And pester me no more.

LEPORELLO.   Well, still I think
You'd have done better to have stayed away.

DON JUAN. Well, thanks indeed! I almost died of boredom.
Ah, what a dull and tedious race of men!
What scenery, what sky! Nothing but smoke . . .
Women? Well let me tell you, Leporello,
The humblest peasant girl of Andalusia
Is well worth all their beauties put together.
At first, it's true, they quite enchanted me,
Those blue-eyed women with their skin so white,
And with their modesty. But most of all,
It was the novelty attracted me.
But soon enough, I realized it was
A real sin to waste my time on them,
For they are more wax dolls than real women.
Not like our girls at all! . . . Hey, Leporello!
You know this place? Have we been here before?

LEPORELLO. Now, how could I forget St. Anthony's,
The convent which you often used to visit?
I had to wait with horses in that grove—
A tedious chore! One thing I know for sure,
Your time with her went faster there than mine
Down here, believe me, sir . . .

DON JUAN.   My poor Ines!
She is no longer here. I loved her so!

LEPORELLO. Ines? The dark-eyed one? Oh, I recall:
For three months all your efforts were in vain
But finally the Devil took a hand . . .

DON JUAN. Those summer nights! . . . I found such strange
            delight
In her sad gaze and in her stiff, cold lips.
I'm still surprised how you could fail to see
Her great, uncanny charm. Oh, I admit
She was no real beauty; one would not
Have called her beautiful to look upon.
Except those eyes of hers, that dark, deep gaze—
I never saw before a look like that.

Her voice was soft and weak, just like a child's
Who's small and sickly. And her husband was
A big, disgusting brute . . . I found too late . . .
Ah, my poor Ines!

LEPORELLO.   But many others
Have followed her.

DON JUAN.   Well, certainly! Why not?

LEPORELLO. And granted life, you will have many more.

DON JUAN. Indeed, I hope so.

LEPORELLO.   Now we're in Madrid,
Which of those beauties shall we try to trace?

DON JUAN. Laura, of course. I'll hurry straight to her.

LEPORELLO. Ah yes?

DON JUAN.   I'll walk right in the door and if
I find another there, I will suggest
He step out of the window.

LEPORELLO.   Oh, of course,
We're cheerful here and mistresses now dead
Are well forgotten. Who's that coming there?

(*Enter a* MONK.)

MONK. She's on her way. Perhaps you are the servants
Of Donna Anna?

LEPORELLO.   No, we are free men
Taking the air.

DON JUAN. But you, you wait for whom?

MONK. For Donna Anna. She comes here to kneel
Before her husband's tomb.

DON JUAN.   What? Donna Anna,
Old Commodore de Solva's faithful widow,
Slain by someone . . . I can't remember whom.

MONK. By Don Juan, that godless libertine.

LEPORELLO. Well, well, I see that Don Juan's renown
The quiet, cool monastic vaults has reached
And anchorites sing praises of his deeds.

MONK. Why, have you ever met him?

LEPORELLO.   Met him? Us?
Oh no. Where is he now d'you know?

MONK.   Exiled
Far, far away.

LEPORELLO. The farther so, the better!
They ought to bag all those lewd fiends and toss

The nasty brood far out into the sea.

DON JUAN (*aside*). Why say a thing like that?

LEPORELLO.   Be quiet, be quiet,
I know what I'm about.

DON JUAN.   You say it's here
The Commodore is buried?

MONK.   On this spot.
His widow had this monument erected
Over his grave. And every day she comes
And weeps and prays that he may rest in peace.

DON JUAN. Amazing widow! Tell me, is she fair?

MONK. A woman's beauty should not move a monk
But since there is a sin in lying too
Then let me tell you that a saint himself
Could not remain umoved by such a beauty.

DON JUAN. Now I see why the dead man was so jealous.
He always locked her in—no one could see her.
I always longed to have a talk with her.

MONK. Never does Donna Anna speak to men.

DON JUAN. But what of you, my friend? She talks to you.

MONK. It's not the same for me, I am a monk.
Here she comes now.

(*Enter* DONNA ANNA.)

DONNA ANNA.   Ah, Father, let me in.

MONK. Yes, yes, at once, Senora, I am coming.
(DONNA ANNA *follows the* MONK.)

LEPORELLO. Is she a beauty?

DON JUAN.   Couldn't see a thing
Except perhaps a slender heel that flashed
Under her widow's weeds.

LEPORELLO.   That should suffice.
The rest, I'm sure, your fancy can fill in.
It is more adept than is any artist,
Working with equal ease from foot or brow.

DON JUAN. Mark my words well: I'll get to know her soon!

LEPORELLO. Ah, here we go again! It is too much!
He's killed her husband but that's naught to him,
And now he wants to watch the widow weep.
Ah, he's quite shameless!

DON JUAN.   It is getting dark.
Come, let us hurry, and before the moon

Rises to turn the inky dark of night
Into a pale penumbra, we must enter
Madrid . . .

LEPORELLO. Ah, what disgrace! For him a true
Grandee of Spain to sneak into Madrid
Fearing the moonlight, like a common thief . . .
Ah, what a rotten life I must endure!
I've had enough of following Don Juan.

SCENE 2. *Laura's room. Supper.*

1ST GUEST. Believe me, Laura, I have never yet
Admired your acting as I have to-night.
How brilliantly you understood your role!

2ND GUEST. What great interpretation and how forceful!

3RD GUEST. What artistry!

LAURA.   Yes, every word and gesture
Came down to me on wings of inspiration,
The words flowed forth as if not learned by rote
But like the beatings of my heart itself.

1ST GUEST. How true! And even now your eyes are gleaming,
Your cheeks aflame, your passion not extinguished.
And since it glows, don't let the embers die.
Sing us a song, oh Laura, sing for us!
Sing anything you like.

LAURA.   Bring my guitar. (*Sings.*)

ALL. Bravo, bravo! Sublime! Superb! Divine!

1ST GUEST. Enchantress, thank you, you have reached our
        hearts.
Of all life's pleasures, music is surpassed
Only by love, itself a melody.
Why, look, Don Carlos too, your gloomy guest,
Seems moved by it.

2ND GUEST.   How beautiful it is,
Melodious! Who wrote the words?

LAURA.   Don Juan.

DON CARLOS. What's that? Don Juan?

LAURA.   Ah, that was long ago.
He was a faithful friend, but fickle lover.

DON CARLOS. Your Juan is nothing but a godless scoundrel,
And you a little fool.

LAURA.   What, are you mad!

I'll bid my servants cut your rasping throat
For all your titles as Grandee of Spain.

DON CARLOS (*rising*). I dare you—call them!

1ST GUEST. Laura, stop it please.
Don Carlos, don't be angry, she's forgotten . . .

LAURA. Forgotten what? That in an honest combat,
Don Juan did kill the brother of Don Carlos?
All I regret is that it wasn't him!

DON CARLOS. I was a fool to lose my temper thus.

LAURA. Aha, so you admit you are a fool,
Then let us make it up.

DON CARLOS. I'm sorry, Laura.
You know I cannot bear to hear that name
With equanimity.

LAURA. But why blame me,
If my friend's name keeps leaping to my lips?

GUEST. Come, Laura, as a sign your anger's gone,
Sing us another song.

LAURA. All right, one more;
It's late already. Well, what should I sing?
Come, listen then. (*Sings.*)

ALL. Oh, wonderful! Divine!

LAURA. Good-night, my friends.

GUESTS. Good-night, our Laura, sweet!

(GUESTS *leave*. LAURA *stops* DON CARLOS.)

LAURA. You madman, Carlos, stay behind with me.
I like you, you remind me of Don Juan,
The way you gnashed your teeth and ranted on.

DON CARLOS. Oh, happy fiend, you must have loved him so!
You loved him, Laura? (LAURA *nods*.) Very much?

LAURA. I did.

DON CARLOS. And do you love him still?

LAURA. You mean right now?
To love two men at once I am unable.
And now it's you I love.

DON CARLOS. Do tell me, Laura,
How old are you today?

LAURA. I am eighteen.

DON CARLOS. You're very young, and young you still will be
Another five or six years hence. Perhaps
For six years more around you they will cluster,

Flatter, caress and shower you with gifts.
They'll serenade you nightly, kill each other
On corners dark and dim. But time will pass,
Your eyes, deep sunk, will be black-rimmed and wrinkled,
And in your tresses black gray streaks appear.
They'll call you aged crone. Tell me, what then?

LAURA. Why think of that? Why do you talk of it?
Are thoughts like that for ever on your mind?
Come to the balcony. Ah look, the sky
Is so serene. The warm, unmoving air
With scent of lemon and of laurel's filled.
High in the dark blue denseness shines the moon
And watchmen's sonorous voices cry "All's well!"
And far off to the North, the Paris skies
Perhaps this night are overhung with clouds.
A cold rain falls, there blows a wicked wind.
But what is that to us? Oh, listen, Carlos,
I order you henceforth to smile. Go on!
That's it!

DON CARLOS. Dear Demon! (*A knocking at the door.*)

DON JUAN.   Laura, here I am!

LAURA. Who's there? Whose voice is that?

DON JUAN.   Unlock the door!

LAURA. What? Can it be? Oh Lord!

DON JUAN.   Good-evening, Laura.

LAURA. It's you, Juan!

DON CARLOS.   What, Don Juan?

(LAURA *flings her arms around* DON JUAN's *neck.*)

DON JUAN.   Sweet Laura! (*Kisses her hand.*)
Who is your visitor?

DON CARLOS.   It's I, Don Carlos.

DON JUAN. Coincidence indeed! Upon the morn,
I'll be at your disposal.

DON CARLOS.   No, right now,
Immediately!

LAURA.   Don Carlos, will you stop!
This is my house and not the public street.
I must ask you to leave.

DON CARLOS (*ignoring her*). Come on, set to!
You have your sword.

DON JUAN.   Impatient, eh? Have at you!
(*They fight.*)

LAURA. Look out, Juan! (*Throws herself on a couch.*)
(DON CARLOS *falls.*)

DON JUAN. Come, Laura! It's all over.

LAURA. What, dead? A fine thing! Here, right in my room!
But now what shall I do, you fiendish rake?
Where shall we put him?

DON JUAN. What if he's alive?

LAURA. Alive, you say? Why, look, you've pierced his heart,
His living blood no longer gushes now
From that three-cornered wound your sword has made.
He breathes no more. What shall we do with him?

DON JUAN. The fault was not my own; he asked for it.

LAURA. Juan, this is too much. You've gone too far.
With you there's always trouble but the fault
Is never yours. But say, whence have you come?
And have you been here long?

DON JUAN. I've just arrived.
I'm here in secret—haven't yet been pardoned.

LAURA. And your first thought was for your Laura, right?
All that is very nice, but leave it now.
I don't believe you—you were passing by
And saw the house.

DON JUAN. Oh, Laura dearest, no!
You ask my Leporello! He will say,
That from a wretched place outside the city
I've slipped into Madrid to find my Laura. (*Kisses her.*)

LAURA. Dearest! How can you, with the dead man here?
What shall we do with him?

DON JUAN. Just leave him there.
At dawn tomorrow, I'll wrap him in a cloak,
And leave his body in some dark, dank alley.

LAURA. But please, look out, don't let yourself be seen.
I'm glad you didn't come a minute sooner.
Your friends were having supper here with me.
They left just now. Suppose you'd met them here.

DON JUAN. Well, tell me, Laura, have you loved him long?

LAURA. Whom do you mean? You can't be serious?

DON JUAN. Come, Laura, tell me now, how many times
You have deceived me while I was away?

LAURA. And what about yourself, you reckless rake?

DON JUAN. Confess . . . No, wait, we'll talk of it again.

Scene 3. *The Commodore's Monument.*

Don Juan (*disguised as a monk*). All's well so far. Since
    I have killed Don Carlos,
I have become a hermit, hiding here.
I see the lovely widow every day
And I believe she too has noticed me.
Up until now, we both have been reserved,
But I've decided I'll speak up today.
How shall I start? "May I presume, Senora? . . ."
Ah, damn it, no, I'll leave it to the moment,
I'll improvise a love song, wait and see.
But I feel sure she should be here by now,
The Commodore must grow impatient waiting.
But Lord, what Titan has this sculptor made!
Look at those shoulders—what a Hercules!
In real life he was but weak and puny
And standing on his toes he never could
Have stretched and reached to place his finger on
The Statue's stony nose. The night we met
Behind the Escurial, he ran upon my sword
And there was stuck—grasshopper on a pin;
And when I think how proud he was, how haughty,
How stern of spirit . . . I see her coming now.

    (*Enter* Donna Anna.)

  Donna Anna. Ah, here he is once more . . . Forgive me,
    Father,
From holy meditations I distract you,
Forgive me if you can.

    Don Juan.   No, I'm the one
Who should crave your forgiveness, oh Senora!
Perhaps I check the flow of your great grief.

    Donna Anna. No, Father, no, my grief's locked in my heart.
When I am close to you, my humble prayers
May rise to Heaven—pray, join your voice with mine.

    Don Juan. Oh, who am I to pray with Donna Anna?
Of such an honor I would be unworthy.
I would not dare with my polluted lips
Your sacred plea to Heaven to repeat.
No, only from afar with pious awe
Dare I to watch you quietly bow your head,
Your tresses raven black against pale marble,
Making me feel an angel has come down

From heaven above and lighted on the tomb.
My heart is moved and it is closed to prayer;
In speechless admiration here I stand
And envy that cool marble that it feels
Your fragrant breath and flowing, loving tears . . .

DONNA ANNA. Strange words indeed . . .

DON JUAN.   Senora?

DONNA ANNA.   You've forgot . . .

DON JUAN. That I most humble hermit that I am
Should still my sinful voice when in this place?

DONNA ANNA. It seems to me . . . I did not understand . . .

DON JUAN. Ah, now I see it—you know everything!

DONNA ANNA. Know what?

DON JUAN.   That I'm no monk, and at your feet
To beg for your forgiveness I have come . . .

DONNA ANNA. Oh Lord, who are you then, get up, get up . . .

DON JUAN. Unhappy victim of a hopeless passion.

DONNA ANNA. How can you! And before my husband's grave!
Please leave at once.

DON JUAN.   One minute, Donna Anna!

DONNA ANNA. But what if someone comes . . .

DON JUAN.   The gate is locked.
One minute just.

DONNA ANNA. What can you want with me?

DON JUAN. To die! Oh, let me die this hour, at once,
Right at your feet. And let my humble ashes
Be buried here. Oh! Not too near to those
Of him you loved, but somewhere at a distance,
Beside that iron gate or by the ditch,
So that your slender foot or dress's hem
May glide across my grave each time you come
To visit this proud tomb and spread your locks
On this cold stone and weep.

DONNA ANNA.   You are quite mad.

DON JUAN. Must it be madness here to wish to die?
Were I insane, I'd surely want to live
And keep the hope to touch your heart with love
So tender and so strong; were I a madman
Beneath your balcony I'd spend my nights
And with my serenades, rob you of sleep.
Instead of skulking from you I'd have drawn
Your gaze upon myself; if I were mad

I never would have suffered silently . . .

DONNA ANNA. Is this what you call silence?

DON JUAN.   Oh, it's chance
If I today have spoken. But for that
My tortured love would be a secret still.

DONNA ANNA. And have you felt it long, this love for me?

DON JUAN. If long or not I really cannot say,
But this I know: that from that moment only
Have I the meaning of this fleeting life
And that of happiness grasped once for all.

DONNA ANNA. Go, leave at once, you are a dangerous man.

DON JUAN. Why dangerous?

DONNA ANNA.   I fear to listen even.

DON JUAN. I will not say a word. Don't send away
A man for whom the sight of you is joy.
I cherish no vain hopes, I ask for naught,
But since I am condemned to live I must
See you . . .

DONNA ANNA. Be off, this is no place for words,
Mad ravings such as these. Come on the morrow
To see me on condition that you swear,
You'll treat me with the same respect as now.
I will be home to you, but after dark.
I've seen no one since I was left a widow.

DON JUAN. God bless you, Donna Anna, you're an angel.
May He pour balm upon your heart as you
Have done upon my lost and tortured heart.

DONNA ANNA. Away with you!

DON JUAN.   Another moment, please!

DONNA ANNA. It seems that I must be the one to leave.
I cannot keep my mind upon my prayers.
My soul you've troubled with your worldly speech.
To such my ear no longer is accustomed.
Tomorrow then . . .

DON JUAN.   I still don't dare believe
That such exultant bliss has now come true.
So we shall meet tomorrow! And not here!
And not in secrecy . . .

DONNA ANNA.   Tomorrow, yes!
What is your name?

DON JUAN.   Diego de Calvado.

DONNA ANNA. Good-night, Don Diego.   (*Exits.*)

DON JUAN.   Leporello, hey!

LEPORELLO. What is it?

DON JUAN.   I'm so happy, Leporello,
She said tomorrow evening she'll receive me.
I'm happy as a child!

LEPORELLO.   Did you then speak
To Donna Anna? I suppose she said
A friendly word or two? Perhaps did you
Bestow on her your blessing?

DON JUAN.   No, man, no,
With her own lips she set a date for me.

LEPORELLO. Ah, widows, they are all the same!

DON JUAN.   Oh God!
I am so happy—I'd embrace the world.

LEPORELLO. What do you think the Commodore would say?

DON JUAN. You think he will be jealous? I do not.
A man of reason he has always been
And has become still more so since he died.

LEPORELLO. Wait, wait! Look at his statue!

DON JUAN.   Well then, what?

LEPORELLO. He seems to glare at you in frozen anger!

DON JUAN. He does? Then please invite him for tomorrow,
Of course to Donna Anna's house, not mine.

LEPORELLO. Invite the statue? Why?

DON JUAN.   Well, to be sure
Not for a chat. Tomorrow bid him come
To Donna Anna's later, after dark,
And stand as sentinel before the door.

LEPORELLO. Good heavens, what a subject for a joke!

DON JUAN. Go on, invite him.

LEPORELLO.   But . . .

DON JUAN.   Go on, be quick!

LEPORELLO. Most noble and most handsome monument,
My master, Don Juan, hereby requests
Your presence at . . . Oh no! I swear, I can't!

DON JUAN. Coward! Go on! I'll teach you!

LEPORELLO.   Pardon me!
My master, Don Juan, is asking you
To come tomorrow—not too early though—

And place yourself on guard before the door
Of your wife's house . . . (THE STATUE *nods agreement*.) Oh!
   Oh!

DON JUAN.   What's going on?

LEPORELLO. Ah! It'll be the death of me!

DON JUAN.   What now?

LEPORELLO (*nodding like* THE STATUE). The statue . . . ah!

DON JUAN.   You nod?

LEPORELLO.   Not I, but it!

DON JUAN. What nonsense is this?

LEPORELLO.   Come and see yourself.

DON JUAN (*to* LEPORELLO). I'll show you, good-for-nothing!
                    (*To* STATUE.)   Commodore,
I cordially invite you to stand watch
Tomorrow at the door while I, inside,
Am being entertained. Well, will you come?
(STATUE *nods*.) Oh, God!

LEPORELLO.   What did I tell you?

DON JUAN.   Let's get out!

SCENE 4. *A room in Donna Anna's House. Don Juan,
   Donna Anna.*

DONNA ANNA. Well, here we are, Don Diego, as you wished.
But I'm afraid my dull, sad conversation
Will bore you; I am but a grieving widow
Unable to forget her loss; my tears,
Like April showers with sun, are mixed with smiles.
Well, why do you say nothing?

DON JUAN.   Silently
I'm savoring the thought of being here
With lovely Donna Anna, who no more
Is kneeling by the stony effigy,
Before the grave of the most lucky dead.

DONNA ANNA. How can you be so jealous of the dead?
Can he torment you even from the grave?

DON JUAN. What right have I to envy him you chose?

DONNA ANNA. I did not choose but did as I was bid
By mother. He was rich while we were poor.

DON JUAN. Ah, lucky man! He brought his empty gifts
To lay before your feet, oh goddess fair.
Yet, it would seem that that gave him the right

To savor all the bliss of paradise.
Had I known you before, with what delight
Would I have given rank and fortune, all
For just one gentle glance from your fair eyes.
I would have been a slave to your commands,
Studied your every whim that I might then
Anticipate them; and I would have made
Your life one long enchantment; but alas,
That fate was not for me.

DONNA ANNA.   Don Diego, stop!
Listening to you, my very thoughts are sins.
A widow must be faithful to the grave.
If you but knew how Don Alvaro loved me!
And I am certain, were it he bereaved,
There would be no enamored lady here.
He'd have been true to matrimonial love.

DON JUAN. Oh, Donna Anna, cease to torture me
By coming back time and again to him.
I dare say I have earned this punishment
But spare me please . . .

DONNA ANNA.   How have you earned it then?
You're tied to none by any sacred bonds.
There is no fault in Heaven's eyes or mine
If you love me.

DON JUAN. In your eyes? Oh, my God!

DONNA ANNA. Why, have you wronged me? Tell me how, I
    pray.

DON JUAN. No, never!

DONNA ANNA.   Diego, tell me, what is this?
Come, tell me, do!

DON JUAN.   No, not for anything.

DONNA ANNA. It's really quite bizarre! I must insist.

DON JUAN. No, no.

DONNA ANNA.   So such is your submission then!
How does this fit with what you said before?
You think this is the way a slave should act?
If you don't answer, you'll provoke my ire.
Tell me at once, what have you done to me?

DON JUAN. I dare not, it will make you hate me so.

DONNA ANNA. No, no, I do forgive you in advance.
I want to know.

DON JUAN. No, you don't want to know

The deadly secret lurking in my heart.

DONNA ANNA. Deadly you say? I really wonder why.
What can it be? How could you have offended?
We've never met and I have never had
A single enemy in all my life
Save only one—my husband's murderer.

DON JUAN (*aside*). Things now come to a head or so it seems.
(*Aloud.*) Say, have you ever met that wretch Don Juan?

DONNA ANNA. No, on that man I've never set my eyes.

DON JUAN. You hate him?

DONNA ANNA.   Yes, to that I'm duty bound.
But do not change the subject, Don Diego,
I want an answer . . .

DON JUAN.   If you met Don Juan,
How would you act?

DONNA ANNA.   Oh, I would take my dagger
And pierce his murderous heart.

DON JUAN.   Well, Donna Anna,
Where is your dagger, for my heart is here!

DONNA ANNA. Diego, what is this?

DON JUAN.   I'm Juan, not Diego.

DONNA ANNA. Oh, God in heaven! Sure, it cannot be!

DON JUAN. I am Juan.

DONNA ANNA.   No!

DON JUAN.   I did kill your husband
And there is no regret in me at all.

DONNA ANNA. Do I hear right? No, no, impossible!

DON JUAN. I am Juan and yes, I love you true.

DONNA ANNA (*falling*). Where am I? Oh, I feel so faint . . .
   (*Faints.*)

DON JUAN.   Great heaven!
What's happened? Donna Anna, please awake.
I am Don Diego, your adoring slave.

DONNA ANNA. Leave me along. (*Weakly.*) You are my enemy.
You took all that I had in life from me.

DON JUAN. Oh, I am anxious to redeem myself.
My darling, kneeling at your feet I wait
For your command to die or still to breathe
For your sake only . . .

DONNA ANNA.   So this is Don Juan . . .

DON JUAN. I'm sure he's often been described to you

As something of a monster and a fiend.
Perhaps this reputation is deserved,
There's so much evil on my tired conscience.
It weighs me down. Of lechery I've been
An ardent follower. But since I've met you
I feel I've been reborn. In loving you,
I fell in love with virtue. Until now
I've never knelt thus tremblingly before it.

DONNA ANNA. I know that Don Juan is eloquent;
I've often heard him called a sly seducer.
You demon, say, how many helpless women
Have you to their perdition coldly sent?

DON JUAN. But I loved none of them till now.

DONNA ANNA.   Do you
Expect me to believe that Don Juan
Is for the first time in his life in love
And not just looking for another victim?

DON JUAN. If to deceive you had been my intent,
Would I have breathed that name, which is to you
More odious than any in the world?
What scheming can you find in this? What craft?

DONNA ANNA. Who knows with you? And yet you have come
    here
To certain death had you been recognized.

DON JUAN. All right, let it be death. Life is small price
To pay for such a moment.

DONNA ANNA.   How can you,
Foolhardy man, steal out of here unharmed?

DON JUAN (*kissing her hand*). Oh, do I hear concern for
    Don Juan?
Well, this must mean there is no hatred left,
In your sweet heart, oh Donna Anna, dear.

DONNA ANNA. Oh, how I wish my heart could hate Don Juan!
But now the time has come for us to part.

DON JUAN. When shall we meet again?

DONNA ANNA.   I do not know.
Some day.

DON JUAN.   Tomorrow.

DONNA ANNA.   Where then?

DON JUAN.   Why not here?

DONNA ANNA. Oh, Don Juan, my heart is weak indeed.

DON JUAN. Seal your forgiveness with a kiss, oh Anna.

DONNA ANNA. Go now!

DON JUAN.   One kiss, a cool and friendly one.

DONNA ANNA. How you insist. All right. I'll kiss you once.
(*A knocking at the door.*)
What is that knocking? Hide yourself, Don Juan.

DON JUAN. Good-night. I'll see you soon, my gentle love.

(*Runs out, then runs back in again.*)

DONNA ANNA. What happened?

DON JUAN.   Ah! (*Enter* THE COMMODORE'S
STATUE. DONNA ANNA *falls.*)

STATUE.   I came as I was bid.

DON JUAN. Oh Lord! Oh Donna Anna!

STATUE.   Let her be.
All's at an end. You're trembling, Don Juan.

DON JUAN. Not I! I called you and I'm glad you came.

STATUE. Give me your hand.

DON JUAN.   Here. Oh, my Lord, how hard,
The pressure of this heavy, marble hand!
Oh, let me go! Release your stony grip.
I'm lost! All's over! Oh, my Donna Anna!

(*They sink through the floor together.*)

CURTAIN

The Inspector General

A COMEDY IN FIVE ACTS

by
NIKOLAI GOGOL

*Don't blame the mirror
If your mug is twisted.*

Popular saying

In his youth Nikolai Gogol made an attempt to become a professional actor, and all his life he was deeply interested in the theater. After his first literary successes as a storyteller he turned to playwriting, and composed between 1832 and 1841 several minor comedies, among them *The Gamblers,* a biting, sharp satire, and the farcical, delightfully funny *Marriage.* He started the latter in 1835 but interrupted it for a new project: he wanted to make a play based on an anecdote of mistaken identity told him by Pushkin. He finished the comedy by the end of the year: it was *The Inspector General.* The censors refused to pass this work by the twenty-six-year-old author, but Zhukovsky, Gogol's friend and a poet with high connections, arranged a reading of the comedy at the Imperial Court, and Nicholas I liked it. This decided *The Inspector General*'s fate. On April 19, 1836, it was performed in the Tsar's presence at the Alexandrinsky Theater in St. Petersburg, and since the Sovereign laughed and clapped, the audience followed—despite the fact that spectators, mostly governmental officials and noblemen, were stunned and shocked. When the curtain fell on this "impudent and impertinent nonsense," as it was later called by the reactionaries, the whole house rose in an uproar. Discussions about *The Inspector General* continued in the streets, in restaurants, in the drawing rooms of the capital, in the press and at all public gatherings. The conservatives denounced the comedy as a dangerous calumny, the liberals hailed it as a timely exposé of social ills. All the young people acclaimed Gogol enthusiastically and defended him against the attacks of the older generation. Most of the literary critics, led by the pugnacious Belinsky, saw in *The Inspector General* a great affirmation of national comedy, a new chapter in the history of Russian realism. And everybody agreed that as a political event of the first magnitude it had far-reaching social implications.

Gogol was greatly perturbed by all this clamor. He confessed later that he did aim in his comedy "to pile up all the vile things in Russia, all the injustices which occur in those places and on those occasions when justice is most needed, and laugh at it all." But confronted with the most contradictory yet invariably passionate reactions to his play, he felt perplexed and unhappy. He tried at first to reassure the detractors of his "pure intentions" and he wrote all sorts of "afterpieces" in which he stated that the positive hero of his comedy was laughter itself and intimated that the supreme Inspector General is to be found in heaven and that the play had a hidden religious meaning. All these explanations failed to produce any effect, and Gogol got so depressed by all the controversy that six weeks after the first performance of his great comedy, he left Russia and fled abroad.

As often happened with Gogol, he was not completely aware of the impact and repercussions of his own work. But *The Inspector General* remained the most popular Russian comedy, and for more than a century it amused, entertained and stirred millions of spectators in theaters all over Russia.

Of course, the immediate impression of *The Inspector General* in the thirties and forties was that of a daring social satire. It revealed to everybody the truth about the provincial administration personified by the coarse and cunning mayor and his corrupted officials. The grotesque gallery of grafters, brutal little tyrants, gossipy landowners, empty-headed females cheated by a boastful impostor, was representative of the whole system of abuse and bribes based on serfdom and despotism. A funny anecdote became an indictment of a regime—and this was the obvious significance of the comedy. But besides its topical or historical value, it was a literary masterpiece of universal importance, and this determined its place in Russian and world letters long after the abolition of serfdom and the transformation of pre-reform Russia. In his caricatures, which were like the masks of the *commedia dell'arte* with their common defects and distortions, Gogol immortalized certain fixed human types, knaves and rogues, morons and brutes; and the spectators were quick to recognize familiar faces. In the last act of the play the mayor shouts at the audience: "What are you laughing at, idiots!? At yourselves . . ." The epigraph to the comedy intimates that the author simply reflected daily reality: "Don't blame the mirror if your mug is twisted." Gogol maintained that Khlestakov was the central figure of *The Inspector General,* that we all have in us the germs of a disease called "the illness of Khlestakov" (or "khlestakovshchina" in Russian). The combination of triviality and *braggadocio* that is so typical of Khlestakov cannot hide his basic emptiness. With all his showing off he is like a bubble that will burst and reveal the void inside it. This void seemed the sign of the Devil to Gogol. For him the flighty impostor was the petty demon of futility and evil, in the same way that the mayor and his acolytes were incarnations of a less subtle, more coarse and obvious villainy.

Hundreds of Russian actors gave different images of the comedy's main protagonists. Sosnitsky in 1836 portrayed the mayor as a shifty, foxy man, a cold-blooded swindler. Shchepkin, the great realist actor, showed him as an ignorant, impulsive rascal, governed by his beastly instincts. The impersonation of Khlestakov proved to be more difficult, and Gogol was not satisfied with the actor Dur, Sosnitsky's partner, who interpreted the impostor in an almost farcical vein. From the first night in Alexandrinsky and throughout the nineteenth century, *The Inspector General* had innumerable performances, but a certain tradition, going back to the forties, prevailed in the interpretation. In 1908 the Moscow Art Theater tried to discover in the comedy a new psychological dimension. This aim was fully attained by Mikhail Chekhov, the nephew of the writer, who gave a stunning image of an almost frightening, pathological and grotesque Khlestakov. His impersonation had definite mystical overtones, raising the impostor to the level of universal wickedness.

Under the Soviets, the interpretation of *The Inspector General* went through various phases before reverting to the strictly traditional and socially-centered method of "Socialist Realism." The only great exception was the adaptation of the comedy by Meyerhold in the late twenties. He called it "a grandiose suite on Gogolian themes," broke the play into fifteen episodes, introduced new personages and made Khlestakov an expert adventurer and politician. The controversy provoked by this challenging production was tremendous, but despite the condemnation of Meyerhold by leading party organs, his attempt to use Gogol's comedy as a synthetic and symbolic picture of Russia had a lasting although often indirect impact on the Soviet theater.

The Inspector General

CHARACTERS

THE MAYOR, Anton Skvoznik-Dmukhanovsky
ANNA ANDREYEVNA, his wife
MARIA, his daughter
SCHOOL SUPERINTENDENT, Luke Khlopov
HIS WIFE
THE JUDGE, Amos Lapkin-Tapkin
DIRECTOR OF CHARITIES, Artemy Strawberry
THE POSTMASTER, Ivan Shpekin
PETER DOBCHINSKY } local landowners
PETER BOBCHINSKY
IVAN ALEXANDROVICH KHLESTAKOV, a government clerk from
    Petersburg
OSIP, his servant
THE DOCTOR, Christian Ivanovich Hübner
LULUKOV
RASTAKOVSKY } respected citizens of the town
KOROBKIN
THE POLICE INSPECTOR, Stepan Sharpears
WHISTLES
BUTTON } Policemen
GRABMUG
ABDULIN, a merchant
A LOCKSMITH'S WIFE, Poshlopkina
A CORPORAL'S WIDOW
MISHKA, the Mayor's servant
AN INN SERVANT
GUESTS (male and female), MERCHANTS, TOWNSFOLK, PE-
    TITIONERS

PERSONALITIES AND COSTUMES
(Notes for Actors)

THE MAYOR: An official no longer young and, in a way,
    quite intelligent. Although he takes bribes, he behaves with

43

dignity; he is quite serious-minded; even tends to moralize; he speaks neither loudly nor softly, neither very much nor very little; his every word has weight. His face is coarse and hard, as is inevitable in one who has worked his way up from the bottom in government service. He changes rather rapidly from fear to joy, from cringing to overbearing airs, being a man of crude, unrefined character. He usually wears his official uniform, with its braid, knee-boots, and spurs. His close-cropped hair is flecked with white.

ANNA ANDREYEVNA: His wife, a provincial coquette, not yet altogether middle-aged. Her head is still full of light novels and scrapbooks, and this forms a curious mixture with her present housewifely preoccupations with her storerooms and servants. Very inquisitive and, on occasion, displays vanity. Sometimes gets the upper hand over her husband but only because he can't find words to answer her. But the advantage she thus gains extends only to unimportant things and she usually contents herself with nagging and sneering at him. During the course of the play she changes into four different dresses.

KHLESTAKOV: A young man of 23 or so, very thin and puny; a bit silly, not ruled by his head—the sort who is rated as quite irresponsible in government service. Speaks and acts entirely without thinking; quite incapable of concentrating on any one idea. His speech is jerky and words fly from his mouth as if by themselves and quite unpredictably. The more the actor playing this role evinces ingenuousness and simplicity, the better will be his performance. He is fashionably dressed.

OSIP: His servant; much like any other middle-aged servant. He has a serious tone; generally keeps his eyes lowered. He is given to moralizing and sometimes lectures his master in his absence. His voice, generally quite even, takes on a stern, abrupt, almost rude tone when he speaks to his master. He is more intelligent and quicker-witted than his master, but he doesn't like to talk much, preferring to mislead people quietly. He wears a shabby gray or blue frockcoat.

BOBCHINSKY and DOBCHINSKY: Both short, squat men, very inquisitive and greatly resembling each other. Both have round little bellies; both gesticulate and speak very fast. Dobchinsky is a little taller and more serious than Bobchinsky; Bobchinsky is more casual and livelier than Dobchinsky. They both wear gray frockcoats, yellow Nankeen trousers, and boots with tassels. On their first appearance, Dobchinsky wears a loose, bottle-green frockcoat and Bobchinsky his former army tunic.

JUDGE LAPKIN-TAPKIN: A man who has read five or six books and so is something of a free-thinker. Loves to make conjectures and for this reason gives great weight to every word he utters. The actor playing him should constantly maintain a meaningful expression. He has a deep voice and speaks in a hoarse, strangled, protracted drawl, like an old clock that wheezes before it strikes.

DIRECTOR OF CHARITIES, STRAWBERRY: A very fat, sluggish, and clumsy man, but, for all that, a sly schemer and a cheat. He looks like a fussy, obliging person and wears a rather loose frockcoat, except in Act IV when he appears in a tight civil service uniform with short sleeves and an enormous collar which almost encases his ears.

POSTMASTER: Simple-hearted to the point of being naïve.

The other parts need no special elaboration; the original types on which they are based are almost always readily available.

THE GUESTS: These should be of various types. They should be tall and short, fat and thin, disheveled and carefully combed. Their costumes should also vary: frockcoats, Hungarian jackets, tailcoats of different colors and styles. There should also be a great deal of variety in the ladies' costumes: some are rather well-dressed, even with claims to fashion, but always with something a little wrong—either the bonnet worn at a wrong tilt or some rather unsuitable handbag. Other ladies appear in dresses which don't belong to any possible fashion at all, with big kerchiefs, caps which look like loaves of sugar, and so on.

THE ACTORS should pay special attention to the final scene. The last words uttered should give everyone a sudden electric shock. The entire group should change positions in a flash. A cry of surprise should be wrung from all the women at once, as if from a single breast. If these directions are not followed, the whole effect may be lost.

❧

ACT I

A room in the Mayor's house.

SCENE 1. *The Mayor, the Director of Charities, the School Superintendent, the Judge, the Police Inspector, the Doctor, two Policemen.*

MAYOR. Gentlemen, I've called you in to tell you a very unpleasant piece of news. There's a government inspector on his way here.

JUDGE. What inspector?

CHARITIES. Which inspector?

MAYOR. An inspector from Petersburg. Traveling incognito. And what's more, with secret instructions.

JUDGE. That's all we need!

CHARITIES. Everything was going along smoothly—and now look!

SCHOOL SUPERINTENDENT. Oh Lord! And with secret instructions too!

MAYOR. I felt it coming somehow: all last night I kept dreaming of two extraordinary rats, the likes of which I've never seen before: so black and of altogether unnatural proportions. They came, they sniffed, and off they went. Here, let me read you a letter I received from Andrei Shmykov—I'm sure you know him, Director of Charities. Here's what he writes: "My dear friend and benefactor," (*He mutters under his breath, scanning letter.*) ". . . to inform you . . ." Ah, here we are: "And, by the way, I hasten to inform you that an official has been sent from the capital to conduct a secret inspection of our whole province and particularly of our district." (*He raises his finger meaningfully.*) "I know from the most reliable source that the inspector has already arrived, although he tries to pass himself off as a private person. And since you're too clever a man to let anything that happens to come within reach of your hands slip by, I'm certain that, like anyone else, you must have a few small things on your conscience . . ." (*Stopping.*) Well, that's all right, we're all friends here . . . "So, if I were you, I'd take every precaution, for he may descend on you at any moment, if he hasn't arrived already. In fact, he may be staying incognito somewhere . . . Yesterday I . . ." Oh well, the rest's just family matters: "My sister Anna and her husband are staying with us; Ivan has grown very fat and plays the fiddle all the time . . ." and so on and so forth. So that's the situation.

JUDGE. Yes, quite a situation. Most extraordinary, really! I'm sure there must be something behind it.

SCHOOL SUPERINTENDENT (*to* MAYOR). But why, Mayor, why? Why an inspector here?

MAYOR. Why? Just our bad luck, that's all. (*Sighs.*) Up till now, we've had nothing to complain of, thank God—they've kept busy with other towns. Looks like it's our turn now.

JUDGE. I believe there's something more subtle to it, Mayor— something political. I'd say it means this: Russia . . . well, yes, Russia is preparing for war, and the government, you understand, is sending an official to find out if there's any treason around.

MAYOR. Huh! What next? And you're supposed to be a smart man. Treason in an out-of-the-way town like this! What d'you think we are—a frontier town? Huh, you can set out from here and travel for three years in any direction and you still won't get to another country!

JUDGE. Well, I still say . . . you didn't quite grasp . . . you don't understand . . . the government is full of clever schemes: it doesn't make any difference that we are so far out—they keep an eye on everything.

MAYOR. Well, whatever they have their eye on, I've warned you, gentlemen. So watch out! For my part, I've taken certain steps, and I advise you to do the same. (*To* CHARITIES.) Especially you, Charities. The inspector's sure to want to have a look at your charitable institutions before he gets to anything else. So you'd better see to it that everything's shipshape: that the patients get clean nightcaps and, in general, look a bit less like a lot of coal miners than they usually do.

CHARITIES. Oh, that's not so terrible, really. We can even put clean nightcaps on them, if it comes to that.

MAYOR. Yes, and you might also write above each bed in Latin or some other such lingo, that's your field, Doctor, the names of the diseases, who fell sick when, which day and the date . . . And, by the way, you shouldn't let your patients smoke such strong tobacco—makes you sneeze your head off when you go in there. Besides, we'd be better off with fewer of them, otherwise, it might reflect on the quality of the medical care.

CHARITIES. Oh, when it comes to medical care, the doctor and I, we have a well-established policy: back to nature. We don't believe in expensive drugs. Man is not all that complicated:

if he's meant to die, he'll die anyway, and if he's meant to recover—he'll recover whatever care he gets. Besides, it'd be hard for the doctor to go into all sorts of explanations with them. He's a German—doesn't speak a word of Russian.

(*The* DOCTOR *produces a sound, something halfway between "ee" and "ay."*)

MAYOR. And you, Judge, I'd advise you to look into things over at the courthouse. The guards have been breeding geese in your waiting rooms and all the little geese keep darting around the place, getting under the litigants' feet. Of course, now, poultry raising, that's praiseworthy in every respect and there's no reason why a guard shouldn't go in for it. But still, you know, in a place like that, it might look a bit awkward . . . I meant to call it to your attention before this, but somehow I never got around to it.

JUDGE. All right, I'll order them all taken off to the kitchen this very day. What about having dinner with me?

MAYOR. And then, another thing—it doesn't look right having all sorts of junk hanging up to dry right in the courtroom itself. And there's a hunting crop hanging over the filing cabinet . . . I know you like hunting, but it'd be better to take it down for now at least. When the inspector's gone, you can put it back again, I suppose. Then there's your court clerk. I know he's very competent, but he reeks like a brewery—that's not right either. I meant to point it out to you long ago, but something came up, I forget what, and . . . There must be something he can take for it, if it really is his natural smell as he says. Maybe he ought to try eating onions or garlic or something. In any case, the doctor could prescribe some special remedies for him.

(DOCTOR *makes same sound as before.*)

JUDGE. No, I don't think it's possible to get that smell off him. He says his nurse dropped him when he was a baby and, ever since, there's been a slight whiff of vodka about him.

MAYOR. Well, all right, I just wanted to call your attention to it. Now, as to this inspector being sent and what Shmykov calls "things on your conscience" in his letter, there's nothing I can say. It'd be useless trying to argue: there isn't a man who doesn't have some little sins or other on his conscience. Why, God Himself arranged things that way, and Voltaire's followers are wasting their saliva denying it.

JUDGE. What do you mean, actually, by little sins, Mayor? There are sins and sins, you know. I'm quite ready to admit that I take bribes—but what kind of bribes? Why, greyhound puppies. Now, that's not at all the same thing, as you well know.

MAYOR. Puppies or whatever—a bribe's a bribe.

JUDGE. Sorry, I can't go along with you there, Mayor. It's not the same thing as accepting a fur coat worth 500 rubles, or a costly shawl for your wife.

MAYOR. And what if the only bribes you take are greyhound puppies, when you don't believe in God. You never go to church. Take me now—my faith is unshakable and I'm in church every Sunday. While you . . . I know you. When you start talking about the creation of the world, it's enough to make one's hair stand on end.

JUDGE. Well, at least I worked it all out by myself.

MAYOR. Well, there're times when you're better off having no brains at all than being too smart. Besides, I only mentioned the municipal court in passing. To tell the truth, no one's likely to poke his nose in there. From that point of view, you've really got a safe spot—God Himself seems to have taken it under His protection. But you now, Luke, as School Superintendent you should keep an eye on the teachers. Of course, they're all very learned and they've been through various colleges, but they have very strange ways—perhaps that's inevitable with such great learning. For instance, one of them, the fat-faced one, I can never remember his name, he can't get along without making faces once he gets up on his platform there. Like this. (*He makes a face.*) Then he puts his fingers up under his tie and starts stroking his beard with the back of his hand. Of course, if he makes a face like that at one of his pupils, it doesn't matter, maybe it's even necessary—I'm not a specialist, I can't tell. But just think what would happen if he did it in front of a visitor. It could be very bad. The inspector, or anyone else, might take it personally and then God knows what might come of it.

SCHOOL SUPERINTENDENT. But what can I do? I've told him many times. Why, just the other day—just as an important visitor came into the classroom he made such a terrible face. Never seen such a face before. I'm sure he meant well, mind you, but I got a whole lecture for allowing free thinking to be sown in the minds of our young people.

MAYOR. And then I must also call your attention to the history teacher. He has a head full of learning, I can see that, and he's picked up a whole body of knowledge. But he explains things with such heat, he forgets himself. I listened to him once and, well, as long as he was talking of the Assyrians and the Babylonians, it was all right, but when he got to Alexander the Great, I can't think what came over him. I thought there was a fire! Really! He leaped off the platform and, with all his strength—bang! with a chair against the floor! Of course, he's a hero, Alexander the Great, but why break chairs? It's a dead loss to the municipal funds.

SCHOOL SUPERINTENDENT. Yes, he's very temperamental. I've talked to him about it several times. But all he says is: "Say what you like, but I'd give my life for learning, any day."

MAYOR. Uhmm, such are the inscrutable ways of fate: if a man's intelligent, he's either a drunk or he makes such faces you have to remove the holy pictures for fear of shocking the saints.

SCHOOL SUPERINTENDENT. It's no blessing to be in the service of learning—you get to be afraid of everything. Everyone interferes and tries to show how terribly clever he is too.

MAYOR. Ah, if that was all. But this damn incognito! He'll pop up suddenly and say: "So there you are, my fine ones! And which of you," he'll say, "is the Judge?"—"Lapkin-Tapkin." —"Well, get me Lapkin-Tapkin! And which is the Director of Charities?"—"Strawberry."—"So, let's see Strawberry!" That's what's really bad.

SCENE 2. *The same and Postmaster.*

POSTMASTER. What's going on, gentlemen? What's this about an inspector coming here?

MAYOR. Haven't you heard?

POSTMASTER. I just heard about it now, from Bobchinsky. He came to see me in the post office a moment ago.

MAYOR. Well then? What do you make of it?

POSTMASTER. What do I make of it? Looks to me like there'll be war with the Turks.

JUDGE. Exactly! Just what I thought!

MAYOR. And you're way off, both of you.

POSTMASTER. It means war with the Turks, I tell you. It's them Frenchies behind it all.

MAYOR. War with the Turks indeed! It's we here who're going to get it in the neck, not the Turks. You can bet your life. That's what the letter says.

POSTMASTER. Well, if that's the way it is—then it's not war with the Turks.

MAYOR. So, Postmaster, what *do* you think, after all?

POSTMASTER. Who am I to say? It's what you think that's important, Mayor.

MAYOR. Me? I'm not scared—well, a little, maybe . . . I'm a bit worried about the merchants and tradespeople. They seem to have it in for me, and yet God knows, if I did make a few of them fork out a little here and there, I did it without the slightest animosity. I'm beginning to wonder. (*Takes* POSTMASTER *by the arm and leads him to one side.*) I'm beginning to wonder whether someone hasn't complained against me behind my back. Otherwise, I don't see why an inspector should be coming this way. Listen, Postmaster, couldn't you—for all our sakes—sort of hold onto every letter, both incoming and outgoing, that passes through your post office, and, you know, sort of unseal it a bit and see what it says, in case it contains a complaint against some of us or even says anything at all. Then, if there's nothing, you could seal it up again. Or, if you don't want to be bothered with it, send it on open.

POSTMASTER. I know, I know . . . You don't have to tell me how it's done. That I do anyway, and not even as a safety measure but simply out of sheer curiosity. You can't imagine how I love to keep up with what's going on in the world. And, take it from me, it makes the most interesting reading! Some letters are real pearls. I find some beautiful bits of writing . . . and then, it does broaden one's horizons. I'd say it makes better reading than the *Moscow News*!

MAYOR. Well then, tell me, haven't you read anything about some official coming this way from Petersburg?

POSTMASTER. No, not from Petersburg. But there's plenty about officials from Kostroma and Saratov. It's a shame though, that you're not a letter-reader yourself; you'd find some really beautiful passages. Why, just recently, an army lieutenant was writing to his friend and he described a ball in the most playful way . . . really, very, very good: "My life, dear friend," he writes, "flows in Elysium, young ladies galore, bands playing, flags flying . . ." Oh, he describes it all with such feeling! I kept that one for myself. Would you like me to read it to you?

MAYOR. No, no, there's no time now. But please, remember, if you should come across a complaint or a denunciation, don't hesitate to hold onto it.

POSTMASTER. I'd be delighted to.

JUDGE. Watch out, that'll get you into trouble one of these days.

POSTMASTER. Oh Lord!

MAYOR. Don't worry, don't worry. It'd be different if you were going to make some sort of a public scandal of it, but, this way, it's strictly a family matter.

JUDGE. Yes, looks like we've got a bad business on our hands.

And to think I came here, Mayor, to present you with a charming little bitch—she's the sister of that dog you know. I suppose you've heard that Cheptovich has started a lawsuit against Varkhovinsky—well, now I'm in clover: I can go hunting hares on either of their estates.

MAYOR. Oh heavens, I've no time for your hares now with this damned incognito hanging over my head. I keep expecting the door to open and . . .

SCENE 3. *The same and Bobchinsky and Dobchinsky, who both enter panting.*

BOBCHINSKY. An extraordinary event!

DOBCHINSKY. Unexpected news!

ALL. What? What is it?

DOBCHINSKY. Something quite unforeseen: we enter the hotel . . .

BOBCHINSKY (*interrupting*). Dobchinsky and I enter the hotel . . .

DOBCHINSKY (*interrupting*). Please, Bobchinsky, let me tell it.

BOBCHINSKY. No, let me please . . . please, please . . . after all, you're not all that good at telling a story . . .

DOBCHINSKY. But you always get mixed up and leave things out.

BOBCHINSKY. I won't leave anything out, really I won't! As long as you don't interrupt me. Just let me tell it my way. Please, gentlemen, tell Dobchinsky not to interrupt me.

MAYOR. For heaven's sake, tell us what this is all about. My heart is in my mouth! Sit down, gentlemen, please. Here, Bobchinsky, here's a chair for you. (*They all sit down around* DOBCHINSKY *and* BOBCHINSKY.) Well, what is it, what is it?

BOBCHINSKY. Let me, let me, I'll tell you the whole thing in the right order. As soon as I had the pleasure of leaving you, when you were so disturbed by that letter you received, well, so then I ran in to see— Please, Dobchinsky, don't interrupt. I've got it all straight in my head. —So I, please note, I ran in to see Korobkin. And when I didn't find Korobkin at home, I went to see Rastakovsky. But Rastakovsky wasn't home either, so I popped in on the postmaster here, to inform him of the news you had received, and on leaving there, I met Dobchinsky . . .

DOBCHINSKY (*interrupting*). Near the stall where they sell pies.

BOBCHINSKY. Near the stall where they sell pies. So, I say to him: "Have you heard the news the Mayor received in a confidential letter?" And it turned out that Dobchinsky had already heard it from your housekeeper Avdotya, who for some reason unknown to me, had been sent to Philip Pochechuyev's.

DOBCHINSKY (*interrupting*). For a keg for French brandy.

BOBCHINSKY (*brushing him aside*). For a keg for French brandy. Well, so Dobchinsky and I set off for Pochechuyev's . . . There now, Dobchinsky, don't interrupt me now. So we were on our way to Pochechuyev's when Dobchinsky says to me: "Let's go to the inn. I haven't eaten since morning," he says, "and so there's a sort of stomach quake going on inside me." Yes, in Dobchinsky's stomach. "At the inn," he says, "they've fresh salmon that's just come in. So we could have a snack." Well then, just as we entered the inn, a young man . . .

DOBCHINSKY (*interrupting*). Not bad looking, wearing civilian clothes . . .

BOBCHINSKY. Not bad looking, wearing civilian clothes, and he walks across the room with such a thoughtful expression on his face—a real physiognomy—and his bearing, and up here, (*He waves his hand around his forehead.*) up here, you can see, he's got plenty. I had a sort of foreboding about him and so I say to Dobchinsky: "There's something out of the ordinary here, that's for sure." But Dobchinsky had already beckoned to the innkeeper, whose name is Vlas. His wife had her baby three weeks ago—a fine, bouncing boy. He's sure to become an innkeeper like his father. So, Dobchinsky calls Vlas over and asks him quietly like: "Who," he says, "is that young man?" "That," Vlas says, "that . . ." Don't interrupt, Dobchinsky, please! You can't tell it, really you can't. You lisp. I know for a fact you've only one tooth in your head, and it's hollow and whistles when you talk. "That young man," Vlas says, "is an official from Petersburg and he goes by the name," he says, "of Ivan Alexandrovich Khlestakov. And," he says, "he's on his way to Saratov Province, and he strikes me as very peculiar. This is the second week he's here, and he never leaves the inn and everything goes on the bill and he hasn't paid a kopek yet." That's all he told me but I saw what it meant in a flash. "Aha!" I said to Peter . . .

DOBCHINSKY. No, Bobchinsky, I said "Aha!"

BOBCHINSKY. All right, so you said it first, but then I said it too. So, he and I both said "Aha!" and then I said: "What's he doing sitting here when he's on his way to Saratov Province?" Obviously he must be the official in question.

MAYOR. What? What official?

BOBCHINSKY. The official about whom you were warned—the Inspector General.

MAYOR (*frightened*). What are you talking about, man! It can't possibly be him!

DOBCHINSKY. It's him! A man who doesn't pay and doesn't leave. Who else could it be? And his travel order is made out for Saratov.

BOBCHINSKY. It's him, all right, I'm sure of it. You should see how observant he is: took in everything at a glance. He saw that Dobchinsky and I were eating smoked salmon—because of the state of Dobchinsky's stomach, as I explained—yes, well he even had a look into our plates. Incredibly observant! Gave me quite a shock.

MAYOR. Oh Lord, have mercy on us miserable sinners! Which room does he have?

DOBCHINSKY. Number 5, under the staircase.

BOBCHINSKY. That's the room where those officers had a fight when they stopped over here last year.

MAYOR. And has he been here long?

DOBCHINSKY. Two weeks already.

MAYOR. Two weeks! (*Aside.*) May the saints preserve us! In those two weeks, the corporal's widow was flogged; the prison inmates weren't issued their rations; the streets were filthy and full of drunks. Ah, what a shame and a disgrace! (*He clutches his head in his hands.*)

CHARITIES. What shall we do, Mayor? Shall we go over to the inn, all of us together?

JUDGE. No, no. Let the mayor go first and then the clergy and the merchants. It says so in the books: *The Acts of John the Freemason* . . .

MAYOR. No, no, please, let me do things my way. I've been in difficult positions before and I've got out of them and even received thanks for my trouble. So perhaps the Lord will see us through this one too. (*Turns to* BOBCHINSKY.) You say he's a young man?

BOBCHINSKY. Yes, twenty-three or four, not much more.

MAYOR. So much the better—it's easier to nose out a young one. When it's an old devil, then it's bad; but a young one's all in the open anyway. You gentlemen prepare yourselves, each in your own sphere, and I'll wander over there by myself—or perhaps with Bobchinsky here—as a private citizen, just to see whether the travelers are being treated properly. Hey, Whistles!

POLICEMAN WHISTLES. Yes, sir?

MAYOR. Go and fetch me the police inspector, or rather, no, I'll need you here. Tell someone else to go and fetch the police inspector as quickly as possible, but be back immediately.

(WHISTLES *hurries out.*)

CHARITIES (*to* JUDGE). Come, Judge, let's go. There may really be trouble.

JUDGE. Ah, you have nothing to worry about! Just put clean nightcaps on your patients and you're all set.

CHARITIES. Nightcaps indeed! I'm supposed to feed my patients clear broth, but the whole hospital reeks of cabbage so awfully that people have to hold their noses.

JUDGE. Well, I must say, I'm not too worried. After all, who'll want to go poking his nose into a district courthouse. And if he does try to look into a file, he'll be sorry he did. I myself have been on the bench fifteen years now, and if I do happen to glance into a file, I soon give it up. King Solomon himself wouldn't be able to make out what's the truth and what's not, in those things.

(*Exit* JUDGE, CHARITIES, SCHOOL SUPERINTENDENT, POST-MASTER, *colliding with the returning* POLICEMAN *at the door*.)

SCENE 4. *Mayor, Bobchinsky, Dobchinsky and Whistles the Policeman.*

MAYOR. Is the carriage outside?

WHISTLES. Yes, sir.

MAYOR. Go out into the street . . . no, wait! Go and get me—but, say, where are the others? Surely you shouldn't be on duty by yourself. Didn't I give orders for Prokhorov to be here too? Where is he?

WHISTLES. Prokhorov's at the police station, but he's not quite fit for duty right now.

MAYOR. How come?

POLICEMAN. Well, it's like this, sir—they brought him in this morning dead to the world. We've poured two buckets of water over him already but he still hasn't sobered up.

MAYOR (*seizing his head*). Oh Lord, oh Lord! Go out into the street quick . . . or, no—first go and fetch my sword and my new hat from the other room. Well, Dobchinsky, let's go.

BOBCHINSKY. Me too, me too! Let me come too, Mayor.

MAYOR. No, no, Peter, it's impossible. It wouldn't look right and, besides, there's not enough room in the carriage.

BOBCHINSKY. Oh, you needn't worry about that. I won't be in your way; I'll just trot along behind the carriage. I just want to have a peek through the door at him, to see how he operates . . .

MAYOR (*to* WHISTLES *who hands him the sword*). Hurry now and get the police together, let each of them take . . . Ah, look how scratched my sword is! Blast that Abdulin, the miserable, petty shopkeeper. He can see his mayor's sword is old, but d'you think he'd think of sending a new one over? Ah, they're an unreliable lot. I bet the chiselers are already fishing their petitions out of their pigeon-holes and preparing them— So, as I said, Whistles, let every man of the force grab a street—I mean, not a street, damn it, a broom—and let them sweep all the streets leading to the inn. And see they sweep them clean, you hear? And you'd better watch out yourself! I know you— you get chummy with them at the inn just so you can slip their silver teaspoons into your boot. Better watch out, I've got my eye on you! And the way you acted with the draper, uh? He said you could have two yards for your uniform and you swiped the whole roll. Just watch out! You're getting a bit above yourself, you know. Well, get going now!

SCENE 5. *The same and Police Inspector Sharpears.*

MAYOR. At last, Inspector! Where have you been hiding for heaven's sake? What's the matter with you?

INSPECTOR. I was just outside, in the street.

MAYOR. Well then, you know a high official has arrived from Petersburg. So, what have you done about it?

INSPECTOR. Just as you ordered—I've sent Button with some policemen to clean up the sidewalk.

MAYOR. And where's Grabmug?

INSPECTOR. Grabmug's off with the fire engine.

MAYOR. And Prokhorov's drunk.

INSPECTOR. That's right.

MAYOR. How could you allow such a thing?

INSPECTOR. Ah, with him you never know. Yesterday there was a fight just outside town. He went out there to restore order and came back plastered.

MAYOR. Listen, here's what you must do. Sergeant Button, he's a tall fellow now, well, put him on the bridge. Let him maintain public order there. Yes, and have that broken old fence quickly taken down—you know, by the shoemaker's shop, and have a post set up, as if we were about to start building something there. The more demolition there is, the more it shows activity on the part of a town's mayor. Oh Lord! I was forgetting that at least forty cart-loads of garbage have been dumped behind that fence. Ah, what a miserable town this is! No sooner do I have a public monument or even just a fence erected somewhere, than they immediately start piling up God knows what there! (*Sighs.*) And if the inspector general asks one of your men whether he's happy with his job, I want him to say, "Yes, sir, very, very happy indeed," because if any of them says anything different, I'll give him plenty to be unhappy about.

. . . Oh, dear, dear, dear, dear, I'm a sinner, a dreadful sinner! (*Picks up a box instead of his hat.*) God grant that I get this business off my hands as quickly as possible, and I'll burn such a candle, bigger than any that's been burned in these parts before. I'll make every lousy shopkeeper in this town fork out a hundred pounds of wax for it. Oh Lord, oh Lord! Let's go, Dobchinsky! (*Begins to put the cardboard box on his head.*)

INSPECTOR. Mayor, that's a box, not a hat.

MAYOR (*throwing it down*). So it's a box! The hell with it! Ah, if they ask why the Welfare Institution chapel hasn't been built yet and what happened to the money assigned for it five years ago, don't forget to say that construction was begun but that it burned down. I submitted a report to that effect. See to it that no one blunders and blurts out that it was never really started. And someone should tell Grabmug to go easy with his fists; with him, both guilty and innocent get black eyes in the name of order. Let's go, let's go, Dobchinsky. (*Exits only to reappear immediately.*) Yes, and the soldiers shouldn't be let out of the barracks except in proper uniform: that good-for-nothing bunch, they just put their tunics on over their nightshirts and underneath there's nothing at all.   (*Exit all.*)

SCENE 6. *Anna Andreyevna, the Mayor's wife, and Maria, his daughter, enter hurriedly.*

ANNA ANDREYEVNA. Where are they? Where are they? Oh good heavens . . . (*Opening the door.*) Anton, my dear! Tony! (*Speaks very quickly to* MARIA.) It's all your fault—dilly-dallying, worrying first about a pin, then about a kerchief. (*Runs over to window and calls out.*) Anton, where are you off to? Has he come? Why, the Inspector General, of course! Does he have a mustache? What sort of a mustache?

MAYOR'S VOICE. Later, later, my dear.

ANNA ANDREYEVNA. Ah, sure, it's always later! I don't wish to wait! Can't you tell me at least—is he a colonel? What? (*Scornfully.*) Huh, he's already left. You'll remember this one! And it's all this wretched girl's fault. "Mama, Mama, wait for me while I pin my kerchief at the back. Just one second," she says. I'll give you just one second! Now we haven't found out a thing! It's all your awful vanity, my girl. As soon as you heard the postmaster was here, you had to start primping before the mirror; first this way, then that! She thinks he's fallen for her—but as soon as you turn your head, he starts making faces at you.

MARIA. Well, what can we do now, Mama? Anyway, we'll find out what's going on in a couple of hours.

ANNA ANDREYEVNA. A couple of hours! Thanks a lot! That's a fine answer! Why don't you say that a month from now we'll know even more about it. (*Leans out of the window.*) Hey, Avdotya! Avdotya, have you heard about someone's arriving? . . . You haven't? Oh, the stupid goose! He waved you away? So let him wave, you should have asked him anyway. You couldn't even find that out! You've nothing but nonsense in your head, thinking of men all the time! What? They went off in a hurry? Well, you could've run after the carriage at least. I want you to go there now, d'you hear? Run along and find out where they went, and this time, really find out what this fellow from Petersburg is like—you hear? Peep through a crack in the door and find out everything—what kind of eyes he has. Whether they're black or not, and then come back right away, understand? Quick, quick, quick! (*She keeps shouting. As the curtain falls, the two women are still standing at the window.*)

CURTAIN

ACT II

A small hotel room. A bed, table, trunk, an empty bottle, Russian boots, a clothesbrush, etc.

SCENE 1. *Osip lying on his master's bed.*

OSIP. Damn it, I'm so hungry my stomach's rumbling—sounds like a whole regiment blowing trumpets. This way we'll never get home. But what can you do? Two months already since we left Petersburg! He's gone through all the money, getting this far, and now he's just lying low with his tail between his legs and doesn't seem to be in any hurry. There'd have been enough, more than enough, for the trip, but no, he has to show off in every town we come to. (*Imitates his master,* KHLESTAKOV.) "Hey, Osip, go get me a room—see it's the best they have—and order dinner, also the best. You know, I can't eat bad food. I have to have the best." That'd be all right if he was worth something, but he's nothing but a common penpusher. And he would make friends with the other travelers, and then it's cards.

And now look what he's played himself into! Ah, I'm fed up with this life! I sure was better off in the village, although there's nothing much in the way of fun there. But then you don't have much trouble there either. You get yourself a woman and then you can spend the rest of your life sleeping and eating pies and nothing else, if that's the way you want it. Yes, no question about it, life in Petersburg tops everything. As long as you have money—and it's a real refined social life: there's the theaters, and them dancing dogs, anything you want. And the people are real polite, too, just like they were all princes or something. You go to the Central Market, the stallkeepers give you *sir,* and on the ferry across the Neva you may find yourself sitting next to some important official. You want company? Just step into the corner store and you'll find some cavalryman there who'll tell you about the army camps and he'll explain the meaning of every star in the sky, so you see it all as clear as if you had them in the palm of your hand. In Petersburg, you have a chance to come across some nice, rich old lady, or sometimes a housemaid'll give you such a look . . . hoo, hoo, hoo! (*Smirks and shakes his head.*) Yes, everyone's polite as hell! You never hear a rude word and everyone calls you "mister." You get sick of walking, you just grab a horse cab and sprawl around in it like a gent. And if you don't want to pay—well, every house has a back gate, so you can skip in the front and out the back, so that even a bloodhound couldn't find you. There's only one thing's lousy and that's that one day you eat until you almost burst while the next you have to starve almost to death. Just like I'm doing now, for instance. And it's all my stupid master's fault. What can you do with a man like that? His papa sends him money, enough to get by on, but as soon as he gets it, he begins to throw it around right and left. He takes cabs everywhere he goes; every day you have to get him theater tickets, and a week later, here he's sending you off to the flea-market to sell his new tailcoat. Sometimes he loses everything, down to his last shirt, and then he's got nothing left but that old jacket and his worn-out overcoat. I swear to God, it's the gospel truth! And just look at that real swanky English cloth! His tail-coat alone cost a hundred and fifty rubles, and at the market you have to let it go for twenty. As to trousers, they fetch so little it's hardly worth bothering. And why all these troubles? Because he doesn't attend to his job: instead of carrying out his duties, he hangs around some of them elegant streets or gets into a card game. Ah, if the old master knew! He wouldn't worry about that son of his being a government official—he'd pull down his pants and give him such a whacking that the official in question would be going around rubbing his seat for a week afterward. If one has a job to do, the best thing is to get on with it. Look now, the innkeeper says he won't let you have anything to eat till you've paid what you owe. And what'll happen if we don't pay? (*Sighs.*) Oh Lord, Lord, if I could just have a drop of cabbage soup. I could eat the whole world, the way I feel. Ah, someone coming . . . Must be him. (*He quickly jumps up from the bed.*)

Scene 2. *Osip and Khlestakov.*

KHLESTAKOV. Here, take this. (*Hands him cap and cane.*) Have you been lolling around on my bed again?

OSIP. Why should I? You think I've never seen a bed before?

KHLESTAKOV. Liar, I know you were. I can see it's all rumpled.

OSIP. What would I want with your bed? Now I suppose, I don't know what a bed is? I've got feet, and I stand on them. I don't need your bed.

KHLESTAKOV (*pacing about the room*). Have a look in the packet there. Is there any tobacco left?

OSIP. How could there be? You smoked the last of it four days ago.

KHLESTAKOV (*paces up and down, twisting his lips into different grimaces. Finally he says in a loud, determined voice*). Hey, Osip! Listen!

OSIP. Yes, sir?

KHLESTAKOV (*in a voice still loud but less determined*). I want you to go there . . .

OSIP. Where?

KHLESTAKOV (*in a voice that is now neither loud nor determined; in fact, it is almost supplicating*). Downstairs, to the restaurant. Tell them . . . well, to serve me my dinner.

OSIP. Oh no, I won't!

KHLESTAKOV. How dare you! Idiot!

OSIP. How? Well, I just won't. And anyhow, it won't make no difference; nothing'd come of it. The innkeeper said he won't serve you dinner no more.

KHLESTAKOV. He won't dare refuse. You're talking nonsense!

KHLESTAKOV (*in a voice that is now neither loud nor de-*

OSIP. He even said he'd go and complain to the mayor. This he says, and your master are a couple of chiselers, and your master's a crook besides. We've seen cheats and finaglers before, he says.

KHLESTAKOV. And I suppose you're very happy, you rat, to be able to repeat all that to me now.

OSIP. "That way," he says, "anyone could come and feed and run himself up a bill and then I wouldn't be able to kick him out because of the money he owes me. I am not going to fool around," he says, "I'm lodging a complaint and they'll get him out of here and toss him straight into jail."

KHLESTAKOV. Come, come, idiot, that's enough from you. Go on now and tell him I want my dinner. Ah, what an uncouth creature!

OSIP. I think it'd be better if I asked the innkeeper to come here. Then you can tell him yourself.

KHLESTAKOV. What do I want to see him for? You go and tell him.

OSIP. No, really, master . . .

KHLESTAKOV. Oh, all right then, damn you! Go and tell him to come here. *(Exit OSIP.)*

SCENE 3. *Khlestakov alone.*

KHLESTAKOV. Oof, I'm so hungry! I hoped a little walk would deaden my appetite, but I'm damned if it has! Hm, if only I hadn't gone through all that cash in Penza, I'd have enough left to get home. That infantry captain really gypped me. The way that fellow cut the cards! We weren't at it more than fifteen minutes before he'd completely cleaned me out. And yet, I'd have given anything to take him on again—but I didn't get the chance. What a lousy little town! They won't even give you credit at the grocer's. How mean can you get! *(He whistles a tune from* "Robert the Devil," *then a Russian folksong, and finally something quite nondescript.)* No one seems to be coming up.

SCENE 4. *Khlestakov, Osip and an Inn Waiter.*

WAITER. The landlord sent me to ask what I could do for you.

KHLESTAKOV. Ah, hello, old man. How are you?

WAITER. Thank you, sir, I can't complain.

KHLESTAKOV. And how're things in the hotel? Everything all right?

WAITER. Yes, everything's fine, thank God.

KHLESTAKOV. Are there many guests?

WAITER. Yes, quite a few.

KHLESTAKOV. Listen, my good man, they still haven't brought

me my dinner, so please, shake 'em up a bit, and see that I get it soon. You see, I have to attend to some business after dinner.

WAITER. But the landlord says he won't let you have anything on credit any more. He even wanted to go and complain to the mayor today.

KHLESTAKOV. Complain? What about? Just think a moment; I have to eat, don't I? Otherwise I may waste away altogether. In fact, I'm very hungry and I'm in dead earnest when I say that.

WAITER. Yes, sir. He said: "I won't serve him dinner unless he pays up for what he's had already." Those were his very words.

KHLESTAKOV. Then go and try to reason with him, persuade him.

WAITER. But what can I say to him?

KHLESTAKOV. Make him see that I just have to eat. We'll see about the money later . . . Or does he imagine that just because he's nothing but a peasant and can go without eating for a day or two, it's all right for me too! He certainly ought to know better than that!

WAITER. All right, I'll tell him what you said.

SCENE 5. *Khlestakov alone.*

KHLESTAKOV. It's going to be really tough if he doesn't give me anything to eat. I don't think I've ever been so hungry. Perhaps I should let some clothes go. My trousers, for instance? No, I guess I'd rather go hungry but arrive home in a suit cut by a Petersburg tailor. It's a pity I couldn't hire a carriage—it sure would have been nice to drive up home in a carriage. Then I could've driven the damn thing right up to the porch of one of the neighboring landowners, with the lamps and all, and with Osip in livery on the step. I can just see them all getting excited: "Who is it? What's going on? Look! A footman in gold livery!" And then that footman announces: (*Draws himself up, pretending to be the footman.*) "Ivan Alexandrovich Khlestakov from Petersburg! Is your master receiving?" Those yokels don't even know what "receiving" means. When some oaf of a landowner comes to visit them, he just goes ambling right into the drawing-room, like a clumsy, great bear . . . and then I'd go up to some pretty daughter of the house: "Mademoiselle, I'm so delighted . . ." (*He stretches out a hand and clicks his heels.*) Ah, damn it! (*Spits.*) I'm so hungry, it's making me feel sick.

SCENE 6. *Khlestakov, Osip. Later, Inn Waiter.*

KHLESTAKOV. Well?

OSIP. They're bringing you your dinner.

KHLESTAKOV (*clapping his hands and leaping onto his chair*). Dinner's coming! Dinner's coming!

WAITER (*entering with plates and a napkin*). This is the last time, the landlord says.

KHLESTAKOV. The landlord, the landlord . . . To hell with your landlord! What do you have there?

WAITER. Soup and roast.

KHLESTAKOV. What, only two dishes?

WAITER. That's right.

KHLESTAKOV. Ah no! What kind of nonsense is that? I won't accept it. You go and ask what he means by it. This won't do!

WAITER. But the landlord . . . he says you're getting more than you should as it is.

KHLESTAKOV. And why isn't there any gravy?

WAITER. There's no gravy.

KHLESTAKOV. How's that? When I was passing by the kitchen, they were preparing all sorts of things. And then, in the dining-room this morning, I saw two short little men eating smoked salmon and all sorts of other things.

WAITER. Yes, that may be so, but still, there isn't any.

KLHESTAKOV. What d'you mean, there isn't any?

WAITER. There just isn't.

KHLESTAKOV. And what about salmon? Fish? Meat balls?

WAITER. Well, all that's for those who're better off.

KHLESTAKOV. Ah, you fool!

WAITER. Yes, sir.

KHLESTAKOV. Ah, you fathead! Why should they eat rather than me? Why can't I have the same as the rest of them, damn it? Aren't they customers, just the same as me?

WAITER. Well no, they're not the same as you, for sure.

KHLESTAKOV. What are they then?

WAITER. Well, they're the usual sort of customers. They pay cash.

KHLESTAKOV. I'm not going to argue with an idiot like you! (*Serves himself some soup and starts to eat.*) What kind of soup is this? It's just dishwater; it tastes like nothing on earth, although it certainly stinks! Take it away and get me some proper soup!

WAITER. I'll take it away, sir, if you wish. The landlord, he said if you didn't like it, you didn't have to have it.

KHLESTAKOV (*shielding the food with his arm*). Come on, come on, leave it alone, idiot. You may be used to behaving like that with others, but you can't do it with me! I wouldn't advise you to! (*He eats.*) You call this soup? (*Goes on eating.*) I don't believe there's another person in the whole world who has ever eaten soup like this. There're feathers floating in it instead of butter. (*Cuts himself some chicken.*) Oh Lord, what chicken! Come on, give me the roast! Hey, Osip, there's some soup left. You can have it! (*Cuts the roast.*) What kind of a roast is this? This isn't roast beef!

WAITER. Well, what is it then?

KHLESTAKOV. God knows what it is, but it's not roast beef. They've roasted a lump of iron instead of beef. (*He eats.*) The things they give you to eat, the chiselers! My jaws ache from trying to chew just one piece. (*Picks his teeth with his fingers.*) Crooks! It's like bits of bark—you can't get it out for anything! Food like that turns your teeth black. Ah, the bandits! (*Wipes his mouth with his napkin.*) There's nothing more?

WAITER. No, nothing.

KHLESTAKOV. Ah, the lousy bunch of thieves! They could at least have given me some gravy or a piece of pie. Loafers! All they ever do is gyp travelers.

(*The* WAITER *clears the table and exits carrying dishes, along with* OSIP.)

SCENE 7. *Khlestakov, then Osip.*

KHLESTAKOV. Really, I feel as if I hadn't eaten at all; it's only sharpened my appetite. If I had some change, at least, I could send him to the market to buy a French roll.

OSIP (*entering*). The mayor of this town has just come over to the inn and he's asking all sorts of things about you.

KHLESTAKOV (*frightened*). Here goes! That lousy innkeeper must have complained. Supposing he really does drag me off to jail? Well, so what, after all? If I'm treated like a gentleman, then I . . . no, no, it'd be awful. There're all sorts of officers and people around town and I, as usual, had to try to show off. And then, there's that merchant's daughter I had a little exchange of winks with . . . No, it'd be awful. Who does he think he is, anyway? How dare he, after all? Who does he think I am—a shopkeeper or a tradesman? (*Bracing himself, he draws himself up.*) I'll tell him straight to his face: How dare you? How . . . (*The door handle turns.* KHLESTAKOV *turns pale and goes limp.*)

SCENE 8. *Khlestakov, Mayor, Dobchinsky.*

(*On entering, the* MAYOR *stops. He and* KHLESTAKOV, *equally frightened, stare popeyed at each other for a few moments.*)

MAYOR (*recovering a little and standing stiffly to attention*). Good-day to you, sir!

KHLESTAKOV (*bowing*). Ah, hello . . .

MAYOR. I hope I'm not disturbing you, sir.

KHLESTAKOV. No, no, not at all!

MAYOR. It is my duty, as mayor of this town, to see to it that travelers and respectable people in general are treated properly and not taken advantage of.

KHLESTAKOV (*at first, stuttering a little, but toward the end of his speech, talking loudly and clearly*). But what can you do now? I really couldn't help it . . . but, of course, I'll pay . . . as soon as I get money from home. (BOBCHINSKY *peeks in at door.*) It's really more the innkeeper's fault than mine: the beef he serves is as tough as a lump of iron. And the soup! God knows what he dumps into it; I had to throw it out the window. He's been starving me for days on end. And you should taste the tea I get, it's really very peculiar—it stinks of fish, not tea. So how am I to blame if . . . It's quite unheard of!

MAYOR (*intimidated*). I'm so sorry to hear it. It's really not my fault though. Nowadays, there's always good beef at the market in my town, the very best, and the merchants who bring it in are people of good behavior and don't drink. I can't even imagine where this innkeeper gets such beef! But if there's something suspect about it, leave it to me. . . . Now, may I suggest that you come with me and I'll provide you with new lodgings.

KHLESTAKOV. Oh no, I'm not coming! I know what you mean by new lodgings—you mean jail. But what right do you have? Indeed, how dare you? . . . After all, I . . . I'm in government service in Petersburg. (*Bracing himself.*) I . . . I . . . I . . .

MAYOR (*aside*). Oh Lord, he seems to be ill-tempered—not at all easy to handle! Looks as if he knows everything already; those damned merchants must've told him.

KHLESTAKOV (*trying to look unafraid*). Yes, even if you brought your entire police force here, I wouldn't go! I'm going to complain to the Minister! (*Bangs his fist on the table.*) What do you want of me, anyway? What is it?

MAYOR (*standing stiffly at attention, his whole body trem-*

bling). Please, sir, please, take into consideration that I have a wife and small children . . . please don't ruin my career.

KHLESTAKOV. No, I won't go there! What next! What business is it of mine? Just because you have a wife and children, I have to go to jail! I've never heard such stuff before! (BOB-CHINSKY's *head pops up in the doorway but immediately vanishes in panic*.) No, thank you very much, I refuse.

MAYOR (*trembling*). It was just my lack of experience, I assure you, sir. Just that. And then, of course, as you know, sir, a government salary is hardly enough to keep oneself in tea and sugar. But even if some bribes were taken, it was really nothing to speak of: to put a little something on the table, or maybe for material for a couple of suits, that sort of thing. As to that corporal's widow who engaged in trade without a license—I'm supposed to have had her flogged, but it's a slander, really, sir, an absolute slander. My enemies thought that one up. They'd do anything to hurt me!

KHLESTAKOV. What do I care about them? (*He thinks for a while*.) But really, I don't see why you have to bring your enemies into this, or that corporal's widow, whoever she may be. . . . You'd better not try having me flogged. That'd be the end of everything! Anyway, I'll pay up, I'll pay up what I owe, but I just don't have any money on me right now. That's why I'm still sitting here—I haven't a kopek to my name.

MAYOR (*aside*). Ah, this is a really subtle one! What a smoke-screen! Just go and make anything out in it if you can! There's no telling which side to approach him from. . . . Well, I'll still have to have a go at it, no matter what. Come what may, I'll take a stab at it. (*Aloud*.) If you're really in need of money, or of anything else, I'd be glad to be of service. It's part of my duty to assist travelers.

KHLESTAKOV. Oh yes? Good! Then lend me some and I'll settle up with the innkeeper right away. I think two hundred rubles would do me fine, even less . . .

MAYOR (*handing him a roll of bills*). There's exactly two hundred rubles in here, I'm quite sure. Please don't bother counting, sir.

KHLESTAKOV (*taking the money*). I'm most grateful. I'll send it back to you as soon as I get home. I just found myself short, you know . . . I see you're an honorable man, sir. Now everything's different.

MAYOR (*aside*). Well, thank God he took the money! Now everything will be all right. Anyway, I slipped him four instead of two hundred.

KHLESTAKOV. Hey, Osip. (*Enter* OSIP.) Call the waiter! (*To*

MAYOR *and* DOBCHINSKY.) Oh, but why are you standing! Please sit down. (*To* DOBCHINSKY.) Do please sit down.

MAYOR. Please don't bother, sir, we can very well stand.

KHLESTAKOV. No, no, please sit down. I see now how open-hearted and hospitable you are. But, at first, I thought you'd come to . . . (*To* DOBCHINSKY.) Do sit down here. (MAYOR *and* DOBCHINSKY *sit down.* BOBCHINSKY *peeps in at door, listening.*)

MAYOR (*aside*). I'll have to be bolder. He wants us to respect his incognito. All right, then, we'll go along with his little game, if that's what he wants. We'll play it that we've no idea who he really is. (*Aloud.*) We were passing by in the line of duty, Dobchinsky here, one of our local landowners, and I, and we stopped over at the inn to see whether the guests were being well taken care of, because I'm not like other mayors, who don't concern themselves with such things. Besides, aside from my official duty, I wish, out of sheer Christian charity, to see that every mortal man is well received in my town, and now, you see, as if in reward, I've had the good luck to make your acquaintance.

KHLESTAKOV. It's lucky for me, too. If it hadn't been for you, I must admit, I'd have been stuck here for a long time. I had no idea how I was going to pay.

MAYOR (*aside*). Ha, that's a good one! Didn't know how he was going to pay! (*Aloud.*) May I inquire where you intend to go after this—which towns you mean to visit?

KHLESTAKOV. I'm on my way to Saratov Province, to my estate there.

MAYOR (*aside, with an ironic expression*). Does he really expect me to believe he's going to Saratov? And he doesn't even blush! I'd certainly better keep a sharp eye open with this one. (*Aloud.*) I'm sure it's a very good thing to visit one's home, sir, although, when traveling, one is always sure to experience all sorts of aggravations—you know, delays in obtaining horses and all that. But then, it is a diversion for the mind. You, I imagine, are mostly traveling for pleasure?

KHLESTAKOV. Oh no, my old man wanted me to come. He's furious with me because I haven't made much headway in the service in Petersburg yet. He thinks as soon as you get there, they go and give you the Order of St. Vladimir. Huh, I'd like to see how he'd stick it out, how he'd make out in the rat race of government service.

MAYOR (*aside*). Ah, the things he dreams up! And now he has to weave his old father into the story! (*Aloud.*) And do you intend to spend long at home?

KHLESTAKOV. I really can't tell; my old man's stubborn and stupid as a log. I'm just going to have to tell him: "Do as you wish, but I can't live outside Petersburg!" And, anyway, why should I waste my life among peasants. That won't do for me any more—I'm thirsting for enlightenment now.

MAYOR (*aside*). That's some yarn he's spun! He lies and lies without tripping up once. And yet he's so insignificant-looking, so puny, I feel I could squash him under my nail. But, just wait, I'll force him to make a slip soon enough. Just keep talking, my lad. (*Aloud.*) I agree with you completely—what would you do, buried in the sticks? Take me for instance: I don't sleep nights, striving for the Fatherland. I give myself ungrudgingly . . . but when it comes to a reward, who knows when I'll get it. (*Glances around the room.*) It seems to me that this room is rather damp?

KHLESTAKOV. It's a miserable room, and you should see the bedbugs! I've never seen the like—they bite like dogs!

MAYOR. But, my goodness, it's shocking that an enlightened man like you should have to put up with that. And from whom? From some sort of good-for-nothing bedbugs, who shouldn't ever have been born in the first place! Besides, isn't it rather dark in here?

KHLESTAKOV. Yes, it sure is dark. And the landlord won't let me have any candles any more. Sometimes I feel like reading a little, or I may get a fancy to write something down—and I can't. It's just too dark.

MAYOR. May I venture to suggest to you . . . But no, I don't dare. . . .

KHLESTAKOV. What is it?

MAYOR. No, no, really, I'm unworthy.

KHLESTAKOV. But tell me what it is, anyway.

MAYOR. If I may make so bold . . . I have a wonderful room for you at home—light, quiet. But no, of course not. I realize myself, it would be far too great an honor. Please don't be angry—I only suggested it out of the simplicity of my heart.

KHLESTAKOV. But I'd be delighted. I'm sure I'd be much better off in a private home than in this dump here.

MAYOR. Oh, I shall be so glad! And my wife will be very pleased, too. That's just the way I am—hospitable since childhood, especially when the guest is a cultured person. And please don't think I'm just trying to flatter you: flattery, now, is one fault I'm free of. I mean it from the bottom of my heart.

KHLESTAKOV. Oh, thanks a lot! I don't like two-faced people either. I really appreciate your frankness and friendliness. I must say, as long as a man treats me with respect and consideration, I can ask nothing more of him.

SCENE 9. *The same and the waiter, brought in by Osip. Bobchinsky's head pops through the doorway.*

WAITER. You sent for me, sir?

KHLESTAKOV. Yes, bring me my bill.

WAITER. But I gave you a new bill just a short while ago, sir.

KHLESTAKOV. I can't remember all your stupid bills. Tell me how much it was.

WAITER. You paid only for your dinner the first day, sir. On the second day you paid for a snack of smoked salmon, and, after that, you had everything on account.

KHLESTAKOV. I'm not asking you all that, you fool. How much is it altogether?

MAYOR. Please, sir, you mustn't bother with such trifles—they can wait. (*To* WAITER.) Out with you, now. The money'll be sent over.

KHLESTAKOV. Yes, I suppose you have the right way of handling these people. (*Puts his money away again. Exit* WAITER. BOBCHINSKY *peeks through the door.*)

SCENE 10. *Mayor, Khlestakov, Dobchinsky.*

MAYOR. Would you care to inspect some of the public services here in our little town, such as the charitable institutions, perhaps?

KHLESTAKOV. But, what is there to see?

MAYOR. Well, you can see how we cope with things, how we're organized . . .

KHLESTAKOV. With the greatest of pleasure. I'm ready. (BOBCHINSKY'S *head pops in at door.*)

MAYOR. And then, if you so wish, we could go on from there to the district school, and you could see the way we've organized the teaching of various subjects there.

KHLESTAKOV. That'd be very, very interesting.

MAYOR. And then, if you like, we can visit the police station and the local prison, so you can see how we take care of our prisoners.

KHLESTAKOV. But why the prison? Let's inspect the charitable institutions.

MAYOR. Just as you please, sir. Now, do you intend to go in your own carriage, or would you rather drive with me in mine?

KHLESTAKOV. I'll come with you.

MAYOR (*to* DOBCHINSKY). Well, Dobchinsky, I'm afraid there'll be no room for you then.

DOBCHINSKY. That's all right. I'll manage.

MAYOR (*aside to* DOBCHINSKY). Listen, you run—and as fast as your legs will carry you—and deliver two notes: one to Charities at the charitable institution and the other to my wife. (*To* KHLESTAKOV.) May I be so bold as to ask your leave to write just a line in your presence? It is to my wife, so that she can make preparations to receive our distinguished guest.

KHLESTAKOV. Oh, why should you trouble? . . . Oh well, there's ink here. As to paper, I don't know. Would this bill do?

MAYOR. It'll do fine. Thank you. (*He writes, at the same time talking to himself.*) Well, we'll see how things go after lunch and a couple of fat-bellied bottles! We have some of that local Madeira. It doesn't look like much, but it'll knock an elephant off its feet. If I can only find out just what sort of man he is and how wary I have to be of him. (*His note written, he hands it to* DOBCHINSKY *who walks over to the door, but just as he puts his hand on the knob, it flies open and* BOBCHINSKY, *who has been listening on the other side of it, comes tumbling onto the scene. All exclaim.* BOBCHINSKY *gets up.*)

KHLESTAKOV. Have you hurt yourself?

BOBCHINSKY. It's nothing, nothing, thank you. Absolutely no need for a fuss. Just a little bang on the bridge of my nose. I'll run over to the doctor's. He has a certain plaster—that'll take care of it.

MAYOR (*to* KHLESTAKOV, *making a reproachful gesture at* BOBCHINSKY). Ah, it's nothing at all. With your leave, sir, shall we go now? I'll tell your servant to take your trunk over to my place. (*To* OSIP.) My dear fellow, take everything over to my place—just ask for the Mayor's, anyone'll show you the way. With your leave, sir! (*Lets* KHLESTAKOV *go ahead, following behind him, then turns back and speaks reproachfully to* BOBCHINSKY.) Ah you! Couldn't you find anywhere better to fall? And then you had to go and sprawl out, looking like a sight! Ah, you!   (*Exits followed by* BOBCHINSKY.)

CURTAIN

ACT III

Same as Act I

SCENE 1. *Anna Andreyevna and Maria standing at the window in the same position in which we left them.*

ANNA ANDREYEVNA. So you see, we've been waiting here for a whole hour because of your stupid fussiness. You'd finished dressing but you still had to keep dawdling around . . . I should never have listened to you! Oh, how infuriating! And now, there's not a soul around—you'd think they were doing it on purpose. The whole place seems dead.

MARIA. Really, Mama, in a minute or two we'll know what's going on. Avdotya will be back any minute now. (*Looks out of the window, then cries out.*) Look, Mama, look! There's someone coming, down there at the end of the street.

ANNA ANDREYEVNA. Where? You're always imagining things. Oh yes, there he is. Who is it, though? He's short . . . he's wearing a tailcoat . . . who on earth could it be? Ah, how annoying, I wish I knew who it was!

MARIA. It's Dobchinsky, Mama.

ANNA ANDREYEVNA. What do you mean, Dobchinsky? The things you make up! It's not Dobchinsky at all. (*Waves her handkerchief.*) Hey you, come over here, quickly!

MARIA. It really is Dobchinsky, Mama.

ANNA ANDREYEVNA. There you go again. You always have to argue about everything. I tell you it's not Dobchinsky.

MARIA. Well, now, well, Mama? You see, it is Dobchinsky.

ANNA ANDREYEVNA. Of course it's Dobchinsky, I can see for myself, can't I? What are you arguing about? (*Calls out of the window.*) Hurry up, hurry up, why are you walking at such a snail's pace? Well then, where is everybody? What? Well, go on, tell me now! What? Very severe? Yes? And what about my husband? My husband! (*Stepping back from the window with some annoyance.*) Oh, he's so stupid! Won't tell me a thing until he gets inside.

SCENE 2. *The same and Dobchinsky.*

ANNA ANDREYEVNA. Ah, you ought to be ashamed of yourself! I was depending entirely on you, as a responsible man!

They all ran out on me and you went right after them! And here I am still waiting for a word of explanation. Shame on you! Here I was godmother to your Johnny and your Lizzie and now look how you behave!

DOBCHINSKY. But, my dear friend, I assure you, I've run so fast to pay my respects to you that I'm completely winded. My respects, Maria.

MARIA. Good day, Peter.

ANNA ANDREYEVNA. Well, what happened? Do tell us. What's going on over there?

DOBCHINSKY. Your husband sends you this note.

ANNA ANDREYEVNA. Yes, yes, but who is he? What's his rank? Is he a general?

DOBCHINSKY. No, he's not, but a general has nothing on him. He's so well educated and has such an impressive way about him!

ANNA ANDREYEVNA. Aha! So he's the man my husband was warned about in that letter?

DOBCHINSKY. No doubt about it. I was the first to discover it, along with Bobchinsky.

ANNA ANDREYEVNA. So, go on, tell me all about it; what do things look like?

DOBCHINSKY. Well, thank heaven, everything seems fine so far. At first, though, he received the mayor a little coldly; yes, he was quite angry and displeased with the hotel. He refused, however, to move to your house, saying he didn't wish to go to jail to cover up for your husband. But later, when he realized it wasn't Anton's fault, they had a little talk and he changed his mind, thank God, and everything went off smoothly. They've gone to inspect the charitable institutions now . . . but before that, I must admit, Anton thought perhaps there'd been some secret denunciation. I was quite scared myself . . .

ANNA ANDREYEVNA. But what did you have to be afraid of, since you're not a government employee?

DOBCHINSKY. Well, yes, but you know . . . when a bigwig like that opens his mouth, it makes one sort of uncomfortable.

ANNA ANDREYEVNA. Ah, I'm sure there's nothing to it really. Tell me rather, what's he like? Is he old or young?

DOBCHINSKY. He's very young. Around twenty-three, I'd say. But he speaks like an old hand at this game. "I don't mind," he says, "I'm ready to go anywhere." (*Waves his hands about.*) Just like that. And about himself, he says, "I like to write and to read a little, but I can't," he says, "because the room is dark."

ANNA ANDREYEVNA. But what's he like himself? Dark? Fair?

DOBCHINSKY. Well, I'd say he's rather mousey-colored. And his eyes dart around so fast—like mice—even makes you quite uncomfortable.

ANNA ANDREYEVNA. Let's see what Anton writes in his note. (*Reads.*) "I hasten to inform you, my dear, that at first I found myself in a quite lamentable position, but trusting to God's mercy, for two pickled cucumbers and one half-portion of caviar, one ruble, twenty-five kopeks . . ." (*Stopping.*) I don't understand a thing, what have pickled cucumbers and caviar got to do with it?

DOBCHINSKY. Oh, that's because Anton had nothing else to write on so he used a hotel bill . . .

ANNA ANDREYEVNA. I see. (*Continues reading.*) "but trusting to God's mercy, it looks as if it will all end well. Please hurry and prepare a room for an important guest; the one with the yellow wallpaper would be the most suitable. Don't bother to add anything to the dinner, because we'll have already had a snack with Strawberry at the charitable institution. But order more wine. Tell Abdulin to send the very best. Tell him, if he doesn't, I'll pull his whole cellar apart. I kiss your hand, my dear, and remain your ever-loving husband, Anton." Oh good Lord! I'd better hurry! Hey, who's there? Mishka!

DOBCHINSKY (*running to door and calling out*). Mishka! Mishka! Mishka!

(*Enter* MISHKA.)

ANNA ANDREYEVNA. Listen. Run over to Abdulin the wine merchant's . . . wait, I'll give you a note. (*Sits at table, writes note, talking at the same time.*) Give this note to the coachman Sidor and tell him to run over to Abdulin's with it and then bring the wine back. And you yourself go right away and give that room a good clean-out. And put a bed in there and a washstand, and the rest . . .

DOBCHINSKY. Anna Andreyevna, I think I'll be running along now. I'd like to see him in action—inspecting.

ANNA ANDREYEVNA. Go ahead, I'm not holding you back.

SCENE 3. *Anna Andreyevna and Maria.*

ANNA ANDREYEVNA. Well, Maria dear, we'd better see about dressing. He's a Petersburg dandy and God forbid he should find anything to turn his nose up at. The proper thing for you would be your blue dress with the flounces.

MARIA. Pooh, Mama, not the *blue* one! I don't like it at all, and besides, the Judge's wife wears blue and Mr. Strawberry's daughter too. No, I'd better wear the flowered one.

ANNA ANDREYEVNA. The flowered one! . . . Really, you're just saying that to be contrary. You'll look much better in the blue, because I intend to wear my pale yellow. I'm very fond of the pale yellow.

MARIA. Oh, Mama, the pale yellow doesn't become you at all.

ANNA ANDREYEVNA. The pale yellow doesn't suit me?

MARIA. No, it doesn't. I bet you anything it won't look nice —you need to have really dark eyes for it.

ANNA ANDREYEVNA. That's a fine thing to say! So now my eyes aren't dark enough? They're as dark as they come. What nonsense you talk! Of course, they're dark: I'm always the Queen of Clubs when I tell my fortune.

MARIA. Oh no, Mama, you're the Queen of Hearts.

ANNA ANDREYEVNA. Nonsense, utter nonsense! I've never been the Queen of Hearts. (*Exits hurriedly with Maria. Speaks from off-stage.*) The things you imagine! The Queen of Hearts indeed! Lord knows, the things you say sometimes!

(*As they exit, the door opens and* MISHKA *throws some rubbish out through it. At the other door,* OSIP *enters with a trunk on his back.*)

SCENE 4. *Mishka and Osip.*

OSIP. Where shall I put this?

MISHKA. In here, old fellow, in here.

OSIP. Hang on, give us a chance to rest a bit first. Ah, what a miserable life! Any load seems heavy on an empty belly.

MISHKA. Tell me, old fellow, will the general be here soon?

OSIP. What general?

MISHKA. Why, your master.

OSIP. My master? What kind of a general is he?

MISHKA. You mean he isn't a general?

OSIP. He's a general only if you start from the other end.

MISHKA. Well, is that more or less than a regular general?

OSIP. More.

MISHKA. I see, so that's why they're raising such a fuss here.

OSIP. Listen, fellow, I can see you're a smart lad—how about getting us something to eat.

MISHKA. Oh, there's nothing ready for you yet, old fellow. Of course, you can't be expected to eat simple food—but as soon as your master sits down to dinner, you'll be given the same food as him.

OSIP. Well, but the simple food—what d'you have?

MISHKA. Just soup and meat pie.

OSIP. Well then, let's have some. Soup and meat pie! Don't

worry, we'll eat anything. Come on, let's take the trunk in. Is there another door to that room?

MISHKA. Yes, there is.

(*They carry trunk into the side room.*)

SCENE 5. *Two policemen. Each opens one side of the double doors. Enter Khlestakov and, behind him, Mayor, then Charities, School Superintendent, Dobchinsky and Bobchinsky with a plaster on his nose. The Mayor points out a scrap of paper on the floor to the policemen. They hurry forward to pick it up, jostling each other in their haste.*

KHLESTAKOV. Fine institutions. I like your way of showing travelers everything there is in your town. In other towns, they didn't show me a thing.

MAYOR. In other towns, if I may make so bold as to remark, the town councilors and officials are more concerned, if you'll forgive the expression, about their own interests. But we here, even if I do say so myself, we have only one desire—to earn the approval of our superiors by vigilance and hard work.

KHLESTAKOV. That was a very good lunch. I really ate my fill. Do you eat like that every day?

MAYOR. It was in honor of such a pleasant guest.

KHLESTAKOV. Ah, I love to eat! After all, that's what we live for—to pluck the flowers of pleasure. What kind of fish was that?

CHARITIES (*approaching him*). It was pike.

KHLESTAKOV. Delicious! Where was that that we had lunch? Was it the hospital?

CHARITIES. It was indeed—a charity institution.

KHLESTAKOV. Oh yes, sure, I saw beds there. I suppose most of your patients have recovered? There weren't many there, were there?

CHARITIES. There are about ten left, not more. The rest have all recovered. That's how we work it—all in good order. Perhaps it may even seem incredible to you, but ever since I took over, the patients have been recovering, like flies. They hardly have time to get into the hospital before they're better again. And it's not so much the medicines as our conscientiousness and good organization.

MAYOR. May I be so bold as to draw your attention to the terrible intricacy of the mayor's duties! There is so much to be done—just think of the sanitation, the repairs and alterations alone . . . in a word, the most brilliant man could get lost in all the complications. But here, thanks be to God, everything's going along just fine. Another mayor, now, might well be looking out for his own advantage—but, believe it or not—even when I go to bed, I still keep thinking: Oh, good Lord, my God, now how can I arrange things so that the government will recognize my zeal and be pleased with me? Will they reward me, or not? That's up to them, of course, but, that's the only way I can find peace of mind. And so, when everything's in order in the town, when the streets are swept, the prisoners well cared for; when there aren't too many drunks—what more can I wish for? I swear it's not honors I'm after. A reward—it's tempting to be sure—but compared to civic virtue, it's nothing but dust and vanity.

CHARITIES (*aside*). Just listen to that loafer laying it on! He's got a real, God-given talent for it!

KHLESTAKOV. That's true. I must admit, I sometimes like to do some philosophizing myself in prose sometimes, or on occasion I toss off a few verses.

BOBCHINSKY (*to* DOBCHINSKY). Very, very apt! Did you hear? His comments are always so much to the point. You can see he's stored up plenty of learning.

KHLESTAKOV. Tell me now, what kind of entertainment do you have around here? Have you, for instance, such a thing as a club where one can get a little game of cards?

MAYOR (*aside*). Hm, we know what you're driving at, my boy! (*Aloud.*) God forbid! Such establishments are quite unheard of around here. Why, I've never so much as held a card in my hand. Don't even know how to play. I feel very strongly about it. Indeed, if by chance, I happen to catch sight of a king of diamonds or something like that, I feel just plain sick. I did once happen to build a house of cards—to amuse the children —but after that I dreamed of the damn things all night long. I don't know how people can waste their valuable time on them.

SCHOOL SUPERINTENDENT (*aside*). And to think that only yesterday, the crook took me for a hundred rubles!

MAYOR. I prefer to use my time in the service of the government.

KHLESTAKOV. Well, no, that's not right either. . . . Well, it all depends on how you look at it. For instance, if a person calls a halt after losing three-quarters of his stake . . . well, then, of course . . . No, but you must admit, it's a great temptation to play sometimes.

SCENE 6. *The same, Anna Andreyevna and Maria.*

MAYOR. May I be so bold as to present my family to you, sir—my wife, my daughter.

KHLESTAKOV (*bowing*). I am delighted to meet you, Ma'am, it's a great pleasure for me . . .

ANNA ANDREYEVNA. But the pleasure is even greater for us. To meet a personality like you . . .

KHLESTAKOV (*showing off*). Oh, no, Madam, I must insist, it's my pleasure that's greater.

ANNA ANDREYEVNA. How can you say such a thing, sir! But I realize that you're just saying that as a compliment. Ah, do sit down, please.

KHLESTAKOV. Just to stand near you is a pleasure. However, if you insist. Ah, it is real bliss to be sitting close to you.

ANNA ANDREYEVNA. Pardon me, but I don't dare to take that as addressed to me. I expect you're finding your little *voyage* quite dull and uncomfortable compared with your life in the capital.

KHLESTAKOV. Most, most uncomfortable. For one accustomed to living in society and all, to find himself suddenly on the road —and, *comprenez vous*, grubby inns and black ignorance. If it were not for this happy chance, which has . . . (*Glances at* ANNA ANDREYEVNA, *preening himself.*) made up for everything . . .

ANNA ANDREYEVNA. Oh yes, indeed, I imagine how painful this trip must've been for you.

KHLESTAKOV. Well, I must say, Ma'am, right at this minute, it's quite pleasant.

ANNA ANDREYEVNA. Do you really mean that? You do me great honor, sir; much more than I deserve.

KHLESTAKOV. Why don't you deserve it? You do deserve it, Ma'am, absolutely!

ANNA ANDREYEVNA. I live in the country—

KHLESTAKOV. Well, but the country also has its points: it has hills, brooks, all that. Oh, of course, it can't be compared with Petersburg. Ah, Petersburg! What a life it is! Perhaps you think I'm a mere copying-clerk, but I assure you, I'm on a friendly footing with the head of our section. He'll come and slap me on the back and say: "Come on, let's dine together." Usually, I just pop into the department for a minute or two to tell them: Do this, do that! There's a special clerk there to write the letters—he's like a mouse—scratching away with his pen all the time, scratch-scratch-scratch, writing and writing. They even wanted to make me head of the department, but I said to myself, why should I bother? As it is, the janitors come flying up the stairs after me—"Allow me, Ivan Alexandrovich, sir—" That's me— "We'll shine your boots for you." (*To* MAYOR.) Why are you standing, gentlemen? Please, sit down.

MAYOR, CHARITIES, SCHOOL SUPERINTENDENT (*speaking together*). We can stand before a high-ranking official like you. We'll stand. Please don't worry about us, sir.

KHLESTAKOV. Don't stand on ceremony. Please sit down. (*They sit down.*) I don't go much for protocol. In fact, I usually try to slip by unnoticed. But it's quite impossible! I just have to go out somewhere and right away, it's: "There goes Ivan Alexandrovich!" And once I was even taken for the Commander-in-Chief. The soldiers fairly leaped out of the guardhouse and presented arms. Afterward, one of the officers, whom I know well, says to me: "Ah, brother, we were sure you were the Commander-in-Chief!"

ANNA ANDREYEVNA. Please, tell us more!

KHLESTAKOV. Well, I know lots of pretty actresses. But then, there are several little vaudeville acts that I . . . I often meet with writers. Pushkin is a good friend of mine. I often say to him: "Well, Pushkin, old fellow, how are things?" And he always comes back at me with: "Well, old man, everything's sort of so-so." He's a very, very original fellow, you see.

ANNA ANDREYEVNA. So you write too? I imagine it must be most exciting to be an author. They publish you in magazines too, no doubt?

KHLESTAKOV. Yes, yes, of course, in magazines too. And I've written many plays: among others, *The Marriage of Figaro, Robert le Diable, Norma,* and many I don't even remember by name. And I wrote them all rather by chance. I never really wanted to write, but theater directors would come and pester me: "Come, old man, please write us something." And so I'd say to myself: "Well, all right, old man, let's go!" And so I'd sit down and write the whole thing in one evening. They couldn't believe their eyes! I write with extraordinary facility: everything that's come out under the name of Baron Brambeus, and then the novel, *The Frigate of Hope,* and the *Moscow Telegraph* . . . It's all me. I wrote the whole lot.

ANNA ANDREYEVNA. Really! So it's you—Baron Brambeus!

KHLESTAKOV. Of course. I help them all out, fixing up their prose. Why, Smirdin the publisher pays me forty thousand for it.

ANNA ANDREYEVNA. Then you probably wrote *Yurii Miloslavsky* too?

KHLESTAKOV. Certainly, I wrote it.

ANNA ANDREYEVNA. I guessed it right away.

MARIA. But, Mama, it says in the book that Mr. Zagoskin wrote it.

ANNA ANDREYEVNA. Here we go! I knew you'd have to start arguing even now.

KHLESTAKOV. Yes, that's true, that's Zagoskin's, but there's another *Yurii Miloslavsky,* and that one's mine.

ANNA ANDREYEVNA. Well, it must be yours that I read. It's wonderfully written!

KHLESTAKOV. I must admit, I live for literature. Mine is the first house in all Petersburg. Everyone knows Ivan Alexandrovich's house. (*Addressing all.*) Any time you're in Petersburg, gentlemen, I invite you, all of you, to come and visit me. And, you know, I give balls, too.

ANNA ANDREYEVNA. I can just imagine the splendor and the good taste of the Petersburg balls!

KHLESTAKOV. Ah, don't even talk of it! For instance, they serve watermelon—seven hundred rubles worth of watermelon! And the soup is brought by boat straight from Paris, right in the tureen; they lift the lid and the steam—it's unlike any steam one finds in nature. I go to balls every day. Then we sit down to a game of whist: the Minister for Foreign Affairs, the French Ambassador, the English Ambassador, the German Ambassador, and I. And you play till you're half dead—never seen anything like it. So you dash upstairs to your room and you just say to the cleaning woman: "Hey, Mavrushka, my overcoat" . . . But what am I talking about? It just altogether slipped my mind that I live in an apartment on the second floor. The staircase of my house alone is worth seeing! And if you could just glance into my reception room before I wake up in the morning. There are counts and princes bumping into each other and buzzing like a lot of bumblebees. All you can hear is buzz-buzz-buzz. . . . Sometimes you'll find a minister there, too. (MAYOR *and others rise diffidently to their feet.*) Even the parcels sent to me are addressed Your Excellency. Once I was in charge of a whole government department. It was very strange. The minister left on a trip, no one knew where. Well, naturally, they started to argue how his place could be filled and by whom? Many of the higher-ups were eager to have a go at it, but when they'd had a taste of what it involved, they saw it was too much for them. It may look like nothing from the outside, but when you look closer . . . damn it all, they soon realized they'd have to turn to me. So they sent their messages to me and, within minutes, the streets were full of couriers, couriers, couriers . . . just imagine, thirty-five thousand couriers!

Can you imagine how I felt? "Ivan Alexandrovich, come and run the department!" I must admit I was a little taken back. I appeared in my dressing gown, intending to refuse, but then I thought to myself: suppose the Tsar hears about it? And then there was my record of service to think of too. . . . "Very well, Gentlemen, all right, I'll take the job, I'll take it," I says. "So be it. But, you'd better watch out now . . . I have," I says, "my ear to the ground! I . . ." And after that, whenever I walked through the department, it was like a real earthquake: they all trembled and shook like leaves. (MAYOR *and others shake with fear.* KHLESTAKOV *becomes even more excited.*) Yes, I don't like to fool around. I gave them all a good talking to. The Imperial Council itself is afraid of me. And with good reason, too. That's the way I am! I don't stop before anyone. I tell them all: "I know everything, I'm all over the place, everywhere. I go to the Tsar's Court every day. Why, they'll make me a field marshal tomorrow." (*Slips off his seat and nearly hits the floor, but is respectfully supported by the officials.*)

MAYOR (*approaching, shaking all over and making an effort to speak*). But y-y-your, y-your . . . excellen—

KHLESTAKOV (*speaking quickly and sharply*). What is it?

MAYOR. But y-y-your, y-y . . .

KHLESTAKOV (*in the same tone*). Can't make out a thing— sheer nonsense.

MAYOR. Y-y-your excellen . . . Excellency, would perhaps wish to rest . . . there's a room here, and everything you need.

KHLESTAKOV. Nonsense, who wants to rest! Although, yes, I do wish to have a rest. The lunch we had, gentlemen, was good. . . . I'm pleased, quite pleased. Excellent fish, excellent!
(*Goes off into side room followed by* MAYOR.)

SCENE 7. *The same, without Khlestakov and Mayor.*

BOBCHINSKY (*to* DOBCHINSKY). There's a man for you, Peter! That's what it means to be a man. I've never been in the presence of such a bigwig before—I almost died of fright. What d'you think he is by way of rank?

DOBCHINSKY. I wouldn't be surprised if he was a general, Peter.

BOBCHINSKY. Well, Peter, I'd say a general couldn't even hold a candle to him. And if he *is* a general, then he must be the generalissimo himself. You heard how he has the Imperial Council under his thumb. Come, let's hurry over and tell the judge and Mr. Korobkin all about it. Good-by, Anna Andreyevna.

DOBCHINSKY. Good-by, dear Anna Andreyevna.

(Exit both.)

CHARITIES (*to* SCHOOL SUPERINTENDENT). It's simply terrifying! There's no telling what he may do! To think he surprised us not even properly dressed for the occasion. Why, he may send off an adverse report, to Petersburg, just as soon as he's had his snooze.

(Exits thoughtfully; SCHOOL SUPERINTENDENT *follows him, saying as he leaves.)*

Good-by, Ma'am.

SCENE 8. *Anna Andreyevna and Maria.*

ANNA ANDREYEVNA. Oh, isn't he nice!

MARIA. He's a darling!

ANNA ANDREYEVNA. What fine manners! You can tell he's a Petersburg dandy right away! Receptions and all that. . . . Oh, how marvelous! I adore that type of young man! He takes my breath away! And, you know, he liked me very much; I noticed, he kept glancing at me.

MARIA. Oh no, Mama, it was me . . .

ANNA ANDREYEVNA. Ah, enough of your nonsense! This really isn't the time or the place for it.

MARIA. But, Mama, it's true.

ANNA ANDREYEVNA. What next! You'd say anything just to contradict me! That's enough of that! When did he look at you? And, anyway, why should he look at you?

MARIA. But it's the truth, Mama. He kept looking at me all the time; when he started talking about literature, he gave me a look, and then he looked at me when he was telling about how he played whist with the ambassadors.

ANNA ANDREYEVNA. Well, maybe once or twice, and even then I bet he was saying to himself: "Ah, I suppose I ought to look at that one a bit, too."

SCENE 9. *The same and Mayor.*

MAYOR (*entering on tiptoe*). Sh-sh-sh . . .

ANNA ANDREYEVNA. What's the matter?

MAYOR. I'm not too happy really about getting him drunk like that. Now, suppose only half of what he said was true? (*Grows thoughtful.*) And how can it not be true? When he's drunk, a man brings up everything and whatever's in his heart is on his tongue too. Of course, there was some exaggeration in what he said, a few small lies, but then a speech is no speech without them. So he plays whist with ambassadors, attends the Tsar's Court . . . And so, the more I think of it . . . Ah, damned if I know! My head's spinning. It feels as if I were standing on top of a belltower . . . It's also a bit like waiting for them to come and hang you.

ANNA ANDREYEVNA. Well, I didn't feel ill at ease with him at all. To me, he is simply a refined man of the world with manners of the very highest tone. As to his rank—what's that to me?

MAYOR. Oh, you women! All you think of is wagging your tongues! It's all just yap, yap, yap! And then, you're liable to blurt out something stupid, for which you may get a good dressing-down at the most, without any lasting damage; but for your poor husband, it will mean the end of his career. And, my dear, you behaved so freely with him—just as if he were a Dobchinsky or someone like that.

ANNA ANDREYEVNA. I'd advise you not to worry yourself about that. We happen to know a thing or two. (*Glances at* MARIA.)

MAYOR (*soliloquizing*). Ah, what's the good of talking to you! My God, what a business! I still haven't got over my fright. (*Opens door and speaks through it.*) Mishka, tell Policemen Whistles and Grabmug to come in here. They're somewhere just outside in the street. (*After a short silence.*) Ah, everything's so cockeyed nowadays! You'd think he'd at least look impressive, but he's such a puny slip of a fellow! How's one supposed to guess who he is? Perhaps he looks different in his dress uniform, but when he wears that miserable little frock-coat, he's exactly like a fly with its wings pulled off. And look how long he held back at the inn, tying us up with all those allegories and equivocations. I thought it'd take a lifetime to find out what he was getting at. But now he's finally broken down. In fact, he even said more than was necessary. Well, he's young . . .

SCENE 10. *The same and Osip. All run toward him, beckoning to him.*

ANNA ANDREYEVNA. Here, come here, my good fellow.

MAYOR. Sh! . . . Well, what's happening? Is he asleep?

OSIP. Not yet, he's still moving around a bit.

ANNA ANDREYEVNA. Listen, what's your name?

OSIP. Osip, Ma'am.

MAYOR (*to* WIFE *and* DAUGHTER). That's enough, that's

enough! (*To* Osip.) Well, my friend, did they give you a good meal?

Osip. They did, I thank you most kindly, they gave me a good meal.

Anna Andreyevna. Well, tell me— I suppose there are lots of counts and princes who come to visit your master?

Osip (*aside*). What'll I tell them? They fed me well just now, and it looks as if they'll feed me again, and even better. (*Aloud.*) Yes, Ma'am, there are counts, too.

Maria. Ah, Osip, you know, your master is a real pet!

Anna Andreyevna. Tell me, Osip, how does he . . .

Mayor. Now, please stop it! You're preventing me from finding anything out with your nonsense. Well, my friend, what . . . ?

Anna Andreyevna. And what's your master's rank?

Osip. The usual sort of rank, Ma'am.

Mayor. Oh, my God, you'll land us all in a real mess with your stupid questions! You don't give me a chance to get a word in about serious things. Well, my friend, tell me, what's your master like? Is he very strict? Does he like to haul people over the coals?

Osip. Well, he likes everything to be in order. Everything has to be shipshape with him.

Mayor. You know, my friend, I like your face. I'm sure you must be a good fellow. Now, tell me . . .

Anna Andreyevna. Listen, Osip, what uniform does your master go around in over there?

Mayor. Enough of your chatter! This is an important matter. A matter of life and death. (*To* Osip.) Now, my friend, I must say, I really like you very much and, you know, an extra drink never hurts when you're on the road, especially with the cold weather we've been having. So here's a couple of rubles for drinks.

Osip (*taking the money*). I thank you most kindly, sir, and may God bless you for helping out a poor man.

Mayor. Oh, I'm only too happy to help . . . Now, my friend, what . . .

Anna Andreyevna. Listen, Osip, what color eyes does your master prefer in a lady?

Maria. Dear Osip! What a charming little nose your master has!

Mayor. Stop it now! Give me a chance! (*To* Osip.) Tell me, my friend, what does your master pay most attention to, that is, what does he like best when he's traveling?

Osip. It depends . . . He'll look at anything he's shown. And what he likes best of all is to be well received. He very much likes good, open-handed hospitality.

MAYOR. Open-handed hospitality?

OSIP. Yes, that's right. Here, take me, I'm only a serf, yet he still keeps an eye out to see that things are good for me, too. You know, sir, sometimes we stop over somewhere, and afterward, he says to me: "Well, Osip, did they treat you good?" "No, Your Excellency, not good at all!" "That proves he's a bad official if he's a bad host, Osip," he says. "You remind me when we get back home." "Ah," I thinks to myself, "never mind! I'm just a simple man."

MAYOR. Good, good, now you're talking! What I gave you was for drinks. Well, here's some more, for snacks.

OSIP. Why are you so good to me, Your Honor? (*Pockets money.*) Well, I guess I'll go and have a drink to your health.

ANNA ANDREYEVNA. Come over here to me, Osip! I have something for you too.

MARIA. Dear Osip, kiss your master for me!

(*A slight cough from* KHLESTAKOV *is heard from the other room.*)

MAYOR. Sh! (*Rises on tiptoe. The rest of the scene is conducted in low voices.*) God forbid you should make a noise! Please, go now! You've done enough harm for one day!

ANNA ANDREYEVNA. Come, Maria! I'll tell you something I've noticed about our guest that is for your ear only.

MAYOR. Oof! They'll talk their heads off! Just try and listen to them—you'll end up having to stuff your ears! (*Turning to* OSIP.) Well, my friend . . .

SCENE 11. *The same and Policemen* Grabmug *and* Whistles.

MAYOR. Sh! Listen to the clumsy clods thumping along in their boots! You come down on each foot like a ton of bricks! Where the hell have you been?

GRABMUG. My orders were . . .

MAYOR. Sh! (*Covers* GRABMUG's *mouth with his hand.*) Just listen to him caw like a crow! (*Imitating him.*) "My orders were!" Such a roar, you'd think he was yelling into a barrel! (*To* OSIP.) Well, my friend, off you go and prepare whatever's needed for your master. Just call for anything at all that's in the house. (*Exit* OSIP.) And you station yourself on the porch, and don't you budge! And don't let any outsiders into the house; especially merchants! If you let a single one of them in, I'll . . . And as soon as you see someone coming with a complaint or even without a complaint—even if he just looks like

someone who might want to lodge a complaint against me—
you kick him right out. Like that! Don't hold yourselves back!
(*Demonstrates with his foot.*) D'you hear? Sh! sh! Quiet! . . .
                    (*Exits on tiptoe after the two* POLICEMEN.)

ACT IV

The same room in the Mayor's house.

SCENE I. *Enter cautiously, almost on tiptoe, the Judge,
Charities, Postmaster, School Superintendent, Dobchinsky
and Bobchinsky, all formally dressed, decorations and all.
The entire scene is conducted in hushed tones.*

JUDGE (*forming the others into a semicircle*). For heaven's
sake, gentlemen, form a semicircle; let's have a little order
here! He's entitled to it! He attends the Tsar's Court and can
afford to bawl out the Imperial Council! Come on, fall in! We
must have some military discipline, and I mean, *military*! You,
Peter, come around on this side, and you, Peter, you stand
here. (*Both* PETERS, DOBCHINSKY *and* BOBCHINSKY, *scurry to
their places on tiptoe.*)

CHARITIES. Whatever you say, Judge, we really ought to *do*
something.

JUDGE. Such as?

CHARITIES. You know very well.

JUDGE. Grease his palm?

CHARITIES. Well, yes, grease his palm perhaps . . .

JUDGE. That's dangerous, damn it, he may raise hell about it.
He's a high official, remember. Unless perhaps we could do it in
the form of a contribution from the local gentry toward some
monument or something like that.

POSTMASTER. Or maybe we could say: "Look, here's some
money came in the mail and no one knows who it belongs to."

CHARITIES. You watch out he doesn't send you somewhere far
away by mail yourself! Listen, in a well-organized community,
these matters can be handled properly. Anyway, what are we
doing here, herded together like so many cows? We should present ourselves one at a time, and then, when each of us is alone
with him, with no witnesses around, as it should be, then . . .
then's the moment. That's how things are done in a well-organized
community. Well, what about you going in first, Judge?

JUDGE. No, it'd be better if you went. After all, it was in your institution that our distinguished visitor broke bread.

CHARITIES. Well then, let Luke be the first. He's the enlightener of the young, after all.

SCHOOL SUPERINTENDENT. No, no, gentlemen, I can't. The way I was brought up, if someone just one rung above me on the ladder addresses me, I feel like fainting and my tongue won't move, as if it were stuck in the mud. No, gentlemen, you must excuse me, you really must.

CHARITIES. So, you see, Judge, there's no one left but you. Besides, as soon as you open your mouth, it's as if Cicero in person were flying off your tongue, riding every word you say.

JUDGE. Some Cicero! Anything else? Just because once in a while I get carried away talking about a pack of hounds or some special hunting dog and become eloquent . . .

ALL (*importuning him*). No, no, it's not only about dogs. You've also spoken about disorder . . . No, Judge, don't let us down! You're like a father to us! . . . Please, Judge!

JUDGE. Let me be, gentlemen!

(*At this moment, a cough and footsteps are heard from* KHLESTAKOV'S *room. All rush, jostling each other, toward the door, where they crowd together, trying to get out. This naturally entails someone's getting squashed. Subdued exclamations are heard.*)

BOBCHINSKY'S VOICE. Ouch! Dobchinsky, you stepped on my toe!

CHARITIES' VOICE. Get off me, gentlemen, let me live to repent my sins. You're crushing me to death!

(*A few cries of "Ow!" and "Ouch!" rise. Finally, they all manage to push their way through and the room is left empty.*)

SCENE 2. *Khlestakov, alone, enters looking sleepy-eyed.*

KHLESTAKOV. That was a good snooze. Where on earth do they get such mattresses and comforters? I was so warm, it made me sweat even! Guess they served me some real good stuff with my lunch—I can still feel my head throbbing. Well, I see a nice time can be had here. Ah, I sure like hospitality and, I must say, I like it even better when it comes right from the heart and isn't done with ulterior motives. Then there's the Mayor's daughter—not bad at all. The mother is still all right too, and if it were possible . . . Yes, I must admit, this is just the life for me.

Scene 3. *Khlestakov and Judge.*

Judge (*aside as he enters*). Oh dear Lord, please see me through this safely. My knees are buckling under me. (*Aloud, drawing himself up and clutching his sword hilt.*) May I have the honor of presenting myself:—Judge of the District Court here, Collegiate Assessor Lapkin-Tapkin.

Khlestakov. Please sit down. So you're the judge here?

Judge. I was elected in 1816 for a three-year term by the local gentry, and have continued in my duties ever since.

Khlestakov. And tell me, is it profitable to be a judge?

Judge. For three three-year terms I was awarded the Order of St. Vladimir, fourth class, with a commendation from my superiors. (*Aside.*) The money's here in my hand, but my hand feels as if it were on fire.

Khlestakov. Oh, I like the Order of St. Vladimir. I'd rather have a St. Vladimir fourth class than a St. Anne third class.

Judge (*thrusting out his clenched fist a little way. Aside*). Oh, my God, I feel as if I were sitting on hot coals.

Khlestakov. What's that you have in your hand?

Judge (*becoming panicky and dropping the bills on the floor*). It's nothing . . .

Khlestakov. What d'you mean nothing? Isn't that money that fell on the floor?

Judge (*shaking all over*). No, no, it's not. (*Aside.*) Oh, my God, he's going to have me arrested! They'll come and cart me away any moment now.

Khlestakov (*picking up the money*). But it *is* money!

Judge (*aside*). Well, that's the end of everything! I'm lost! I'm lost!

Khlestakov. You know what—lend me this . . .

Judge (*hurriedly*). Of course, of course, with the greatest of pleasure. (*Aside.*) Courage, courage! Mother of God, get me out of this!

Khlestakov. You see, I've spent all I had on me, on the road, first for one thing, then . . . Of course, I'll send it back to you as soon as I get home.

Judge. Please, not at all . . . it's an honor, anyway . . . Of course, to the extent of my feeble powers, with zeal and diligence, I will endeavor . . . to serve my superiors . . . (*Rises and draws himself up to attention.*) I don't wish to impose further upon your time and patience. Do you have any further orders?

Khlestakov. What orders?

JUDGE. I thought you might have some orders for the local district court.

KHLESTAKOV. But why? I have absolutely no need of the district court for the moment. No, none. Thank you most kindly.

JUDGE (*bows and says aside as he exits*). Well, the town is ours!

KHLESTAKOV (*as* JUDGE *exits*). Nice man, the judge!

SCENE 4. *Khlestakov and Postmaster. Postmaster enters, wearing his formal uniform. Draws himself up, clasping his sword.*

POSTMASTER. May I have the honor of presenting myself: Court Councilor Shpekin, Postmaster.

KHLESTAKOV. Ah, how do you do? How nice it is to have pleasant company. Do sit down. Tell me, do you live here permanently?

POSTMASTER. Oh yes, sir, I do indeed.

KHLESTAKOV. Well, I must say, I like this little town very much. Of course, it's rather small; but what of that? What d'you expect, every town isn't Petersburg, after all. Isn't that right?

POSTMASTER. Absolutely right.

KHLESTAKOV. Of course, it's only in the capital that you'll find all the high-tone people and no provincial geese. Don't you think so?

POSTMASTER. Exactly so. (*Aside.*) Hm, he doesn't seem to be at all stuck-up. Asks my opinion about all sorts of things.

KHLESTAKOV. But, on the other hand, you will agree that it's quite possible to live happily, even in a small town.

POSTMASTER. Oh yes, indeed, sir.

KHLESTAKOV. In my opinion there's only one essential condition: people must respect you and like you sincerely, isn't that so?

POSTMASTER. No doubt about it, sir.

KHLESTAKOV. Well, I must admit, I'm very glad to find you share my opinions. Of course, people often think me eccentric, but that's just the way I am. (*Glances at* POSTMASTER, *then says aside.*) I'll ask the postmaster for a loan! (*Aloud.*) You know, the strangest thing has happened to me—I spent all my money getting here. Could you possibly lend me three hundred rubles?

POSTMASTER. But certainly, sir. In fact, it will make me immensely happy to do so. Here you are, sir. From the bottom of my heart, I'm glad to be of service.

KHLESTAKOV. I'm most grateful. I must admit I hate to deny

myself anything when I'm traveling, and indeed, why should I? What do you think?

POSTMASTER. Exactly, sir, why should you? (*Rises, draws himself up, clasping sword.*) I don't wish to further impose upon your time and patience. Do you have any comments as regards the Postal Service?

KHLESTAKOV. No, none.

(*Postmaster bows and exits.*)

KHLESTAKOV (*lighting up a cigar*). That postmaster is a very nice fellow too. Anyway, he's very obliging. I like that.

SCENE 5. *Khlestakov and School Superintendent, who is almost shoved through the door. A quite loud whisper is heard behind him: "Go on! What're you afraid of!"*

SCHOOL SUPERINTENDENT (*drawing himself up rather shakily, and clutching his sword*). May I have the honor of presenting myself:—Titular Councilor Khlopov, School Superintendent.

KHLESTAKOV. Please come in. Sit down, sit down. Wouldn't you like a cigar? (*Offers cigars.*)

SCHOOL SUPERINTENDENT (*to himself irresolutely*). There's one in the eye for you! That, I never expected. Shall I take a cigar or not?

KHLESTAKOV. Do have one, they're not too bad, you know. Of course, they're not as good as what I get in Petersburg. Now, over there, old man, I smoke a marvelous cigar—they cost twenty-five rubles the hundred. When you've smoked one, you simply want to kiss your own hand; that's how good they are. Here's a light. (*Holds out candle for him.* SCHOOL SUPERINTENDENT *tries to light up, shaking all over.*)

KHLESTAKOV. No, no, that's the wrong end!

SCHOOL SUPERINTENDENT (*dropping cigar in his fright, making a spitting motion and waving his hand, to himself*). Ah, hell! I'm ruined and all because of my damned shyness!

KHLESTAKOV. Well, I can see you don't go for cigars much. Me, I must admit, they're my weakness. That and—well, when it comes to the female sex, I just can't remain indifferent. What about you? Which do you like best, brunettes, or blondes? (SCHOOL SUPERINTENDENT *doesn't know what to say at all.*)

KHLESTAKOV. No, tell me frankly, brunettes or blondes?

SCHOOL SUPERINTENDENT. I wouldn't presume to know.

KHLESTAKOV. Oh no, I won't let you wriggle out of it now! I want absolutely to know your tastes.

SCHOOL SUPERINTENDENT. If I may be so bold as to remark . . . (*Aside.*) Don't know what I'm saying myself.

KHLESTAKOV. Aha! So you don't want to tell me! Probably some little brunette has been giving you a bit of bother. Admit it! Isn't it so? (SCHOOL SUPERINTENDENT *remains silent*.)

KHLESTAKOV. Aha! I see you're blushing! So why don't you tell me all about it?

SCHOOL SUPERINTENDENT. I'm quite overcome, Your Hon . . . Excell . . . (*Aside*.) My damned tongue's betrayed me, betrayed me!

KHLESTAKOV. Overcome? It's true that there's something in my eyes that intimidates people. At any rate, I know that not a single woman can resist them, isn't that so?

SCHOOL SUPERINTENDENT. Oh, exactly so, sir.

KHLESTAKOV. You know, the oddest thing has happened to me during my travels; I've spent every penny! Could you lend me three hundred rubles?

SCHOOL SUPERINTENDENT (*plunging his hand into his pocket. Aside*). It'll be something if I don't have it! Oh yes, I have it, I have it. (*Takes bills from his pocket and hands them shakily to* KHLESTAKOV.)

KHLESTAKOV. Thank you very, very much.

SCHOOL SUPERINTENDENT (*drawing himself up and clutching his sword*). I have no wish to impose upon you further.

KHLESTAKOV. Good-by, then.

SCHOOL SUPERINTENDENT (*almost running out of the room. Aside*). Well, thank God! Now perhaps he won't even look at the schools.

SCENE 6. *Khlestakov and Charities. Charities draws himself up and clutches sword.*

CHARITIES. May I have the honor of presenting myself:— Court Councilor Strawberry, Director of Charities.

KHLESTAKOV. How d'you do? Do sit down.

CHARITIES. It was I who had the honor of escorting you around the charitable institutions entrusted to my care and of receiving you personally there.

KHLESTAKOV. Ah yes, I remember you. That was a very good lunch you gave us.

CHARITIES. I'm glad to make every effort in the service of the Fatherland.

KHLESTAKOV. I must admit, good food is my weakness. But wait—it seems to me that the last time I saw you you were a bit shorter. Could I be right?

CHARITIES. Indeed, you could very well be, sir. (*Pause*.) All I can say is that I spare no effort and carry out my duties with zeal. (*Moves his chair closer to* KHLESTAKOV *and speaks in a low voice.*) May I tell you that the postmaster is a real loafer: he completely neglects his duties; the mail is delayed. . . . Perhaps you'd like to look into it yourself. And it's the same with the judge, who was in here just a little while ago. He spends his whole time hunting hares; he keeps dogs in his chambers and—although he's a friend and even a relative of mine—I feel it's my duty to the Fatherland to warn you about his conduct, which is, to say the least, most reprehensible. For instance, there's a landowner named Dobchinsky in this town, whom I know you've met. Well, whenever this Dobchinsky steps out of his house, the judge steps in and visits Dobchinsky's wife for hours on end—I'm willing to swear to it. You just have to look at the children: none looks like Dobchinsky and every one of them, including the tiny, baby girl, is the image of the judge.

KHLESTAKOV. Well, I'll be damned!

CHARITIES. And then there's our school superintendent. I really can't imagine how the government could have entrusted him with such a post. He's, to say the least, a radical and he fills the heads of our young people with such pernicious doctrines that I wouldn't care to describe them in your presence. Do you, perhaps, wish me to put all this down on paper?

KHLESTAKOV. Very good, let's have it on paper. I'd like that very much. You know, when I get bored, I just love to have something amusing to read. . . . What's your name? I keep forgetting.

CHARITIES. Strawberry.

KHLESTAKOV. Ah yes, Strawberry. Well now, tell me, Mr. Strawberry, do you have children?

CHARITIES. Why, of course. Five of 'em. Two are grown-up already.

KHLESTAKOV. Grown up? Ah, you don't say! And what are they now?

CHARITIES. Perhaps you wish to inquire what their names are?

KHLESTAKOV. Yes, what are their names?

CHARITIES. Nikolai, Ivan, Elizaveta, Maria, and Perpetua.

KHLESTAKOV. Very nice.

CHARITIES. I don't wish to impose my presence upon you any longer, to take up your time, which would otherwise be devoted to your sacred duties . . . (*Bows and prepares to leave.*)

KHLESTAKOV (*accompanying him to the door*). Not at all, not at all. Why that's ridiculous. Please, I'd be glad to . . . I'm very fond of company. (*Exit* CHARITIES. KHLESTAKOV *goes back to door and, opening it, calls after him.*) I say! What's your name again? I keep forgetting.

CHARITIES. Strawberry.

KHLESTAKOV. If you'd be so kind, Mr. Strawberry—the strangest thing has happened to me. I spent all my money on the way here. Don't you have four hundred rubles you could lend me by any chance?

CHARITIES. I do indeed.

KHLESTAKOV. Ah, what a lucky coincidence. Thank you very much.

SCENE 7. *Khlestakov, Bobchinsky and Dobchinsky.*

BOBCHINSKY. May I have the honor of presenting myself:— Peter Bobchinsky, the son of Ivan Bobchinsky, a resident of this town.

DOBCHINSKY. And I'm Peter Dobchinsky, son of Ivan Dobchinsky, a local landowner.

KHLESTAKOV. But we've already met. I even remember your falling, sir—how's your nose?

BOBCHINSKY. Better, thank God. I beg you not to concern yourself over it. It's healed up already, completely healed up.

KHLESTAKOV. Well, that's a good thing. I'm glad. . . . (*Abruptly and unexpectedly.*) Do you have any money on you?

BOBCHINSKY. Money? What money?

KHLESTAKOV. A loan of a thousand rubles.

BOBCHINSKY. No, I really don't have that much. Maybe you have, Dobchinsky?

DOBCHINSKY. I'm afraid I don't have that much on me. As you know, Bobchinsky, all my money went into government bonds.

KHLESTAKOV. Well then, if you don't have a thousand, a hundred rubles would do.

BOBCHINSKY (*searching through his pockets*). Don't you have a hundred rubles, Dobchinsky? I only have forty altogether.

DOBCHINSKY (*looking in wallet*). All I have is twenty-five.

BOBCHINSKY. Come, look more thoroughly. I know you have a hole in your right-hand pocket and probably some's fallen through into the lining.

DOBCHINSKY. No, really, there's none in the lining either.

KHLESTAKOV. Well, it doesn't matter. I just thought you might have. Well, never mind, make it sixty-five . . . (*Takes money.*)

DOBCHINSKY. May I make so bold as to consult you concerning a very delicate matter.

KHLESTAKOV. Yes, what is it?

DOBCHINSKY. It's a matter of great delicacy: my oldest son, sir . . . well, it so happens he was born before I was even married . . .

KHLESTAKOV. So?

DOBCHINSKY. That is, only in a manner of speaking, for he was born to me exactly as if we were married and afterwards, I concluded the bonds of marriage and all that, just as it should be. So now, I would like him to be, sir, an altogether legitimate son of mine, and to be called just like me, Dobchinsky that is.

KHLESTAKOV. All right, let him be called that! It can be done.

DOBCHINSKY. I wouldn't have bothered you about it, except it's such a shame because of his abilities. He's a boy that . . . I have great hopes for him. He can recite different poems by heart and if he gets hold of a knife somewhere, he'll make little carriages and things, like a real magician. Bobchinsky, here, can tell you.

BOBCHINSKY. Oh yes, he has great abilities.

KHLESTAKOV. Good, good, I'll do my best in the matter. I'll speak to . . . I'm sure it can be done . . . (*Turning to* BOB-CHINSKY.) And you, did you wish to ask me something?

BOBCHINSKY. Yes, indeed. I have a most humble request.

KHLESTAKOV. What is it?

BOBCHINSKY. Please, when you get back to Petersburg, I beg you most humbly to tell all those various bigwigs there, the senators and admirals, tell them, you know, "Your Honor, or Your Excellency, there's a Peter Bobchinsky living in such-and-such a town." Just tell 'em, Peter Bobchinsky lives there.

KHLESTAKOV. Very well.

BOBCHINSKY. And if by chance you should happen to see the Tsar, tell the Tsar too, tell him: "Your Imperial Majesty, Peter Bobchinsky lives in such-and-such a town."

KHLESTAKOV. Very well.

DOBCHINSKY. Excuse us for bothering you like this.

BOBCHINSKY. Excuse us for bothering you like this.

KHLESTAKOV. Not at all, not at all. I'm delighted. (*Sees them to the door.*)

SCENE 8. *Khlestakov alone.*

KHLESTAKOV. There're a lot of officials here and it looks as if they take me for some government bigwig. True, yesterday I threw a little dust in their eyes. But still what idiots! I think I'll write to Petersburg, to Trapichkin, and tell him the whole story. He writes that sort of piece for magazines, so let him take a crack at them. Hey, Osip, bring me paper and ink! (Osip *pokes his head in at door.*)

Osip. Yes, sir.

Khlestakov. That Trapichkin now—if he once gets his teeth into someone, just watch out! He wouldn't spare his own father if he had a chance of being witty. And he's partial to money too. Incidentally these officials are nice people; it was really nice of them to lend me money like that. Let's see how much do I have now? That's three hundred from the judge, three hundred from the postmaster—that makes six hundred, seven hundred, eight hundred—what a greasy bill—eight hundred, nine hundred . . . Oho! Here we go, over a thousand. Well now, my dear Captain, just you wait till I get hold of you. Now we'll see who'll fleece whom!

SCENE 9. *Khlestakov. Osip enters with paper and ink.*

Khlestakov. Well, you see, idiot, how they wine and dine me now! (*Starts writing.*)

Osip. Yes, thank God! But you know what, sir?

Khlestakov. What?

Osip. You should leave this town. Really, it's time to be off.

Khlestakov (*writing*). What nonsense! Why?

Osip. Mark my words, sir. Leave the lot of 'em and God bless 'em, I say—it's enough now. What do you want with them now? The hell with them! You don't know what may come up —someone else may drive in. Really, sir! And, you know, they have good post-horses here, we could use them.

Khlestakov (*writing*). No. I'm not ready to go yet. Maybe tomorrow.

Osip. But why wait till tomorrow? Really, sir, let's leave. Maybe it's all a great honor for you but nevertheless, you know, it'd really be better to leave right away. . . . After all, they must've taken you for someone else and then, your father'll be angry because you've dilly-dallied so long . . . so, we really ought to be on our way, sir. And they'll give us good horses here.

Khlestakov (*writing*). Well, all right then. But first send this letter off and, at the same time, get an order for post-horses. And see to it that they give us good horses. Tell the drivers I'll give them a silver ruble each if we go fast as couriers, and if they sing as we drive! (*Goes on writing.*) I can just see Trapichkin's face—he'll die laughing!

Osip. I'll send it with one of the servants here, sir, and I'd better start packing. That way, no time'll be wasted.

KHLESTAKOV (*writing*). All right. Just bring me a candle.

OSIP (*exits and speaks off-stage*). Hey there, listen brother, take a letter to the post and tell the postmaster it's to go free of charge. Then tell 'em to send over their best troika for my master—a courier's troika—and tell them the master won't be paying the fare, the government'll refund them. And see that they hurry it up or the master'll get mad. Wait, the letter's not ready yet.

KHLESTAKOV (*still writing*). I wish I knew where he's living now, on Post Office Street or Pea Street. He changes apartments pretty often—avoids paying the rent that way. I'll take a chance and address it to Post Office Street. (*Folds letter and addresses it.* OSIP *enters with candle.* KHLESTAKOV *seals letter. The voice of* POLICEMAN GRABMUG *is heard off.*)

GRABMUG'S VOICE. Where d'you think you're going, big beard. I'm not to let anyone in, I tell you.

KHLESTAKOV (*giving* OSIP *letter*). There you are. Send it off.

MERCHANT'S VOICES. Come, let us through. You can't stop us going in. We're here on business.

GRABMUG'S VOICE. Off with you! Off with you! He's not receiving! He's asleep. (*The noise increases.*)

KHLESTAKOV. What's going on out there, Osip? Go and see what it's all about.

OSIP (*looking out window*). There are some merchants trying to get in but the policeman won't let 'em. They're waving some papers in the air. Looks like they want to see you.

KHLESTAKOV (*going up to window*). What's the matter, friends?

MERCHANTS' VOICES. We appeal to your gracious kindness, sir, tell the policeman that you wish to receive our petitions.

KHLESTAKOV. Let them in. I'll see them. Osip, tell them I'll see them.   (*Exit* OSIP.)

KHLESTAKOV (*takes petitions handed to him through window, opens one and reads*). "To His Noble Serene Highness, Master of Finances, from the Merchant Abdulin . . ." What the hell is this? There's no such title!

SCENE 10. *Khlestakov and Merchants. Behind the Merchants, a basket of wine and loaves of sugar are brought in.*

KHLESTAKOV. What can I do for you, my friends?

MERCHANTS. We humbly beseech Your Honor . . .

KHLESTAKOV. What is it you wish?

MERCHANTS. Do not abandon us, sir! We're victims of horrible oppression!

KHLESTAKOV. From whom?

ONE OF MERCHANTS. Oh, it's all the Mayor, sir! There's never been a mayor like him before. He does such things to us that we can't even repeat, sir. The soldiers he quarters on us all the time, eat us out of house and home—so there's nothing for us to do but hang ourselves, the way he treats us! He grabs you by the beard and shouts: "Ah, you damned Tartar!" Really, sir! It'd make sense, of course, if we were in any way disrespectful, but we always do our duty: his spouse and his daughter are welcome to whatever material they need for their dresses—that goes without saying. But it's never enough for him! He just comes into the shop and takes everything his eye happens to fall on. He may see a bolt of cloth, for instance, and he'll say: "That's a nice little bit of stuff you've got there, friend. Bring it over to my place." Well, what can you do? But a bolt like that can have a good forty yards in it.

KHLESTAKOV. Really? What a crook!

MERCHANTS. We can swear to it, sir. We can't remember ever having a mayor like him before. As soon as we catch sight of him, we try to hide everything in the shop. And he doesn't limit himself to delicacies either—he'll take any old rubbish: prunes that've been lying there in the barrel for about seven years, which even the clerk wouldn't touch. He'll grab a whole handful. On his birthday we bring him over just about everything you can think of; there's not a thing more he needs. But no! He still wants more, and so he makes us repeat the whole business on his Saint's Day—St. Anton's. So what can you do? You bring him more on St. Anton's.

KHLESTAKOV. But he's a real bandit!

MERCHANTS. And just try arguing with him and he'll quarter a whole regiment in your house. And if you protest, he closes down your store. "Ha," he says, "I'm not going to subject you to corporal punishment or torture; it's forbidden by law. But I'll have you down to eating nothing but bread and herring, my friend!"

KHLESTAKOV. What a crook! He should be sent to Siberia!

MERCHANTS. Wherever Your Honor wishes to send him, it's all right with us, just so he's farther away from here. Deign to accept a token of our esteem, sir. Allow us to present you with this sugar and wine.

KHLESTAKOV. No, no, you mustn't even think of it. I never take bribes. Now if, for instance, you offered to lend me three hundred rubles, that would be quite a different matter. I can accept a loan.

MERCHANTS. Oh please, sir. (*Taking money from their pockets.*) But what's three hundred rubles? You'd better take five hundred; only help us.

KHLESTAKOV. Thank you. I've no objection to a loan. I accept.

MERCHANTS (*offering him the money on a silver tray*). Well but, please, do take this little tray as well.

KHLESTAKOV. Well, all right, I could take the tray.

MERCHANTS (*bowing*). Well then, just this once, take the sugar, too.

KHLESTAKOV. Oh no, I never take bribes of any . . .

OSIP. But why not, Your Excellency? Please take it! Everything comes in useful when you're traveling. Here, you, bring the sugar loaves and the basket over here! Yes, the whole lot! It'll all come in useful. What's that there? A coil of rope? Give it here! Rope can come in handy on the road, too. If the cart or something breaks, you can tie it up.

MERCHANTS. Well then, be so kind, Your Honor—that is, if you don't grant our petition and help us, we just don't know what to do with ourselves. We might just as well hang ourselves.

KHLESTAKOV. I promise I'll do my best.   (*Exit* MERCHANTS.)
(WOMEN'S *voices are heard off-stage.*)

WOMEN'S VOICES. You don't dare keep me out! I'll complain to *him* about you. Don't you push me so roughly!

KHLESTAKOV. Who's out there? (*Goes over to window.*) What's the matter, my good woman?

VOICES OF TWO WOMEN. I beg your indulgence, Your Honor! Please, sir, hear me out.

KHLESTAKOV (*through window*). Let her in.

SCENE 11. *Khlestakov, Locksmith's Wife, Corporal's Widow.*

LOCKSMITH'S WIFE (*bowing low*). I beg your favor!
CORPORAL'S WIDOW. I beg your favor!

KHLESTAKOV. But, who are you?

CORPORAL'S WIDOW. The widow of Corporal Ivanov.

LOCKSMITH'S WIFE. I'm the wife of the local locksmith, Fevronya Poshlopkina, sir.

KHLESTAKOV. Wait a minute. One at a time. Now you, what can I do for you?

LOCKSMITH'S WIFE. My humble request concerns the mayor, sir. May God send him every evil and may bad luck always pursue him, the crook, and his children, his uncles, and his aunts!

KHLESTAKOV. Why? What happened?

LOCKSMITH'S WIFE. Why, the crook, he sent my husband off into the army, where they shaved his head and all, although his turn hadn't come around yet at all. And, in fact, it's against the law to draft a married man.

KHLESTAKOV. But how could he do that?

LOCKSMITH'S WIFE. He did it, the crook, he did, may God make him suffer for it in this world and the next! And if he has an aunt, may every sort of harm befall her, and if his father's still alive, may the pig choke for good and croak. The tailor's son should have been taken, he's a drunken lout anyway; but his parents gave the mayor an expensive present. So then he tried to get hold of Panteleeva's son—she's a shopkeeper —but she sent the mayor's wife three bolts of linen, so then he started on me. "What," he says, "do you want your husband around for? He's not suitable for you." As if I didn't know whether he's suitable or not. That's my business not his, the dirty crook. "Your husband," he says, "is a thief. Maybe he hasn't stolen anything yet," he says, "but he's bound to, any time now. And the army'll take him next year anyway." And how'm I going to manage without my husband? The dirty crook! I'm just a weak woman, you beast, may none of your family ever get to heaven, and if you've got a mother-in-law, may your mother-in-law also . . .

KHLESTAKOV. All right, all right. And what about you? (*Turns to the other woman.*)

LOCKSMITH'S WIFE (*as she exits*). Please don't forget, sir. Be so kind!

CORPORAL'S WIDOW. I've come, sir, to complain about the mayor . . .

KHLESTAKOV. Yes, what is it? Why? Be brief.

CORPORAL'S WIDOW. He had me flogged, sir.

KHLESTAKOV. What?

CORPORAL'S WIDOW. It was a mix-up, sir. The women were quarreling at the market, and the police didn't get there in time, so they grabbed me. They really gave it to me—I couldn't sit down for two days after that.

KHLESTAKOV. So, now what am I supposed to do about it?

CORPORAL'S WIDOW. There's nothing can be done, of course. But you could order him to pay a fine for that mistake. There's no reason why I shouldn't take advantage of my bad luck, and I sure could do with the money now.

KHLESTAKOV. All right, all right. You may go now. I'll see to it. (*Hands holding petitions are thrust through the window.*) Good heavens, who else is out there? (*Goes to window.*) No, no, I don't want to see any more! That's enough, enough!

(*Leaving window.*) Damn it all, I'm fed up with the lot of 'em. Don't let anyone in, Osip!

OSIP (*shouting out of window*). Go away, go away. This isn't the time. Come tomorrow! (*The door opens and there appears a strange figure in a heavy overcoat, with an unkempt beard, a swollen lip, a bandaged face. In the background behind him several others are to be seen.*)

OSIP. Off with you, off with you! Where d'you think you're going? (*He pushes him in the stomach, stumbling out into the hall with him and slamming the door behind him.*)

SCENE 12. *Khlestakov and Maria.*

MARIA. Oh!

KHLESTAKOV. Why, what frightened you so, Ma'am?

MARIA. Oh, I wasn't frightened.

KHLESTAKOV (*putting on airs*). Pardon me, Ma'am. I'm happy that you should take me for the sort of man, who . . . May I be so bold as to ask where you were going?

MARIA. I wasn't really going anywhere.

KHLESTAKOV. Well then, why weren't you going anywhere?

MARIA. I was wondering whether Mother was here . . .

KHLESTAKOV. Ah no! I want you to tell me: why weren't you going anywhere?

MARIA. I think I'm disturbing you; you were engaged in some important business.

KHLESTAKOV (*putting on airs*). Your eyes are more important to me than any business. . . . You couldn't possibly disturb me; it'd be quite impossible. On the contrary, you can only delight me.

MARIA. Ah, that's the way they talk in the capital.

KHLESTAKOV. That's the way to talk to one as beautiful as you. May I have the great happiness of offering you a chair? Although I realize you should have a throne rather than a chair.

MARIA. Really, I don't know . . . I really ought to go. (*Sits.*)

KHLESTAKOV. What a wonderful kerchief you have!

MARIA. You're making fun of me. You're just laughing at us provincials.

KHLESTAKOV. Oh, Madam, I would so love to be that kerchief of yours, so that I might hug your lily-white, little neck.

MARIA. I'm sure I don't know what you're talking about: it's just an ordinary kerchief. . . . Strange sort of weather today.

KHLESTAKOV. And your lips, Ma'am, are fairer than any weather.

MARIA. Oh, you keep saying those things. But I'd like to ask you to write me some verses in my autograph book rather, to remember you by. You must know many.

KHLESTAKOV. Anything you want, Ma'am. What verses would you like?

MARIA. Well, some sort of . . . good ones, new ones.

KHLESTAKOV. What's a verse or two to me? I know so many.

MARIA. So tell me, what will you write then?

KHLESTAKOV. But what's the point of my reciting it. I know it without that.

MARIA. I'd very much like to hear it . . .

KHLESTAKOV. Well, I have lots of them, all kinds. For instance, I could give you this one: "Oh, thou who vainly in your sadness, Murmurest against God's goodness. Oh, man . . ." Well, yes, then there are others . . . can't remember right now. Anyway, all that's unimportant. I'd rather offer you my love instead, which, when you glance at me . . . (*Moves his chair closer to hers.*)

MARIA. Love! I don't understand a thing about love . . . I've never been able to understand what it's all about. (*Moves her chair farther away from his.*)

KHLESTAKOV. Why do you move your chair away? We'd be better off sitting close to one another.

MARIA (*moving farther*). Why close? It's all the same if we're farther apart.

KHLESTAKOV. Why farther? It's all the same if we're close.

MARIA (*moving farther*). But what's the point of it?

KHLESTAKOV (*moving closer*). It just seems to you that we're so close—all you have to do is imagine that we're farther apart. Oh, how happy I should be, Ma'am, if I could clasp you in my embrace.

MARIA (*looking out of window*). What was that? I thought I saw something fly by? Was it a magpie or some other bird?

KHLESTAKOV (*kissing her on the shoulder and looking out of the window*). That's a magpie.

MARIA (*rising indignantly*). Ah no, that's really too much! . . . What nerve!

KHLESTAKOV (*holding her back*). Forgive me, Ma'am. I did it out of love, out of sheer love!

MARIA. You take me for a little provincial . . . (*Tries to leave.*)

KHLESTAKOV (*holding on to her*). Yes, out of love. I was just joking, Maria, please. Don't be angry! I'm prepared to go down on my knees to ask your forgiveness. (*Falls to his knees.*) Forgive me, please forgive me. You see, I'm on my knees before you.

SCENE 13. *The same and Anna Andreyevna.*

ANNA ANDREYEVNA (*seeing* KHLESTAKOV *on his knees*). Oh, what a sight!

KHLESTAKOV (*rising*). Hell!

ANNA ANDREYEVNA (*to daughter*). What's the meaning of this, young lady? What's going on here?

MARIA. Mama, I . . .

ANNA ANDREYEVNA. Leave the room! Do you hear! Leave, leave, and don't let me see you here again. (MARIA *exits in tears.*) Excuse me, but, I must admit, I was so shocked . . .

KHLESTAKOV (*aside*). This one looks pretty appetizing too— not bad at all. (*Throws himself on his knees.*) Look at me, Ma'am, I am consumed by love.

ANNA ANDREYEVNA. What are you doing on your knees! Get up, get up, the floor's not as clean as all that.

KHLESTAKOV. No, no, on my knees I stay! I wish to know for certain, on my knees, what my fate is to be—life or death.

ANNA ANDREYEVNA. I'm sorry but I'm still not quite sure what you have in mind. If I'm not mistaken, you are declaring your love for my daughter?

KHLESTAKOV. No, it's you I love. My life hangs by a hair. If you will not crown my undying love, I will no longer be worthy of existence. With my heart in flames, I ask your hand!

ANNA ANDREYEVNA. But allow me to draw your attention to the fact that I am, in a sense, sort of . . . I'm married.

KHLESTAKOV. That doesn't matter. In love, nothing makes any difference. Karamzin himself said: "The laws are to blame." We will go far off to a shady stream. Your hand, please, I beg you . . .

SCENE 14. *The same and Maria. Maria comes running in.*

MARIA. Mama, Papa says you . . . (*Seeing* KHLESTAKOV *on his knees, cries out.*) Oh, what a sight!

ANNA ANDREYEVNA. What do you want? What is it? Why? What bad manners! You just burst in here like a scalded cat! And what's so strange, anyway? Well, what do you want this time? Really, just like a little three-year-old! One'd never believe she was past eighteen! When are you finally going to learn a bit of sense? When are you going to start behaving like a nice, decently brought-up young person? When will you ever learn the rules of good behavior and respectability?

MARIA (*through tears*). Honestly, Mama, I didn't know.

ANNA ANDREYEVNA. Your head's so empty the drafts blow around in it! You're as bad as the judge's daughter. Why do you imitate those hussies when you have before you a wonderful example to follow—just model yourself on your own mother.

KHLESTAKOV (*clasping* MARIA's *hand, to* ANNA ANDREYEVNA). Madam, please, do not oppose our happiness! Bestow your blessing on our undying love!

ANNA ANDREYEVNA (*surprised*). Then it's her . . .

KHLESTAKOV. It's up to you to decide: is it to be life or death?

ANNA ANDREYEVNA. So you see, you little idiot, it's because of you, you worthless creature, that our dear guest has been pleased to go down on his knees. And you come bursting in like a madwoman! Really, it'd serve you right if I refused— you're not worthy of such happiness.

MARIA. I'll never do it again, Mama. I promise I won't.

SCENE 15. *The same and Mayor.*

MAYOR (*breathlessly*). Your Honor! Don't ruin me! Please, don't ruin me!

KHLESTAKOV. What's this all about?

MAYOR. I know, sir, the merchants have been complaining to you about me. On my honor, I assure you, sir, half of what they say isn't true. They cheat the customers themselves, they weight their scales, sir, and shortchange them. And the corporal's widow too, sir, she lied about my having her flogged, I swear she's lying. The truth is, she flogged herself, sir.

KHLESTAKOV. The hell with the corporal's widow. Who cares about her?

MAYOR. You musn't believe it, you mustn't! They're such liars . . . a child wouldn't trust them. The whole town knows what liars they are. And as to being a crook, may I make so bold as to say that they're crooks themselves, such as the world has never seen before.

ANNA ANDREYEVNA. Do you know what an honor His Excellency is bestowing on us? He has asked for our daughter's hand.

MAYOR. What? What? . . . You're out of your mind, my dear. I beg you not to be angry, Your Excellency, my wife is a little weak in the head. Her mother was the same way.

KHLESTAKOV. But it's true. I am asking for her hand. I love her.

MAYOR. I can't believe it, sir.

ANNA ANDREYEVNA. What do you mean, you can't believe it, since you're being told?

KHLESTAKOV. I'm perfectly serious . . . I'm drunk with love.

MAYOR. I don't dare believe it. I am unworthy of such an honor.

KHLESTAKOV. If you will not agree to give me your daughter's hand, heaven knows what may happen.

MAYOR. I can't believe it. Your Excellency is just having his little joke.

ANNA ANDREYEVNA. Good Lord, what a blockhead! You're being told . . .

MAYOR. I can't believe it!

KHLESTAKOV. Give me her hand—I'm a desperate man and I'm ready for anything. If I shoot myself, they'll have you up in court.

MAYOR. Oh, good Lord! I'm innocent—body and soul. Please don't be angry! Please do just as you wish, Your Excellency! My head's in a whirl, really. . . . It's all beyond me! I never used to be such a fool!

ANNA ANDREYEVNA. Well, give them your blessing!

(KHLESTAKOV and MARIA approach him.)

MAYOR. May God bless you—and I'm innocent. (KHLESTAKOV kisses MARIA. The MAYOR looks at them.) Good gracious! It's really so! (Rubs his eyes.) They're kissing. Oh Lord, they're kissing! A real engaged couple! (Cries out, skipping about in his joy.) Ah, Anton, Anton! Ah, Mayor! Look how things have turned out!

SCENE 16. *The same and Osip.*

OSIP. The horses are ready.

KHLESTAKOV. Oh good, I'll be right there.

MAYOR. What? Are you leaving?

KHLESTAKOV. Yes.

MAYOR. But what about . . . that is . . . I believe you yourself hinted something about a wedding?

KHLESTAKOV. Oh, I'll only be gone a short while . . . one day. I'm going to see my uncle. He's a rich old man. I'll be back tomorrow.

MAYOR. We would not presume to hold you back. We wish you a safe return.

KHLESTAKOV. Thank you, thank you, I'll be right back. Farewell, my love . . . no, I simply have no words to express my feelings. Good-by, dearest one. (Kisses her hand.)

MAYOR. Perhaps you need something for your trip? Maybe you need some money?

KHLESTAKOV. Oh no, why should you? (*Thinks a little.*) Well, after all, I suppose I could do with some.

MAYOR. How much would suit you?

KHLESTAKOV. Well, you gave me two hundred before—that is, not two, but four hundred. I don't wish to take advantage of your mistake—so, let's say, lend me enough now to make it an even eight hundred.

MAYOR. Right away! (*Takes money from wallet.*) Ah, how lucky—brand new bills!

KHLESTAKOV. Oh yes. (*Takes and scrutinizes bills.*) That's wonderful! They say new bills bring good luck.

MAYOR. Yes, indeed.

KHLESTAKOV. Good-by, Mayor, thank you very much for your hospitality. I must tell you, from the bottom of my heart—I've never been so pleasantly received anywhere. Good-by, Anna Andreyevna. Good-by, Maria, my love.   (*Exits.*)

(*Off-stage is heard.*)

KHLESTAKOV'S VOICE. Farewell, my angel, my Maria!

MAYOR'S VOICE. What's this? You're going off in an ordinary post-chaise?

KHLESTAKOV'S VOICE. Oh yes, I'm used to it by now. Springs make my head ache.

COACHMAN'S VOICE. Whoa . . .

MAYOR'S VOICE. Well, at least take something to cover the seat, if only a rug. Allow me to tell them to bring you a rug.

KHLESTAKOV'S VOICE. Oh no, don't bother. It's nothing. Well, all right, thank you, tell them to bring a rug.

MAYOR'S VOICE. Hey, Avdotya! Go to the storeroom and get the best rug, the one with the blue background, the Persian one. Hurry up now!

COACHMAN'S VOICE. Whoa . . .

MAYOR'S VOICE. Would you be so good as to tell me when we can expect you?

KHLESTAKOV'S VOICE. Tomorrow or the day after.

OSIP'S VOICE. Ah, is that the rug? Give it here. That's right, put it there! This way! Now let's have some straw over on this side.

COACHMAN'S VOICE. Whoa . . .

OSIP'S VOICE. Over this side! Here! More! That's fine, very nice! (*Beats the rug with his hand.*) Now you can sit down, sir.

KHLESTAKOV'S VOICE. Good-by, Mayor.

MAYOR'S VOICE. Good-by, sir!

WOMEN'S VOICES. Good-by, Ivan Alexandrovich!

KHLESTAKOV'S VOICE. Good-by, Mother dear!

COACHMAN'S VOICE. Giddup, my fine ones!
(*A harness bell jingles.*)

CURTAIN

ACT V

The same room.
SCENE 1. *Mayor, Anna Andreyevna, and Maria.*

MAYOR. Well, Anna? What d'you think of that? We're in clover
this time for sure! Tell the truth now—would you ever have
imagined anything like that? Here you were, just a simple
mayor's wife and now, lo and behold, you're the mother-in-law
of a devil of a fellow!

ANNA ANDREYEVNA. You're wrong! I've known all along. It
seems so extraordinary to you because you're just a common
man who has never met real people of quality.

MAYOR. I'm a person of quality myself, my dear. But, seriously,
when one comes to think of it, Anna, what a fine pair of birds
we are now! We can really fly high now, damn it all! Just
wait, now I'll make it hot for all those who were so eager to
hand in petitions and complaints. Hey, who's there? (*Enter*
POLICEMAN.) Oh, it's you, Ivan. Go and get the merchants in
here. I'll teach the dogs! So they decided they'd complain against
me, did they? Bunch of damned Judases! Well, just wait, my
fine friends! What you got before was nothing to what you'll
get now. Write down the names of everyone who came to complain against me and, above all, of the scribes who turned out
the petitions for them. And, also, I want you to announce to one
and all the honor God has sent their mayor; instead of giving
his daughter in marriage to some ordinary person, she's going
to marry a man such as the world has never seen before, a
man who can do everything, but everything! Announce it all
over the town, so that everyone'll know. Go and cry the news,
ring the bells! Ah, damn it all! When we celebrate, we celebrate! (POLICEMAN *exits.*) So that's how it is, Anna. Now,
what d'you think, where shall we live? Here or in Petersburg?

ANNA ANDREYEVNA. In Petersburg, naturally. How could we
possibly stay here?

MAYOR. All right then, so it'll be Petersburg, although we
could get along fine here, too. If we move to Petersburg, of
course, I'll have to send my mayor's job to hell, eh, Anna, what
do you say?

ANNA ANDREYEVNA. Naturally. What would you want with being mayor?

MAYOR. Do you think, Anna, I could get myself a high rank now? He's chummy with all the ministers and he goes to the Palace and, with all those connections, he could get me a real big promotion, so that, in time, I might even wind up among the generals. D'you think it's possible?

ANNA ANDREYEVNA. Why, of course it's possible.

MAYOR. Ah, damn it all, it'd be fun to be a general! That entitles you to wear that ribbon across your shoulder. What color ribbon would you prefer for me, Anna—red or blue?

ANNA ANDREYEVNA. Why, the blue, of course.

MAYOR. Eh? So that's what you want! But the red one would do me fine, too. As long as you're a general, what's the difference? When a general goes somewhere, couriers and aides gallop ahead of him and requisition all the horses at the post-stations. No one else can have horses—they all have to wait, all those petty officials, army captains, mayors of small towns. But if you're a general, you're all right. You dine at governors' mansions wherever you go and if you feel like giving trouble to some mayor, just go ahead! Ha-ha-ha! (*He laughs heartily.*) That's what's so alluring about it, damn it all!

ANNA ANDREYEVNA. Oh, your tastes are so terribly common! You must realize, though, that we'll have to alter our way of life. You'll no longer hang around with a wretched dog-lover of a judge and go hunting hares, or with that old Strawberry there. Oh no, your friends will be nicely mannered people of the finest breeding—such as counts and other society people. But I'm really worried about you; sometimes you use expressions that one never hears in polite society.

MAYOR. What of it? Words never harmed anyone.

ANNA ANDREYEVNA. That's all very well for a mayor, but over there it'll be a completely different sort of life.

MAYOR. Yes, they say that over there they have two kinds of fish—eels and smelts—which are so good that one bite starts your mouth watering.

ANNA ANDREYEVNA. You've got nothing but fish on your mind. But I want our house to be the first in the capital, and I want my own room to be so fragrant with ambergris that visitors will have to screw up their eyes before they dare to step inside. (*Screws up her eyes and sniffs.*) Ah, won't that be marvelous!

SCENE 2. *The same and Merchants.*

MAYOR. Ah! Hello, fellows!

MERCHANTS (*bowing*). Greetings, sir.

MAYOR. Well, how are you, my fine friends? How's life treating you? Not too good, I understand. You even had to complain, you pot-merchants! You drapers! You cheats! You chiselers! You crooks! So, you complained, uh? And what was the trouble? Too much was being taken from you? So, you figured they'd shove me in jail! . . . But you know what? Now you'll have seven devils and one witch on your backs and . . .

ANNA ANDREYEVNA. Oh my goodness, Anton, what language you use!

MAYOR (*displeased*). I can't be bothered with choosing nice words now! Do you know that the high official you were complaining to is about to marry my daughter? Well, how does that make you feel? And what d'you have to say now? Now, I'm going to do the talking. Listen to me: you crooks are always cheating people. You get a government contract and then you cheat the Fatherland out of a hundred thousand rubles by supplying rotten cloth. And if, after that, you give me a measly twenty yards, you expect me to give you a medal for it! If they knew about it, they'd give you such a—— And just look at the pot-bellied fathead: he's a merchant, don't you dare touch him! "We," he says, "are as good as anyone; even the gentry have nothing on us!" But a gentleman, you ugly-mug, a gentleman's got learning. Maybe they do whip him in school, but there's a point to it, makes him learn what he needs to know. And what are you? You start out cheating from the beginning and your boss beats the daylights out of you for not swindling people. When you're still a shrimp, before you even know who your own father is, you're already going around short-changing people. And as soon as you've grown yourself a round little belly and stuffed your pockets, you start putting on airs like nobody's business! What d'you think you are—the eighth wonder of the world? Just because you drink up sixteen samovars a day, you think you're someone, uh? Well, I'll show you what you can do with your importance!

MERCHANTS (*bowing*). We're sorry, Mr. Mayor!

MAYOR. Complaints, eh? You, for instance, tell me—who was it who helped you in that swindle when you built the bridge? You sent in a bill for twenty thousand rubles for the lumber and, whichever way you look at it, it wasn't even worth a hundred rubles all told. Well, let me remind you, you bearded goat: it was me! You forgot, uh? I could easily have reported you and had you packed off to Siberia, too. Well, speak up, what do you have to say? Uh?

ONE MERCHANT. We were wrong, Mr. Mayor, we're

sorry. The Devil got us all mixed up. We swear we won't complain again and we'll do anything you say to make up for it. Just don't be angry with us.

MAYOR. Don't be angry! You're groveling at my feet now simply because I happen to be on top. But if things had gone your way, even a little bit, you'd bury me in the mud, you crook, and then put a beam on top of me to keep me there.

MERCHANTS (*bowing to the ground*). Please, Mr. Mayor, don't ruin us!

MAYOR. "Don't ruin us!" Now it's "don't ruin us," but what were you saying before? I'd like to . . . (*Waves his hand in disgust.*) Well, may God forgive you. Enough of this. I don't bear grudges. But, from now on, you'd better watch out! I'm not giving my daughter in marriage to some ordinary man, so let the congratulations be in keeping, understand? Don't think you can get away with a measly sturgeon or a loaf of sugar. All right then, get along with you now!

(*Exit* MERCHANTS.)

SCENE 3. *The same: Judge, Charities, later Rastakovsky, a respected citizen.*

JUDGE (*still in doorway*). Is the rumor true, Mayor? An extraordinary bit of good fortune seems to have come your way.

CHARITIES. May I have the pleasure of congratulating you on such exceptional good luck? I was so happy when I heard. (*Approaches* ANNA ANDREYEVNA *and kisses her hand.*) Anna Andreyevna! (*Goes over to* MARIA *and kisses her hand.*) Maria!

(*Enter* RASTAKOVSKY.)

RASTAKOVSKY. Congratulations, Mayor. God grant you and the young couple long life. And may your posterity be numerous, both grandchildren and great-grandchildren! Anna Andreyevna! (*Kisses* ANNA ANDREYEVNA'S *hand.*) Maria! (*Kisses* MARIA'S *hand.*)

SCENE 4. *The same and Korobkin, a respected citizen, his wife and Lulukov, another respected citizen.*

KOROBKIN. Allow me to congratulate you, Mayor! Anna Andreyevna! (*Kisses her hand.*) Maria! (*Kisses her hand.*)

KOROBKIN'S WIFE. I congratulate you on this new happiness, from the bottom of my heart, Anna Andreyevna.

LULUKOV. May I have the honor of congratulating you, Anna Andreyevna! (*Kisses her hand and then, turning to the audience, clicks his tongue with a devil-may-care air.*) Maria!

May I have the honor of congratulating you. (*Kisses her hand and again turns toward the audience with the same devil-may-care air.*)

SCENE 5. *Many visitors, wearing frockcoats and tailcoats, who first kiss Anna Andreyevna's hand, saying: "Anna Andreyevna!" then Maria's, saying "Maria!" Bobchinsky and Dobchinsky elbow their way through the crowd.*)

BOBCHINSKY. May I have the honor of congratulating you!
DOBCHINSKY. May I have the honor of congratulating you.
BOBCHINSKY. On the happy event!
DOBCHINSKY. Anna Andreyevna!
BOBCHINSKY. Anna Andreyevna! (*They kiss her hand simultaneously, knocking their heads together.*)
DOBCHINSKY. Maria! (*Kisses her hand.*) I have the great honor of congratulating you. . . . You are very, very fortunate: now you'll go around in gold dresses, eat all sorts of delicate dishes and spend your time in the most entertaining ways!
BOBCHINSKY (*interrupting*). Maria, allow me to congratulate you and may God grant you every luxury, plenty of money and a wee son, wee as that (*Shows how wee with his hands.*), tiny enough to sit in the palm of your hand and cry all the time "wah, wah, wah!"

SCENE 6. *Several more visitors, who come and kiss Anna Andreyevna's and Maria's hands. School Superintendent and his wife.*

SCHOOL SUPERINTENDENT. May I have the honor . . .
SCHOOL SUPERINTENDENT'S WIFE (*running ahead of him*). Congratulations, Anna Andreyevna! (*They kiss.*) I was so glad and excited when I heard. They told me: "Anna Andreyevna is giving away her daughter in marriage." "Oh, my goodness," I thought to myself. I was so glad that I said to my husband, "Listen, Luke, my love," I said, "how marvelous for Anna Andreyevna!" Then I thought to myself, "Well, thank God!" And I told him: "I'm so delighted, I just can't wait to tell Anna Andreyevna personally." . . . "Goodness gracious," I thought to myself, "Anna Andreyevna always expected to make a good match for her daughter, and just look at that: she's got just what she wanted." And I was so pleased, really, that words failed me. I cried and cried, really howled. Luke says to me: "What on earth are you howling about, Nastenka?" he says.

"I don't know myself, Luke love," I said, "tears are just flowing by themselves, like a river, if you see what I mean."

MAYOR. I pray you all to be seated! Hey, Mishka, bring some more chairs!

(VISITORS *take seats.*)

SCENE 7. *The same, Police Inspector and Policemen.*

POLICE INSPECTOR. May I have the honor of congratulating you, Your Honor, and wishing you many years of prosperity.

MAYOR. Thank you! Thank you! Ladies and gentlemen, please sit down! (GUESTS *take seats.*)

JUDGE. Now, Mayor, tell us please, how this whole business started, how it progressed, step by step, in fact—the works.

MAYOR. Well, the whole business went off quite remarkably. He was pleased to propose in person.

ANNA ANDREYEVNA. And in the most respectful, refined manner. He expressed himself quite marvelously. He said: "I, Anna Andreyevna, am doing this exclusively out of respect for your virtues." And he's such a wonderfully well-bred man, of the noblest principles. "Believe me, Anna Andreyevna," he said to me, "to me, my life is worth no more than a kopek! I'm only doing this out of my great respect for your rare qualities."

MARIA. But Mama! He said that to me, not to you!

ANNA ANDEYEVNA. Be quiet! What do you know about it? Don't poke your nose into something that's none of your business! "I, Anna Andreyevna," he told me, "am amazed!" Ah, he put it so flatteringly! And when I remarked that we'd never hoped for such an honor, he suddenly fell to his knees and declared most nobly: "Anna Andreyevna," he said, "don't make me miserable! Agree to respond to my feelings. If you don't, I'll put an end to my own life!"

MARIA. But, Mama, he was saying that about me.

ANNA ANDREYEVNA. Of course, he mentioned you, too. I don't deny that!

MAYOR. We were even quite alarmed when he said he'd shoot himself. "I'll shoot myself," he says, "I'll just shoot myself!"

MANY GUESTS. Well I never!

JUDGE. That's quite something!

SCHOOL SUPERINTENDENT. Well, really, fate must have ordained it all.

CHARITIES. Not fate, old man, fate's blind—the mayor has earned it by his services to the Fatherland! (*Aside.*) Ah, some pigs get all the luck!

JUDGE. I'd like to sell you that little hound we were dickering over, Mayor.

MAYOR. I have no time to be bothered with dogs, now.

JUDGE. Well, if you don't want that one, we'll agree on some other dog.

KOROBKIN'S WIFE. You just can't imagine, Anna Andreyevna, how happy I am over your good fortune.

KOROBKIN. But where, if you'll allow me to inquire, is the distinguished guest right now? I heard he'd left for some reason or other.

MAYOR. Yes, he left for a day, on very important business.

ANNA ANDREYEVNA. He's gone to see his uncle, to ask his blessing.

MAYOR. To ask his blessing, but he'll be . . . (*Sneezes. All cry "God bless you!"*) Thank you very much! But he'll be back by tomorrow. (*Sneezes. All shout "Bless you!" again. Some voices are heard above the others.*)

POLICE INSPECTOR. We wish you good health, Your Honor!

BOBCHINSKY. A hundred years and a sack of gold!

DOBCHINSKY. God lengthen your days to forty times forty!

CHARITIES. The hell with you!

KOROBKIN'S WIFE. Devil take you!

MAYOR. My profoundest thanks and the same to you!

ANNA ANDREYEVNA. We're planning to live in Petersburg from now on. I must admit, the small-town atmosphere here is a bit dull! I confess, I find it quite unbearable. . . . And then, in Petersburg, my husband will . . . well, he'll probably be made a general.

MAYOR. Yes, dammit, I must say I'd like that a lot—to be made a general.

SCHOOL SUPERINTENDENT. May God grant you that!

RASTAKOVSKY. What is impossible for man is possible for God!

JUDGE. To a big ship, a big voyage!

CHARITIES. Honor to those that deserve it!

JUDGE (*aside*). He'll have pulled off quite a trick, if he really does get to be a general. A generalship'd fit him like a saddle fits a cow! Oh no, he's still a far cry from that. There're many smarter than him there who're still not generals.

CHARITIES (*aside*). The damn swine is trying to sneak into a generalship already! And who knows, he may make it with those stuffed turkey airs of his, damn him to hell! (*Turning to him.*) Well, when that happens, Mayor, don't forget your old friends!

JUDGE. And if some business or other should turn up, don't withhold your patronage!

KOROBKIN. Next year I'll be sending my son to the capital, to enter government service. So please take him under your protection, be a father to the poor boy.

MAYOR. For my part, I'm prepared to do anything that's within my power.

ANNA ANDREYEVNA. Oh Anton, you're always ready to make promises. But you certainly won't have time to bother with such matters then, and so why should you take them upon yourself?

MAYOR. But why, my dear? Sometimes it's possible to help.

ANNA ANDREYEVNA. Of course it's possible, but, after all, you can't extend your patronage to all the small fry.

KOROBKIN'S WIFE. Did you hear how she referred to us?

LADY GUEST. She's always been like that. I know her. You invite her to tea and she'll put her feet on your table.

SCENE 8. *The same and Postmaster, who bursts in breathlessly with an opened letter in his hand.*

POSTMASTER. My friends, the most amazing thing! The man we took for the Inspector General wasn't one at all.

ALL. What d'you mean, not the Inspector General?

POSTMASTER. He wasn't an inspector at all! I found it out from this letter.

MAYOR. What do you mean? What do you mean? What letter?

POSTMASTER. Why, his own letter. He sent it to be mailed and so I glance at the address and what do I see? "Post Office Street, Petersburg." That really gave me a shock. I was sure he'd found out something about our postal service here and was reporting it to the government. So, of course, I opened it.

MAYOR. But how did you dare to open the letter of such a high official?

POSTMASTER. I don't know myself: I was impelled by some supernatural force. I was just about to call the messenger to tell him to send it express, but then I was overcome by curiosity. I've never felt so curious in my life before. A voice inside me said: "I mustn't, I mustn't!" But it kept tugging at me and I really couldn't help it! In one ear a voice kept repeating: "Don't open it or you'll be a dead duck!" While in the other ear some demon kept nagging: "Open it, open it, open it!" And as I pressed down on the seal, I could feel fire running through my veins, and then, as soon as I'd broken it, I felt frozen, yes, I swear, I was absolutely frozen, and my hands were shaking and everything went fuzzy.

MAYOR. But how did you dare to open the letter of such a powerful personage?

POSTMASTER. Well, that's just it—he's neither powerful nor even a personage hardly.

MAYOR. What is he then?

POSTMASTER. Well, nothing much. God knows what he is!

MAYOR (*vehemently*). What do you mean by nothing much? How dare you say God knows what he is! I'll put you under arrest . . .

POSTMASTER. What? You'll put me under arrest?

MAYOR. Yes, I!

POSTMASTER. You couldn't if you tried!

MAYOR. Haven't you heard—he's going to marry my daughter and I'm going to have a very high post myself; I can have you packed up and sent to Siberia.

POSTMASTER. Wait, Anton! What's all this about Siberia? Siberia's far away. You'd better let me read the letter. Ladies and gentlemen, will you let me read it?

ALL. Read it! Read it!

POSTMASTER (*reading*). "I'm writing to you posthaste, my dear Trapichkin, to tell you of the amazing things that have been happening to me. On the way here I had a little game of cards and was cleaned out by an infantry captain; things were so bad that the innkeeper wanted to have me clapped in jail. Then, all of a sudden, because of my Petersburg mug and clothes, the whole town mistook me for some Inspector General. So now I'm living at the mayor's, having a great time. I have my eye on both his wife and daughter and am quite open about it. I just haven't been able to make up my mind which one to start off with. I think maybe I'll try the mother first, because she seems to be ready and eager to accommodate me right now. Remember that time when we were broke and had to sponge for our dinners? Remember the time when that pastry cook wanted to throw me out because of some tarts I'd eaten and had asked him to charge to the account of the King of England? Well, now things have taken quite a different turn. They lend me all the money I want. They're a terribly funny bunch—you'd die laughing. I know you write little pieces for the magazines: well then, find a place for this lot in your writings. First—the mayor. He's as stupid as an ox."

MAYOR. Impossible! That can't be in there!

POSTMASTER (*showing him the letter*). Read for yourself.

MAYOR (*reading*). "As an ox." Impossible! You wrote it yourself!

POSTMASTER. How could I have written it?

CHARITIES. Read!

SCHOOL SUPERINTENDENT. Read!

POSTMASTER (*continuing to read*). "The Mayor. He's as stupid as an ox . . ."

MAYOR. Damn it all, did you have to repeat it! As if it wasn't bad enough that it's there at all!

POSTMASTER (*continuing to read*). Umm . . . umm, u . . . "an ox. The postmaster's a fine fellow, too . . ." (*Stops reading.*) Yes, well here he says some unprintable things about me, too.

MAYOR. Oh, no! You read it!

POSTMASTER. But what would be the point?

MAYOR. No, damn it, if you're going to read, read! Read it all!

CHARITIES. Allow me to read it. (*Puts on glasses and reads.*) "The postmaster is the spitting image of our departmental doorman, Mikheyev, and I bet he drinks just as much vodka, too, the crook."

POSTMASTER (*addressing the audience*). Huh! He's just a nasty little boy who needs a good whipping, that's all he is!

CHARITIES (*continuing to read*). "The Director of Ch-ch-chari . . ."

(*Stammering.*)

KOROBKIN. Why have you stopped?

CHARITIES. Awful handwriting . . . anyway, it's obvious, he's just a nasty piece of work.

KOROBKIN. Give it to me! It seems to me my eyes are better than yours. (*Takes hold of letter.*)

CHARITIES (*refusing to relinquish it*). No, no, we can skip that passage. Further on it's legible again.

KOROBKIN. I know, I know—allow me.

CHARITIES. Well, if it's to be read, I can read it myself. Really, further on it's easy to make out.

POSTMASTER. No, no, read it all! After all, all the first part was read aloud.

ALL. Give him the letter, Charities, give it to him! (*To* KOROBKIN.) Go on, read!

CHARITIES. All right then. (*Gives him the letter.*) Here, please . . . (*Covers part of letter with his hand.*) Start here. (*All crowd around him.*)

POSTMASTER. Read it, read it. What nonsense! Read the whole thing.

KOROBKIN (*reading*). "The Director of Charities, one Strawberry, is a pig in a skull cap."

CHARITIES (*addressing the audience.*). That's not even witty!

'A pig in a skull cap! Whoever heard of pigs wearing skull caps!

KOROBKIN (*continuing to read*). "The School Superintendent fairly reeks of onions."

SCHOOL SUPERINTENDENT (*to the audience*). By God, I've never even had an onion in my mouth.

JUDGE (*aside*). Well, thank God there's nothing about me at least!

KOROBKIN (*reading*). "The Judge . . ."

JUDGE. Look at that . . . (*Aloud.*) I say, friends, this letter seems to go on and on. The hell with it! Why should we read all that bunk!

SCHOOL SUPERINTENDENT. No, no!

POSTMASTER. No, keep reading!

CHARITIES. Yes, might as well read it to the end now.

KOROBKIN (*continuing*). "Judge Lapkin-Tapkin is the last word in *mauvais ton* . . ." (*Stops.*) That must be French, I suppose.

JUDGE. God knows what it means anyway! If it means nothing worse than crook we'll be doing all right, but maybe it's something worse than that.

KOROBKIN. (*continuing to read*). "However, they're an amiable and hospitable lot. Well, that's all for now, Trapichkin my friend. I think I'll follow your example and try my hand at writing. In the long run this sort of life becomes boring and one longs for some spiritual sustenance. I've come to the conclusion that it's essential to engage in some higher activity. Write to me at Podkatilovka in Saratov Province. (*Turns letter over and reads address.*) "To Ivan Trapichkin, Esq., Courtyard Apartment, Third Floor, on the right, 97 Post Office Street, Petersburg."

A LADY. What an unexpected twist!

MAYOR. When he was cutting our throats, he certainly did a thorough job. I'm floored, floored, completely floored! I can't make out a thing, my eyes are all blurred. I can see nothing but pigs' snouts instead of faces. . . . Get him back here, get him! (*Waves his hands.*)

POSTMASTER. How can we get him back! I specially ordered the supervisor to give him the best coach and some demon must have prompted me to send ahead an order for post-horses for him.

KOROBKIN'S WIFE. Well, really, this is a quite unprecedented mix-up.

JUDGE. But, damn it, that man borrowed three hundred rubles off me!

CHARITIES. And another three hundred from me.

POSTMASTER (*sighing*). Oh Lord, and three hundred from me, too!

BOBCHINSKY. And from Peter here and me, he borrowed sixty-five, between us.

JUDGE (*spreading out his arms in a helpless gesture*). But how could it have happened, my friends? How, after all, could we have been so stupid?

MAYOR (*clasping his head in his hands*). What a . . . no, no, what an old fool I am! I'm an old ass that's gone soft in the head! . . . Thirty years I've been in the service of my country and not one merchant, not a single contractor has been able to put one over on me. I've cheated the swindlers, swindled the crooks, and hooked cheats who were ready to rob the whole world. I've duped three governors! But who cares about governors! (*Waves his hand in disgust.*)

ANNA ANDREYEVNA. But it just can't be, Anton. He's engaged to our Maria . . .

MAYOR (*in heartfelt tones*). Engaged indeed! You can run after him with your tongue hanging out and your toes spread fanwise—that's how he's engaged! *Now* she's throwing the engagement in my face! (*In a frenzy.*) Take a look, take a look, let the whole world, all Christendom, everyone, look what a fool they made of the mayor! A fool, that's what he is, a fool—the old wretch! (*Shakes his fist at himself.*) Ah, you fat-nosed idiot! You took that miserable wisp of a creature for someone important! There now, he's driving along the road with jingle bells and all! And he'll tell the story to the whole world! And I'll be a laughing stock. But that's nothing yet—some pen-pusher'll turn up, some scribbler, and he'll put me into his comedies and he'll have no respect for my name or position, and all those morons will show their ugly teeth and grin and clap their stupid hands! What are you laughing at, idiots!? At yourselves, perhaps! . . . Ah, you! . . . (*Angrily stamps his feet.*) If I could just get my hands on all those scribblers! Those pen-pushers, those damned liberals—they're the devil's own brood! I'd like to tie you all up in knots, to grind you to a powder, and send the lot of you to hell! Ah, I wish I could knock you into a cocked hat . . . (*Shakes his fist and stamps his heel.*)

(*After a short silence.*)

Even now, I can't get a hold of myself. You see how true it is—if God wants to punish someone, he first takes away his reason. What was there even remotely resembling an inspector general about that tramp? Not a thing! He wasn't even the littlest bit like one! But everyone started shouting: "The inspector general, the inspector general!" Who was the first to say he was the inspector general? Who was it?

CHARITIES (*shrugging*). I couldn't tell you how it all came about if you killed me. I'm still in a daze.

JUDGE. Who started it? I can tell you who started it—these two fellows did! (*Indicates* DOBCHINSKY *and* BOBCHINSKY.)

BOBCHINSKY. Oh no, leave me out of it! It never even occurred to me!

DOBCHINSKY. I had nothing to do with it! Absolutely nothing!

CHARITIES. Oh yes, I'm sure it was you.

SCHOOL SUPERINTENDENT. That's right. You came running out of the inn like a couple of madmen—"He's here and he hasn't paid his bill . . ." You caught us a fine bird!

MAYOR. Of course it was you! You, the town's gossips! You damned liars!

CHARITIES. I wish you'd go to hell with your stories about inspector generals and the rest.

MAYOR. All you ever do is tear around the town mixing people up, you damned chatterboxes! You're forever spreading gossip, you clip-tailed magpies!

JUDGE. Lousy slobs!

SCHOOL SUPERINTENDENT. Dupes!

CHARITIES. Pot-bellied puffballs!

(ALL *surround them.*)

BOBCHINSKY. It wasn't me, by God; it was Peter here.

DOBCHINSKY. Oh no, Peter, you were the first to . . .

BOBCHINSKY. Certainly not, you were the first.

LAST SCENE. *The same and Gendarmes.*

GENDARME. The inspector general has arrived from Petersburg and, in the name of the Tsar, summons you into his presence. He is staying at the hotel.

(*All are thunderstruck by his words. A single cry of surprise escapes from the lips of all the ladies. The entire group abruptly shifts position, then freezes on the spot. The* MAYOR *stands like a post in the center of the stage, his arms flung wide and his head thrown back. On his right, his* WIFE *and* DAUGHTER, *their whole bodies straining toward him. Behind them, the* POSTMASTER *transformed into a question mark directed at the audience. Behind him, the* SCHOOL SUPERINTENDENT *looking bewildered and innocent. Behind him, on the far side of the stage,* THREE WOMEN GUESTS, *leaning to-*

ward each other with highly sarcastic expressions, look at the
MAYOR's *family. On the* MAYOR's *left,* DIRECTOR OF CHARITIES
STRAWBERRY, *his head slightly on one side, as if listening to
something. Behind him, the* JUDGE, *his arms akimbo, squatting
low, almost sitting on the floor, and moving his lips as if
about to start whistling or to say: "Well, I'll be damned, now
we're really in for it!" Behind him* KOROBKIN, *turning toward
the audience with one eye screwed up and pointing meaningfully at the* MAYOR. *Behind him, at the far side of the stage,*
DOBCHINSKY *and* BOBCHINSKY *reaching their arms out toward each other, their mouths gaping, and their eyes popping
out. The other* GUESTS *just stand like posts. The group stands
in this position as if turned to stone for almost a minute and
a half.)*

CURTAIN

A Month in the Country

A COMEDY IN FIVE ACTS

by
IVAN TURGENEV

Ivan Turgenev's first play, *Carelessness*, appeared in 1843 and was soon followed by other comedies—nine in the next ten years. These included *Broke, An Amicable Settlement, The Family Charge, Where It Is Thin There It Breaks, The Bachelor, A Month in the Country, The Country Woman, A Conversation on a Highway* and *An Evening in Sorrento*. Of all these pieces, *A Month in the Country* is the most successful both from a literary and a theatrical point of view.

Turgenev began writing for the theater as a representative of the "natural" school, at first in the wake of Gogol. At the same time when melodrama and vaudeville dominated the Russian stage and great Western playwrights were distorted by censorship (Belinsky, the critic, spoke in the forties of "plucked" Schiller and "plundered" Shakespeare), Turgenev's plays made a substantial contribution to the realistic movement. In *A Month in the Country* he went beyond a faithful representation of reality and showed his ability to create a psychological drama. Critics usually see in this comedy merely a picture of the Russian nobility, a portrayal of intelligent but bland "superfluous men" confronted by a new type, the student Belaev, the harbinger of a change in social conditions. The relationship between the ineffectual Rakitin and the bored Natalia Petrovna was viewed by Turgenev's contemporaries as a manifestation of the weaknesses and artificiality of a certain way of life. The feeling which tied Vera to Belaev, on the other hand, was hailed as deep, sincere and healthy. Thus the two main couples of the comedy were opposed to each other, and although Belaev seemed at the end defeated, his failure was attributed to external intervention and not to his own errors, while Rakitin's fiasco was interpreted as a consequence of his personal flaws and defects. This kind of social analysis, however, misses the very essence of the comedy and presents a distorted image of its protagonists. In fact, Turgenev did not make Belaev a perfect hero, nor did he denigrate Rakitin: in the play the latter exits with great dignity, and there are tragic overtones in his fate.

Turgenev's principal accomplishment was to have written a

psychological drama in the guise of a drawing-room comedy placed in a familiar "gentlefolk's nest" environment. The main conflicts in *A Month in the Country* are not social but psychological and moral, and the plot cannot be reduced to the usual opposition of two generations; it is not simply a preview of Turgenev's *Fathers and Sons*. The verbal duel between Rakitin and Natalia Petrovna reflects a clash of personalities. The cunning and scheming of Natalia Petrovna, her jealousy and unscrupulous warfare against her rival are counterbalanced by Vera's innocence and simplicity which (as in the case of Bolshintsev) reverse the situation. The difference between the awakening of love in the seventeen-year-old Vera and in Natalia Petrovna, mature woman of thirty, is shown in a delicate, allusive manner; the relations between the two heroines are depicted with subtle psychological nuances. Sharp and often tense dialogues reflect the changes in the emotions and moods of the protagonists, but the inner movement of the play (for instance, the gradual transformation of Natalia Petrovna's feelings with the growth of her passion) is propelled without any external action.

Instead of the complicated plot and contrived stage effects customary in the theater of the fifties, Turgenev concentrated on a simple story without any spectacular climaxes, and built the whole dramatic development on a disclosure of true emotions and motivations, with just the right dose of comic relief. As a dramatist he refused to explain everything: he left a great deal to the imagination of the spectator; the material, physical action was transacted behind the wings; and the psychological undercurrents became the main carriers of the story. He structured the dialogue in accordance with his artistic intention, avoiding long speeches and monologues, interrupting important conversations and making his heroes and heroines leave a great deal unfinished and unsaid. The true significance of many scenes in *A Month in the Country* is intimated as much by omissions as by the spoken word. Prolonged intervals, lyrical passages, and natural settings are introduced as scenic devices. All these features make Turgenev a direct precursor of Chekhov.

Turgenev did not have much luck with his comedy. First, there was the fight with the censor before the play was passed for publication in 1855, five years after it had been written. Even then it was badly mutilated. For example, Turgenev was forced to drop the figure of Islaev" and to make Natalia Petrovna a widow. The final and revised text of the comedy could not be printed until 1869. Secondly, his contemporaries failed to see the novelty of treatment and tone in *A Month in the Country,* and this became quite obvious in its first production in 1872 when the actors interpreted it all wrongly. Finally, in 1879 an abridged version of the comedy was shown in the Alexandrinsky theater in St. Petersburg (in the presence of the author), and its success was due to the inspired acting of Maria Savina, a great artist and a friend of the aging writer. Later she shifted with equal success from her initial part of Vera to that of Natalia Petrovna. Another great actress, Yermolova, was instrumental in bringing the comedy to the Moscow Maly Theater at the beginning of our century. But the decisive moment in the history of the play came in 1909 with its production by Stanislavsky in the Moscow Art Theater. Stanislavsky subordinated the acting and the whole style of the performance to what he called "the inner action, the inner design" of the work. "The thin amorous lace knit so masterfully by Turgenev," he wrote, "demands a special manner of acting without which the spectator would not be able to enjoy the complex twists of all these loving, suffering and jealous hearts. Turgenev's plays become un-theatrical if presented on the stage with the usual histrionic devices. They were for that very reason judged un-theatrical in the old Theater." *A Month in the Country* shown in splendid period setting by Matislav Dobuzhinsky, with Stanislavsky as Rakitin, Olga Knipper, Chekhov's widow, as Natalia Petrovna, and Richard Boleslavsky as Belaev, was enthusiastically received by the public. Since that time it has been a fixture in the repertory of all Russian theaters.

A Month in the Country

CHARACTERS

ARKADY ISLAEV, 36 years old; a rich landowner
NATALIA PETROVNA ISLAEV, 29 years old; his wife
KOLIA, 10; their son
VERA, 17; their ward
ANNA SEMYONOVNA ISLAEV, 58; Islaev's mother
LIZAVETA BOGDANOVNA, 37; her companion
SCHAAF, 45; the German tutor
MICHEL RAKITIN, 30; a friend of the family
ALEXEI BELAEV, 21; a university student and tutor to Kolia
BOLSHINTSOV, 48; a neighbor
DOCTOR SPIGELSKY, 40
MATVEI, 40; a footman
KATIA, 20; a maid

The action takes place on the Islaevs' estate, in the early 1840's. Between Acts I and II, II and III, and IV and V, there is a day's interval.

ACT I

The drawing-room of the Islaevs' house. Right, a card table and a door leading to the study; center rear, a door to the ballroom; left, two windows and a round table. In each corner, a sofa. Anna Semyonovna Islaev, Lizaveta Bogdanovna, and Schaaf are seated at the card table playing preference. Natalia Petrovna Islaev and Rakitin are seated at the round table left. She is embroidering on a frame, he has a book in his hands. The wall clock strikes three.

SCHAAF (*speaking with a German accent*). I veel dake heartz.

ANNA SEMYONOVNA. What, hearts again? Well, I must say, my

dear fellow, this way you'll be the ruin of us all!

SCHAAF (*phlegmatically*). Et ov heartz.

ANNA SEMYONOVNA (*to* LIZAVETA BOGDANOVNA). Just look at him! How can one play with such a man? (LIZAVETA BOGDANOVNA *smiles*.)

NATALIA (*to* RAKITIN). Why don't you go on? Read some more.

RAKITIN (*slowly raising the book*). *Monte-Cristo se redressa haletant* . . . Do you really want to hear it, Natalia?

NATALIA. No, not really.

RAKITIN. Why are we reading it then?

NATALIA. I'll tell you why: a few days ago a certain lady said to me, "Haven't you read *Monte-Cristo?* You simply must read it, it's wonderful." I said nothing then but now I can tell her that I've read it and I didn't find anything wonderful about it.

RAKITIN. Of course, if you've already managed to make up your mind about it . . .

NATALIA. Really, you're the laziest man I ever . . .

RAKITIN. But I'm quite prepared to go on. (*Finds place in book*.) *Se redressa haletant, et* . . .

NATALIA (*at once interrupting him*). Have you seen Arkady today?

RAKITIN. Yes, I ran into him over by your mill dam. They're repairing it, you know. He was explaining something to the workmen and to put his point across, he felt he had to get knee-deep into the sand.

NATALIA. He throws himself into everything he does with too much enthusiasm. He's overzealous. It's hardly a good quality —don't you agree?

RAKITIN. I do indeed.

NATALIA. Oh, how boring of you to always agree with everything I say. Better read.

RAKITIN. I see, now you want me to disagree with you. By all means.

NATALIA. It's always what I want. What I really want is for you to want something. Anyway, now I want you to read.

RAKITIN. Yes, Ma'am. (*Turns to book again*.)

SCHAAF. Heartz!

ANNA SEMYONOVNA. What again! This is absolutely unbearable! (*To* NATALIA.) Natalia, Natalia . . .

NATALIA. What is it?

ANNA SEMYONOVNA. Just imagine, Schaaf is absolutely ruining us. Each time it's either seven or eight in hearts.

SCHAAF. Ant dees dime id iz zefen.

ANNA SEMYONOVNA. D'you hear that? It's awful, really!

NATALIA. Yes, quite awful.

ANNA SEMYONOVNA. So that's that then. (*To* NATALIA.) By the way, where's Kolia?

NATALIA. He's gone for a walk with his new tutor.

ANNA SEMYONOVNA. Ah. Well, shall we go on, Lizaveta?

RAKITIN (*to* NATALIA). What tutor?

NATALIA. Oh, I forgot to tell you—we've engaged a new tutor without even consulting you.

RAKITIN. To replace Dufour?

NATALIA. No. This one is to teach Kolia Russian. The princess is sending us a Frenchman from Moscow.

RAKITIN. And this Russian—what's he like? Is he an old man?

NATALIA. No, he's young. Anyway, he's only been engaged for the summer.

RAKITIN. Ah, it's a vacation job, is it?

NATALIA. Yes, that's right. And, you know what, Rakitin—you like to observe people, to analyze them, dig into their souls . . .

RAKITIN. Really, what makes you . . .

NATALIA. Oh yes, you do. Well, see what you think of him. I rather like him—he's slim, well-built, and there's something so open and cheerful about him. You'll see for yourself. He's a bit awkward, though, and I suppose you'll condemn him outright for that.

RAKITIN. You really have it in for me today, Natalia.

NATALIA. No, seriously, see what you think of him. My impression is that he may turn out a very nice person. Although, who can ever tell?

RAKITIN. You've aroused my curiosity.

NATALIA. Have I now? (*Dreamily.*) Well, go on, read some more.

RAKITIN. *Se redressa haletant, et . . .*

NATALIA (*suddenly looking around*). And where's Vera? I haven't seen her since this morning. (*Smiling at* RAKITIN.) Put the book away. I can see we'll never get to read it today. Tell me something instead.

RAKITIN. All right. But what shall I tell you? Ah yes! I spent a few days at the Krinitsyns' and, believe it or not, they're bored with each other already.

NATALIA. What makes you say that?

RAKITIN. Boredom's something you can't hide. Anything else, but not boredom.

NATALIA (*looking at him*). But you think anything else can be hidden?

RAKITIN (*after a brief pause*). Yes, I'd say so.

NATALIA (*lowering her eyes*). Well, so what did you do at the Krinitsyns'?

RAKITIN. Nothing. It's awful when one's bored in the company of one's friends. You feel at ease with them, not in the least awkward; you like them; there's nothing to irritate you; and yet, you're so bored it wearies you, your heart nags dully; it's a bit like being hungry all the time.

NATALIA. So, you're often bored with your friends, are you?

RAKITIN. As if you didn't know what it's like to be with someone you love but who rather bores you just the same!

NATALIA (*slowly*). Love . . . that's a big word. You're being a bit too complicated for me.

RAKITIN. Complicated? Why complicated?

NATALIA. That's just what's wrong with you. You know what, Rakitin—you're very smart, but . . . (*Pauses.*) sometimes when we talk, it's just like making lace. Ever seen it done? Lacemakers work in stuffy rooms, hardly moving an inch all day. Lace is beautiful but one swallow of cool water on a hot day is much better.

RAKITIN. Look, Natalia, today you're . . .

NATALIA. What?

RAKITIN. You're angry with me about something.

NATALIA. Oh, you clever people! With all your cleverness, you understand so little about others. Of course I'm not angry with you.

ANNA SEMYONOVNA. Ah! Finally the sheep is shorn! You're in trouble now! (*To* NATALIA.) Natalia, this villain here has met his fate.

SCHAAF (*acidly*). Eet eez ze fault of Lizafeta Bogdanovna.

LIZAVETA BOGDANOVNA (*irritated*). I'm sorry, but I couldn't possibly have known that Anna Semyonovna had no hearts.

SCHAAF. In ze future, I do not infite Lizafeta Bogdanovna for mine partner.

ANNA SEMYONOVNA (*to* SCHAAF). But what did she do wrong?

SCHAAF (*in exactly the same tone*). In ze future I do not infite Lizafeta Bogdanovna for mine partner.

LIZAVETA BOGDANOVNA. Well, what's that to me! What next!

RAKITIN. You know, Natalia, the more I look at you today, the less I recognize you.

NATALIA (*with some curiosity*). Is that so?

RAKITIN. Yes, really, there's some change in you.

NATALIA. Is there? Well then, do me a favor. Since you know me so well, see if you can guess just how I've changed and what can have caused it. All right?

RAKITIN. Well . . .

(KOLIA *runs in noisily from the ballroom and goes straight to* ANNA SEMYONOVNA.)

KOLIA. Grandma, Grandma! Look what I've got! (*Showing her a bow and arrows.*) Look!

ANNA SEMYONOVNA. Let's see, darling. Oh, what a wonderful bow! Who made it for you?

KOLIA. He did, he did . . . (*Indicates* BELAEV *who has stopped in the ballroom doorway.*)

ANNA SEMYONOVNA. Oh! How cleverly it's made.

KOLIA. I aimed at a tree with it, Grandma, and I hit it twice. (*Jumps up and down.*)

NATALIA. Let me have a look, Kolia.

KOLIA (*running to her and speaking while she examines the bow*). Oh, *Maman,* you should've seen Mr. Belaev climb a tree! He's going to teach me how and he's going to teach me to swim, too. He's going to teach me everything, everything! (*Jumps up and down.*)

NATALIA (*to* BELAEV). I'm very grateful to you for taking so much trouble with Kolia.

KOLIA (*eagerly interrupting her*). Oh, I like him, *Maman,* I do like him!

NATALIA (*stroking* KOLIA's *head*). He's a bit of a softie. I'll be very glad if you can make a hardy, agile boy out of him for me.

(BELAEV *bows.*)

KOLIA. Let's go to the stables, sir. Let's take Favorite some bread.

BELAEV. All right, let's go.

ANNA SEMYONOVNA (*to* KOLIA). Come here to me. Give me a kiss first.

KOLIA (*running out*). Later, Grandma, when I come back. (*Runs out into the ballroom.* BELAEV *follows him.*)

ANNA SEMYONOVNA (*looking after* KOLIA). He's so sweet! (*To* SCHAAF *and* LIZAVETA BOGDANOVNA.) Isn't he?

LIZAVETA BOGDANOVNA. Oh yes, indeed.

SCHAAF (*after a pause*). I pass.

NATALIA (*to* RAKITIN, *with a trace of anxiety*). Well, what did you think of him?

RAKITIN. Of whom?

NATALIA (*after a pause*). The Russian tutor.

RAKITIN. Oh, I'm sorry, I forgot. I was so absorbed with your question. (NATALIA *looks at him with a hardly perceptible ironic smile.*) Although, I must say, his face . . . yes . . . yes, he has a good face. He seemed very nice. But he's awfully shy, isn't he?

NATALIA. Yes, rather.

RAKITIN (*looking at her*). Still, I can't account for . . .

NATALIA. What if you and I took him in hand, Rakitin? Would you like to? We'll complete his education. It's a real opportunity for sedate, sober-minded people like us! After all, we are very sedate, don't you think?

RAKITIN. I gather this young man interests you. I'm sure he'd be very flattered if he knew.

NATALIA. Not in the least, believe me! You shouldn't judge by the way one of us would have acted in his place. He's not a bit like you and me, Rakitin. That's just the trouble with us—we keep examining ourselves so carefully and, after that, we imagine that we know all about people.

RAKITIN. "Another man's heart is like a dark forest." But what are you driving at? Why do you keep taking digs at me?

NATALIA. And at whom am I to take digs, if not at my friends? And you are my friend, aren't you? (*Presses his hand.* RAKITIN *brightens up and smiles.*) An old friend.

RAKITIN. I'm only afraid that you may get sick of your old friend.

NATALIA (*laughing*). It's the sweetest things that make one sick.

RAKITIN. Maybe. But that doesn't make it any better for them.

NATALIA. Oh, stop it! (*Lowering her voice.*) As if you didn't know, *ce que vous êtes pour moi.*

RAKITIN. You play with me like a cat with a mouse, Natalia. But I'm not complaining.

NATALIA. Poor little mousie!

ANNA SEMYONOVNA. And twenty from you, Schaaf! Aha!

SCHAAF. In ze future, I do not infite Lizafeta Bogdanovna for mine partner.

(*Enter footman* MATVEI *from ballroom. Announces* DOCTOR.)

MATVEI. Dr. Spigelsky, Ma'am.

DOCTOR (*entering behind* MATVEI). You don't announce doctors! (*Exit* MATVEI.) My profoundest respects to the whole family. (*Kisses* ANNA SEMYONOVNA'S *hand.*) Good-day, Ma'am. Any luck today?

ANNA SEMYONOVNA. Luck indeed! I'm hardly managing to break even. And I'm glad to get off so lightly, with that villain over there. (*Indicates* SCHAAF.)

DOCTOR (*to* SCHAAF). Really, Schaaf, is that the way to play with ladies? That's awful! I would never have thought it of you.

SCHAAF (*growling through clenched teeth*). Vith laties, vith laties!

DOCTOR (*approaching the round table at the left*). How are you, Natalia? Hello, Rakitin.

NATALIA. How are you, Doctor?

DOCTOR. That's a question I like to hear—it means you must be well yourself. How am I getting along? A self-respecting doctor never gets sick. He just ups and dies all of a sudden. Ha-ha.

NATALIA. Do sit down. I'm in good health . . . just a little depressed perhaps. But that, in itself, is a sign of trouble, isn't it?

DOCTOR (*sitting down beside* NATALIA). Let's feel your pulse. (*Doing so.*) Oh dear, oh dear, these nerves! You hardly ever go out for a walk, Natalia, you seldom laugh—that's all that's wrong with you. What are you staring at, Rakitin? Well, I suppose I could prescribe some drops for you.

NATALIA. I've no objection to laughing. (*Animatedly.*) Well, after all, you've got a sharp tongue, Doctor. I like and admire you for that. So tell me something amusing. Rakitin here has done nothing but philosophize all day long.

DOCTOR (*giving* RAKITIN *a sidelong glance*). Ah, I see it's not just the nerves that are upset—I detect a touch of biliousness, too.

NATALIA. Good heavens, you too? Examine away, Doctor, but please keep your findings to yourself. We all know how terribly penetrating you are. The pair of you, you're both very perspicacious.

DOCTOR. Yes, Ma'am.

NATALIA. Tell us something amusing.

DOCTOR. Yes, Ma'am. But you've caught me a bit off balance. No sooner do I put my foot in the door, than it's, come on, tell us something amusing. Give me a chance, at least, to take a pinch of snuff. (*Does so.*)

NATALIA. What preparations!

DOCTOR. But you must understand, Ma'am—it all depends what you call amusing. It's a question of what you tell to whom. For instance, take your neighbor Khlopushkin—you just have to show him your finger and he bursts out laughing, laughs till he's hoarse, with the tears pouring out of his eyes, while you're quite another matter. Well, all the same, let's have a go at it. I suppose you know Platon Verenitsyn?

NATALIA. Yes, I think I've met him—anyway, I've heard of him.

DOCTOR. Well, he has a sister who's quite mad. In fact, I think they're either both mad or both sane, because the two of them are so alike it's amazing. But, anyway, that's beside the point. Who's considered mad and who isn't is a matter of luck. Well, this Verenitsyn has a daughter—a greenish little thing, you know, with pale little eyes, and a red little nose and small, yellow teeth—in a word, a charming young woman; she plays the piano and lisps too, so, you see, everything's just right. She stands to inherit an estate with two hundred serfs, and then her aunt's as well, with a hundred and fifty more. Of course, her aunt is still alive and likely to live for a long time—the insane always live long—but God is merciful. She made her will out in favor of her niece, although just the day before she was in such a state I had to pour cold water over her—absolutely uselessly, I may say, for she's completely incurable. Well, so Verenitsyn's daughter was quite an eligible young lady. He began taking her out on visits and suitors started to appear, among them a certain Perekuzov, a dried-out stick of a young man, very timid but with the highest principles. And so papa liked our Perekuzov, and daughter liked him, too. Well, it seemed there was nothing in the way. Off to the altar and God bless them! And, indeed, everything was going along fine. Mr. Verenitsyn had got to the point where he was nudging Mr. Perekuzov in the belly and slapping him on the back, when, lo and behold, an officer appeared out of the blue, called Ardalion Protobekasov. He first laid eyes on Verenitsyn's daughter at the Marshal of Nobility's Ball, danced three polkas with her, and said to her, rolling his eyes I bet: "Oh, I'm so unhappy," and that was enough to sweep our young lady off her feet. There were tears, sighs, moans. Nobody looks at Perekuzov any more, nobody says a word to him. The mere word "wedding" causes endless wrigglings. Good Lord almighty, what a mess! Well, Verenitsyn thinks to himself, if it's to be the officer, it's to be the officer. He's also a man of means, thank God. So they invite him, "Won't you do us the honor," they say. He'll do them the honor. He comes, does a bit of courting, falls in love, and finally offers heart and hand. So, you imagine Verenitsyn's young lady happily accepts? That's what you think! No, there're more tears, sighs, fainting fits. The father's at his wits' end. What is it, after all? What's the matter now? And what d'you think she answers? "Oh," she says, "Father, I don't know which of them I love, this one or the other." "What?" "Honest to God, I don't know. It'd be better if I didn't marry either of them. And yet I'm in love!" Verenitsyn, it goes without saying, is beside himself. And the suitors don't know what's what any more, either. But she won't budge. So you see what strange things are happening all around us.

NATALIA. I don't see what you find so surprising about it—as if one couldn't love two people at the same time!

RAKITIN. Ah, you think . . .

NATALIA (*slowly*). Yes, I think . . . and yet—I don't know, perhaps it just shows that you don't love either of them.

DOCTOR (*taking snuff and looking from* NATALIA *to* RAKITIN *and back*). So that's how it is, so that's how it is.

NATALIA (*in a lively tone to* DOCTOR). That was a good story, but you didn't make me laugh just the same.

DOCTOR. No, I didn't and I wonder if anyone else could. Anyway, that's not what you really want.

NATALIA. What do I want then?

DOCTOR. God knows.

NATALIA. Ah, what a bore you are! No better than Rakitin.

DOCTOR. You flatter me. (NATALIA *makes an impatient gesture.*)

ANNA SEMYONOVNA (*getting up*). Well, at last. (*Sighing.*) I've sat so long my feet have gone to sleep. (LIZAVETA BOGDANOVNA *and* SCHAAF *also rise.*) Oo-oof!

NATALIA (*getting up and walking over to them*). What an idea to sit so long without moving.

(DOCTOR *and* RAKITIN *get up.*)

ANNA SEMYONOVNA (*to* SCHAAF). That's seventy kopeks coming from you, my dear fellow. (SCHAAF *bows coldly.*) You're not going to be the one to collect every time. (*To* NATALIA.) You seem a little pale today, my dear. Are you all right? Doctor, is she all right?

DOCTOR (*who has been whispering about something with* RAKITIN). Oh yes, perfectly.

ANNA SEMYONOVNA. That's good then. Well, I'm going to have a little rest before dinner. I'm very tired. Let's go, Lizaveta. Off, my legs, my legs.

(*Goes into the ballroom with* LIZAVETA BOGDANOVNA. NATALIA *accompanies her to the door.* DOCTOR, RAKITIN *and* SCHAAF *remain down stage.*)

DOCTOR (*offering* SCHAAF *snuff*). Well, Schaaf, *wie befinden sie sich?*

SCHAAF (*taking snuff with an important air*). Gut. Und how are you?

DOCTOR. Not bad, thanks. (*In a low voice to* RAKITIN.) So you really don't know what's the matter with Natalia today?

RAKITIN. No, I've no idea.

DOCTOR. Well, even if you don't know . . . (*Turns and goes to meet* NATALIA *who is coming back toward them.*) I have a little bit of business to talk over with you, Ma'am.

NATALIA (*crossing to window*). Really? What is it?

DOCTOR. I would like to talk to you privately.

NATALIA. So that's how it is. You frighten me.

(RAKITIN *meanwhile has taken* SCHAAF *by the arm and is walking up and down the room with him, whispering something to him in German.* SCHAAF *laughs and says, in a low voice:* "Ja, ja, ja! ja wohl, ja wohl, sehr gut.")

DOCTOR (*lowering his voice*). Actually, it's a matter that does not concern you alone.

NATALIA (*looking out into the garden*). What do you mean?

DOCTOR. Well, it's like this. A certain good friend of mine has asked me to find out . . . that is . . . what your plans are for your ward, Vera.

NATALIA. What plans?

DOCTOR. Well, without beating around the bush, my friend . . .

NATALIA. Do you mean, by any chance that he has matrimonial views concerning her?

DOCTOR. That's exactly it.

NATALIA. You must be joking.

DOCTOR. Not in the least.

NATALIA (*laughing*). But really! She's still a child! What an extraordinary errand!

DOCTOR. What's so strange about it? This friend of mine . . .

NATALIA. I know you're a practical man, Doctor. Now, who is this friend of yours?

DOCTOR (*smiling*). Please, please. You still haven't given me anything positive to go on.

NATALIA. But I've told you she is still a child, and you're perfectly well aware of it yourself, Mr. Diplomat. (*Turning away.*) Speaking of her, here she is in person. (VERA *and* KOLIA *come running in from the ballroom.*)

KOLIA (*running to* RAKITIN). Tell them to bring us some glue, we need glue.

NATALIA (*to* VERA). Where have you been? (*Stroking her cheek.*) You're all flushed.

VERA. In the garden. (DOCTOR *bows to her.*) Hello, Doctor.

RAKITIN (*to* KOLIA). What do you want glue for?

KOLIA. We need it. Mr. Belaev is making us a kite. Tell them . . .

RAKITIN (*moving toward the bell*). Wait a moment, I'll get it for you.

SCHAAF. *Erlauben sie.* Kolia haf his Cherman lesson not brepared. (*Takes* KOLIA *by the arm.*) *Kommen sie.*

KOLIA (*sadly*). *Morgen, Herr Schaaf, morgen.*

SCHAAF (*sharply*). *Morgen, morgen, nur nicht heute, sagen alle faule Leute. Kommen sie.* (KOLIA *pulls back.*)

NATALIA (*to* VERA). Who have you been with all this time? I haven't seen you since this morning.

VERA. With Mr. Belaev and Kolia.

NATALIA. Ah! (*Turning.*) Kolia, what does this mean?

KOLIA (*lowering his voice*). Herr Schaaf . . . Mama . . .

RAKITIN (*to* NATALIA). They were making a kite and now Herr Schaaf wants to give him an assignment.

SCHAAF (*self-righteously*). *Gnädige Frau* . . .

NATALIA (*sternly to* KOLIA). Please do as you're told. You've done enough running around for one day. Now go with Herr Schaaf.

SCHAAF (*leading* KOLIA *out into the ballroom*). *Es ist unerhört!*

KOLIA (*in a whisper to* RAKITIN *as he leaves*). Tell them to bring the glue anyway. (RAKITIN *nods.*)

SCHAAF (*pulling* KOLIA *behind him*). *Kommen sie, mein Herr.*

(*Exits with him into the ballroom.* RAKITIN *exits after them.*)

NATALIA (*to* VERA). Sit down, you must be tired. (*Sits down herself.*)

VERA (*sitting down*). Oh no, not at all.

NATALIA (*to* SPIGELSKY *with a smile*). Doctor, have a look at her. Doesn't she look tired?

DOCTOR. But it's very good for her, I'm sure.

NATALIA. That's very possible. (*To* VERA.) Still, what were you doing in the garden?

VERA. Oh, we were playing. Running around. First we watched them working on the dam, then Mr. Belaev climbed a tree after a squirrel. He went way up high and then he began shaking the top. Were we scared! Finally the squirrel fell out and Treasure nearly caught it. But it got away.

NATALIA (*glancing at* DOCTOR *with a smile*). And then?

VERA. Then Mr. Belaev made Kolia a bow. He made it so quickly! And after that he stole up to the cow in the meadow and suddenly jumped on her back. The cow got frightened and ran and started bucking but he just held on to her and laughed . . . (*Laughs herself.*) After that, Mr. Belaev was going to make us a kite and we came in here to get some glue.

NATALIA (*patting her cheek*). A child, an absolute child, don't you think so, Doctor?

DOCTOR (*slowly, looking at* NATALIA). Yes, I must agree with you.

NATALIA. Now you can see for yourself.

DOCTOR. But why should that prevent her from . . . On the contrary, I'd say . . .

NATALIA. You would, would you? (*To* VERA.) Well, so I gather you had a wonderful time?

VERA. Oh yes, Mr. Belaev is such fun.

NATALIA. He must be. (*Pauses.*) Sometimes, Vera, I can't really believe you're seventeen! (VERA *looks at her slightly surprised.*) You're still a child, just a child. (RAKITIN *enters from the hall.*)

DOCTOR (*fussily*). Oh, I forgot, your coachman is sick and I haven't been in to see him yet.

NATALIA. What's the matter with him?

DOCTOR. He has a fever, but it's not serious.

NATALIA (*as he leaves*). Will you have dinner with us, Doctor?

DOCTOR. If I'm invited.   (*Exits into the ballroom.*)

NATALIA. *Mon enfant, vous feriez bien de mettre une autre robe pour le dîner.* (VERA *rises.*) Come over here, Vera. (*Kisses her on the forehead.*) Ah, child, child! (VERA *kisses her hand and goes into the study on the right.*)

RAKITIN (*to* VERA *in a low voice, winking*). I've had everything that's needed sent to Mr. Belaev.

VERA (*in a low voice*). Oh, thank you very much.   (*Exits.*)

RAKITIN (*going up to* NATALIA. *She holds out her hand to him and he takes it and presses it*). At last we're alone. Natalia, please tell me—what's the matter?

NATALIA. Nothing, Michel, nothing. And if there was something, it's all over now. Sit down. (RAKITIN *sits down next to her.*) It happens to everyone—storm clouds are bound to wander across the sky sometimes. Why are you looking at me like that?

RAKITIN. Looking at you? I'm happy.

NATALIA (*smiling at him in answer*). Open the window, Michel, it's so nice outside. (RAKITIN *gets up and opens the window.*) Ah, a breeze! (*Laughing.*) You'd think it'd just been waiting for a chance to burst in. (*Looking around.*) Look how it's taken possession of the room—you'll never drive it out again now.

RAKITIN. And you, you're calm and gentle now—like evening after a thunderstorm.

NATALIA (*dreamily*). "After a thunderstorm." But was there a storm?

RAKITIN (*shaking his head*). One was gathering.

NATALIA. Really? (*Pauses, looking at him.*) You know, Michel, I can't even imagine a more kind-hearted man than you existing. I mean it. (RAKITIN *makes a gesture to stop her.*) No, let me have my say. You're so understanding, so affectionate, so reliable. You never change. I owe you so much.

RAKITIN. Why have you chosen this particular moment to tell me this, Natalia?

NATALIA. I don't know. I just feel happy. I'm relaxed now. Please, let me run on . . .

RAKITIN (*pressing her hand*). You're my good angel.

NATALIA. (*laughing*). You wouldn't have said that this morning. But you know me well enough, Michel, so I'm sure you'll forgive me. Relations between us are absolutely pure and straightforward, and yet they're not quite natural. We can look Arkady and anyone else in the eye, and yet . . . (*Grows thoughtful.*) That's what makes me feel so depressed sometimes, and so awkward. Then I become nasty and childish—I'm quite ready to take out my bad temper on anyone, and especially on you. I hope you don't mind my picking you for the honor?

RAKITIN (*eagerly*). Oh, on the contrary . . .

NATALIA. Yes, sometimes it's a pleasure to torment someone you love. Someone you love . . . Why, I'm just like Pushkin's Tatiana: I can also say: "I love you, why should I disguise it?"

RAKITIN. Natalia! You mean . . .

NATALIA (*interrupting him*). Yes . . . I love you. But you know what? It sometimes seems very strange to me. I love you —and it's such a simple, restful feeling. It doesn't disturb my peace. It warms me, and yet . . . You've never made me cry, and yet, it would seem, I should have . . . (*Interrupting herself.*) Why is it like that?

RAKITIN (*a little sadly*). That's a question that doesn't require an answer.

NATALIA (*dreamily*). Well, but we've known each other for a long time now.

RAKITIN. Four years. Yes, we're old friends.

NATALIA. Friends. No, you're more than a friend to me.

RAKITIN. Let it be, Natalia. I'm afraid you will shatter my frail happiness.

NATALIA. No, no, no. The trouble is you're too good. You're too indulgent, you spoil me. You're too good, d'you hear?

RAKITIN (*smiling*). Yes, Ma'am.

NATALIA (*looking at him*). I don't know about you, but I don't wish for any other happiness. Many would envy me. (*Holds out both hands to him.*) Isn't that so?

RAKITIN. I am in your power. Do what you will with me.

(*The voice of* ARKADY ISLAEV, NATALIA'S *husband, is heard in the ballroom saying:* "So you sent for him?")

NATALIA (*rising abruptly*). It's him! I can't bear to see him now. I'm going! (*Goes into the study.*)

RAKITIN (*Looking after her*). What on earth's the matter with her? Is this the beginning of the end, or the end itself? (*Pauses.*) Or is it the beginning?

(*Enter* ISLAEV *with a preoccupied look. He removes his hat.*)

ISLAEV. How are you, Michel?

RAKITIN. We've seen each other before today, remember?

ISLAEV. Oh, excuse me. I've been up to my ears all day. (*Pacing the room.*) It's very strange! The Russian peasant is quite sharp and shrewd and I have great respect for him. And yet, there are times when you can talk to him till you're blue in the face, explaining something. You get the impression that you've made it all as clear as can be and then it turns out it was no use at all. The Russian peasant doesn't have that . . . that . . .

RAKITIN. You're still busy with the mill dam, I suppose?

ISLAEV. That . . . you might call it . . . he has no love of work. Yes, it's precisely love for it that's lacking. He doesn't give you a chance to explain what you want properly. "Yes, sir," he says. But then you find he simply hasn't understood a thing. Take the German now—he's quite different! The Russian has no patience. But I have great respect for him, for all that. Where's Natalia, d'you know?

RAKITIN. She was in here a minute ago.

ISLAEV. But what time is it? It must be dinner time. Been on my feet since morning, got a mountain of work to do. And I still haven't been over to the new construction site. It's awful how time flies—impossible to keep up with everything! (RAKITIN *smiles.*) Ah, I see you think that's funny. But what can I do, man? I am what I am. I'm a practical man. I was born a landowner, and I'm not suited for anything else. There was a time when I had other dreams, but they didn't come off. I burned my fingers—and how! Where's Belaev gone?

RAKITIN. And who's Belaev?

ISLAEV. Oh, he's the new Russian tutor. He's still pretty uncivilized but he'll adjust. Quite a smart lad. I asked him to have a look and see how the construction was going today. (*Enter* BELAEV.) Ah, here he is! Well? How's it going over there? I bet they're loafing around? Uh?

BELAEV. No, sir, they're working.

ISLAEV. Have they finished the second framework?

BELAEV. They're working on the third already.

ISLAEV. And did you tell them about the beams?

BELAEV. Yes, I did.

ISLAEV. Well, what did they say?

BELAEV. They say they've never done it any other way.

ISLAEV. Hm. Was Ermil the carpenter there?

BELAEV. Yes, he was.

ISLAEV. Ah! Well, thank you very much. (*Enter* NATALIA.) Ah, Natalia, how are you?

RAKITIN. What's the matter with you? Are you going to ask everyone how they are twenty times today?

ISLAEV. I told you, I'm snowed under. Oh, by the way, have I shown you my new winnower? Let's go, it's very interesting. Imagine, it creates a hurricane, a real hurricane. We'll have time before dinner. Like to see it?

RAKITIN. Sure.

ISLAEV. And what about you, Natalia? Coming along?

NATALIA. What do I understand about your winnowers! You go ahead, but mind you don't stay too long!

ISLAEV (*going out with* RAKITIN). We'll be right back.

(BELAEV *makes a movement to go with them.*)

NATALIA (*to* BELAEV). And where are you going, Mr. Belaev?

BELAEV. I . . . I . . .

NATALIA. Well, of course, if you feel like a stroll.

BELAEV. Oh no, Ma'am—I've been outdoors all morning.

NATALIA. Oh! Well, in that case, do sit down. Here. (*Indicating a chair.*) You and I haven't had a proper talk yet. We still haven't got to know each other properly. (BELAEV *bows and sits down.*) And I would like to get to know you.

BELAEV. That . . . that's very kind of you, Ma'am.

NATALIA (*smiling*). You're afraid of me now—I can see that. But wait a while. When we know each other better, you won't be any more. Tell me, how old are you?

BELAEV. Twenty-one.

NATALIA. Are your parents living?

BELAEV. My mother is dead, my father's alive.

NATALIA. And is it long since you lost your mother?

BELAEV. Yes, a long time.

NATALIA. But you remember her?

BELAEV. Oh, but yes, of course I do.

NATALIA. And does your father live in Moscow?

BELAEV. No, Ma'am, in the country.

NATALIA. Oh! And do you have any brothers or sisters?

BELAEV. One sister.

NATALIA. And are you very fond of her?

BELAEV. Oh yes, I am. She's much younger than I am.

NATALIA. What's her name?

BELAEV. Natalia.

NATALIA (*in a lively tone*). Natalia? How strange. That's my name, too, you know. (*Stopping.*) So you're very fond of her?

BELAEV. Yes, I am.

NATALIA. Tell me, what do you think of my Kolia?

BELAEV. A very nice boy.

NATALIA. Isn't he? And so affectionate! He's already become quite attached to you.

BELAEV. I will do my best . . . I'm very glad . . .

NATALIA. You understand—naturally, I'd like to make a real man of him. Of course, I don't know whether I'll succeed. But, whatever else, I want him to always remember his childhood with pleasure. Let him develop freely—that's the important thing. Myself, I was brought up quite differently. My father wasn't a wicked man, but he was peevish and strict. Everyone in the household, from my mother on down, was afraid of him. Whenever we were summoned to go to him, my brother and I always secretly crossed ourselves. Now and then my father would show me some affection but I remember that it only made me feel tense and embarrassed. When my brother grew up, he broke with my father, as you may have heard. I'll never forget that terrible day. As to me, I always remained an obedient daughter, till the day my father died. He called me his comfort, his Antigone. —He went blind in the last years of his life. —But his tenderest marks of affection weren't enough to wipe out the impressions of my young years. I was afraid of him even when he was old and blind, and I never felt at ease in his presence. Perhaps the effects of that timidity, of that long constraint, have not completely disappeared to this day. I know that, at first glance, I seem—how shall I put it?—cold, perhaps. But here I am talking about myself, instead of discussing Kolia with you. I only wanted to say that I know from personal experience how good it is for a child to grow up free and untrammeled. You, for instance, I don't imagine they were very strict with you in your childhood, were they?

BELAEV. I don't quite know how to put it, Ma'am. Certainly, no one was strict with me. Actually, no one bothered about me much.

NATALIA (*timidly*). But, surely, your father . . .

BELAEV. He had no time for it, Ma'am. He spent more and more of his time with the neighboring landowners . . . on business, that is. Although, actually, he also went not on business but . . . Well, one might say, that was his way of earning his living. He rendered them certain services, you know.

NATALIA. Oh! So then there was no one to see to your upbringing.

BELAEV. No, no one, to tell the truth. And, I suppose it's quite noticeable. I feel my deficiencies quite keenly.

NATALIA. Perhaps, but then . . . (*Stops, then resumes the conversation, a little embarrassed.*) Oh, by the way, was that you singing in the garden yesterday?

BELAEV. When do you mean, Ma'am?

NATALIA. In the evening, by the pond. Was it you?

BELAEV. Yes, Ma'am, it was. (*Speaking quickly.*) I didn't think . . . the pond is so far from the house, I didn't think one could hear from here.

NATALIA. But you're not apologizing? You have a very pleasant, carrying voice, and you do sing well. Have you ever studied music?

BELAEV. No, Ma'am, not really. I sing by ear and only simple songs.

NATALIA. You sing them wonderfully. Sometime I'll ask you . . . not now, but when we know each other better, when we become closer friends. We will become closer friends, won't we? I have great confidence in you—my chatting away like this should convince you of that. (*She extends her hand to shake hands with him.* BELAEV *takes it hesitatingly and then, after a moment of perplexity during which he cannot decide what to do with it, he kisses it.* NATALIA *blushes and withdraws her hand. Meanwhile, the* DOCTOR *has entered from the hall, stopped and taken a step back.* NATALIA *gets up quickly and so does* BELAEV.)

NATALIA (*with embarrassment*). Oh, it's you, Doctor. Mr. Belaev and I have been . . . (*Stops.*)

DOCTOR (*loudly and with familiarity*). You have no idea, Natalia, what's going on in your own house. I go to the servants' quarters and ask for the coachman who is sick. I look around and there's my patient sitting at the table and stuffing both cheeks with pancakes and onions. Go and practice medicine after that! Go and be dependent on people being sick and the modest income it's supposed to bring you in!

NATALIA (*with a forced smile*). Oh, really. (BELAEV *makes a movement as if to leave the room.*) Mr. Belaev, I forgot to tell you . . .

(VERA *runs in from the ballroom.*)

VERA. Mr. Belaev, Mr. Belaev! (*Seeing* NATALIA's *look, she stops abruptly.*)

NATALIA (*a little surprised*). What's going on? What do you want?

VERA (*blushing, lowering her eyes, and indicating* BELAEV). I was looking for Mr. Belaev.

NATALIA. Why?

VERA. Kolia . . . that is, Kolia asked me . . . about the kite . . .

NATALIA. Ah! (*In a low voice to* VERA.) *On n'entre pas comme cela dans une chambre. Cela ne convient pas.* (*Addressing the* DOCTOR.) What time is it, Doctor? Your watch is always right. It must be dinner time.

DOCTOR. Just one moment, Ma'am, and I'll tell you. (*Takes watch out of pocket.*) Right now . . . right now, the exact time is . . . exactly twenty minutes past four.

NATALIA. You see? Dinner time. (*Approaches mirror and fixes her hair. Meanwhile* VERA *whispers something to* BELAEV. *They both laugh.* NATALIA *looks at them in the mirror.* DOCTOR *watches her out of the corner of his eye.*)

BELAEV (*in a low voice, laughing*). Really?

VERA (*also in a low voice, nodding*). Yes, yes, she fell off.

NATALIA (*turning toward* VERA *with feigned indifference*). What's this? Who fell?

VERA (*confused*). Well, Mr. Belaev put up a swing and Nanny decided . . .

NATALIA (*turning to* DOCTOR *without waiting to hear the end of what* VERA *is saying*). Oh, Doctor, would you come over here a minute? (*Leads him away to the other side of the room, then addresses* VERA *again.*) Nanny's not hurt, I hope?

VERA. Oh no!

NATALIA. Good. But still, Mr. Belaev, you shouldn't have . . .

MATVEI (*entering from ballroom and announcing*). Dinner is served, Ma'am.

NATALIA. Ah good! But where is Mr. Islaev? There now, he and Rakitin will be late again.

MATVEI. They are already in the dining-room, Ma'am.

NATALIA. And mother?

MATVEI. She is also in the dining-room, Ma'am.

NATALIA. Good, then let's go in. (*Indicates* BELAEV.) Vera, *allez en avant avec monsieur.*

(*Exit* MATVEI, *followed by* BELAEV *and* VERA.)

DOCTOR (*to* NATALIA). There was something you wanted to say to me?

NATALIA. Oh yes! Well, you see . . . we'll have to talk further about . . . about your offer.

DOCTOR. Concerning Vera?

NATALIA. Yes, I'll think about it, I'll think about it.

(*Both go out into the ballroom.*)

CURTAIN

ACT II

The garden. Left and right, benches under the trees; center, raspberry bushes. Katia and Matvei enter right. Katia carries a basket.

MATVEI. Well then, Katia, what's it to be? Do me a favor, let's have an answer—please!

KATIA. I really don't know what to say, Matvei.

MATVEI. You know very well how I feel about you, if you see what I mean. I know I'm older than you—there's no denying that, but I can still hold my own with the next man. I'm in the prime of life, so to speak. And furthermore, I'm not one of those rough fellows, as you well know. So I really don't see what else you could want.

KATIA. Believe me, Matvei, I appreciate your asking me very much, but . . . but I think we should wait a while.

MATVEI. But what's there to wait for? First of all, let me remind you, you never said anything about waiting before. And as for respecting you, Katia, you have nothing to worry about there. I'll give you such respect you'll have nothing left to wish for. Moreover, I don't drink and, then, the masters think well of me, never have a word of reproach.

KATIA. Really, Matvei, I just don't know what to say.

MATVEI. Ah, Katia, it's only lately you've started this sort of business.

KATIA (*blushing a little*). What d'you mean only lately? Why only lately?

MATVEI. Well now, that I can't tell. But I do know you acted different with me before.

KATIA (*hurriedly, glancing off-stage*). Look out! The German's coming!

MATVEI (*sadly*). Ah, that long-nosed stork! We'll come back to this another time. (*Exits right. KATIA moves away toward the raspberry bushes. SCHAAF enters left, a fishing rod over his shoulder.*)

SCHAAF. Rasperry? Rasperry fery gut frut. You likes rasperry?

KATIA. Yes, I like them.

SCHAAF. Heh, heh! Und I alzo. I everzing likes vot you likes. (*Seeing that she wishes to go.*) Oh, Katia, vait a leetle.

KATIA. I don't have time, sir. The housekeeper'll be after me.

SCHAAF. Oh, zat is nozzing. I too, I go . . . (*Indicating rod.*) . . . how you say, catch, you unnerstant, catch, zat iz, feesh catch. You likes? Feesh?

KATIA. Yes.

SCHAAF. Heh, heh, I too, I too. You know vat I tell you, Katia—in German ist a zong. (*Sings.*) *Kathrinchen, Kathrinchen, wie lieb' ich dich so sehr!* Zat iz, in Ruschisch, O Katia, my leetle Katia, you iz gut, I luf you. (*Tries to put an arm around her.*)

KATIA. Stop it, stop it! You should be ashamed of yourself. Look, the masters are coming! (*Escapes into the raspberry bushes.*)

SCHAAF (*in a low voice, adopting a stern expression*). *Die dumme!*

(NATALIA *enters right, arm-in-arm with* RAKITIN.)

NATALIA (*to* SCHAAF). Ah, Herr Schaaf! You off to catch some fish?

SCHAAF. Yes, Ma'am.

NATALIA. And where is Kolia?

SCHAAF. Wiz Lizafeta Bogdanovna. Lezzon ov piano.

NATALIA. Oh! (*Looking around her.*) Are you alone here?

SCHAAF. All alone.

NATALIA. You haven't seen Mr. Belaev?

SCHAAF. No, ma'am.

NATALIA (*after a pause*). We'll go along with you, if you don't mind, Herr Schaaf, and see how good you are at fishing.

SCHAAF. I am very pleased you come.

RAKITIN (*in a low voice to* NATALIA). What a strange idea.

NATALIA (*to* RAKITIN). Come on, let's go, *beau ténébreux.*
(*All three exit right.*)

KATIA (*cautiously poking her head out of the raspberry bushes*). Ah! They've gone. (*Comes out of the bushes, then stops, growing thoughtful.*) Ooof, that German! (*Sighs and starts picking raspberries again, singing softly.*)

> It's not fire that's burning,
> It's not pitch that bubbles.
> It's my eager heart that's yearning,
> Boiling, bubbling o'er my troubles . . .

Ah, Matvei's right! (*Continuing to sing.*)

> Boiling, bubbling o'er my troubles.
> Not yearning for Mama,
> Nor indeed for Papa . . .

Hm, nice big raspberries these. (*Continuing her song.*)

Not yearning for Mama,
Nor indeed, for Papa . . .

Phew! it's hot! Stifling. (*Continuing to sing.*)

Not yearning for Mama,
Nor indeed for Papa,
Boiling, bubbling o' . . .

(*Suddenly looks around her, falls silent and half hides herself behind a bush.* BELAEV *and* VERA *enter left.* BELAEV *carries the kite in his hand.*)

BELAEV (*to* KATIA, *as they pass the raspberry bushes*). Why did you stop, Katia? (*Singing.*)

Boiling, bubbling o'er a maiden . . .

KATIA (*blushing*). That's not how we sing it.

BELAEV. How then? (KATIA *laughs and does not answer.*) What are you doing? Picking raspberries? Let's have one to taste.

KATIA (*offering him the basket*). Have them all.

BELAEV. Oh no, that's too much. Would you like some, Vera? (VERA *takes some from the basket, then he takes some.*) Thanks, that's enough. (*Hands the basket back to* KATIA.)

KATIA (*pushing his hand away*). But have them all, take them.

BELAEV. No, really, thanks. (*Gives her the basket.*) Thank you. (*To* VERA.) Shall we sit down here on this bench, Vera? You see (*Indicating kite.*) I have to tie its tail on and you can help me. (*They go and sit down on the bench.* BELAEV *gives her the kite to hold.*) That's right. Be sure to hold it straight now. (*Starting to tie on the tail.*) What's the matter?

VERA. Like this, I can't see you.

BELAEV. What do you have to see me for?

VERA. I mean . . . I want to see how you tie it.

BELAEV. Oh! Well, wait a minute. (*Adjusts kite so that she can see him.*) Katia, why don't you sing? Come, sing. (*Coming a little way out of the bushes,* KATIA *starts to sing softly.*)

VERA. Tell me, did you fly kites in Moscow too, sometimes?

BELAEV. No chance for kites there! Hold this string here. That's the way. You think we have nothing else to do in Moscow?

VERA. Well, what do you do there?

BELAEV. What do we do? We study, attend lectures.

VERA. What do they teach you there?

Belaev. All sorts of things.

Vera. You must be very good in your studies. Better than all the others.

Belaev. No, not very good. Certainly not better than all the others! I'm rather lazy.

Vera. Oh, I can't really believe you're lazy.

Belaev. I am though. I guess I was born that way.

Vera (*after a pause*). Well, do you have friends in Moscow?

Belaev. Sure. Ah, this string isn't strong enough.

Vera. And are you fond of them?

Belaev. Sure, aren't you fond of yours?

Vera. My friends? I don't have any friends.

Belaev. Well, I meant . . . more casual . . . school friends or something?

Vera (*slowly*). Yes.

Belaev. So you do have some girls you're friendly with?

Vera. Yes, but, I don't know why, lately I haven't given them much thought. I didn't even answer Liza Moshnin's letter, and she asked me particularly.

Belaev. Anyway, what do you mean, you have no friends? What about me?

Vera (*smiling*). Oh, you're quite a different matter. (*After a pause.*) Mr. Belaev!

Belaev. Yes?

Vera. Do you write poetry?

Belaev. No, why?

Vera. Just asking. (*After a pause.*) In boarding school there was a girl who wrote poetry.

Belaev (*pulling a knot tight with his teeth*). Oh, I see. Was it good?

Vera. I don't know, but when she read it to us, we cried.

Belaev. What made you cry?

Vera. We were sorry for her—so sorry!

Belaev. Did you go to school in Moscow?

Vera. Yes, at Madame Bolus'. Natalia Petrovna took me out of school last year.

Belaev. Do you like Natalia Petrovna?

Vera. Oh yes, she's so good. I like her very, very much.

Belaev (*with a little laugh*). I bet you're a bit afraid of her?

Vera (*also with a slight laugh*). A little.

Belaev (*after a pause*). And who was it sent you to school?

Vera. Natalia Petrovna's late mother. I grew up in her house. I'm an orphan.

Belaev (*letting his hands fall*). An orphan? You don't remember your mother or father?

VERA. No, I don't.

BELAEV. My mother's dead, too. So you see, we're both orphans. Well, it's just too bad—we mustn't let it get us down.

VERA. Orphans are supposed to be quick to make friends with each other.

BELAEV (*looking at her*). Really? Do you think that's so?

VERA (*looking him in the eyes and smiling*). I think it is.

BELAEV (*laughing and again busying himself with the kite*). Let's see, how long have I been here now?

VERA. Twenty-eight days, counting today.

BELAEV. What a memory! There. Our kite's ready. Just look what a tail! Let's go and get Kolia to show it to him.

KATIA (*coming up to him with the basket*). Would you like some more raspberries?

BELAEV. No, thank you, Katia.

(KATIA *withdraws silently.*)

VERA. Kolia's with Lizaveta Bogdanovna.

BELAEV. Fancy keeping a child indoors in this weather!

VERA. Lizaveta Bogdanovna would only be in our way.

BELAEV. I wasn't talking about her.

VERA (*hurriedly*). Kolia wouldn't be allowed to come without her. Anyway, she was full of praise for you yesterday.

BELAEV. Was she?

VERA. You don't like her?

BELAEV. Oh, I've nothing against her or her snuff. Good luck to her! Why do you sigh?

VERA (*after a pause*). No reason. How clear the sky is!

BELAEV. And that makes you sigh? (*Pause.*) Perhaps you're bored?

VERA. Me? Bored? Oh no! Sometimes I sigh without even knowing why myself. But I'm certainly not bored. On the contrary. (*After a pause.*) I don't know, I seem to be under the weather lately. Yesterday I went upstairs to get a book and all of a sudden—just imagine—I sat down right there on the stairs and burst into tears. I've no idea what I was crying about, but the tears kept pouring out of my eyes for a long time afterward. What does it mean? The rest of the time, I'm quite happy.

BELAEV. It's from growth. You see, you're growing. That happens. I thought your eyes looked a little swollen yesterday evening.

VERA. Ah, you noticed?

BELAEV. Sure.

VERA. You notice everything.

BELAEV. Oh no, not everything.

VERA (*thoughtfully*). Mr. Belaev . . .

BELAEV. Yes?

VERA (*after a pause*). What on earth was it I wanted to ask you? You know, I've completely forgotten what it was!

BELAEV. Are you really so absent-minded?

VERA. No, but . . . Oh yes, here's what I wanted to ask you—I believe you told me once that you have a sister?

BELAEV. Yes, I have.

VERA. Well, tell me—does she look like me?

BELAEV. Oh no, you're much prettier.

VERA. Oh, how can you say that? She's your sister. I wish I was in her place.

BELAEV. What are you talking about? You think you'd like to be in our cramped little cottage now?

VERA. No, that's not what I meant. But is your house really so small?

BELAEV. Very small. Nothing like this place.

VERA. Who wants so many rooms anyway?

BELAEV. What do you mean? You'll soon find out for yourself why one needs lots of rooms.

VERA. Soon? When?

BELAEV. When you have a house of your own to run.

VERA (*dreamily*). You think so?

BELAEV. You'll see. (*After a pause.*) Well, shall we go and get Kolia now? What d'you say?

VERA. Mr. Belaev . . .

BELAEV. Why don't you call me Alexei?

VERA. Oh yes, may I?(*She suddenly starts.*) Oh!

BELAEV. What's the matter?

VERA (*softly*). Natalia Petrovna's coming this way.

BELAEV (*also softly*). Where?

VERA (*indicating with her head*). Over there—she's coming along the path with Mr. Rakitin.

BELAEV (*rising*). Let's go and get Kolia. He must have finished his lesson by now.

VERA. Yes, let's go. I'm afraid she may be annoyed with me. (*They get up and quickly exit left.* KATIA *again hides herself in the raspberry bushes.* NATALIA *and* RAKITIN *enter right.*)

NATALIA (*stopping*). Isn't that Belaev and Vera walking away?

RAKITIN. Yes, it's them.

NATALIA. It looks as if they were running away from us.

RAKITIN. Possibly.

NATALIA (*after a pause*). Well, I must say, I don't think Vera should . . . after all, alone in the garden with a young man . . . Of course, she's just a child, but still, it's not done. I'll have to speak to her about it.

RAKITIN. How old is she?

NATALIA. Seventeen! She's seventeen already. Isn't it hot today. I'm tired. Do let's sit down awhile. (*They sit down on the bench where* VERA *and* BELAEV *had been sitting.*) Has the Doctor left?

RAKITIN. He has.

NATALIA. Oh, you should have held on to him. For the life of me I can't think why such a man should have decided to be a country doctor. He's most amusing. I find him terribly funny.

RAKITIN. And here I thought you were in no mood for laughing today.

NATALIA. What made you think that?

RAKITIN. I just thought so.

NATALIA. Because I can't stand any show of feeling today? Yes, I warn you there isn't a thing that can touch me. But that in no way prevents me from laughing. On the contrary. Besides, I had something to talk over with him.

RAKITIN. May I ask what?

NATALIA. No, you may not. As it is you know everything I think, everything I do. It gets monotonous.

RAKITIN. Forgive me, I didn't think . . .

NATALIA. I'd like to keep at least something secret from you.

RAKITIN. What are you saying? One would think from the way you talk that I knew everything . . .

NATALIA (*interrupting him*). Well, don't you?

RAKITIN. You're laughing at me.

NATALIA. Do you really want me to believe you don't know everything that's going on inside me? In that case, I must say I can't congratulate you—for someone who watches me from morning till night . . .

RAKITIN. Is that a reproach?

NATALIA. A reproach? (*After a pause.*) I see you're not really so perceptive as all that.

RAKITIN. Well, that may be, but since I watch you from morning to night, allow me to share with you one observation I have made.

NATALIA. About me? Please do.

RAKITIN. You won't be angry?

NATALIA. No. At least, I hope not.

RAKITIN. Lately, Natalia, you've been in a state of constant irritation. It's an involuntary, inner irritation—as if you were battling with yourself, as if you were perplexed about something. I didn't notice anything of the sort before I went to visit the Krinitsyns—it's something recent. (NATALIA *traces lines in the gravel with her parasol.*) Sometimes you sigh so deeply, the way a person who is very, very tired sighs, a person who can't find rest.

NATALIA. And what do you conclude from all this, Mr. Observer?

RAKITIN. Nothing. I'm just worried.

NATALIA. I thank you kindly for your concern.

RAKITIN. And then . . .

NATALIA (*with some impatience*). Oh, do let's change the subject. (*Silence.*)

RAKITIN. You're not planning to drive out anywhere today?

NATALIA. No.

RAKITIN. Why not? It's a nice day for a drive.

NATALIA. I'm too lazy. (*Pause.*) Tell me, do you know Bolshintsov?

RAKITIN. Our neighbor, Afanasy Bolshintsov?

NATALIA. Yes.

RAKITIN. You know very well I do. Only two days ago, I was playing preference with him right here in your house.

NATALIA. I'd like to know what kind of a man he is.

RAKITIN. Bolshintsov?

NATALIA. Yes, yes, Bolshintsov.

RAKITIN. Well, I must admit, this is something I didn't expect!

NATALIA (*impatiently*). What didn't you expect?

RAKITIN. That you would ever start asking about Bolshintsov. That stupid, fat, ponderous fellow! Though, all the same, I can say nothing bad about the man.

NATALIA. He's nowhere near as stupid and ponderous as you think.

RAKITIN. Perhaps not. I must admit I really haven't studied the gentleman very carefully.

NATALIA (*an ironic note in her voice*). Ah, you haven't been observing him?

RAKITIN (*with a forced smile*). I really wonder what made you bring the matter up.

NATALIA. I was just wondering. (*Another silence.*)

RAKITIN. Look, Natalia, look at the dark green of that oak against the deep blue of the sky. It's flooded by sunlight and yet its colors are so deep. How much indestructible life and strength there is in it, especially when you compare it with that young birch sapling there. It looks as if it were about to vanish in the radiance; its tiny leaves shine with a liquid sort of brilliance, as if they were melting, and yet, it's beautiful, too.

NATALIA. You know what, Rakitin? I noticed long ago that you have a very acute feeling for what's called the beauty of nature. And you talk very cleverly, very elegantly, about it . . .

so cleverly and so elegantly that I imagine Nature must be inexpressibly grateful to you for your exquisitely apt descriptions of her. You trail after her like a scented, red-heeled marquis after a buxom peasant lass. Only, it sometimes seems to me your subtle comments are wasted on her, just as the courtly addresses of the marquis are wasted on the peasant girl. Nature is much simpler, coarser even, than you suppose, and that's because, thank God, she's healthy. Birch trees don't melt or faint like nervous ladies.

RAKITIN. *Quelle tirade!* Nature is healthy. That is, in other words, I'm a morbid creature.

NATALIA. You're not the only morbid creature—we're neither of us any too healthy.

RAKITIN. Ah, I'm well acquainted with the art of saying the nastiest things to a person in the most innocent way. For instance, instead of telling him straight to his face he's stupid, one just remarks with an amiable smile, "Look, aren't *we* stupid?"

NATALIA. You're offended with me? Really, what nonsense! I only meant to say that we're both . . . well, if you don't like the word morbid, that we're both getting old—very, very old.

RAKITIN. Old? I don't consider myself old.

NATALIA. Well, listen anyway. Here, on this very bench where we're sitting now, a few minutes ago, two creatures who are really young were sitting.

RAKITIN. You mean Belaev and Vera? Well, they're certainly younger than we are. Of course, there's a few years difference in our ages. But that doesn't make us old.

NATALIA. The difference is not just in years.

RAKITIN. Oh, now I understand. You envy their . . . their naïveté, their freshness, their innocence, in a word, their silliness.

NATALIA. Do you think so? You really think them silly? You think everyone's stupid today. You didn't understand what I meant. And, anyway, what's so terrible about being silly? What's the good of having brains, if they can't help you to enjoy life? There's nothing more tiresome than gloomy intelligence.

RAKITIN. Hmm. Why don't you say directly what you mean? My company doesn't amuse you—isn't that it? Why should intelligence in general suffer for the sake of little me?

NATALIA. Oh, but you've got me completely wrong. (KATIA *comes out from the raspberry bushes.*) What, have you been picking raspberries, Katia?

KATIA. Yes, Ma'am.

NATALIA. Let me see. (KATIA *comes over to her.*) What nice

raspberries! How red, but your cheeks are even redder. (KATIA *smiles and lowers her eyes.*) Well, off you go now. (*Exit* KATIA.)

RAKITIN. There's another young person—the kind you like.

NATALIA. Certainly. (*She gets up.*)

RAKITIN. Where are you off to?

NATALIA. First of all, I want to see what Vera's doing. It's time she went inside. And secondly, I must admit that, somehow, I don't like this conversation of ours. I think we should cut down on our discussions about Nature and Youth and all that for a while.

RAKITIN. Perhaps you'd rather walk by yourself?

NATALIA. Well, to tell you the truth, yes, I would. We'll be seeing each other again soon. Shall we part friends? (*Extends her hand to him.*)

RAKITIN (*rising*). Of course. (*Shakes hands with her.*)

NATALIA. Good-by then. (*She opens her parasol and exits left.*)

RAKITIN (*pacing up and down for a while*). What's the matter with her? (*Pause.*) It's a passing mood! A mood? I've never noticed anything of the sort in her before. In fact, she's always been the most even-tempered woman I know. What's behind it? (*Paces some more, then suddenly stops.*) Ah, how funny people are who have but one idea in their heads, one aim in life, one preoccupation. People like me, for instance. She was right—you spend from morning to night observing all the petty little details in people and you become petty yourself. That's just the way it is. But I can't live without her. In her presence I am more than happy. It's a feeling that can't be called just happiness; I belong to her entirely. To part from her would, without exaggeration, be just like parting from life. What's the matter with her? What does this inner perturbation mean? What forces her to be so caustic? Perhaps she's beginning to get bored with me? Hmm. (*Sitting down.*) I've never deluded myself—I know very well how she feels about me. But I hoped that, in time, that calm feeling would develop into—— As if I had any right to hope! I have to admit I'm in a pretty ridiculous position—might even say contemptible. (*Pause.*) Well, what's the good? She's an honest woman and I'm no Casanova. (*Grinning bitterly.*) Alas! (*Rising abruptly.*) Ah, that'll do! Clear that junk out of your head once and for all, Rakitin! (*Walking around.*) What a beautiful day today! (*Pause.*) Ah, she knew how to hurt me. My "exquisitely apt" descriptions! She's very clever, especially when she's in a bad temper. And what's this sudden admiration for simplicity and innocence? Perhaps that Russian tutor . . . She talks a lot about him, although I must say I don't see anything so special about him. He's just another student. Surely she . . .

no, that's impossible! She's just in a bad mood—doesn't know what she wants herself, so she claws at me. Like a child pushing its nanny. Hmm, that's not a very flattering comparison! But it's best to leave her alone. When this fit of melancholy restlessness passes, she'll be the first to laugh at that long-legged colt, that downy youth. Well, Rakitin, you've got it all worked out quite neatly, but are you right? Who knows? We'll see. This isn't the first time you've gone rambling on only to find suddenly that all your assumptions and conclusions wouldn't do and you'd just have to fold your arms and wait quietly to see what would happen. And meanwhile, you must admit, you're in a pretty awkward and unpleasant situation . . . and, for the moment, you'll just have to put up with it. (*Looking around.*) Oh, here comes our straightforward young man himself. He's picked a good time. I've never had the opportunity to have a talk with him. Well, let's see what sort of a person he is. (BELAEV *enters left.*) Ah, Belaev! Have you come out for a stroll in the fresh air, too?

BELAEV. Yes, I have.

RAKITIN. Well, actually, the air's not really so fresh today, I must say. It's dreadfully hot, but in the shade here, under these limes, it's more or less bearable. (*Pause.*) Have you seen Natalia Petrovna?

BELAEV. I met her just now. She went into the house with Vera.

RAKITIN. But wasn't it you I saw here with Vera half an hour ago?

BELAEV. Yes, it was. I had been for a walk with her.

RAKITIN. Ah! (*Takes his arm.*) Well, how do you like life in the country?

BELAEV. Oh, I like the country. There's only one drawback here and that's the poor hunting.

RAKITIN. Oh, you hunt?

BELAEV. Oh, yes. And you?

RAKITIN. I? No, I must admit, I'm a poor shot and, then, I'm too lazy.

BELAEV. I'm lazy too, but not when it comes to walking.

RAKITIN. Ah! In what are you lazy then—reading?

BELAEV. No, I like to read. But I don't like working for a long stretch at a time, especially when I have to work on one particular subject.

RAKITIN (*smiling*). Well, and what about talking to the ladies, are you lazy there?

BELAEV. Oh, now you're making fun of me. I'm simply scared of the ladies.

RAKITIN (*a little confused*). What makes you think . . . why should I make fun of you?

BELAEV. Oh well, you might. There's nothing so terrible about that! (*Pause.*) Can you tell me where one can get gunpowder here?

RAKITIN. In town probably. I know they sell some sort of gunpowder, but perhaps you need good quality?

BELAEV. No, it's not for hunting. I want to make some fireworks.

RAKITIN. Oh, d'you know how to?

BELAEV. Yes, I've already picked out a place on the other side of the pond. I hear it's Natalia Petrovna's birthday next week and I thought it would fit in nicely.

RAKITIN. She'll be very pleased at your thoughtfulness. You know, Belaev, she likes you.

BELAEV. That's very kind. Oh, by the way, Mr. Rakitin, I believe you receive a magazine out here? I wonder if you would lend it to me?

RAKITIN. Certainly, be glad to. They publish some very good poetry.

BELAEV. I don't go much for poetry.

RAKITIN. How's that?

BELAEV. Oh, I don't know. Humorous verse always strikes me as being so forced, and, anyway, you don't see it often. And as to romantic poetry, I don't know, I don't trust it somehow.

RAKITIN. You prefer the short stories?

BELAEV. Oh yes, I like a good story, but what I really like is the critical essays.

RAKITIN. Really?

BELAEV. I like the man who writes them.

RAKITIN. And do you write at all yourself?

BELAEV. Oh no! Why write if you haven't any talent? People would just laugh. In fact, there's one thing I find quite curious and perhaps you can explain it to me: a man may seem very intelligent and yet, just let him take pen in hand and, believe me, you have to turn the icons' faces to the wall, the results are so terrible! No, writing isn't for me. I'm happy if I understand what's been written already!

RAKITIN. Well, I can tell you one thing—very few young men have as much common sense as you!

BELAEV. Thanks for the compliment. (*Pause.*) I picked out that spot by the pond for the fireworks because I know how to make Roman candles which will burn on the water.

RAKITIN. That should make a very pretty show. May I ask you, Belaev, do you speak French?

BELAEV. No, I don't. I once translated a novel by Paul de Kock—*The Dairymaid of Mont Fermel*—perhaps you know it. They paid me fifty rubles for it, although I really don't know a word of French. Just imagine, I translated "quatre-vingt dix" as "four-twenty ten." I took the job because I needed it. But, you know, it's a shame I don't speak French. I wish I did. But I'm so damn lazy. For instance, I'd like to read George Sand in the original. But the pronunciation alone . . . How on earth can one cope with it? *An, on, en, in* . . . it's too much!

RAKITIN. Well, something can certainly be done about that.

BELAEV. Do you have the time by any chance?

RAKITIN (*looking at watch*). Half-past one.

BELAEV. Now why should that Lizaveta Bogdanovna keep Kolia at the piano so long? By now he must be dying to get out of there.

RAKITIN (*gently*). Well, but one must study too, you know.

BELAEV (*sighing*). Oh, why do you have to remind me of it? Of course, it's lucky everyone's not a loafer like me.

RAKITIN. Come, come.

BELAEV. I assure you, I know myself.

RAKITIN. But I think, indeed I'm quite sure, that what you consider a fault in yourself, your easy-going ways, is just what makes people like you.

BELAEV. Who, for instance?

RAKITIN. Well, Natalia Petrovna, for example.

BELAEV. Natalia Petrovna? Well, with her I certainly don't feel easy-going, as you put it.

RAKITIN. Is that so?

BELAEV. Yes, but don't you think that culture is the most important thing in a person? It's all very well for you, but I really don't understand how you can say that. (*Getting up abruptly.*) What was that? Sounded like a corn crake. (*Starts to leave.*)

RAKITIN. May have been, but where are you going?

BELAEV. To get my shotgun. (*Moves toward exit left.* NATALIA *enters left, coming toward him.*)

NATALIA (*breaking into a smile as she catches sight of him*). Where are you off to?

BELAEV. I . . .

RAKITIN. He's going to get his shotgun. He heard a corn crake.

NATALIA. Oh, please don't shoot it in the garden. Let the poor bird be. Besides, you might frighten Grandma.

BELAEV. As you wish, Ma'am.

NATALIA (*laughing*). Oh really, Mr. Belaev! "As you wish,

Ma'am"—what an expression. How can you talk like that? But just you wait, Mr. Rakitin and I are going to take you in hand. Yes, yes, we've already discussed the matter more than once. There's a whole conspiracy against you, I warn you. Will you allow me to take over your education?

BELAEV. Oh, Ma'am, I . . .

NATALIA. Well, in the first place, don't be so timid. It doesn't suit you a bit. Yes, indeed, we'll have to take you in hand. (*Indicating* RAKITIN.) After all, we're a couple of oldsters and you're a young man. You'll find it'll all work out very well. You'll see to Kolia and I . . . we, we'll see to you.

BELAEV. That'd be very kind of you.

NATALIA. All right then. Now, what were you and Mr. Rakitin talking about here?

RAKITIN (*smiling*). He was telling me about how he managed to translate a French book without knowing a word of French.

NATALIA. Ah! Well, we'll have to teach you French. By the way, what have you done with your kite?

BELAEV. I put it in the house. I thought that you . . . that you weren't pleased.

NATALIA (*a little embarrassed*). What made you think that? Because I told Vera . . . because I asked her to come inside with me? Oh no, you're wrong, that was because . . . (*Eagerly.*) You know what? Kolia must have finished his lesson by now. Let's go and get him and Vera and the kite. Would you like to? And we'll all go out to the meadow together. Shall we?

BELAEV. With pleasure, Natalia Petrovna.

NATALIA. Fine. Let's go then. (*Holding out her arm.*) Come, take my arm, you awkward creature! Off we go!

(*They exit quickly left.*)

RAKITIN (*following them with his eyes*). What liveliness! What gaiety! I've never seen that expression on her face before. And what a sudden change! (*Pause.*) Souvent femme varie . . . But I . . . there's no doubt I rub her the wrong way today. That's for sure. (*Pause.*) Ah, nonsense! We'll see what happens. (*Slowly.*) But surely it isn't . . . (*With a wave of the hand.*) Can't be! But that smile, that friendly, gentle, radiant look. Oh, God forbid I should start suffering pangs of jealousy, especially senseless jealousy! (*Looking around suddenly.*) Ah, what are you doing here?

(*The* DOCTOR *and* BOLSHINTSOV *enter left.* RAKITIN *goes to meet them.*)

RAKITIN. Hello, hello. Well, Doctor, I didn't expect to see you again today. (*Shakes hands with him.*)

DOCTOR. Well, I must say, I didn't expect to come back either. But then I stopped by at his place (*Indicating* BOL-SHINTSOV.) and he was sitting in his carriage, just about to leave to come over here. So I turned right around and came back with him.

RAKITIN. Well, I'm glad to see you anyway.

BOLSHINTSOV. It's true, I was on my way . . .

DOCTOR (*drowning him out*). The servants told us that everyone was in the garden. Anyway, there was no one in the drawing-room.

RAKITIN. What, didn't you run into Natalia?

DOCTOR. When?

RAKITIN. Why, just now.

DOCTOR. No. But we didn't come straight from the house. Bolshintsov here wanted to see whether there were any mushrooms in the grove.

BOLSHINTSOV (*perplexed*). Me?

DOCTOR. Come now, we all know how you love mushrooms. So Natalia has gone into the house? Well, no matter. We can go back.

BOLSHINTSOV. Yes, of course.

RAKITIN. She went to pick up the others to go for a stroll with her. They want to fly a kite, it seems.

DOCTOR. Good thing, too. It's good to be outdoors in this weather.

RAKITIN. Wait a moment. I'll go in and tell her you're here.

DOCTOR. Oh, why should you disturb yourself?

RAKITIN. Not at all. I have to go in anyway.

DOCTOR. Well, in that case, don't let us detain you. No standing on ceremony, you know.

RAKITIN. Good-by then.   (*Exits left.*)

DOCTOR. Good-by. (*To* BOLSHINTSOV.) Well, Bolshintsov . . .

BOLSHINTSOV (*interrupting him*). Why on earth did you have to drag those mushrooms into it? What was it all about—what mushrooms?

DOCTOR. Would you rather I'd said that my friend Bolshintsov got the jitters, so that instead of coming by the direct road, we had to take the bylanes?

BOLSHINTSOV. That's so, but why mushrooms? But I don't know, perhaps I'm wrong.

DOCTOR. Yes, my friend, you're probably wrong. You'd better remember that if we came here, it was on your insistence. So just watch out you don't fall on your face!

BOLSHINTSOV. Yes, Doctor, I know, but then, you told me . . . I'd like to know where I stand.

Doctor. My dear man, it's a bit more than ten miles from your place to here, and for every mile we went you asked me that at least three times. You really think you have to repeat it again? Well, listen then—but this is the very last time I'll tell you—here's what Natalia told me: "I . . ."

Bolshintsov (*nodding his head*). Yes.

Doctor (*sadly*). Yes. . . . What's "yes" about it? I haven't told you anything yet. "I," she said, "don't know Mr. Bolshintsov very well, but he seems to be a good man. On the other hand, I don't have the least intention of forcing Vera, so let him come and visit us and if he gains . . ."

Bolshintsov. Gains? She said gains?

Doctor. "If he gains her favor, neither Anna Semyonovna nor I will stand in the way."

Bolshintsov. Not "stand in the way"? Did she actually say that—"not stand in the way"?

Doctor. Yes, yes, of course. You're really funny! She said, "Neither Anna Semyonovna nor I will stand in the way of their happiness."

Bolshintsov. Hmm.

Doctor. "Their happiness." So now you see what you're faced with, Bolshintsov. It's up to you now to convince Vera that her happiness lies in marrying you. You have to gain her favor.

Bolshintsov (*winking*). Yes, yes, exactly, to gain it. I agree entirely.

Doctor. You insisted I bring you here today. Well, now we'll see how you go about it.

Bolshintsov. Go about it? Yes, yes, indeed, I must gain her favor. Only, you know what, Doctor? You're my closest friend and I must confess to you that I have one weakness. Here, you see, I asked you to bring me here today, as you put it . . .

Doctor. You didn't ask—you demanded. You demanded insistently.

Bolshintsov. Well, yes, all right, have it your way. But, you understand, when we were at home, I felt I was quite prepared. . . . But now I'm afraid.

Doctor. Afraid of what?

Bolshintsov (*glancing up at him from under lowered brows*). The risk.

Doctor. Wha-a-at?

Bolshintsov. The risk. It's a big risk. I must confess to you, Doctor, you my . . .

Doctor. Your "closest friend." Yes, yes, we know all that. What else?

BOLSHINTSOV. Yes, yes, you're right. I must confess, Doctor, that I . . . well, in general, I've had very few dealings with ladies, with the female sex in general, so to speak. To tell you the truth, Doctor, quite frankly, I can't even imagine what one's supposed to talk about with a person of the female sex—and even less, face-to-face, especially when it's a young lady.

DOCTOR. You amaze me. I don't know what there is you're not supposed to talk about with a person of the female sex, especially a young lady, especially face-to-face.

BOLSHINTSOV. Well, but, it's all very well for you, but I'm not like that and that's why I've turned to you. They say that it's the first step that counts in these affairs. So couldn't you suggest a word or two, to start the conversation off, something pleasant, for instance, some sort of a remark—and then I could go on from there. After that, I think I could manage by myself.

DOCTOR. No, I won't suggest what you should say because it won't be the slightest use to you. But I can give you a piece of advice if you want.

BOLSHINTSOV. On yes, please do. And when it comes to showing my appreciation, you know . . .

DOCTOR. We'll see, we'll see, I'm not going to bargain with you!

BOLSHINTSOV (*lowering his voice*). As far as the team of horses goes, you can rest assured . . .

DOCTOR. Ah, leave it now! You understand, Bolshintsov, there's no denying that you're a nice fellow . . . (BOLSHINTSOV *bows slightly.*) that you have many good points . . .

BOLSHINTSOV. Oh, come, come!

DOCTOR. And, moreover, I believe you have three hundred serfs on your estate?

BOLSHINTSOV. Three hundred and twenty.

DOCTOR. And they're not mortgaged?

BOLSHINTSOV. I don't have a kopek of debt.

DOCTOR. So, you see, it's just as I said—you're an excellent fellow and a first-rate suitor. But, as you said yourself, you've had very little to do with ladies.

BOLSHINTSOV (*with a sigh*). That's right. I, you might say, have shied away from the female sex since childhood.

DOCTOR (*with a sigh*). So, you see. Now, that's no great drawback in a husband—on the contrary. But there are circumstances, such as your first declaration of love, when you really have to have something to say. See what I mean?

BOLSHINTSOV. Oh yes, I agree absolutely.

DOCTOR. Otherwise, you know, Vera might just think you didn't feel well and nothing more. And then your figure—although it's most dignified, yet there's nothing about it to please the eye particularly, you know, which is what we need now.

BOLSHINTSOV (*sighing*). Yes, that's what we need now.

DOCTOR. At least, that's what young ladies like. Yes, and then, your age. . . . In a word, we can't rely on our charms too much. So, really, a few pleasant words won't help. But you have something else that you can depend on, something much firmer and more hopeful, namely your sterling qualities, and your three hundred and twenty serfs. If I were in your shoes, I'd simply say to Vera . . .

BOLSHINTSOV. In private?

DOCTOR. Oh yes, it must be in private. "Vera," I'd say, (BOLSHINTSOV's *lips move, silently repeating the* DOCTOR's *every word.*) "I love you and I ask your hand. I'm a simple, kind, quiet man and I'm not poor by any means. With me, you would be completely free. I would try to gratify your every wish. Please make all the inquiries you want about me and, if you can see your way to it, take a little more notice of me than you have heretofore—and give me whatever answer you see fit, whenever you see fit. I'm prepared to wait and would even consider it a pleasure to do so."

BOLSHINTSOV (*repeating the last words aloud*). A pleasure to do so! Yes, yes, yes, that's it. There's only one thing, Doctor —it seems to me you used the word quiet—you say I'm a quiet man.

DOCTOR. Well, you are a quiet man, aren't you?

BOLSHINTSOV. Well, yes, of course, but, just the same, it seems to me . . . Well, d'you think it's appropriate? Wouldn't it be better to say, for instance . . .

DOCTOR. What?

BOLSHINTSOV. Well, for instance . . . (*Pause.*) Oh well, after all, quiet will do really.

DOCTOR. Ah, Bolshintsov, take my advice. The more simply you express yourself, the less flowery you make your little speech, the better—believe me. And above all, don't insist: whatever else you do, don't insist. Vera is very young still, you might frighten her away. Give her plenty of time to think over your proposal. Yes, and there's one more thing—I almost forgot. Well, look, since you've asked for my advice, let me say that you ought to pay more attention to your vocabulary, my friend. For instance, you often say terrific instead of terrible and like instead of as. Of course, one hears it, but you'd better follow the way educated people talk. And then, I remember, you once referred to a certain hospitable landowner as a "*bongbivant*." You said, "What a *bongbivant* he is." It's a good word, of course, but unfortunately it doesn't mean a thing. As you know, French isn't my strong point either, but I understand enough to know that you should have said *bonvivant*. Avoid eloquence, and I promise you you'll succeed. (*Looking around.*) Ah, here they come. (BOLSHINTSOV *wants to escape.*) But where are you going? After mushrooms again? (BOLSHINTSOV *smiles, blushes, and stays.*) First and foremost—don't lose your nerve.

BOLSHINTSOV (*hurriedly*). Listen, does Vera know anything about it yet?

DOCTOR. Of course not!

BOLSHINTSOV. You know, I'm depending on you. (*Blows his nose.*)

(NATALIA, VERA, BELAEV *carrying the kite, and* KOLIA *enter left. Behind them come* RAKITIN *and* LIZAVETA BOGDANOVNA. NATALIA *is in a very gay mood.*)

NATALIA (*to* BOLSHINTSOV *and the* DOCTOR). Ah, hello, gentlemen. Hello, Doctor, I wasn't expecting you today, but I'm always glad to see you. Hello, Mr. Bolshintsov. (BOLSHINTSOV *bows, rather embarrassed.*)

DOCTOR (*to* NATALIA, *indicating* BOLSHINTSOV). Bolshintsov here insisted on bringing me over.

NATALIA (*laughing*). I'm much obliged to him. But does one really have to drag you here?

DOCTOR. One certainly doesn't as a rule! But since I'd just come from here.

NATALIA. Ah, Mr. Diplomat, you're all mixed up.

DOCTOR. I notice you're in a cheerful mood and that gladdens my heart.

NATALIA. And it's such a rare occurrence that you notice it specially?

DOCTOR. Oh no, I didn't say that, but . . .

NATALIA. *Monsieur le diplomate,* you're getting more and more mixed up.

KOLIA (*who has been impatiently jumping around near* BELAEV *and* VERA *all this time*). But, *Maman,* what are we waiting for, when are we going to fly the kite?

NATALIA. Whenever you like. Come, Mr. Belaev, and you too, Vera, let's go to the meadow. (*Addressing the others.*) I hardly imagine the rest of you would be amused by such an occupation. Lizaveta Bogdanovna and you, Rakitin, I leave our good Mr. Bolshintsov in your charge.

RAKITIN. But why should you think it wouldn't amuse us, Natalia?

NATALIA. Oh, you're such a serious-minded lot. You must consider such things as silly, childish games. Of course, we're not stopping you from coming with us if you wish to. (*To* BELAEV *and* VERA.) Let's go.

(NATALIA, VERA, BELAEV *and* KOLIA *exit right*.)

DOCTOR (*looking at* RAKITIN *a little surprised, then addressing* BOLSHINTSOV). Well, Bolshintsov, give Lizaveta Bogdanovna your arm.

BOLSHINTSOV (*hurriedly*). With the greatest of pleasure. (*Takes* LIZAVETA BOGDANOVNA'S *arm*.)

DOCTOR (*to* RAKITIN). And, if you're agreeable, you and I will walk along together, Rakitin. (*Takes his arm*.) Just look— they're fairly running along the path. Let's go and watch them fly the kite, even though we are such serious-minded people. Bolshintsov, won't you lead the way?

BOLSHINTSOV (*to* LIZAVETA BOGDANOVNA, *as they start to walk*). One might say the weather today is most pleasant, don't you think?

LIZAVETA BOGDANOVNA (*mincing*). Oh most pleasant.

DOCTOR (*to* RAKITIN). Rakitin, I have something I must talk to you about. (RAKITIN *suddenly laughs*.) What are you laughing about?

RAKITIN. Nothing, nothing. It just struck me as funny that we should be bringing up the rear like this.

DOCTOR. Well, you know, the vanguard very easily becomes the rear-guard. It's all a question of a change of direction.

(*They all exit right*.)

CURTAIN

ACT III

The same as Act I. The Doctor and Rakitin enter from the ballroom.

DOCTOR. So what d'you say, Rakitin? Will you help me out in this?

RAKITIN. But how can I help you?

DOCTOR. How? Well, put yourself in my position. You know, I'm not directly involved—I'm just trying to help out. Ah, my kind heart will be the death of me!

RAKITIN (*laughing*). Come, you've a long way to go before that happens.

DOCTOR (*also laughing*). Who knows, who knows? But I really am in a rather awkward position. Natalia wanted me to bring Bolshintsov here and she authorized me to give him the answer and now, from one side I get nothing but sulky looks, as if I'd made a blunder, and from the other, Bolshintsov keeps nagging at me. They're avoiding him and they refuse to speak to me.

RAKITIN. Well, what on earth made you take on this business? After all, between us, you know very well he's just plain stupid.

DOCTOR. Why between us? You think it's a secret? But since when is it only intelligent people that marry? Marriage is one pleasure you could leave the poor fools at least. And then, you say I took on the business. But that's not true at all. Here's what happened—a friend asks me to put in a good word for him. Well? Should I have refused? I'm a kind-hearted sort of fellow and I wouldn't know how to. So I try to make good on a promise to a friend and what do I get? "Thank you kindly, but please don't bother yourself any further." Well, I can understand that, so I don't bother myself any further. But then, all of a sudden, they start encouraging me and themselves put forward a suggestion. I obey and they're indignant again. But, after all, what have I done wrong?

RAKITIN. But who said you'd done anything wrong? I only wonder why you're going to so much trouble.

DOCTOR. Because . . . because the man won't leave me in peace.

RAKITIN. Come, come.

DOCTOR. And then, he's an old friend of mine.

RAKITIN (*with a skeptical smile*). Oh yes? Well that's different then.

DOCTOR (*also smiling*). Well, why pretend after all? There's no fooling you anyway. All right then, he promised me . . . that is, one of my horses is finished, and so, he's promised me . . .

RAKITIN. A new horse?

DOCTOR. Well, no . . . a whole team of three.

RAKITIN. Why didn't you say so to start with?

DOCTOR (*eagerly*). But please don't imagine for a minute I'd ever have agreed to act as go-between—it goes against my whole nature (RAKITIN *smiles.*) —if I wasn't sure that Bolshintsov was an impeccably honorable man. And anyway, all I want is a definite answer: yes or no.

RAKITIN. You mean to say it's reached that stage already?

DOCTOR. But what do you imagine? Marriage hasn't even been mentioned as yet—it's merely a question of permission for him to come over here on visits.

RAKITIN. But who would want to forbid it?

DOCTOR. Oh you . . . forbid! Of course, if it had been someone else . . . but Bolshintsov, poor soul, he's such a timid, harmless fellow, right out of a fairy-tale world and still believing in Santa Claus. He has no confidence in himself; he needs encouraging. And then, his intentions are absolutely honorable.

RAKITIN. Yes, and his horses are good, too.

DOCTOR. Yes, and his horses are good. (*Takes a pinch of snuff, then proffers the snuffbox to* RAKITIN.) Would you like some?

RAKITIN. No thanks.

DOCTOR. So that's how it is, Rakitin. I have no desire to deceive you. And indeed, why should I? The whole business is perfectly straightforward. He's a man of substance, with the highest principles, and very gentle. So, if they want him—good. If they don't, they've only to say so.

RAKITIN. Well, that's all very wonderful, but where do I come in? I don't see how I can help.

DOCTOR. Ah, Rakitin, as if you didn't know how much Natalia thinks of you! Why, sometimes she even listens to you. So, be a good fellow. (*Putting his arm around* RAKITIN's *shoulders.*) Put a word in for him.

RAKITIN. And you think he's a suitable husband for Vera?

DOCTOR (*taking on a serious expression*). I'm sure of it. You don't think so now, but you'll agree with me in time. After all, you know yourself that the most important thing in a marriage is a good solid character. And, God knows, Bolshintsov is solid! (*Looking round.*) Ah, that looks like Natalia coming this way now. Rakitin, old man, be a friend! Remember, there's a pair of chestnuts and a sorrel involved—don't let me down.

RAKITIN (*smiling*). All right, all right.

DOCTOR. I'm relying on you. (*Escapes into the ballroom.*)

RAKITIN (*looking after him*). Ah, what a schemer! Little Vera and Bolshintsov! And yet, what's so terrible? I've seen worse marriages. I'll do as he asks, and after that—well, it's none of my business! (*Turns.* NATALIA *enters from the study and, seeing him, stops.*)

NATALIA (*hesitatingly*). Oh it's you . . . I thought you were in the garden.

RAKITIN. My presence annoys you?

NATALIA. Oh, what next! (*Advances to front of stage.*) Are you by yourself?

RAKITIN. The doctor was here till just a moment ago.

NATALIA (*knitting her brows slightly*). Ah, our provincial Talleyrand! Is he still around? What on earth was he telling you?

RAKITIN. I see the provincial Talleyrand, as you call him, is not in favor today and yet, yesterday, I understand . . .

NATALIA. He's funny, amusing, it's true, but he pokes his nose into other people's business. I don't like that. And then, for all his obsequiousness, he's very presumptuous and intrusive. He's an awful cynic.

RAKITIN (*going up to her*). That's not what you were saying yesterday.

NATALIA. So, maybe not. (*In a lively tone.*) Well, what did he say to you?

RAKITIN. He was talking about Bolshintsov.

NATALIA. Oh, that fool!

RAKITIN. You weren't talking about *him* like that yesterday either.

NATALIA (*with a forced smile*). Yesterday was different.

RAKITIN. But apparently when it comes to me there's no difference.

NATALIA (*lowering her eyes*). How's that?

RAKITIN. You're treating me just the same today as you did yesterday.

NATALIA (*extending her hand to him*). I understand . . . but you're wrong. Yesterday, I would never have acknowledged the thought that I was guilty toward you . . . (RAKITIN *wishes to stop her.*) No, don't try to argue. I know and you know what I mean, and today I do acknowledge it. I've thought over many things today. Believe me, Michel, no matter what silly ideas go through my head, no matter what I say or do, there's no one I depend on as I depend on you. (*Lowering voice.*) I don't . . . like anyone more than I like you. (*Short pause.*) Do you believe me?

RAKITIN. I believe you, but you seem so sad today. What's the matter?

NATALIA (*ignoring him and continuing*). I'm convinced of only one thing, Rakitin, and that's that one can never be sure of oneself or of what one will do next. We often don't even understand our past, so how can we be responsible for the future? The future cannot be fettered.

RAKITIN. That's true.

NATALIA (*after a long silence*). Listen, I want to be absolutely frank with you. Perhaps this will hurt you a little, but I know you'd be more hurt if I hid it from you. I'll admit to you, Michel, this young student, Belaev, he's made a pretty strong impression on me.

RAKITIN (*in a low voice*). I know that already.

NATALIA. Oh, you noticed it? When?

RAKITIN. Yesterday.

NATALIA. Oh!

RAKITIN. The day before yesterday, you remember, I told you

I saw a change in you. But then I didn't know how to account for it. But yesterday, after our talk, and then in the meadow . . . Ah, if you could have seen yourself! I didn't recognize you; you were completely different. You laughed, you skipped and jumped around like a little girl, your eyes shone and your cheeks were burning, and you looked at him with such trusting curiosity, with such radiant abandon, and . . . (*Glancing at her.*) You see, even now, your face lights up at the very thought of it. (*Turns away.*)

NATALIA. Oh no, Rakitin, please don't turn away from me. Listen—why exaggerate? I find his youthfulness infectious, and that's all. I myself was never young, Michel, even when I was a little girl. You know the whole story of my life. This whole business has gone to my head like wine, because I'm not used to it, but I know it'll pass quickly, just as it came. It's not even worth discussing. (*Pauses.*) But please, just don't turn away from me. Don't take away your support. Help me.

RAKITIN (*softly*). Help you . . . cruel words! (*Loud.*) You don't know what's happening to you yourself, Natalia. You say it's not worth talking about it, and yet you ask for help. Apparently you feel you need it!

NATALIA. Well . . . yes . . . I'm turning to you as a friend.

RAKITIN (*bitterly*). Yes, I see. I'll try to justify your trust in me. But give me a chance to recover a little.

NATALIA. Recover? But do you really feel you've had some sort of a blow from which you have to recover? Do you really think anything's changed?

RAKITIN (*bitterly*). Oh no! Everything's just the same!

NATALIA. But, Michel, what on earth do you think? Surely you can't suppose . . . ?

RAKITIN. I suppose nothing.

NATALIA. Do you really despise me so much that . . .

RAKITIN. Stop it, for God's sake! Better talk about Bolshintsov. You know, the doctor is expecting an answer about Vera.

NATALIA (*sadly*). You're angry with me.

RAKITIN. I? Certainly not. I'm only sorry for you.

NATALIA. Oh, that's really mean. Aren't you ashamed of yourself, Michel? (RAKITIN *says nothing and she shrugs her shoulders and continues with annoyance.*) You say the doctor is expecting an answer? But who asked him to interfere?

RAKITIN. He assures me that you yourself . . .

NATALIA (*interrupting*). Well, I don't know, maybe I did. . . . Although I don't think I told him anything definite. And then, I can change my mind. Yes, and after all, good Lord, where's the tragedy? He gets involved in all sorts of things but he should know, being a doctor, that everything doesn't always turn out well.

RAKITIN. He only wants to know what answer . . .

NATALIA. What answer! . . . (*Pauses.*) Michel, enough! Give me your hand. Why this indifference and icy politeness? What have I done wrong? Do you really think it's my fault? I came to you in the hope of hearing some kind advice. I didn't hesitate for a second. I didn't even think of trying to hide anything from you, and you . . . I see I was wrong to be so open with you. It would never even have occurred to you . . . you didn't suspect a thing. It wasn't true when you said you knew. And now, God knows what you're thinking.

RAKITIN. Oh please!

NATALIA. Well, give me your hand then. (*He doesn't budge and she continues, a little offended.*) So you're definitely turning away from me? Well then, so much the worse for you. But I don't blame you. (*Bitterly.*) You're jealous!

RAKITIN. What right have I to be jealous, Natalia? What are you talking about?

NATALIA (*after a pause*). All right, have it your own way. And as far as Bolshintsov's concerned, I haven't spoken to Vera yet.

RAKITIN. Would you like me to send her here right away?

NATALIA. What's the hurry? But, just as you like.

RAKITIN (*going toward the door of the study*). So you wish her sent to you?

NATALIA (*irritated*). Yes. (RAKITIN *goes into the study.* NATALIA *remains motionless for a little while, then sits down, takes a book from the table, opens it and lets it fall on her knees.*) Him too! But what can it be? This one . . . and the other! And I was relying on him. And then there's Arkady! Oh Lord! I'd completely forgotten about him! (*Straightening up.*) I can see it's time to put a stop to the whole thing. (VERA *enters from study.*) Yes, it's high time.

VERA (*timidly*). You wanted me, Natalia Petrovna?

NATALIA (*looking round quickly*). Ah, Vera! Yes, I want to talk to you.

VERA (*going up to her*). Are you all right?

NATALIA. Yes, of course. Why do you ask?

VERA. I thought . . .

NATALIA. Oh no, it's nothing, it's just rather hot, that's all. Sit down. (VERA *sits down.*) Tell me, Vera, you weren't busy, were you?

VERA. Oh no, not at all.

NATALIA. I ask because I would like to have a talk with you, a

serious talk. Well, you see, my dear, up till now, we've considered
you as just a child, but you're seventeen, you know, and you're a
smart girl. It's time to think about your future. You know I
love you like a daughter—my house will always be a home for
you, but all the same, in the eyes of others, you're an orphan—
and you're not rich. In time, perhaps, you may come to dislike
living permanently with other people. Well, wouldn't you like
to be the mistress of your own house?

VERA (*slowly*). I don't quite understand.

NATALIA (*after a pause*). I have been asked for your hand.
(VERA *looks at her in amazement*.) Ah, you didn't expect that,
did you? Well, I'll admit, it came as a surprise to me, too.
You're still so young. I don't need to tell you that I have not the
slightest intention of trying to push you. In fact, I think it's a little soon for you to be getting married. But I promised to tell you.
(VERA *suddenly buries her face in her hands*.) Vera, what on
earth? You're not crying? (*Takes her hand*.) But you're trembling! But Vera, you're not afraid of me, are you?

VERA (*tonelessly*). I am in your hands, Natalia Petrovna.

NATALIA (*taking* VERA'*s hands away from her face*). Vera, you
should be ashamed of yourself—fancy crying like this. And how
can you say you're in my hands? What do you think I am?
Here I'm talking to you as I would to a daughter, and you . . .
(VERA *kisses her hand*.) Well! You're in my hands, are you?
Well then, come, laugh at once. I command you! (VERA *smiles
through her tears*.) That's better. (NATALIA *puts an arm around
her and draws her toward herself*.) Vera, my child, I want you
to behave with me exactly as you would with your own mother,
or no, better, pretend I'm your older sister and let's have a good
talk together about all these wonderful things. All right?

VERA. All right.

NATALIA. Well, listen then . . . Come, sit closer to me. That's
better. Now, first of all, since I'm your sister, there's certainly
no need for me to assure you that you're at home here. Indeed,
how could a girl like you not be welcome in anyone's home?
So, you shouldn't think even for a moment that your presence
might be a burden or that anyone might want to get rid of you.
You hear? But just the same, one fine day, your big sister
comes to you and says: Just imagine, Vera, someone has asked
for your hand. Well? What would you say then? Perhaps that
you're still too young and haven't even started thinking about
marriage yet?

VERA. Yes.

NATALIA. But don't always answer, yes, like that. Who ever
heard of anyone talking to a sister that way?

VERA (*smiling*). Well, but I mean yes.

NATALIA. Well and your sister thinks you're right, so the suitor is refused and that's the end of that. But suppose the suitor is a nice man and well-off? Suppose he's prepared to wait and is only asking for permission to see you now and then in the hope that, with time, you'll come to like him?

VERA. But who is it?

NATALIA. Ah, you're curious! Can't you guess?

VERA. No, I can't.

NATALIA. You saw him just today. (VERA *blushes*.) It's true he's not very handsome, nor very young. It's Bolshintsov.

VERA. Mr. Bolshintsov?

NATALIA. Yes, that's right.

VERA (*looks at* NATALIA *for a little while, suddenly bursts out laughing, then quickly suppresses her laughter*). Are you joking?

NATALIA (*smiling*). No, but I can see there's nothing more for Bolshintsov to do here. If you'd burst into tears at the mention of his name, there might have been some hope for him, but you just laugh. So there's only one thing left for him to do—to take himself off home and good luck to him.

VERA. I'm sorry but really, I would never have expected. . . . Really, isn't he too old to get married?

NATALIA. Good heavens, how old do you think he is? Why, he's not even fifty. In the prime of life.

VERA. Well, maybe, but he has such an odd face.

NATALIA. We won't talk about him any more. We can just forget him as though he'd never even existed. And, in fact, it's quite natural—how could a girl of your age like a man like Bolshintsov? At your age, one still hopes to marry for love, not for convenience, right?

VERA. Well, surely, you . . . you married Arkady Sergeich for love, didn't you?

NATALIA (*after a pause*). Of course I did. (*She again falls silent and squeezes* VERA's *hand*.) Yes, Vera, just now I said you were still very young, but young people are often right in these matters. (VERA *lowers her eyes*.) So, the matter is decided. Bolshintsov can retire from the scene. I must admit I didn't altogether relish the idea of his fat old face next to yours, so young and fresh, although, mind you, he's a good man. Now do you see how silly it was of you to be afraid of me? You see how quickly we've straightened things out. (*Reproachfully*.) You were really treating me like a guardian. And you know how I hate the very word.

VERA (*hugging her*). Forgive me.

NATALIA. That's all right, then. You're sure now? You're not afraid of me?

VERA. No, I'm very attached to you and not afraid of you in the least.

NATALIA. Well, thanks for that. So from now on then, we're close friends and we won't hide anything from each other. And what if I asked you: Vera dear, come, whisper in my ear—is it only because Bolshintsov is much older than you and not exactly handsome that you don't want to marry him?

VERA. My goodness, isn't that enough?

NATALIA. Yes, it is, I don't dispute that. But is there no other reason?

VERA. I don't even know him really.

NATALIA. I know that, but you haven't answered my question.

VERA. No, there's no other reason.

NATALIA. Truly? Well, in that case, I'd advise you to think it over. I know it'd be hard to fall in love with him, but I must say once again, he's a good man. Of course, if you loved someone else, then it'd be another matter. So no one has stirred your heart yet?

VERA (timidly). How do you mean?

NATALIA. You don't love anyone as yet?

VERA. I love you . . . and Kolia, and Anna Semyonovna, too.

NATALIA. No, you don't understand, I'm not talking about that kind of love. What I mean is, well, for example, among all the young men you've met here or at friends' houses, is there really not a single one you like?

VERA. No, I like some of them, but . . .

NATALIA. Well, for instance, what about that tall officer— what's his name?—at the Krinitsyns'. I noticed you danced with him three times.

VERA. With an officer?

NATALIA. Yes, you know, the one with the big mustache.

VERA. Oh, that one! No, I didn't like him.

NATALIA. Well, and what about Shalansky?

VERA. Shalansky's very nice, but he . . . I don't think he even noticed me.

NATALIA. Why not?

VERA. He . . . well, he seems to be mostly interested in Liza Belsky.

NATALIA (looking at her). Ah, you noticed that, did you? (Pause.) Well, and Rakitin?

VERA. Oh, I'm very fond of him.

NATALIA. Yes, I know, like a brother. Well, then, there's Belaev?

VERA (*blushing*). Oh yes, I like him!

NATALIA (*watching her closely*). Yes, he's very nice. But he's so shy with everyone.

VERA (*innocently*). Oh no, he's not shy with me.

NATALIA. Really?

VERA. We have long conversations. Probably you think he's shy because he . . . Well, he's afraid of you. Of course, he hasn't got to know you yet.

NATALIA. And how do you know he's afraid of me?

VERA. He told me so.

NATALIA. He told you so! He seems to be a good deal more outspoken with you than he is with others.

VERA. I don't know how he is with others, but with me . . . Perhaps it's because we're both orphans. And then, well, he treats me as if I were still a child.

NATALIA. Do you think so? Well, anyway, I like him very much, too. He seems to be a very kind person.

VERA. Oh yes, very! If you only knew. Everyone here likes him. He's so friendly with them all, he talks to them and he's always ready to help. The day before yesterday, he lifted up an old beggar woman who'd fallen on the high road and carried her to the hospital in his arms. And once he picked a flower for me that was growing on a really steep bluff—I had to close my eyes I was so afraid he'd fall and hurt himself. But he's so agile. Well, you must've seen in the meadow yesterday, how agile he is.

NATALIA. Yes, that's true.

VERA. You remember that big ditch he jumped over when he was running with the kite? But that's nothing to him.

NATALIA. And he really picked a flower that was growing in a dangerous spot for you? Well, he must like you a great deal, too.

VERA (*after a pause*). And he's always so cheerful, always good-tempered.

NATALIA. Then, really, I find it quite strange that when I'm there . . .

VERA (*interrupting*). I've already told you, he doesn't know you yet. But wait, I'll tell him . . . I'll tell him there's no reason to be afraid of you, shall I? That you're really very kind.

NATALIA (*with a forced laugh*). Thank you.

VERA. You'll soon see. He does what I say, even though I am younger than him.

NATALIA. I didn't know the two of you were such friends. But mind now, Vera, you be careful. Of course, he's a very nice young man but, you know, at your age . . . It's not fitting. People might think . . . I told you about it yesterday, remember, in the garden? (VERA *lowers her eyes.*) On the other hand, I have no wish to stand in the way of your inclinations, I have full confidence in you, and in him. Still, all the same . . . don't be angry with me, my dear, for being fussy. It's the function of us older people to bore the young with our lectures. Anyway, there's no need for all this, since you simply like him and nothing more—isn't that right?

VERA (*timidly raising her eyes*). He . . .

NATALIA. There, you're looking at me with that same expression you had before. Is that the way to look at a sister? Vera, listen to me. Here, rest your head on my shoulder. (*Strokes her head.*) What if your sister, your real sister, whispered in your ear: Is there really no one you love, Vera dear? Uh? What would you say? (VERA *looks hesitatingly at* NATALIA.) Ah, those eyes are trying to tell me something. (VERA *suddenly buries her head in* NATALIA'*s bosom.* NATALIA *turns pale, then, after a pause, goes on.*) So you do love him? Tell me, you do, don't you?

VERA (*without raising her head*). Oh, I don't know what's the matter with me myself.

NATALIA. Ah, poor girl, you're in love! (VERA *presses her head still closer to her.*) You're in love, but what about him, Vera, how does he feel?

VERA (*still without raising her head*). Why do you ask me? I don't know. Maybe . . . I don't know, I don't know. (NATALIA *winces, then remains motionless.* VERA *raises her head and suddenly notices the change in her face.*) Why, what's happened?

NATALIA (*recovering*). Happened? Nothing. Why? No, nothing.

VERA. But you've turned so pale. What is it? Shall I ring? (*Gets up.*)

NATALIA. No, no, don't. It's nothing. I'll be all right. In fact, I'm all right now.

VERA. Well, at least let me call someone.

NATALIA. No, please don't . . . I . . . I'd like to be left alone. Leave me now, you hear me? We'll come back to this. Go now.

VERA. You're not angry with me?

NATALIA. Why should I be? No, not at all. On the contrary, I appreciate your trust in me. Only, please, leave me now. (VERA *tries to take her hand but she turns away as if she had not noticed her gesture.*)

VERA (*tears in her eyes*). Natalia Petrovna!

NATALIA. Please, leave me alone, please.

(VERA *goes slowly into the study.*)

NATALIA (*remaining alone and motionless for a short while*).

Now I see it all. Those two children love each other. (*Stops and passes a hand across her face.*) Well, why not? So much the better. I hope they'll be very happy! (*Laughing.*) Ah, how could I have even thought . . . (*Stops again.*) It didn't take her long to let the cat out of the bag. I admit I never suspected . . . in fact, the news has quite shaken me. But wait a while, it's not over yet. Oh, my God, what am I saying? What's the matter with me? I don't recognize myself. Have I come to that? (*Pause.*) What am I doing? I want to give that poor girl away in marriage to an old man. I'm trying to use the doctor . . . he suspects, makes hints . . . Then there's Arkady, and Rakitin. Ah . . . (*She shudders and suddenly throws back her head.*) But, it's really too much. Me jealous of Vera? Can I be . . . can I really have fallen in love with him? (*Pause.*) What, do you still doubt it? Yes, you're in love, you wretched woman! How it happened, I don't know. It's as if I'd been poisoned. Suddenly everything's shattered and confused. He's afraid of me. Everyone's afraid of me. And what could he possibly see in me? What would he want with someone like me? He's young and she's young. And I! (*Bitterly.*) Ah, how could he understand me? They're both silly just as Rakitin says. Ah, that one, I can't stand him for being so clever! And Arkady, my good, trusting Arkady! Oh God, I wish I were dead! (*Rising.*) But, good heavens, I must be going out of my mind! Why exaggerate, after all? Well, all right, I've received a blow. I'm not accustomed . . . it's the first time I . . . yes, the first time! It's the first time I've ever been in love! (*Sitting down again.*) He must leave. Yes. And Rakitin, too. It's time I took hold of myself. I allowed myself to step out of line—and now look how far I've gone. And what is it I like about him? (*Growing thoughtful.*) So that's what it is, this frightening feeling. Oh Arkady! I'll fling myself into his arms and beg him to forgive me, to protect me, to save me—him and no one else! All the rest are outsiders to me and they must remain outsiders. But is there really . . . can there really be no other way out? This girl—she's just a child. She could be mistaken. It's all a lot of childish nonsense. Why am I . . . I'll have the matter out with him, I'll ask him . . . (*Reproachfully.*) What's this? You still have hopes? You still want to hope? And what am I hoping for! Oh God, oh God, don't let me despise myself! (*She buries her face in her hands.* RAKITIN, *pale and alarmed, enters from the study.*)

RAKITIN (*coming up to* NATALIA). Natalia . . . (*She does not move. To himself.*) What could have happened between her and Vera? (*Aloud.*) Natalia . . .

NATALIA (*raising her head*). Who is it? Oh, it's you.

RAKITIN. Vera tells me that you're not well . . . I . . .

NATALIA (*turning away*). I'm quite well. I don't know where she got the idea . . .

RAKITIN. No, Natalia, you're not well. Just look at yourself.

NATALIA. Well, perhaps, but what is it to you? What do you want? Why did you come here?

RAKITIN (*emotionally*). I'll tell you why I came. I came to ask you to forgive me. Half an hour ago I was unspeakably stupid and rude. Forgive me. You see, Natalia, no matter how modest a man's wishes and hopes may be, it's hard for him not to lose his head, if only for a moment, when they're suddenly torn from him. But I've recovered my senses now, I understand my position and how wrong I was, and now I want only one thing—your forgiveness. (*He sits down quietly beside her.*) Look at me, don't you turn away now. This is your same old Rakitin, your friend, the man who wants nothing but to be allowed to be, as you put it, a prop for you. Don't deprive me of your trust. Let's make up—and forget that I ever said anything that may have offended you.

NATALIA (*who has been sitting motionless, staring at the floor all this time*). Yes, yes. (*Stopping.*) Oh, excuse me, Rakitin, I didn't hear a word of what you were saying.

RAKITIN (*sadly*). I said . . . I was asking you to forgive me, Natalia. I was asking you whether you would allow me to remain your friend.

NATALIA (*turning slowly toward him and placing her hands on his shoulders*). Rakitin, tell me—what's the matter with me?

RAKITIN (*after a pause*). You're in love.

NATALIA (*slowly repeating after him*). In love . . . But this is madness, Rakitin. It's impossible. Can it really happen like that, suddenly? So, you say I'm in love . . . (*Falls silent.*)

RAKITIN. Yes, you're in love, my poor woman. Don't deceive yourself.

NATALIA (*avoiding his eyes*). But what can I do now?

RAKITIN. I can tell you, Natalia, if you'll promise . . .

NATALIA (*interrupting him, still without looking at him*). You know that this girl, my Vera, loves him. They're in love with each other.

RAKITIN. That's just one more reason . . .

NATALIA (*interrupting him again*). I've suspected it for a long time, but now she's admitted the whole thing to me, just now.

RAKITIN (*in a low voice, as if talking to himself*). Poor woman!

NATALIA (*passing her hand over her face*). But it's time to take hold of myself. I believe you wanted to tell me something? Give me your advice, Rakitin, for God's sake—what shall I do?

RAKITIN. I'm prepared to give you my advice, but on one condition.

NATALIA. What's that?

RAKITIN. Promise me you won't suspect my motives. Tell me you know that I have no ulterior motive and only want to help you. You help me, too. Your trust will give me strength—if not, I'd rather say nothing.

NATALIA. Go on, tell me.

RAKITIN. You don't doubt me?

NATALIA. Tell me.

RAKITIN. Well then, listen. He must leave. (NATALIA *looks at him in silence.*) Yes, he must go. I'm not going to start lecturing you about . . . about your husband, about your duties. Such words would be out of place on my lips. But these two children love each other. You just told me so yourself. Well now, imagine yourself coming between them. Why, it'd be the end of you!

NATALIA. Yes, he must leave. (*After a pause.*) And what about you? Will you stay?

RAKITIN (*confused*). Me? (*After a pause.*) Yes, I must leave, too. For the sake of your peace of mind, your happiness, Vera's happiness, both of us must leave forever.

NATALIA. Rakitin, I had reached such a point that I . . . I was almost prepared to give that poor girl, that orphan, entrusted to my care by my own mother—to give her in marriage to a stupid, ridiculous old man! But I didn't have the heart, Rakitin! The words froze on my lips when she burst out laughing in answer to my proposal. But I made arrangements with the doctor, I put up with his meaningful grins, I bore his smirks, his hints, his compliments. Oh, I feel I'm standing on the brink of an abyss! Save me!

RAKITIN. You see, Natalia, I was right. (*She says nothing and he continues hurriedly.*) He must leave. We must both leave. There's no other way out.

NATALIA (*despondently*). But what sense would my life have then?

RAKITIN. My God, have you really reached that point? Natalia, you'll get over it, believe me. It'll pass. What do you mean—what sense would your life have?

NATALIA. Yes, yes, what sense will my life have when everyone has left me?

RAKITIN. But, your family . . . (NATALIA *lowers her eyes.*) Listen, if you want, I could stay for a few days after he's left, in order to . . .

NATALIA (*gloomily*). Oh yes, I see! You're counting on the force of habit, on our former friendship. You're hoping I'll come to my senses, that I'll come back to you—isn't that right? Oh yes, I understand very well!

RAKITIN (*blushing*). Natalia! Why should you insult me so?

NATALIA (*bitterly*). I understand, all right, but you're deluding yourself.

RAKITIN. What? After your promise, after I spoke up for your sake, for you alone, for your happiness, for the sake of your reputation and finally . . .

NATALIA. Ha, how long have you been worried about my reputation? How is it you never brought it up before this?

RAKITIN (*rising*). Look here, I'm leaving today, this very minute and you'll never see me again. (*Starts to leave.*)

NATALIA (*holding out her hand to him*). Forgive me, Michel! I don't know what I'm saying myself. You see what a state I'm in. Forgive me.

RAKITIN (*quickly returning to her and taking her hand*). Natalia . . .

NATALIA. Oh, Michel, I can't tell you how miserable I am. (*Leans her head against his shoulder and presses her handkerchief to her eyes.*) Help me! Without you I'm lost.

(*At this moment, the door to the ballroom opens and ARKADY ISLAEV and his mother, ANNA SEMYONOVNA, enter.*)

ISLAEV (*loudly*). I've always been of that opinion . . . (*Stops in surprise at the sight of RAKITIN and NATALIA. NATALIA looks round, then hastily leaves the room. RAKITIN, terribly confused, remains where he is.*)

ISLAEV (*to RAKITIN*). What's the meaning of this? What's this little scene all about?

RAKITIN. Er, well, it's nothing. It's just . . .

ISLAEV. Is something the matter with Natalia?

RAKITIN. No but, you see . . .

ISLAEV. Why did she rush out of here like that? What were you talking about? She was crying, wasn't she? You were comforting her. What's it all about?

RAKITIN. Nothing, really.

ANN SEMYONOVNA. Well but, how can it be nothing, Rakitin? (*After a pause.*) I'll go and see. (*Moves toward the study door.*)

RAKITIN (*stopping her*). No, please, it'd be much better if you left her alone now.

ISLAEV. But what does this mean? For goodness sake, tell me!

RAKITIN. Nothing, I swear. Listen, I promise I'll explain the whole thing to both of you—and today. I give you my word.

But right now, please, if you trust me at all, don't ask me anything, and don't bother Natalia either.

ISLAEV. Well, all right, but it's really rather surprising. I've never seen Natalia in such a state before. It's really very strange indeed.

ANNA SEMYONOVNA. And, above all, what could have made Natalia cry? Why did she leave the room? We're not strangers, after all.

RAKITIN. How can you even suggest such a thing! But, you see, we hadn't finished our talk. I must ask you, both of you—please, leave us alone for a little while.

ISLAEV. So that's how it is! So there's some secret between the two of you?

RAKITIN. Yes, a secret, but you'll find out soon enough.

ISLAEV (*after thinking a while*). Come, Mother, let's leave them to their secret conference.

ANNA SEMYONOVNA. But . . .

ISLAEV. Come, come. You heard Rakitin promise to explain everything.

RAKITIN. You may rest assured . . .

ISLAEV (*coldly*). Oh, I'm not worried in the slightest! (*To* ANNA SEMYONOVNA.) Come.   (*They exit.*)

RAKITIN (*watching them leave, then quickly crossing to study door*). Natalia, Natalia, come out of there, please.

NATALIA (*comes out of study. She is very pale*). What did they say?

RAKITIN. Nothing. Calm yourself. Of course, they were a little surprised. Your husband thought perhaps you were ill. He noticed that you were upset. Come, sit down. Why, your legs can hardly hold you. (NATALIA *sits down.*) I told him . . . I asked him not to disturb us for a while, to leave us alone.

NATALIA. And he agreed?

RAKITIN. Yes. I admit I had to promise him I'd explain everything by tomorrow. Tell me, why did you rush out like that?

NATALIA (*bitterly*). Why? Well, all right, so you explain it to him then.

RAKITIN. I'll think of something, don't worry. That's not what's important right now. We must take advantage of this respite. You see yourself, things can't go on like this. You can't go through this sort of torment any more, not a person like you. Myself, I . . . But that's not important now. Just remain firm and I'll be all right. Listen now, since you agree with me . . .

NATALIA. About what?

RAKITIN. That it's essential that . . . that Belaev and I should go. You agree? If you do, there's no sense delaying. If you'll allow me, I'll have a talk with Belaev right away. He's an honorable man. He'll understand.

NATALIA. You want to speak to him about it? You? But what could you say to him?

RAKITIN (*embarrassed*). Well, I . . .

NATALIA (*after a pause*). Listen, Rakitin, doesn't it strike you too that we're behaving like a pair of lunatics? I got panicky and frightened you too, when perhaps there's nothing to it at all.

RAKITIN. What do you mean?

NATALIA. But, really, what are we doing? The atmosphere in this house was so peaceful and quiet and now, all of a sudden . . . How did all this start? Really, we've all gone out of our minds! But now, enough of this fooling. Let's go back to living the way we did before. And then there won't be anything for you to explain to Arkady. I'll go and tell him all about this childish nonsense myself and the two of us will have a good laugh over it. My husband and I need no go-between.

RAKITIN. Natalia, now you do frighten me. You smile, but you're as pale as death. Remember what you told me just quarter of an hour ago.

NATALIA. What of it? But I see what it's all about now. It's you who are causing all this storm so that, at least, you won't drown alone.

RAKITIN. More suspicions, more reproaches. God bless you, Natalia, but you're hurting me. Or is it that you're sorry now for having been too frank with me?

NATALIA. I'm sorry about nothing.

RAKITIN. What does your behavior mean then?

NATALIA (*with feeling*). Listen, Rakitin, if you say one word to Belaev, either in my name or about me, I'll never forgive you.

RAKITIN. Ah! I see! Well, you don't need to worry about it, Natalia. I won't say a word to your Belaev and, in fact, I won't even say good-by to him when I leave today. I have no intention of thrusting my services upon you.

NATALIA (*a little confused*). Perhaps you think I've changed my mind about . . . about his leaving?

RAKITIN. I think nothing at all.

NATALIA. Well, let me tell you that I myself feel so strongly that he must leave that I have definitely decided to dismiss him. (*Pause.*) Yes, and I'll dismiss him myself.

RAKITIN. You?

NATALIA. Yes. And right away, what's more. Please send him here to me.

RAKITIN. What? Right away?

NATALIA. Yes. I'd like to do it now. Please, Rakitin, ask him to come and see me. I'm in full possession of my senses, as you can see. And then, the others won't interfere if I get it over with now. This is the moment for it. I'd appreciate it very much if you sent him in here. I'll ask him about it.

RAKITIN. But I'm sure he won't tell you anything. He told me himself that he feels awkward in your presence.

NATALIA (*suspiciously*). Oh, so you've already talked to him about me? (RAKITIN *shrugs his shoulders.*) Ah, I'm sorry, Michel, I'm sorry. Send him here to me. You'll see. I'll dismiss him and the whole thing will be finished. It'll all be over and forgotten, like a bad dream. Please, send him to me. I absolutely must have the matter out with him. You'll be pleased with me, believe me.

RAKITIN (*who has kept his gaze fixed on her all the time, coldly and sadly*). All right, have it your way. (*Crosses to ballroom door.*)

NATALIA (*as he goes*). Thank you, Michel.

RAKITIN (*turning*). At least spare me your thanks. (*Goes quickly into the ballroom.*)

NATALIA (*alone, after a pause*). He's very noble. But did I really ever love him? (*Gets up.*) He's right. The other one must leave. But how am I going to dismiss him? I only want to find out whether he really does like the girl. Perhaps it's all a lot of nonsense. How could I have become so upset? What's all the fuss about? Well, it's too late now. But I'd like to know what he'll say. Anyway, he must leave. He must; he must. Perhaps he won't want to answer me. After all, he's afraid of me. Well, so? So much the better. There's no need to get involved in a whole long conversation with him. (*Puts her hand to her forehead.*) And I have a splitting headache. Perhaps I should put it off till tomorrow? Yes, that'd be better. Today I keep thinking everyone's watching me all the time. Ah, have I come to this? No, it's better to get it over with. One last effort and I'll be free! Oh yes, how I long to be free, to have peace again. (BELAEV *enters from hall.*) Here he comes . . .

BELAEV (*approaching her*). Mr. Rakitin tells me that you wanted to see me.

NATALIA (*making a slight effort*). Yes, I have to have a talk with you.

BELAEV. A talk?

NATALIA (*avoiding his eyes*). Yes, a talk. (*Pause.*) I must tell you, Belaev, I . . . I'm displeased with you.

BELAEV. May I ask why?

NATALIA. Hear me out. I . . . I really don't know where to

begin. Incidentally, I must tell you, first, that my dissatisfaction does not result from any neglect of duty on your part. On the contrary, I've been very pleased with your way of handling Kolia.

BELAEV. Then, what can it be?

NATALIA (*glancing at him*). Oh, don't worry, you haven't done anything very terrible. You're young and you've probably never lived in someone else's house before. You couldn't have foreseen . . .

BELAEV. But, Ma'am.

NATALIA. I understand your impatience but give me a chance, finally, to tell you what this is all about. Well then, I must tell you that Vera . . . (*Glancing at him.*) Vera has admitted everything to me.

BELAEV (*in surprise*). Vera? What can she have admitted to you? And how does it concern me?

NATALIA. You really don't know? You can't guess?

BELAEV. I have no idea.

NATALIA. In that case, excuse me. If you really can't guess, I apologize. I must have been wrong. But, please take note, I don't believe you. I understand that you feel obliged to say that. I admire your discretion.

BELAEV. I'm sorry but I'm completely at a loss.

NATALIA. Really? Do you expect me to believe that you haven't noticed Vera's inclination toward you.

BELAEV. Vera's inclination toward me? I just don't know what to say. Please, I thought I'd always behaved toward Vera as . . .

NATALIA. As you do toward everyone else, right? (*Short pause.*) Well, whatever the truth is—whether you are really unaware or are just pretending to be—let me tell you something. That little girl loves you. She confessed it to me herself. Well, so I must ask you, now, as an honest man, what do you intend to do?

BELAEV (*embarrassed*). What do I intend to do?

NATALIA (*folding her arms*). Yes.

BELAEV. This is so unexpected, Ma'am.

NATALIA (*after a pause*). Belaev, I see I haven't tackled this matter properly. You don't understand. You think I'm annoyed with you about this but I'm just . . . well, a little worried. And that's only natural. Please, let's sit down and talk it over calmly. (*They sit down.*) I'll be frank with you, and you, too, please try to have a little more confidence in me. Really, you don't have to be so reserved. Vera is in love with you and, of course, that's not your fault. I'm prepared to assume that it's not your fault. But, you see, she has no parents and I'm her guardian. I'm responsible for her, for her future, for her happiness. She's still very young and I'm quite sure the feeling you have aroused in her will vanish quite quickly. At her age, love doesn't last long. But you understand, it was my duty to put you on your guard. It's dangerous to play with fire, you know, and I have no doubt that now you are aware of this inclination of hers, you'll behave differently with her, you'll avoid walks alone in the garden, that sort of thing. Am I right? I can rely upon you. With another I might have hesitated to speak so directly.

BELAEV. Believe me, Ma'am, I greatly appreciate . . .

NATALIA. I assure you, I have full confidence in you. So this can remain a secret between us.

BELAEV. I must admit, everything you've said seems very strange to me. Of course, I wouldn't dream of doubting your word, but . . .

NATALIA. Listen, I've told you all this now on the assumption that, on your side, there's nothing. (*Breaks off.*) Because, of course, if that weren't so . . . Of course, I know you very little as yet, but I know you sufficiently to feel that I need have no reason to stand in your way. You aren't rich, but you're young and you have your future before you, and when two people love one another . . . I repeat, I considered it my duty to fore-warn you, as an honest man, of the consequences of your ac-quaintance with Vera, but if you . . .

BELAEV (*perplexed*). I'm afraid I really don't understand what you mean.

NATALIA (*hurriedly*). Oh, please understand, I'm not demand-ing a confession of you. I can see from your behavior how things are without one. (*Glancing at him.*) Incidentally, I should tell you—Vera had the impression that you weren't al-together indifferent to her.

BELAEV (*remains silent for a while, then gets up*). Then I see, Ma'am, that it will be impossible for me to stay here in your house any longer.

NATALIA (*flaring up*). You could at least have waited until I dismissed you myself. (*Gets up.*)

BELAEV. You have been frank with me. Now let me be frank with you. I don't love Vera—at least, I don't love her in the sense you suggest.

NATALIA. But I never . . . (*Stops.*)

BELAEV. And if Vera has taken a liking to me, if she has got the impression that I, as you put it, am not indifferent to her, I would like to dispel that impression. I will tell her how things really stand myself. But, as you must realize yourself, Ma'am, after such an explanation, staying here would be very awkward for me. My position would be impossible. I can't tell you how sad I'll be to leave here but there's nothing else I can do. I'll always remember you with gratitude. I'll go now. I will come and say good-by to you later.

NATALIA (*with feigned indifference*). As you wish, but I must say, I didn't expect this. This was not at all what I expected to come out of our talk. I only wanted to put you on your guard, since Vera is still a child. In fact, I may have attached too great importance to the whole matter. I really see no need for you to leave. But suit yourself.

BELAEV. But really, I feel it's impossible for me to stay.

NATALIA. Apparently leaving us is an easy matter for you!

BELAEV. No, Ma'am, it won't be easy at all.

NATALIA. I'm not in the habit of detaining people against their wills, but I must say, your going distresses me.

BELAEV (*overcoming a certain amount of indecision*). I have no desire to cause you the slightest distress, Ma'am. I'll stay.

NATALIA (*suspiciously*). Oh! (*Pause.*) I'm a bit taken aback to find you can reverse your decisions so quickly. Thank you very much but . . . let me think it over. Perhaps you're right—perhaps you should leave. I'll think it over and let you know. I hope you won't mind if we leave the matter unsettled until this evening?

BELAEV. I am prepared to wait as long as is convenient. (*Bows and starts to go out.*)

NATALIA. Promise me . . .

BELAEV (*stopping*). What?

NATALIA. You said you wanted to talk this over with Vera. I'm not sure that that would be the right thing. Anyway, I'll let you know my decision. I'm beginning to think that it really would be better if you left. Good-by for now. (BELAEV *bows again and goes into the hall.* NATALIA *follows him with her eyes.*) Well, there was nothing to it, then! He doesn't love her! (*Pacing the room.*) So, instead of dismissing him, I myself insisted he stay on. He'll stay. But what shall I tell Rakitin? What have I done? (*Pause.*) And what right did I have to go telling them all about that poor little girl's falling in love? I wheedled an admission out of her myself, a partial admission, and then I went and . . . so mercilessly, so brutally . . . (*Covering her face with her hands.*) Perhaps he was beginning to feel for her. And what right did I have to nip that flower in the bud? Yes and then, have I nipped it in the bud? He may have lied to me. After all, didn't I lie to him? But no, he's too decent for that. He's not like me! And what was I in such a hurry about? Why did I have to come out with everything at once? (*Sighs.*)

Ah, what of it? If I could only foresee . . . Ah, how dishonest I was with him, how I lied, and he! He was so sincere and un-affected. I admire him for that. Ah, he's a real man! I didn't know him before. He must go. If he stays, I feel I shall go so far that I'll lose all self-respect. Unless he goes, I'm lost! I'll write him a note before he has a chance to see Vera. He must leave!   (*Goes quickly into the study.*)

CURTAIN

ACT IV

A large, empty pavilion with bare walls and an uneven stone floor. The ceiling is supported by six brick columns covered with flaking whitewash, three on each side. Left, two open windows and a door to the garden. Right, a door onto the passage leading to the main house. Center stage, an iron door to a storeroom. By the first column on the right, a green garden bench. In one corner, a few spades, watering cans, and flowerpots. Evening. The red rays of the setting sun slant through the window onto the floor.

KATIA (*entering through door right, hastens to window and stands looking out into the garden for a little while*). No, can't see him. Yet they said he'd gone to the greenhouse—can't have come out again yet. Ah well, I'll wait till he comes by. He's bound to pass here. (*Sighs and leans on windowsill.*) They say he's leaving. (*Sighs again.*) Dunno how we'll get along without him. Poor young lady! The way she begged me. And why shouldn't I help her? Let him have one last talk with her. Whew, it's terrible hot today! Oh well, looks like a few drops of rain falling. (*Looks out of the window again, then suddenly draws back.*) Oh Lord, surely they're not coming in here? Yes, they sure are. Oh Lordy me! (*Starts to run out, but doesn't manage to reach the door to the corridor before the* DOCTOR *and* LIZAVETA BOGDANOVNA *enter from the garden.* KATIA *hides behind a column.*)

DOCTOR (*looking around*). What is this? Some sort of a store-room?

LIZAVETA BOGDANOVNA (*indicating the iron door*). No, there's the storeroom. It seems Mr. Islaev had this pavilion built when he returned from abroad.

DOCTOR. Oh, now I see, a little bit of Venice. Good heavens! (*Sits down on bench.*) Come, let's sit down. (LIZAVETA BOGDA-NOVNA *sits down.*) Come, you must admit, that shower came just at the wrong time. It interrupted our little talk at a most sentimental moment.

LIZAVETA BOGDANOVNA (*lowering her eyes*). Oh, Doctor.

DOCTOR. But there's no reason why we shouldn't resume it now. By the way, did you say old Mrs. Islaev was in a bad mood today?

LIZAVETA BOGDANOVNA. Yes, very bad. She even had her dinner taken up to her room.

DOCTOR. Oh really? That's bad luck!

LIZAVETA BOGDANOVNA. This morning she found Natalia Petrovna crying, and Mr. Rakitin was there. Of course, he's like one of the family, but still . . . Anyway, he promised to explain it all.

DOCTOR. Oh, I see. Well, anyway, there's no need for her to upset herself. In my opinion, Rakitin's never been a dangerous man, and now less than ever.

LIZAVETA BOGDANOVNA. What makes you say that?

DOCTOR. I'm telling you. He talks much too sensibly. Some break out in a rash to get it out of their systems—while these smart ones, now, work it off with their tongues, it all goes into talk. Let me give you a piece of advice, Lizaveta Bogdanovna, don't be afraid of the talkers, they're not dangerous. The quiet ones now, they're a bit crazy often and full of temperament. They're the dangerous ones.

LIZAVETA BOGDANOVNA (*after a pause*). So Natalia Petrovna isn't well?

DOCTOR. She's about as sick as you or me.

LIZAVETA BOGDANOVNA. She didn't eat a thing at dinner.

DOCTOR. Sickness isn't the only thing that makes a person lose his appetite.

LIZAVETA BOGDANOVNA. Did you have dinner at Bolshintsov's?

DOCTOR. Yes, I did. I drove over there. And if I came back, it was for your sake, I swear.

LIZAVETA BOGDANOVNA. Oh, stop it, Doctor! Shall I tell you something, though? Natalia Petrovna's angry with you about something. At dinner, she said something about you that wasn't exactly complimentary.

DOCTOR. Really? Evidently, these fine ladies don't like it if a man is too observant. You have to do what they want and help them all they want, and then on top of that you have to pretend you don't understand what's going on! Ah, they're a fussy lot! However, we'll see. So Rakitin's going around with his head hanging, is he?

LIZAVETA BOGDANOVNA. They all seem to be decidedly out of

sorts. I can't think what can have come over the lot of them.

DOCTOR. If you know too much, you'll grow old too quickly. Anyway, forget 'em. Let's talk about ourselves. It's still raining a bit. Shall we?

LIZAVETA BOGDANOVNA (*coyly lowering her eyes*). What did you want to talk about, Doctor?

DOCTOR. Don't mind my saying so, but why must you be so coy, why suddenly lower your eyes like that? After all, we're not youngsters any more! All that ceremony, tender little remarks, sighs—that's not for us. Let's talk calmly, in a business-like way, as suits people of our age. So, here's the question: we like each other or, at least, I'm assuming you like me.

LIZAVETA BOGDANOVNA (*a little coyly*). Really . . .

DOCTOR. Yes, well, all right, all right. I suppose, since you're a woman you have to, that is . . . (*Demonstrates with his hand.*) make a bit of a dance of it. Well, anyway, we like each other. And from other points of view too, we're a good match. Of course, I'd have to admit that I don't exactly come from a very distinguished family but then you're no princess either. I don't have much money—if I had, you understand yourself, I'd . . . (*Snorts.*) However, I have quite a good practice, not all my patients die. And, according to what you say, you have fifteen thousand in ready cash. All that put together, doesn't sound bad at all. Then, I imagine you must be sick of living in other people's houses. Fussing over the old woman, playing whist with her and taking all her nonsense can't be much fun either. Now, for my part, it's not so much that I'm sick of a bachelor's life as that I'm beginning to get on—well, yes, and then, you can't find an honest cook these days. So you see, everything seems to point to it. There's just one difficulty, as I see it, and that's that we don't really know each other. That is, you don't know me. Because I know you all right. I know all about you and I won't say that you're altogether without drawbacks. You've become a little sour with being an old maid for so long—but that's no tragedy. A wife is like clay in the hands of a good husband. Still, I'd like you to know me well before we're married, or otherwise you'll reproach me afterward. I don't want to rush you into it.

LIZAVETA BOGDANOVNA (*with dignity*). But, Doctor, let me tell you, I too have had the opportunity to get to know you.

DOCTOR. You? Nonsense, women don't see these things. For instance, I bet you take me for a cheerful man, a fun-lover, right?

LIZAVETA BOGDANOVNA. I've always considered you a pleasant man . . .

Doctor. So there you are! You see how easy it is to make a mistake. Just because I play the fool in front of others, tell them funny stories, do them little services, you thought I was really a cheerful, happy-go-lucky man. Well, if I didn't need them, I wouldn't even look at them. And as it is, if I can do it safely, I make fun of them. But I have no illusions—I know some people who need me at every step, who miss me whenever I'm not around, but who still think they have a right to despise me. But I pay them back with the same coin! Take Natalia Petrovna for example. You think I don't see through her? (*Imitating her.*) "Dear Doctor, I'm really very fond of you. You have such a sharp tongue." He-he-he, coo, my dove, coo. Ooh, these fine ladies! The way they smile at you and blink their eyes—but there's distaste written clear across their faces all the time. They're so superior with us. I know why she's ill-disposed toward me today. Really, these ladies are amazing! Just because they bathe in eau-de-cologne every day and talk so condescendingly, dropping their words like coins for you to pick up; they imagine you can't catch them by the tail just like anyone else. Huh, that's what they think! They're mortal sinners just like all the rest of us!

Lizaveta Bogdanovna. Doctor, you surprise me.

Doctor. I knew I would. You see now that I'm not cheerful at all, nor particularly kind either, for that matter. I don't want to pretend to you that I'm something that I've never been. Whatever poses I may take on for these ladies and gentlemen, no one has ever been able to say I was a clown and no one's ever tweaked my nose. I can even say they're a little afraid of me. They know I can bite. One time, three years ago, a certain gentleman, from the South, you know—just a rich farmer really—started acting the fool at the dinner table and he took a radish and stuck it in my hair. So, what d'you think? There and then, and without losing my temper, mind you, I challenged him very politely to a duel. He was almost paralyzed with fear. Then our host made him apologize to me. It had a terrific effect! Well, I'll admit, I knew beforehand that he'd never fight. So, you see, my pride is boundless, but my life hasn't worked out so wonderfully. I'm not particularly gifted either. I was a so-so sort of student. And—I won't hide anything from you —I'm not too competent a doctor; if you were ever to fall ill, I wouldn't treat you myself. If I'd been more gifted and done better in my studies, I'd have been practicing in the capital. Well, of course, for around here, I'm good enough. Now, as far as my personal habits are concerned, I must give you fair warning: at home I'm gloomy, taciturn, and demanding. As long as

I'm humored and fussed over, I don't get mad. I like my old habits to be considered and I like my food well prepared. On the other hand, I'm not given to jealousy and I'm not stingy, and when I'm not around, you can do anything you like. As you can understand, there's no question of romantic love between us, but, nevertheless, I imagine it's still possible to live under one roof with me. Just as long as I'm humored and you don't cry in front of me—that's one thing I can't stand! Otherwise, I'm not difficult. So there's my confession for you. Well, what do you have to say now?

LIZAVETA BOGDANOVNA. What can I say, Doctor? If you haven't been slandering yourself purposely . . .

DOCTOR. But how have I slandered myself? Don't forget that another in my place would have kept quiet about his faults without a qualm, as long as you hadn't noticed them yourself. And then after the wedding, just try and do something—after the wedding, it's too late! But I'm too proud for that. (LIZAVETA BOGDANOVNA *looks at him.*) Yes, yes, too proud, whatever kind of a look you may give me. Before my future wife, I have no intention of dissembling and lying—I wouldn't do that for fifteen thousand, nor even for a hundred thousand. But to a stranger, I'll bow to the ground for a sack of flour. That's the way I am. I'll grin at a stranger but all the time I'm thinking to myself: Ah, you're a real dolt, brother, look how you rise to the bait! But to you, I say what I think. That is, excuse me, I won't tell even you everything I think, but at least I won't deceive you. You probably think I'm quite a crank, I realize that. But just wait. One of these days, I'll tell you the whole story of my life and you'll be surprised that I've managed to stay even what I am. You weren't born with a silver spoon in your mouth either, I don't suppose, and yet, my dear, you can't even imagine what real grinding poverty is like. Anyway, I'll tell you all about it some other time. Now, you think over all I've told you, consider the matter well, in solitude, and let me know your decision. As far as I've been able to observe, you're a sensible woman. You . . . by the way, how old are you?

LIZAVETA BOGDANOVNA. I . . . I'm . . . thirty.

DOCTOR (*calmly*). That's not true—you're all of forty.

LIZAVETA BOGDANOVNA (*flaring up*). I'm certainly not forty! I'm thirty-six.

DOCTOR. Well, that's still not thirty. Now that's a habit you'll have to get out of, especially since a married woman of thirty-six isn't too old at all. And you shouldn't take snuff. (*Getting up.*) The shower's over, it seems.

LIZAVETA BOGDANOVNA (*also rising*). Yes, it's over.

DOCTOR. So you'll give me your answer one of these days?

LIZAVETA BOGDANOVNA. I will tell you my decision no later than tomorrow.

DOCTOR. Ah, I like that. That's smart, very smart! That's my girl! Well, come, give me your arm. Let's go back to the house.

LIZAVETA BOGDANOVNA (*giving him her arm*). All right, let's go.

DOCTOR. Oh yes, by the way, I didn't kiss your hand, but I believe it's the thing. Well, just for this once! (*Kisses her hand. She blushes.*) There we are. (*Goes toward the door to the garden.*)

LIZAVETA BOGDANOVNA (*stopping*). So you really don't think Mr. Rakitin is a dangerous man?

DOCTOR. No, I don't think so.

LIZAVETA BOGDANOVNA. You know what? It seems to me that for some time Natalia Petrovna . . . It seems to me that Mr. Belaev . . . She seems to be very interested in him, uh? Vera too, wouldn't you say so? Perhaps that's what started it all today.

DOCTOR. There's one thing I forgot to tell you—I'm terribly inquisitive myself, but I can't stand inquisitive women. That is, I'll make myself clear—I think a wife should be curious and observant. That can even be useful to her husband. But only with others. You understand? With others. And, incidentally, if you absolutely want to know my opinion about Natalia Petrovna, Vera, Belaev, and the residents of this house in general, let me sing you a little song. I have a dreadful voice, so don't hold it against me.

LIZAVETA BOGDANOVNA (*surprised*). A song!

DOCTOR. Listen! Here's the first verse:

> There was an old woman who had a gray goat,
> There was an old woman who had a gray goat!
>
> > That's so! Just so! A little gray goat!
> > That's so! Just so! A little gray goat!

Second verse:
> The goat took a notion to go to the woods,
> The goat took a notion to go to the woods.
>
> > That's so! Just so! To go to the woods!
> > That's so! Just so! To go to the woods!

LIZAVETA BOGDANOVNA. Really, I don't understand at all.

DOCTOR. Listen to the third verse then.

The gray wolves came by and ate up the goat,
The gray wolves came by and ate up the goat.
(*Jumps up.*)

That's so! Just so! They ate up the goat!
That's so! Just so! They ate up the goat!

Come, let's go now. Bye and bye I have to have a little talk with Natalia. Who knows, she may not snap at me this time? If I'm not mistaken, she still needs me. Let's go.

(*They go out into the garden.*)

KATIA (*cautiously coming out from behind the column*). Whew, I thought they'd never move out of here. Ah, that sawbones is a nasty piece of work. He kept on and on and on, and what didn't he comd out with! And some singing! But I hope I haven't missed Mr. Belaev in the meanwhile. No, he was bound to come this way. (*Going to window.*) So that Lizaveta Bogdanovna will be the sawbones' wife. (*Laughing.*) Wow, who'd have thought it? Still, I wouldn't like to be in her shoes. (*Looking out of window.*) Ah, the grass got a good wash. Smells good all right. That's the wild cherry trees make it smell so good. Oh, there he is. (*She waits a little while.*) Mr. Belaev! Mr. Belaev!

BELAEV'S VOICE (*from the wings*). Did someone call me? Ah, it's you, Katia. (*Comes up to window.*) What is it?

KATIA. Come in here, sir. I've got something to tell you.

BELAEV. Sure. (*Leaves window and a moment later enters at door.*) Here I am.

KATIA. You wasn't caught in the shower?

BELAEV. No, I was in the hothouse with Potap. What is he—your uncle, right?

KATIA. Yes, sir, he's my uncle.

BELAEV. How pretty you look today! (KATIA *smiles and lowers her eyes. He takes a peach out of his pocket.*) Want a peach?

KATIA (*refusing*). Thank you kindly, but eat it yourself.

BELAEV. But I took the raspberries you gave me yesterday. Come, take it. I picked it for you, really.

KATIA. Well, thank you kindly then. (*Takes peach.*)

BELAEV. That's better. Well, what was it you wanted to tell me?

KATIA. Miss Vera asked me to . . . She wants to see you.

BELAEV. Oh! Well, I'll go and find her right away.

KATIA. No, no, she's coming here. She wants to talk to you.

BELAEV (*a little surprised*). She wants to meet me here?

KATIA. Yes, sir. You see, nobody comes in here. You won't be disturbed. (*Sighs.*) She's real fond of you, Mr. Belaev. Oh, she's

such a nice young lady. I'll go get her now, all right? You will
wait, won't you?

BELAEV. Of course, of course.

KATIA. Right away. (*Crosses stage then stops.*) Mr. Belaev,
is it true what they say—that you're going away?

BELAEV. Going away? No. Who told you that?

KATIA. You're not going? Well, thank God! (*Embarrassed.*)
We'll be right back.   (*Exits through door leading to the house.*)

BELAEV (*remaining motionless for a while*). It's amazing! The
most amazing things are happening to me. I never expected
anything like this. Vera loves me. Natalia Petrovna knows about
it. Vera told her so herself. Amazing! Vera's such a good, sweet
child, but . . . well, for instance, what can this note be all
about? (*Takes a small scrap of paper from pocket.*) It's from
Natalia Petrovna and in pencil, too. "Don't leave, don't decide
anything, before we've had a talk." But what can she want
to talk to me about? (*After a pause.*) Ah, the stupid ideas I get
sometimes! I must say, the whole business has me bewildered. If
someone had told me a month ago that I . . . that I . . . Since I
saw Natalia Petrovna, I haven't been the same. Why should my
heart beat so? And now Vera wants to see me. What can I tell
her? Well, at least I'll find out what it's all about. Perhaps Natalia Petrovna's angry with me. But why should she be? (*Rereads
note.*) It's all very, very strange. (*The door opens noiselessly. He
hastily hides the note. In the doorway,* VERA *and* KATIA *appear.
He crosses to them.* VERA *is very pale, keeps her eyes on the
ground and remains fixed on the spot.*)

KATIA. Don't worry now, Miss Vera. You go and talk to him
and I'll keep watch. Don't worry. (*To* BELAEV.) Oh, Mr.
Belaev! (*She closes the window and goes out into the garden,
closing the door behind her.*)

BELAEV. Vera . . . you wanted to see me? Come over here,
sit down. (*Takes her hand and leads her to the bench.* VERA
sits down.) That's the way. (*Looking at her in surprise.*)
What, have you been crying?

VERA (*keeping her eyes lowered*). It's nothing. I came to
ask your forgiveness.

BELAEV. For what?

VERA. I heard you'd had an unpleasant talk with Natalia
Petrovna. I understand you're leaving, that you've been dismissed.

BELAEV. Who told you that?

VERA. She herself. I ran into her after she talked to you. She
told me you didn't want to stay here any more yourself. But I
think you must have been dismissed.

BELAEV. Tell me, does everyone in the house know about it?

VERA. No, just Katia. I had to tell her. I wanted to talk to you, to ask your forgiveness. You can imagine how bad I feel about it all. After all, I feel it's all my fault.

BELAEV. Why is it your fault?

VERA. I couldn't know that Natalia Petrovna would . . . But I don't hold it against her. So please, don't you hold it against me either. This morning, I was just a silly child, and now . . . (*Stops.*)

BELAEV. Nothing's decided yet, Vera. I may stay.

VERA (*sadly*). Ah, you may think so. But it's all settled. Look how you're talking to me now—but d'you remember just yesterday, in the garden? (*Falls silent.*) Oh, I can see Natalia Petrovna's told you everything.

BELAEV (*embarrassed*). Vera . . .

VERA. She's told you everything—I can see it. She wanted to catch me out and, like an idiot, I rose to the bait. But she gave herself away too. I'm not such a child, after all. (*Lowering voice.*) Oh no!

BELAEV. What do you mean by that?

VERA (*looking at him*). Was it really your idea to leave?

BELAEV. It was.

VERA. But why? (BELAEV *doesn't answer.*) You won't tell me?

BELAEV. You were right, Vera. Natalia Petrovna told me everything.

VERA (*weakly*). What, for example?

BELAEV. Please understand. I can't, really.

VERA. Did she tell you I was in love with you?

BELAEV (*hesitatingly*). Yes, she did.

VERA (*quickly*). But it's not true.

BELAEV (*embarrassed*). Really?

VERA (*covering her face with her hands and whispering tonelessly through her fingers*). Well, at least, I never told her that, I don't remember . . . (*Raising her head.*) Oh, how cruel it is of her! And that's really the reason why you're leaving?

BELAEV. Please try to understand, Vera.

VERA (*looking at him*). He doesn't love me! (*Again buries face in hands.*)

BELAEV (*sitting down beside her and taking her hands*). Vera, give me your hand. Listen, there shouldn't be any misunderstanding between us. I love you like a sister. I love you because it's impossible not to love you. Excuse me, if I . . . I've never found myself in such a position before. I don't want to offend you. And I'm not going to pretend to you—I knew that you liked me, that you'd taken a bit of a fancy to me. But, think, what could come of it? I'm only twenty-one and I haven't a kopek to my name. Please don't be angry. I honestly don't know what to say to you.

VERA (*taking her hands away from her face and looking at him*). As if I were demanding anything of you, good Lord! But why so cruelly, so mercilessly . . . (*She stops.*)

BELAEV. I didn't want to hurt you.

VERA. But I'm not blaming you. You haven't done anything. I'm the one who's to blame, and I'm being punished for it, too! And I can't blame her either. I know she's a kind woman but she couldn't help herself. It's turned her head completely.

BELAEV (*puzzled*). Turned her head?

VERA (*without looking at him*). She loves you.

BELAEV. What did you say?

VERA. She's in love with you.

BELAEV. What are you saying?

VERA. I know what I'm talking about. In this one day, I've grown up. I'm not a child any more, believe me. She's jealous —and of me of all people! (*With a bitter smile.*) What do you say to that?

BELAEV. But it's impossible.

VERA. Impossible? Why then did she suddenly decide to marry me off to that fellow—what's his name—that Bolshintsov? Why did she send the doctor to talk to me? Why did she try to talk me into it herself? Oh, I know what I'm saying all right! If you could have seen how her whole face changed when she said . . . Oh, you can't imagine how cunningly, how craftily she tricked me into admitting it. Yes, she's in love with you herself. It's all too obvious.

BELAEV. You're mistaken, I assure you.

VERA. No, I'm not. Believe me, I'm not. If she didn't love you why should she tear into me like that? What have I done to her? (*Bitterly.*) Jealousy excuses everything. Ah, there's no doubt about it. And now, why does she have to send you away? She thinks that you and I . . . well, there's nothing for her to worry about! You might just as well stay! (*Buries her face in her hands.*)

BELAEV. So far she hasn't dismissed me. I've already told you that nothing's decided yet.

VERA (*suddenly raising her head and looking at him*). Really not?

BELAEV. Yes, really. But why are you looking at me like that?

VERA (*as if talking to herself*). Oh, I understand. Yes, yes, she's still hoping . . . (*The door to the corridor is opened quickly and* NATALIA *appears in it. Seeing* VERA *and* BELAEV, *she stops. They do not see her.*)

BELAEV. It can't be, really!

VERA. Yes, I see it all now. She's worked it out coolly and she's realized that I'm no danger to her. And, really, who am I to worry her? A silly little girl—while she!

BELAEV. But how can you even think . . .

VERA. Yes, and then, who knows? Perhaps she's right. Perhaps you do love her.

BELAEV. Me?

VERA. Yes you, are you in love with her? Could you fall in love with her? Why don't you answer?

BELAEV. But, good Lord, what do you want me to answer? You're all upset. Come, for goodness sake calm yourself.

VERA (*turning away from him*). Oh, stop treating me like a child. Answer me sensibly. You just want to get me out of the way so you're trying to comfort me! (*Starts to leave but, catching sight of* NATALIA, *stops.*) Oh! (BELAEV *looks round quickly.*)

NATALIA (*taking a few steps forward*). Yes, it's me. (*She makes an effort to speak.*) I came to fetch you, Vera.

VERA (*slowly and coldly*). And what made you come precisely here? You must have looked all over for me?

NATALIA. Yes, I looked for you everywhere. You should be more careful, Vera. This is not the first time I've spoken to you about it. And you, Mr. Belaev, you've forgotten your promise. You've deceived me.

VERA. No, after all, that's enough, Natalia Petrovna. Stop it now! (NATALIA *looks at her in amazement.*) You've treated me like a child long enough. (*Lowering voice.*) From today on, I'm a woman . . . a woman like you.

NATALIA (*embarrassed*). Vera . . .

VERA (*almost in a whisper*). He never broke his promise to you. It wasn't he who sought this meeting with me. Why should he? He doesn't love me, as you know—you've no need to be jealous.

NATALIA (*in growing amazement*). Vera!

VERA. Take my word for it, you don't have to pretend any more. What's the point now? I see through it, believe me. I'm no longer your ward, whom you watch over (*with irony.*) like an older sister. (*Moving toward her.*) I'm your rival.

NATALIA. Vera, you're going too far.

VERA. Perhaps, but who drove me to it? I don't know myself how I dare talk to you like this. Maybe it's because I've nothing to hope for any more, because you've seen fit to trample me underfoot. And you've succeeded completely. But listen— I've no intention of putting up a great pretense the way you have. For your information, I've told him (*Indicating* BELAEV.) everything.

NATALIA. But what could you possibly tell him?

VERA. What? (*With irony.*) Well, just what I happened to notice. You hoped to get everything out of me without giving yourself away. But you were wrong. You overestimated yourself.

NATALIA. Vera, Vera, control yourself.

VERA (*in a whisper, moving still closer to her*). Tell me, then, that I'm wrong. Tell me that you don't love him. After all, he's told me that he doesn't love me! (NATALIA, *confused, remains silent.* VERA *remains motionless for a while, then suddenly places her hand on her forehead.*) Oh, I'm sorry . . . I . . . I don't know what's the matter with me. Please, forgive me. (*Bursts into tears and rushes out through the door into the corridor. Silence.*)

BELAEV (*crossing to* NATALIA). Please believe me that . . .

NATALIA (*gazing at the floor without moving, and stretching a hand out toward him*). Stop. Vera is right. It's time for me to stop pretending. I have wronged her, and you too—you have every right to despise me. (BELAEV *makes an involuntary gesture.*) I have disgraced myself in my own eyes and now I feel there's only one way for me to regain your respect: sincerity—whatever the consequences. Anyway, this is the last time I'll ever see you, the last time I'll ever speak to you. I love you. (*She is still avoiding his eyes.*)

BELAEV. You love me?!

NATALIA. Yes, I love you. Vera wasn't deceiving either herself or you. I fell in love with you the very first day you arrived, but I didn't realize it myself until yesterday. I'm not trying to find excuses for my behavior. It has been despicable, but perhaps you'll understand and forgive me now. Yes, I was jealous of Vera and it did occur to me to marry her off to Bolshintsov, to have her further away from me and from you. Yes, I used my advantage in years, in position, to worm her secret from her—but then, it took me by surprise and I gave myself away. I love you. But, you know, it is pride alone which is forcing me to make this confession. The comedy I've been playing has ended by trapping me, too. It's impossible for you to stay here now. Anyway, after what I've just told you, I'm sure you'll feel rather ill at ease in my company. You'll want to be as far away as possible yourself. I feel sure of it, and my being so sure has made me bold. I admit I didn't want you to carry away an unpleasant memory of me. Well, now you know everything. Perhaps I have come between you and Vera, perhaps, if none of this had happened, you would have fallen in love with her. I have only one excuse—the whole thing was beyond my control. (*She stops. She has spoken in a fairly calm, even voice, without looking at* Belaev. *He says nothing. She continues with some agitation and still without looking at him.*) Well, why don't you say something? Although, I understand. There's nothing you could say. It's very painful for a man to have a woman for whom he feels nothing tell him she loves him. I appreciate your silence. But believe me, when I told you I loved you, I wasn't being calculating like before. I wasn't counting on anything . . . On the contrary, I was discarding a mask which it was against my nature to wear anyway. Yes and, then, what's the good of pretending and putting on airs now that everything's out in the open and there's no one to deceive any more? It's all over between us now. I won't detain you any longer. You may leave this room without saying a word to me, without even saying good-by. I would not consider it impolite for a moment—on the contrary, I would appreciate it. There are instances when sympathy is out of place—worse than rudeness. Evidently we were not destined to get to know each other. Farewell. My only hope is that now you will no longer remember me as a domineering, hypocritical, scheming person. Good-by for ever. (Belaev, *agitated, tries to speak but cannot.*) You're not going?

Belaev (*who bows and starts to leave, but then, after a short struggle with himself, returns*). No, I can't leave like this. (*For the first time,* Natalia *glances at him.*) Not like this! Listen, a minute ago you said that you didn't want me to take a bad impression of you away with me—but I don't want you to think of me either as a man who . . . Oh, my God! I don't know how to put it. Forgive me, I'm no good at finding words for this sort of thing. I've never met a woman like you before. You say it's not our fate to get to know each other but, really, how could I, an ordinary, hardly educated boy, even hope to come close to you? Think who you are—and who I am! How could I even dare to presume . . . You are so refined. But why go into that? Just look at me, look at my shabby jacket . . . and at your dresses, your perfume. I ask you! Yes, yes, I was afraid of you—and I still am. I can say without the slightest exaggeration that I regarded you as some superior being and then . . . then you tell me that you love me . . . You, Natalia Petrovna—love me! I can feel my heart beating as it's never beaten before. And it's not wonder, not pride. What do I care about pride now? But I can't go like this, whatever you say!

NATALIA (*after a pause, as if to herself*). What have I done?

BELAEV. Please, please, believe me . . .

NATALIA (*in a different voice*). Mr. Belaev, if I didn't know you to be an honorable man, a man who wouldn't stoop to lying, I wouldn't know what to think. Perhaps I would have regretted my frankness. But I trust you. I don't want to hide anything from you—I'm grateful to you for what you have just told me. I understand now why we haven't become close. It wasn't me personally who intimidated you, just my position. (*Stops.*) So much the better—now I shall find it easier to part from you. Good-by. (*Makes a movement to leave.*)

BELAEV (*after a pause*). I know I can't stay here, but I can't convey to you what's going on inside me. You love me! It even frightens me to say those words. This is all so new to me. It's as if I were seeing you, hearing you speak, for the first time, but there's one thing I'm sure of—I must leave. I feel I couldn't be responsible for what would happen.

NATALIA (*in a weak voice*). Yes, Belaev, you must leave. Now that we've discussed the whole matter, you can go. But can it really be that, after all I've done . . . Oh, believe me, if I could have foreseen all that you have told me now, this confession of mine would have died within me. I only wanted to clear up all these misunderstandings. I wanted to confess, to punish myself. I wanted to snap the last thread clean. If I'd had any idea . . . (*She covers her face with her hands.*)

BELAEV. I believe you, I believe you. Why, only fifteen minutes ago, I myself could never have imagined . . . Today, when I saw you before dinner, for the first time I felt something unusual, something quite new, as if a hand had caught my heart in its grip and my chest was afire. It's true, before that, I felt intimidated by you. I even thought I didn't like you. But when you told me today that Vera had the impression . . . (*Stops.*)

NATALIA (*with an involuntary smile of happiness on her lips*). Enough, enough. We shouldn't even think about it. We mustn't forget that we are talking to each other for the last time, that tomorrow you are leaving.

BELAEV. Oh, yes! Tomorrow I shall leave! I can still leave now. We'll get over this. You see, I don't want to exaggerate. I'll leave, and we'll just have to hope for the best. I will take nothing with me but a memory—I shall always remember that you fell in love with me. But how could I not have got to know you until now? Now you're looking at me and I can't imagine there was ever a time when I avoided your eyes, when I felt awkward in your presence.

NATALIA (*smiling*). But you just told me you were still afraid of me.

BELAEV. I? (*After a pause.*) Exactly. I'm amazed at myself. I'm talking so boldly to you. I don't recognize myself.

NATALIA. And you're sure you're not deluding yourself?

BELAEV. About what?

NATALIA. About your being ... (*Shuddering.*) Oh Lord, what am I doing? Listen, Belaev, help me. When has a woman ever found herself in such a position? I no longer have the strength, really ... Perhaps it's all to the good that it should come to an end so abruptly, but at least we've got to know each other. Give me your hand—and good-by forever.

BELAEV (*taking her hand*). I don't know how to say good-by to you now. My heart is overflowing. I wish you ... (*Stops and presses her hand to his lips.*) Good-by. (*Moves toward the garden door.*)

NATALIA (*looking after him*). Belaev ...

BELAEV (*turning*). Yes?

NATALIA (*after a pause, in a weak voice*). Stay.

BELAEV. What?

NATALIA. Stay, and let God be our judge! (*She hides her face in her hands.*)

BELAEV (*quickly crossing to her and stretching out his arms*). Natalia ...

(*At this moment the garden door opens and* RAKITIN *appears in the doorway. He stares at them for a moment, then briskly crosses to them.*)

RAKITIN (*loudly*). We've been looking for you everywhere, Natalia. (NATALIA *and* BELAEV *look round.*)

NATALIA (*taking her hands away from her face and apparently regaining control*). Oh, it's you. Who's looking for me? (BELAEV, *confused, bows to* NATALIA *and starts to leave.*) You're going, Mr. Belaev? Well, don't forget—you know ... (*He bows to her again and goes out into the garden.*)

RAKITIN. Your husband is looking for you. I must say I didn't expect to find you here. I was just going by ...

NATALIA (*smiling*). And you heard our voices. I met Mr. Belaev here ... and we had a little talk. Today, it seems, is a day for talks. But now we can go back to the house. (*Goes toward the door to the corridor.*)

RAKITIN (*a little agitated*). May I ask what decision?

NATALIA (*feigning surprise*). What decision? I don't understand.

RAKITIN (*sadly, after a long silence*). Then, in that case, I understand everything.

NATALIA. Here we go again! More mysterious hints! Well, all right, I had a talk with him and now everything's back to normal again. It was all nothing, exaggeration, and all that you and I were discussing before is just childish nonsense. Let's forget it once and for all.

RAKITIN. I'm not cross-examining you, Natalia.

NATALIA (*forcing herself to sound relaxed*). Now what was it I wanted to tell you? I've forgotten. Well, what's the difference? Let's go. It's all finished with . . . over.

RAKITIN (*gazing fixedly at her*). Yes, it's all over. How annoyed you must be with yourself now for your frankness earlier. (*He turns away.*)

NATALIA. Rakitin . . . (*He meets her eyes again. She appears at a loss for words.*) You haven't spoken to Arkady yet?

RAKITIN. No, not yet. I haven't had time to prepare for it. You must realize I have to invent something.

NATALIA. Ah, this is unbearable! What do they want of me? They watch my every step. Rakitin, really, I must apologize to you.

RAKITIN. Oh, please don't worry, Natalia. Why should you? It's just the normal course of things. But it's rather obvious that Belaev is something of a novice in this role. He really shouldn't have become so panicky and fled like that. Well, never mind, given a little time . . . (*Quickly, in a low voice.*) you'll both learn to sham. (*Loudly.*) Let's go now. (NATALIA *moves toward him, then stops. At that moment,* ISLAEV's *voice is heard outside the garden door: "You say he went this way?" Then* ISLAEV *and the* DOCTOR *enter.*)

ISLAEV. You're right, here he is. Oh, and I see Natalia's here, too! (*Crosses to her.*) What is this—a continuation of this morning's talk? It's evidently an important subject.

RAKITIN. I ran into Natalia here . . .

ISLAEV. Ran into her? (*Looking around.*) Very likely. A real thoroughfare here!

NATALIA. Well, you came in here yourself.

ISLAEV. I came here because . . . (*Stops.*)

NATALIA. You were looking for me?

ISLAEV (*after a pause*). Yes, I was. Don't you want to come back to the house now? The tea's ready and it's getting dark.

NATALIA (*taking his arm*). Yes, let's go.

ISLAEV (*looking around*). You know, we could make two good rooms for the gardeners out of this pavilion, or another servant's room. What do you think, Doctor?

DOCTOR. Sure you could.

ISLAEV. Let's go through the garden, Natalia. (*Crosses to the garden door. Throughout the entire scene, he has not once looked at* RAKITIN. *In the doorway, he turns half-way around.*) Well, what are you waiting for, fellows? Let's go and have our tea.

(*Exits with* NATALIA.)

DOCTOR (*to* RAKITIN). Well, Rakitin, shall we go? Evidently you and I are to bring up the rear.

RAKITIN (*with feeling*). Ah, Doctor, Doctor, I must say, I'm sick and tired of you.

DOCTOR (*with feigned amiability*). Ah, well, if you only knew how sick and tired I am of myself! (RAKITIN *can't help smiling.*)

(*They exit through the garden door.*)

CURTAIN

ACT V

The same as in Acts I and III. Morning. Islaev sits at the table looking over some papers. He rises abruptly.

ISLAEV. No! I just can't get down to work today. I feel as if a nail had been driven into my head. (*Pacing up and down.*) Well, I certainly didn't expect this; never thought I'd be worried like this. The whole question is what I should do—that's what I have to decide. (*Grows thoughtful, then suddenly calls out.*) Matvei!

MATVEI (*entering*). Yes, sir?

ISLAEV. Call the manager, I want to see him. Yes, and tell them to hold on and not start digging at the dam until I get there. Right, you can go.

MATVEI. Very good, sir. (*Exits.*)

ISLAEV (*crossing to the table again and leafing through the papers*). Yes, I have a real problem here!

ANNA SEMYONOVNA (*entering and moving toward* ISLAEV). Arkady . . .

ISLAEV. Ah, it's you, Mother. How are you today?

ANNA SEMYONOVNA (*sitting down on the sofa*). I'm fine, thank God. (*Sighs.*) I'm fine. (*Sighs again, louder.*) Thank God. (*Seeing that* ISLAEV *is not listening to her, she sighs very deeply, emitting a slight moan.*)

ISLAEV. Why are you sighing? What's the matter?

ANNA SEMYONOVNA (*sighing again, but less deeply this time*). Oh, Arkady, as if you didn't know why.

Islaev. What do you mean?

Anna Semyonovna (*after a pause*). I'm your mother, Arkady. Well, I know you're a grown man already, with plenty of sense, but I'm your mother just the same. How much there is in that one little word *mother*!

Islaev. Please, Mother, say what you have to say.

Anna Semyonovna. You know very well what I have in mind, my dear. Natalia—oh, of course, she's wonderful and up till now her behavior has been absolutely beyond reproach. But she's still so young, Arkady! And, as you know, young people . . .

Islaev. I know what you're trying to say. You think that her relations with Rakitin . . .

Anna Semyonovna. God forbid! Nothing of the sort even occurred to me.

Islaev. You didn't let me finish. You think there's something a little unusual about her relations with Rakitin. Secret conferences, tears—you think there's something strange about it.

Anna Semyonovna. Well, and what did he tell you, in the end? What was their conversation about? He hasn't told me a thing.

Islaev. I haven't asked him, Mother, and he doesn't seem to be in any hurry to satisfy my curiosity.

Anna Semyonovna. So what do you intend to do now?

Islaev. Why nothing.

Anna Semyonovna. What do you mean, nothing?

Islaev. Exactly what I say. Nothing.

Anna Semyonovna (*getting up*). Well, I must say, I'm surprised. Of course, you're the master in your own house and know better than I what's good and what's bad in what's going on. However, think of the consequences.

Islaev. Really, Mother, I think you're all excited about nothing.

Anna Semyonovna. But, my dear, as a mother . . . (*Pause.*) Well, I had thought of offering to act as a go-between.

Islaev (*with feeling*). No, as far as that goes, I must ask you not to trouble yourself, Mother. I'd appreciate it very much.

Anna Semyonovna. Whatever you say, Arkady. I'll not say another word. I've done my duty. I've warned you, and from now on, I'll keep my mouth shut. (*A brief pause.*)

Islaev. You won't be driving out anywhere today?

Anna Semyonovna. But I must warn you, my dear, you're too trusting. You judge others too much by yourself. Believe me, real friends are all too rare in this day and age.

Islaev (*impatiently*). Oh, Mother . . .

Anna Semyonovna. All right, all right, I won't say a word. Indeed, what business does an old woman like me have mixing up in it? I must really be getting soft in the head! Of course, I was brought up on different principles and, heaven knows, I tried to instill them in you. Well, well, you have work to do. I won't get in your way. I'm going. (*Crosses to door, then stops.*) So? Well, do what you wish. (*Exits.*)

ISLAEV (*looking after her*). Ah, it's amazing how even those who love you enjoy poking at your wounds with all their fingers, one after the other! And the funny thing about it is that they're convinced that they're relieving your pain. Ah well, I don't hold it against Mother; she means well. And how can she help wanting to give advice? Anyway, that's not the problem here. (*Sitting down.*) What shall I do? (*Becoming thoughtful, he gets up.*) Ah, the simpler the better! I'm no good at diplomatic finesse. I'd be the first to get myself tangled up in it. (*Rings the bell.* MATVEI *enters.*) Is Mr. Rakitin in the house, do you know?

MATVEI. Yes, sir. I saw Mr. Rakitin in the billiard room a moment ago.

ISLAEV. Oh good, well ask him to step in here a minute then.

MATVEI. Very good, sir. (*Exits.*)

ISLAEV (*pacing back and forth*). I'm not used to this sort of mess. I hope to God we're not going to have too much of it. I may be strong but I can't stand up under this sort of thing. (*Places a hand on his chest.*) Brr!

(RAKITIN *enters from the ballroom, looking embarrassed.*)

RAKITIN. You wanted to see me?

ISLAEV. Yes. (*Pause.*) After all, Michel, you owe me something.

RAKITIN. I do?

ISLAEV. What do you mean? Can you really have forgotten your promise about . . . Natalia's crying, and in general . . . Well, when Mother and I found you, remember, you said that you had some *secret,* the two of you, and that you'd explain it all.

RAKITIN. A secret, I said?

ISLAEV. That's what you said.

RAKITIN. But what kind of secret could we have between us? We had a talk.

ISLAEV. What about? And why was she crying?

RAKITIN. You know, Arkady, there are moments in the life of every woman, even if she is perfectly happy.

ISLAEV. Wait, Rakitin, enough of this. I can't bear to see you in such a position. Your embarrassment weighs on me more than on you yourself. (*Taking his hand.*) We're old friends, aren't we? We've known each other since we were boys—I'm not good at shamming, and you've always been frank with me, too. Let me ask you one question. And first of all, I give you my word I won't doubt the sincerity of your answer for a moment. Well then, do you love my wife? (RAKITIN *glances at him.*) You understand—do you love her like . . . well, in a word, do you love her in a way that it would be difficult to admit to her husband?

RAKITIN (*in a toneless voice, after a pause*). Yes, I love your wife . . . in that way.

ISLAEV (*also after a pause*). Thank you, Michel, for being frank about it. You're an honorable man. But, all the same, what are we going to do now? Sit down, let's talk the matter over, the two of us. (RAKITIN *sits down.* ISLAEV *paces the room.*) I know Natalia; I know what a marvelous person she is. And I don't have any delusions about myself. I can't compete with you, Michel—no, don't interrupt me, please—I'm not your equal: you're more intelligent than I am and nicer, and better company too, when you come down to it. I'm just an ordinary man but Natalia loves me—at least, I think she does. But she has eyes to see after all, and how could she help liking you. And I'll tell you something else—I noticed your mutual attraction long ago. But I've always trusted you both completely and as long as things didn't come to a head. . . . Ah, I don't know how to put it! (*Stops.*) But, after yesterday's little scenes, after your second meeting in the evening, what can I do? If, at least, I'd been alone when I surprised you—but no, there were witnesses involved, my mother and that crook of a doctor. Well then, what have you got to say, Michel?

RAKITIN. You're absolutely right, Arkady.

ISLAEV. It's not a question of who's right, but of what's to be done about it. I must tell you, Michel, I may be a plain man but I know better than to ruin someone else's life—and that there are times when it's a sin to insist on one's rights. And don't think I got that out of a book either. My conscience tells me it's so. To leave a person free . . . well, it's all right to leave a person free, but we have to think this whole matter through carefully first. It's too important.

RAKITIN (*getting up*). I've already thought it all out.

ISLAEV. What d'you mean?

RAKITIN. I must leave. I'm leaving.

ISLAEV (*after a pause*). You think you should? Just like that, walk out on us for good?

RAKITIN. Yes.

ISLAEV (*pacing the room again*). That's some decision to take. And yet, perhaps you're right. We'll miss you. And, God knows, perhaps it won't accomplish anything anyway. But you're in the best position to decide. Seems to me it's the right thing to do. You present a danger to me. (*Smiling sadly.*) Yes, you're a real threat. Here, I just this minute said . . . you know, about leaving a person free. But it would have killed me! For me, life without Natalia would be unthinkable. And there's another thing—for some time, and especially during the last few days, I've noticed a great change in her. She's deeply perturbed about something all the time, and that worries me. Isn't it so? I'm not imagining it, am I?

RAKITIN (*bitterly*). No, you're not imagining it!

ISLAEV. You see! So you're leaving then?

RAKITIN. Yes.

ISLAEV. Hmm. But how suddenly this has all descended upon us! No wonder you were so confused when mother and I burst in on you like that.

MATVEI (*entering*). The manager is here, sir.

ISLAEV. Tell him to wait! (*Exit* MATVEI.) Look, Michel, you won't go away for long, uh? After all, it's nothing, man!

RAKITIN. I really don't know, but I think it'll be for a long time.

ISLAEV. But, wait, you don't take me for an Othello or something, do you? Really, I don't think any two friends can ever have had such a conversation since the world began! So, you see, we can't just part like this . . .

RAKITIN (*shaking hands with him*). Let me know when it's all right for me to come back.

ISLAEV. Ah, who is there here to replace you? You don't imagine Bolshintsov could, do you?

RAKITIN. There are others.

ISLAEV. Who? That pretentious idiot Krinitsyn? Belaev's a pleasant enough young fellow, of course, but he can't hold a candle to you!

RAKITIN (*scathingly*). You think not? You don't know him, Arkady. You keep an eye on him. Take my advice. You hear me? He's a most remarkable man!

ISLAEV. Bah! And you and Natalia were wanting to take him in hand, remember? (*Glancing toward the door.*) That's him coming this way now. (*Hurriedly.*) Well then, my dear fellow, it's settled. You'll leave for a little while, some day soon. There's no rush—we must prepare Natalia for it. I'll reassure my mother. And I wish you the best of luck! You've lifted a weight from my heart. Embrace me, my friend! (*Hastily embraces him and then turns toward* BELAEV *as he approaches.*) Ah, it's you. Well, well, how's everything?

BELAEV. Fine thank you, sir.

ISLAEV. Well, but where's Kolia?

BELAEV. He's with Herr Schaaf.

ISLAEV. Oh good! (*Takes his hat.*) Well, good-by for now, gentlemen. I haven't done a thing yet today. Haven't been to the dam or to the construction site either. And what's more, I haven't done my paperwork. (*Takes papers and puts them under his arm.*) Bye now! Matvei! Matvei! Come with me! (*Exits.* RAKITIN *remains wrapped in thought, front stage.*)

BELAEV (*crossing to* RAKITIN). How are you today, Mr. Rakitin?

RAKITIN. Thank you, as usual. And you?

BELAEV. I'm fine.

RAKITIN. One can see that!

BELAEV. What do you mean?

RAKITIN. Nothing . . . you're a picture of well-being. Ah, and I see you're wearing a new coat today. And what's this—a flower in your buttonhole! (BELAEV, *blushing, pulls it out.*) But why did you do that? Really, it's very nice. (*After a pause.*) By the way, Belaev, I'll be going into town tomorrow if you need anything.

BELAEV. Tomorrow?

RAKITIN. Yes and from there I may go on to Moscow.

BELAEV (*surprised*). To Moscow? But I thought you told me just yesterday that you were planning to stay here at least a month?

RAKITIN. Yes, but some business has come up . . .

BELAEV. Are you going for long?

RAKITIN. I don't know. Perhaps.

BELAEV. Does Natalia Petrovna know?

RAKITIN. No, but what makes you ask?

BELAEV (*a little confused*). No reason . . . just wondering.

RAKITIN (*after pausing and looking around*). Look here, Belaev, there's no one else in the room but the two of us, so don't you think it's rather stupid for us to go on playing this comedy?

BELAEV. I don't understand.

RAKITIN. Really now? You really don't know why I'm going away?

BELAEV. No, I don't.

RAKITIN. Strange. But I'm prepared to believe you. You may really not know. Would you like me to tell you why I'm going?

BELAEV. Please do.

RAKITIN. Well—now, I'm counting on your discretion. When you came in, you saw I was talking with Islaev. It was a quite important discussion and it's as a result of it that I'm leaving.

And do you know why? I'm telling you all this because I consider you a decent man. He's taken it into his head that I . . .
well, yes, that I'm in love with his wife. How does that strike
you? Quite an odd idea, isn't it? But I'm thankful to him for
coming straight to me instead of pretending and spying on us
and all that. Well, so tell me, what would you have done in
my place? Of course, his suspicions are without foundation, but
they've alarmed him. And a decent man must be willing to
suffer inconvenience for the sake of his friends' peace of mind.
So that's why I'm leaving. I'm sure you'll approve of my decision. Am I right in thinking you'd have done the same in my
place and left?

BELAEV (*after a pause*). Maybe.

RAKITIN. I'm very glad to hear it. Of course, there's no arguing that my leaving is ridiculous in a way—as if I considered
myself a threat—but you see, Belaev, a woman's honor is
sacred. And then—of course, I'm not saying this of Natalia
Petrovna—but I've known innocent, pure-hearted women, real
babes despite all their cleverness who, precisely because of that
purity and innocence, were more likely than others to give way
to a sudden passion. And so, who knows, in such cases, a little
extra caution can't do any harm, especially when . . . By the
way, Belaev, perhaps you still imagine that love is the world's
greatest blessing?

BELAEV (*coldly*). I haven't tried it yet, but I assume to be
loved by the woman you love is a very great happiness.

RÁKITIN. May you retain such a pleasant conviction for
many years! In my opinion, any love, happy or unhappy, is a
real affliction when you give yourself over to it entirely. You
wait! You may still find out how those gentle little hands can
torment you, with what solicitude they can rend your heart
hour by hour. You wait! You'll find out how much burning
hatred is concealed under the most ardent love! You'll remember
me when you're yearning for peace, for the dullest, emptiest
peace, like a sick man yearning for health; when you find yourself envying any man who is free and light-hearted. You wait!
You'll find out what it's like to be tied to a skirt, what it means
to be enslaved, infected—and what a shameful, exhausting
servitude it is! You'll find out in the end what a high price
one must pay sometimes for the merest trifles. But I don't
know why I'm telling you all this. You won't believe me, anyway. It's just that it's very important to me that you should
agree with me on this point. Yes, yes, one has to be very careful
on these occasions.

BELAEV (*who has kept his eyes fixed on* RAKITIN *the whole time*). Thank you for the lecture, Mr. Rakitin, although I wasn't in any need of it.

RAKITIN (*taking his arm*). Forgive me, please, I didn't intend. . . . I'm not in a position to give lessons to anyone. I just got carried away.

BELAEV (*with slight irony*). And there was nothing behind it?

RAKITIN (*a little embarrassed*). Right. There was nothing behind it. I only wanted to . . . So far, Belaev, you haven't had the opportunity to get to know women—they're a whimsical lot.

BELAEV. But whom do you have in mind, anyway?

RAKITIN. Why, no one in particular.

BELAEV. Just a general remark, right?

RAKITIN (*with a forced smile*). Perhaps. I really don't know how I came to fall into this lecturing tone, but as long as I've started, allow me to give you one piece of sound advice on parting. (*Stopping and waving his hand.*) Ah! But what kind of an advisor am I, anyway? Please excuse my talking your head off like this.

BELAEV. No, no, please go on.

RAKITIN. So, you don't need anything in town?

BELAEV. No, nothing, thank you. But I'm sorry you're leaving.

RAKITIN. Nice of you to say so. Believe me, I'm sorry, too. (NATALIA *and* VERA *enter from the study.* VERA *is very pale and looks sad.*) Nice meeting you. (*Again shakes hands with him.*)

NATALIA (*watching them for a moment and then going up to them*). Good-morning, gentlemen.

RAKITIN (*turning quickly*). Good morning, Natalia. Good morning, Vera. (BELAEV, *looking embarrassed, bows to* NATALIA *and then to* VERA, *in silence.*)

NATALIA (*to* RAKITIN). What have you been doing with yourself today?

RAKITIN. Nothing special.

NATALIA. Well, Vera and I have been out in the garden already. It's so nice out today. We walked under the limes and they smell so sweet. It's so pleasant to walk in the shade and listen to the bees buzzing over your head. (*Timidly to* BELAEV.) We were hoping we'd see you there. (BELAEV *doesn't answer.*)

RAKITIN (*to* NATALIA). Ah, I see that today you too are receptive to the beauties of Nature. (*After a pause.*) Belaev couldn't possibly join you in the garden—he's wearing his new coat.

BELAEV (*flaring up a little*). Well, of course, it's the only decent coat I have and it could get torn in the garden. But what did you mean by that?

RAKITIN (*blushing*). No, no, I didn't mean anything. (VERA *moves in silence to the sofa on the right, sits down and starts working on some embroidery.* NATALIA *gives* BELAEV *a forced smile. There is a short, rather painful silence, then* RAKITIN *continues with cutting casualness.*)

RAKITIN. Oh yes, I forgot to tell you, Natalia—I'm leaving today.

NATALIA (*a little anxiously*). You're leaving? Where are you going?

RAKITIN. I have to go to town on business.

NATALIA. Not for long I hope?

RAKITIN. That depends on how things go.

NATALIA. Well, mind you come back soon. (*To* BELAEV, *without looking at him.*) Belaev, were those your drawings Kolia was showing me? Did you do them?

BELAEV. Yes, I just did them to pass the time.

NATALIA. But they're charming. You have real talent.

RAKITIN. I see you discover new virtues in Mr. Belaev every day.

NATALIA (*coldly*). Perhaps. So much the better for him. (*To* BELAEV.) You probably have other drawings. Do show them to me some time. (BELAEV *bows.*)

RAKITIN (*who has been on pins and needles all this time*). Well, it occurs to me that it's time I went and packed. (*Goes toward ballroom door.*)

NATALIA PETROVNA (*after him*). But you'll come back to say good-by to us?

RAKITIN. Of course.

BELAEV (*after some hesitation*). Wait for me, Mr. Rakitin, I'll come with you. There's something I'd like to talk to you about.

RAKITIN. Oh really! (*They go out into the ballroom.* NATALIA *remains standing center stage for a while then goes and sits down on the left.*)

NATALIA (*after a few moments of silence*). Vera!

VERA (*without raising her head*). What?

NATALIA. For God's sake, Vera, don't be like this. Please Vera . . . (VERA *says nothing.* NATALIA *rises, crosses the stage and quietly kneels down in front of her.* VERA *tries to raise her to her feet, then turns away and covers her face with her hands.* NATALIA *speaks, still kneeling.*) Forgive me, Vera. Don't cry. I know I have wronged you but can't you forgive me?

VERA (*through tears*). Get up, get up.

NATALIA. Not until you forgive me. You're unhappy, I know, but is it any easier for me? Think of it, Vera, now that you know everything—the only difference between us is that you haven't wronged me, while I . . .

VERA (*bitterly*). The only difference! Oh no, there's another difference between you and me. You're so affectionate today, so kind and gentle . . .

NATALIA (*interrupting*). That's because I feel I'm guilty . . .

VERA. Really? Is that the only reason?

NATALIA (*getting up and sitting down beside her*). But what other reason could there be?

VERA. Oh, stop tormenting me! Don't ask!

NATALIA (*sighing*). Oh, I see you can't bring yourself to forgive me.

VERA. You're so kind and gentle today because you feel yourself loved.

NATALIA (*overcome with embarrassment*). Vera!

VERA (*turning toward her*). Well, it's the truth, isn't it?

NATALIA (*sadly*). Believe me, I'm just as unhappy as you are.

VERA. He loves you!

NATALIA. Why should we go on tormenting each other like this? It's time we came to our senses. Think of the predicament I'm in—that we're both in. Do you realize that two people here know our secret already—through my fault, of course. (*Stops.*) Wouldn't it be better if, instead of torturing each other with suspicions and reproaches, we tried to find a way out of this unbearable situation, a way to save ourselves? You must realize that I can't stand all this worry and upset. Or have you forgotten who I am? But you're not listening to me.

VERA (*looking down dreamily*). He loves you.

NATALIA. He's going away, Vera.

VERA (*turning her head*). Oh, leave me alone! (NATALIA *looks at her hesitatingly. At that moment*, ISLAEV'S *voice calls from the study*: "*Natalia, Natalia, where are you?*")

NATALIA (*quickly getting up and crossing to the study door*). Here I am. What do you want?

ISLAEV'S VOICE. Come here a minute, there's something I have to tell you.

NATALIA. Coming. (*She turns toward* VERA, *stretching out her hand.* VERA *doesn't stir.* NATALIA *sighs and goes out into the study*).

VERA (*alone, after a pause*). He loves her! And I have to stay here in her house! Oh, it's really too much! (*She covers her face with her hands and remains like that, motionless. The* DOCTOR'S *head appears in the ballroom doorway. He looks around carefully and then approaches* VERA *on tiptoe. She doesn't notice him.*)

DOCTOR (*placing himself in front of her with his arms crossed and a sarcastic smile on his face*). Ah, here you are, Vera!

VERA (*raising her head*). What? Oh, it's you, Doctor.

DOCTOR. What is it, young lady, aren't you well?

VERA. Yes, I'm all right.

DOCTOR. Let's feel your pulse. (*Does so.*) Hmm, so fast? Ah, Vera, Vera, you don't want to listen to my advice—and yet I've only your good at heart.

VERA (*looking at him firmly*). Doctor . . .

DOCTOR (*promptly*). I'm listening, Vera—oof, what a look! I'm listening.

VERA. The gentleman you mentioned—Bolshintsov—your friend, is he really a good man?

DOCTOR. My friend Bolshintsov? The best and nicest man in the world. An example to hold up to the virtuous.

VERA. He isn't bad-tempered, is he?

DOCTOR. The most easy-going person I've ever met. In fact, he's not a man, but dough you can mold in your hands. If you go searching with a lantern in broad daylight you won't find another such kind-hearted fellow anywhere. He's a lamb.

VERA. You can vouch for him?

DOCTOR (*placing one hand on his heart and raising the other*). As I would for myself!

VERA. In that case, you may tell him . . . I'm prepared to marry him.

DOCTOR (*in joyful amazement*). What? Can it be?

VERA. Yes, but I want it to be as soon as possible, d'you hear? As soon as possible.

DOCTOR. Tomorrow if you like. Well, well! Ah, Vera, you're a very smart young lady! I'll run and find him right away. Ah, how pleased he'll be! Well, this has really turned out most unexpectedly! You have no idea how he worships you, Vera.

VERA (*impatiently*). I'm not asking you about that.

DOCTOR. All right, Vera, all right. But I can tell you, you'll be happy with him. You'll thank me one day. (VERA *again makes an impatient gesture.*) All right, I won't say a word. So, may I really tell him?

VERA. Yes, you may.

DOCTOR. Wonderful. I'll be off right away. Good-by. (*Listens.*) Anyway, there's someone coming. (*Goes into the study, stopping in the doorway and making an astonished face.*) Good-by.
(*Exits.*)

VERA (*looking after him*). Anything at all, rather than stay here. (*Gets up.*) Yes, I've made up my mind. I won't remain in this house, not for anything. I can't bear her meek looks, her smiles. I can't stay here and watch her basking in her happiness. And she is happy, however much she may try to look sad and miserable. And really, her demonstrations of affection for me are more than I can stand.

(BELAEV *appears in the ballroom door, looks around, then crosses to* VERA.)

BELAEV (*softly*). Vera, are you alone?

VERA (*who looks round, trembling, then, after a pause, speaks*). Yes.

BELAEV. Good, I wouldn't have come in otherwise. I've come to say good-by, Vera.

VERA. To say good-by?

BELAEV. Yes, I'm leaving.

VERA. Leaving? You're leaving, too?

BELAEV. Yes, me too. (*In great inner agitation.*) Vera, you must see that I can't stay. I've caused enough trouble here as it is. Not only have I disturbed your peace of mind and Natalia Petrovna's too, without meaning to, but I've also caused a break between old friends. Because of me, Mr. Rakitin is leaving and you've quarreled with your guardian. It's time to put an end to the whole business. Once I've left, I hope, everything will quiet down again and return to normal. I didn't come here to turn the heads of wealthy ladies and young girls. You'll both forget me and after a while, perhaps, you'll wonder what it was all about. I can't understand it even now. I don't want to deceive you, Vera—I'm afraid, terribly afraid at the idea of staying here. I wouldn't be able to answer for myself, because, you know, I'm not used to this sort of thing at all. It makes me feel terribly awkward. I have the impression that everyone's looking at me all the time. And then, finally, it would be impossible for me now, with the two of you here . . .

VERA. Oh don't worry about me! I won't be here much longer.

BELAEV. What do you mean?

VERA. That's my business. But I won't be in your way, believe me.

BELAEV. So, you see, how could I possibly stay? Judge for yourself. It's as if I'd brought a plague down on this house—everyone's running away. It's I alone who should go, while there's still time. I've just had a long talk with Mr. Rakitin and you can't imagine how bitter he feels. He teased me about my new coat—and I deserved it! He's right. Yes, I must leave. Believe me, I can't wait for the moment when I'll be rolling along the high road in the wagon. I'm stifling here; I'm longing for some fresh air. I can't stand it, I feel so unhappy about it all and, at the same time, so relieved to be going. I'm like a man setting out on a long sea-journey—it makes him miserable to leave his friends and he's apprehensive before the unknown, and yet the waves lap so gaily against the shore, the wind blowing in his face is so fresh, that, by itself, the blood stirs in his veins, heavy though his heart may be. Yes, I'm definitely going. I'll go back to Moscow, rejoin my friends there, get down to work.

Vera. So I see you love her, Alexei. You love her and you're still leaving.

Belaev. Stop it, Vera. Why talk like that? Surely you can see that it's all over? It's all flared up and burned out in a flash. Let's part friends. It's time. I've come to my senses. Keep well, be happy, and we'll see each other again some time. I'll never forget you, Vera. I've become very attached to you, believe me. (*Shakes her hand and adds hurriedly.*) Please give Natalia Petrovna this note for me.

Vera (*looking at him embarrassed*). A note?

Belaev. Yes, I . . . I can't say good-by to her.

Vera. But are you leaving right away.

Belaev. Yes, I am. But only Rakitin knows about it and he thinks I'm doing the right thing. I'll go to Petrovsky from here on foot and I'll wait for Rakitin there, then we'll go on to town together. I'll write from there, and they'll send me on my things. You see, it's all arranged already. You can read the note if you want. It has only a couple of words in it anyway.

Vera (*taking the note from him*). So you're really going?

Belaev. Yes, yes. Give her the note and tell her . . . No, don't tell her anything. What would be the point? (*Listens.*) Someone's coming. Good-by. (*Dashes to the door where he stops for a moment, then rushes out. Vera remains where she is with the note in her hand.*)

(*Enter Natalia.*)

Natalia (*going up to Vera*). Vera dear . . . (*Glances at her and stops.*) What's the matter? (*Vera silently hands her the note.*) A note? Who's it from?

Vera (*tonelessly*). Read it.

Natalia. You worry me. (*Reads the note to herself, then suddenly presses her hands to her face and lets herself fall into an armchair. A long silence follows.*)

Vera (*moving closer to her*). Natalia Petrovna . . .

Natalia (*without taking her hands away from her face*). He's leaving! And without even saying good-by to me. Oh, oh! At least he said good-by to you.

Vera (*sadly*). He wasn't in love with me.

Natalia (*lowering her hands and getting up*). He has no right to leave like this. I want . . . He can't just . . . What entitles him to break off so stupidly? Does he want to show me he despises me? I . . . how can he know that I would never have been able to . . . (*Sits down in the armchair again.*) Oh, my God! My God!

VERA. But you yourself told me just a few moments ago that he ought to leave. Don't you remember?

NATALIA. Oh, everything's fine for you now. He's leaving. Now you and I are in the same boat. (*Her voice breaks.*)

VERA. Just now you said, and these are your very words: wouldn't it be better, instead of torturing each other, if the two of us tried to find a way out of this situation, a way to save ourselves? Well, now we've been saved.

NATALIA (*turning away from her, almost with hatred*). Ah . . .

VERA. I understand you, but don't worry—I'll not burden you with my presence much longer. We can't go on living together.

NATALIA (*raising her hand to extend it to her but then letting it fall in her lap*). Why do you say that, Vera? Surely you're not going to leave me too? You were quite right—we're safe now. It's all over. Everything's back to normal.

VERA (*coldly*). Don't worry. (*Looks at* NATALIA *in silence.* ISLAEV *enters from the study.*)

ISLAEV (*looking at* NATALIA, *then speaking in a low voice to* VERA). D'you mean to say she knows he's leaving?

VERA (*perplexed*). Yes, she knows.

ISLAEV (*to himself*). What was he in such a hurry about? (*Aloud.*) Natalia. (*He takes her hand and she raises her head.*) It's me, Natalia. (*She tries hard to smile.*) You're not well, my dear? I really think you ought to lie down for a while.

NATALIA. I'm all right, Arkady. It's nothing.

ISLAEV. But you're terribly pale. Come, do as I suggest. Have a little rest.

NATALIA. Well, I suppose you're right. (*She tries to get up but cannot.*)

ISLAEV (*helping her*). You see? (*She leans on his arm.*) Shall I help you to your room?

NATALIA. Oh, I'm not all that bad yet! Come, Vera. (*Goes toward the study.* RAKITIN *enters from the ballroom.* NATALIA *stops.*)

RAKITIN. Natalia, I've come to say . . .

ISLAEV (*interrupting*). Ah, Michel, come over here a minute. (*Leads him to one side and speaks to him with annoyance, in a low voice.*) Why did you have to tell her all at once like that? I did ask you, after all. What was the hurry? I found her all upset.

RAKITIN (*surprised*). What're you talking about?

ISLAEV. You told Natalia you were leaving.

RAKITIN. And you imagine that's what caused it?

ISLAEV. Sh! She's watching us. (*Loudly.*) Don't you want to go to your room and lie down a bit, Natalia?

NATALIA. Yes, I'm going.

RAKITIN. Good-by, Natalia! (NATALIA *takes hold of the door handle without answering him.*)

ISLAEV (*putting a hand on* RAKITIN'S *shoulder*). You know, Natalia, he's the best friend we ever had.

NATALIA (*with sudden passion*). Yes, I know, he's a wonderful person, you're all wonderful people, the whole lot of you, and yet . . . (*She abruptly covers her face with her hands, pushes the door open with her knee, and quickly leaves the room.* VERA *follows her out.* ISLAEV *silently sits down and leans his elbows on the table.*)

RAKITIN (*looking at him for a little while then shrugging his shoulders with a bitter smile*). Well, that puts me in a fine position! Really, refreshingly cool! Some way to part from someone who has loved her for four years! Fine, fine, the windbag has got what he was asking for! A good thing, too! It was high time such an unhealthy, anemic relationship came to an end. (*Aloud, to* ISLAEV.) Well then, good-by, Islaev.

ISLAEV (*raising his head. He has tears in his eyes*). Good-by, Rakitin. Ah, this is harder than I expected. It's like a sudden storm on a fine day. But time will smooth everything out. Anyway, thank you a thousand times, you're a true friend!

RAKITIN (*to himself, through clenched teeth*). This is too much. (*Sharply loud.*) Good-by. (*Goes toward the ballroom door but runs into the* DOCTOR *who is coming in.*)

DOCTOR. What's happened? I was told Natalia was sick.

ISLAEV (*getting up*). Who told you that?

DOCTOR. The girl . . . the maid.

ISLAEV. No, it's nothing, Doctor. I think it's best not to disturb her right now.

DOCTOR. Oh, that's fine then! (*To* RAKITIN.) I hear you're going into town?

RAKITIN. Yes, on business.

DOCTOR. Oh, on business!

(*At this moment,* ANNA SEMYONOVNA, LIZAVETA BOGDANOVNA, KOLIA *and* SCHAAF *hurry in from the ballroom.*)

ANNA SEMYONOVNA. What's happened? What's the matter with Natalia?

KOLIA. What's the matter with Mama?

ISLAEV. There's nothing the matter with her. She was here a minute ago. What's the matter with all of you?

ANNA SEMYONOVNA. But, Arkady, we were told Natalia was sick.

ISLAEV. Well, you shouldn't have believed it.

Anna Semyonovna. Why take it like that? Our concern is perfectly natural.

Islaev. Yes, of course, of course.

Rakitin. Well, I suppose it's time for me to go.

Anna Semyonovna. You're leaving?

Rakitin. Yes, I'm leaving.

Anna Semyonovna (*to herself*). Ah, now I understand.

Kolia (*to* Islaev). Papa . . .

Islaev. What do you want?

Kolia. Why did Mr. Belaev go?

Islaev. Go? Where has he gone?

Kolia. I don't know. He just gave me a kiss, put on his cap and went out. But it's time for my Russian lesson now.

Islaev. Well, he'll probably be right back. Anyway, we can send someone after him.

Rakitin (*to* Islaev *in a low voice*). Don't do that, Arkady, he won't be coming back. (Anna Semyonovna *tries to overhear what he is saying. The* Doctor *and* Lizaveta Bogdanovna *exchange whispers.*)

Islaev. What on earth is this all about?

Rakitin. He's leaving, too.

Islaev. Leaving? Where's he going?

Rakitin. To Moscow.

Islaev. How can he be going to Moscow? Has everyone gone out of his mind today?

Rakitin (*lowering his voice still further*). Confidentially, Vera has fallen in love with him. Well, so, being a decent man, he's decided to go away. (Islaev *spreads his arms wide, then drops into an armchair.*) So now you see why . . .

Islaev (*jumping up again*). I see nothing. My head's spinning with all this. How on earth can I make out anything? Everyone's scuttling off, this one here, that one there, like a lot of partridge. And all because they're decent people. And it all has to happen on one and the same day.

Anna Semyonovna (*coming up to them from one side*). What's that? You say Mr. Belaev . . . ?

Islaev (*shouting nervously*). It's nothing, Mother, nothing! Schaaf, please take over from Belaev and look after Kolia. Please, take him upstairs now.

Schaaf. Yez, Herr Izlaev. (*Takes* Kolia's *hand.*)

Kolia. But, Papa . . .

Islaev (*shouting*). Go on, go on! (Schaaf *takes* Kolia *out of the room.*) I'll come a bit of the way with you, Rakitin. I'm going to tell them to saddle a horse and I'll meet you by the dam. And while I'm away, Mother, please, for heaven's sake, leave

Natalia alone—and you too, Doctor. Matvei, Matvei! (*Goes out hurriedly.* ANNA SEMYONOVNA *sits down looking dignified and hurt.* LIZAVETA BOGDANOVNA *stations herself behind her chair.* ANNA SEMYONOVNA *raises her eyes to heaven, as if she wished to have nothing further to do with it all.*)

DOCTOR (*furtively and craftily to* RAKITIN). Well, Rakitin, can I give you a lift as far as the highway with my new team?

RAKITIN. What, you mean you have the horses already?

DOCTOR (*modestly*). Vera and I talked the matter over . . . So would you like a lift?

RAKITIN. Sure! (*Bows to* ANNA SEMYONOVNA.) Anna Semyonovna, may I have the honor . . .

ANNA SEMYONOVNA (*maintaining her stately air and remaining seated*). Good-by, Mr. Rakitin. I hope you have a good journey.

RAKITIN. Thank you very much. Lizaveta Bogdanovna . . . (*Bows to her. She curtsies to him. He goes out through the ballroom door.*)

DOCTOR (*kissing* ANNA SEMYONOVNA's *hand*). Good-by, Ma'am.

ANNA SEMYONOVNA (*a little less majestically but still sternly*). Are you leaving too, Doctor?

DOCTOR. Yes, I am. My patients, you know . . . And then, my presence is no longer needed here. (*Bows to them, winking discreetly at* LIZAVETA BOGDANOVNA, *who smiles at him.*) Good-by. (*Runs out after* RAKITIN.)

ANNA SEMYONOVNA (*waiting till he has left, then, crossing her arms, turning slowly to* LIZAVETA BOGDANOVNA). And you, my dear, what do you make of all this business?

LIZAVETA BOGDANOVNA (*sighing*). I really don't know what to say.

ANNA SEMYONOVNA. You know Belaev's leaving, too?

LIZAVETA BOGDANOVNA (*sighing again*). Well, it's very possible that I won't be here for very much longer either. I too am leaving. (ANNA SEMYONOVNA *looks at her in absolute amazement.* LIZAVETA BOGDANOVNA *stands in front of her with her eyes lowered.*)

CURTAIN

The Thunderstorm

A DRAMA IN FIVE ACTS

by
ALEXANDER OSTROVSKY

The Thunderstorm was first performed at the Moscow Maly
Theater on November 16, 1859, and published in a literary magazine in January 1860. It was immediately acclaimed as the playwright's masterpiece, and the critic Dobroliubov set a model for
its interpretation in his essay "The beam of light in the realm
of darkness." In his previous article on Alexander Ostrovsky's comedies Dobroliubov defined the kingdom of darkness as
the patriarchal world of Russian merchants and middle-class
tradesmen, ruled by paternalistic traditions, prejudice, religious
rigidity and petty despotism. In his opinion the dramatic colli-
sions in Ostrovsky's plays were always provoked by the clash between the two opposing camps—the old and the young, the
rich and the poor, the willful ones and the meek ones. In *The
Thunderstorm* Ostrovsky depicted again the prison-like atmosphere of a small town on the banks of the Volga River, enslaved by conservatism and backwardness. In the figures of Dikoy
and Kabanova he brought out the ignorance, the ruthlessness and
the obtuseness of those wealthy masters who behave like poten-
tates and dictate the law to their subordinates. "If I decide
to forgive you, I'll forgive you," said Dikoy, "and if decide to
step on you, I'll crush you." Katerina, the heroine of the drama,
and the daughter-in-law of Kabanova, cannot stand the stifling
air of her new family; she is a sensitive, poetic nature, seeking
happiness and love. Her short-lived passion for Boris, during
the absence of her husband, is simply the expression of her
yearnings for freedom and for escape. Dobroliubov saw Katerina as a positive, creative and deeply national character.
She cannot accept her environment; she rejects the kingdom of
darkness. It is true that she falls its victim, but her suicide is a
form of protest. The very appearance of such a woman as
Katerina among the Dikoys and Kabanovs was a hopeful sign;
the kingdom of darkness was doomed, and this feeling made the
play rather optimistic despite all its tragic accents.

Dobroliubov's point of view was expressed so convincingly
that it was accepted without much discussion by his contemporaries, and it dominated all further analysis of *The
Thunderstorm*. Only toward the end of the nineteenth century

when the topical interest of the play had diminished did the critics and actors attempt a fresh approach to it. They became aware that Katerina was an ardent nature and a pure heart, and that her tragedy lay in the clash between idealistic illusion and coarse reality. The religious, mystical young woman who dreams of beauty and harmony is hurt not only by the oppressive rules established by Kabanova but also by the subserviency of her spineless husband and by the flightiness and lack of courage of her fickle lover. She is still under the influence of religious prohibitions and is tormented by her sin of adultery—hence her suicide as an act of repentance and also as a way out of an impossible situation: she knows what kind of life awaits her under Kabanova's domination. And it is rather difficult to see any sunbeam in this dark and poignant human tragedy.

It is significant that the natural settings of *The Thunderstorm* acquire a dramatic and symbolic significance. There is a deliberate link between the landscape of the play and its plot. The theme of *The Thunderstorm* is brought in by Kuligin, the self-made man, the mechanic who talks of lightning rods to the ignorant Dikoy, and it is during the raging tempest that Katerina makes her public confession and finally throws herself into the river. There is a kinship between the elemental force of nature and the elemental passions of Katerina. And the symbolic value of the landscape is emphasized by the appearance of a mad lady who walks through the stage repeating dire threats. The feeling of a "horror of life" is undoubtedly present in this Russian tragedy.

The high quality of *The Thunderstorm* is sustained by rich dialogue which takes on poetic charm in Katerina's speeches, and by the individualized portrayal of all the characters. No wonder the work became extremely popular not only with audiences but also with the players. For decades Katerina was a supreme test for actresses, many of whose careers were made or destroyed by their impersonation of this complex young woman. Katerina is still one of the favorite figures of the Russian repertory. The most memorable productions of *The Thunderstorm* in the twentieth century were the pre-revolutionary performances directed by Kommissarzhevsky and Meyerhold in 1915, and after the revolution by Tairov in 1924.

The Thunderstorm

CHARACTERS

DIKOY, a merchant and an important figure in the town
BORIS, his nephew, a fairly well-educated young man
MRS. KABANOV, a rich merchant's widow
BARBARA, her daughter
TIKHON, her son
KATERINA, his wife
KULIGIN, a self-taught watchmaker, trying to discover perpetual motion
VANIA KUDRASH, a young man, Dikoy's clerk
SHAPKIN, a tradesman
FEKLUSHA, a pilgrim-woman
GLASHA, a maid at the Kabanovs'
A LADY, a half-mad old woman of 70, attended by two footmen
TOWNSPEOPLE, of both sexes

The action takes place in the town of Kalinov on the banks of the Volga, in summertime. There is an interval of ten days between Acts III and IV. All except BORIS wear Russian-style clothes.

ACT I

A public park atop the steep bank of the Volga. Beyond the Volga, a stretch of rural scenery. On stage, two benches and a few bushes. Kuligin is sitting on a bench gazing out across the river. Vania and Shapkin are strolling about.

KULIGIN (*singing*). Upon a velvet hilltop
    Among the valleys low . . . (*Stops singing.*)
It's a real wonder, I swear. I'm telling you, Vania, I've come here to look at the Volga every day for fifty years now and I still can't get my fill of looking.

VANIA. What d'you mean?

KULIGIN. What an incredible view! Such beauty, it makes my heart sing.

VANIA. You don't say!

KULIGIN. It's a marvel and that's all you have to say! Either you're so used to it you don't see it any more or you just have no feel for all the beauty there is in nature.

VANIA. Ah, what's the good trying to talk to you. You're a real showpiece around here, a chemist!

KULIGIN. No, an engineer, a self-taught one.

VANIA. It all comes to the same thing. (*Silence.*)

KULIGIN (*pointing to one side*). Take a look, Vania, who's that flailing his arms about over there?

VANIA. Why, that's Dikoy bawling out his nephew.

KULIGIN. Fine place he picked!

VANIA. Doesn't make any difference to him where he does it. There's nothing to stop him. He has Boris to take it out on now and he really makes the most of it.

SHAPKIN. You won't find another bully like our Mr. Dikoy, no matter how hard you look. It don't take nothing to make him tear into a man.

VANIA. He's real mean!

SHAPKIN. And that Kabanov woman's not so hot either!

VANIA. Yes, but she at least makes out she does it because she's religious like, respectable, while this one's like a vicious dog that's broken loose.

SHAPKIN. There's no one to keep a hold on him, so he just goes storming around.

VANIA. Ah, what we need's a few more fellows like me around—we'd soon cure him of his tricks.

SHAPKIN. And what would you do?

VANIA. We'd give him a good scare.

SHAPKIN. How'd you do that?

VANIA. A bunch of four or five of us would just have a little talk with him, you know, face to face, in an alley somewhere, and he'd turn silky soft in no time. What's more, he wouldn't dare breathe a word to nobody about the lesson we'd given him and he'd keep a sharp eye out wherever he went after that.

SHAPKIN. Ah, now I see he had a point wanting to send you in the army.

VANIA. All right, he wanted to but he didn't and so I'm here. He won't send me now because he's got a feeling in his stomach that he'd not get off lightly if he tried. He may be a terror to you, but me, I know how to talk to him.

SHAPKIN. Is that so?

VANIA. What d'you mean, is that so? Everybody knows I don't take no nonsense from him or anyone else. But he still keeps me on, don't he? Must be because he needs me, then. So I've got no reason to be scared of him—let him be scared of me.

SHAPKIN. As if he didn't call you names whenever he feels like it!

VANIA. Of course he does. Swearing's like breathing to him. But I don't let him get away with it. Every word he says, I give him back ten, so he just gets disgusted and gives up. You won't catch me knuckling under to him.

KULIGIN. What's the sense following his example? I'd rather just put up with it than be like him.

VANIA. Well then, if you're so smart, you teach him manners first and then come and tell us how you done it. It's a pity those daughters of his are just kids. Ah, if only one of them was grown-up!

SHAPKIN. And what if one was?

VANIA. I'd have shown him. I know how to handle myself with dames.

(DIKOY *and* BORIS *walk past;* KULIGIN *takes off his cap.*)

SHAPKIN (*to* VANIA). Let's make ourselves scarce or who says he won't pick on us. (*They move off.*)

DIKOY. So you thought you'd come here and loaf, you good-for-nothing sponger! Like hell I'll let you!

BORIS. But it's a holiday today. What's there for me to do in the house?

DIKOY. You'd find plenty to do if you looked around. I've warned you once and I've warned you twice: stay out of my way! But with you, it goes in one ear and out the other. What's the matter, isn't there enough room for you here? Wherever I go, there you are already. Ah, damn you, you fool, what're you standing there like a post for? Well, d'you hear me?

BORIS. Yes, I hear you. What more can I do?

DIKOY (*looking at him*). Get out of my sight! I don't even want to talk to a Jesuit like you. (*He walks away.*) What did you have to come and hang around my neck for?

(*Spits in disgust and exits.*)

KULIGIN. How can you have anything to do with him, sir? We here just can't understand it. Why d'you want to stay with him and put up with all that?

BORIS. Who's talking of wanting, Kuligin. I don't have any choice.

KULIGIN. But, if you don't mind me asking, sir, why don't you? If you can tell us why, sir, please do.

Boris. Why shouldn't I tell you? Did you know my grandmother, Anfisa Mikhailovna?

Kuligin. How could I help knowing her?

Vania. We sure did.

Boris. Well then, she quarreled with my father because he married a lady. And so my parents went to live in Moscow. My mother used to say she couldn't stand my father's family after she'd spent three days with them, they seemed such a bunch of savages to her.

Kuligin. I'm not surprised she should've felt like that, sir. You've gotta be used to their ways, sir.

Boris. Well, my parents gave us a good education in Moscow —they didn't grudge us a thing. They sent me to business school there and my sister to a girls' boarding school, but then they both got cholera and died suddenly, and my sister and I were left orphans. Then we heard that our grandmother here had died too, and that in her will she'd provided that our uncle should pay us our share when we came of age—on one condition.

Kuligin. What condition, sir?

Boris. That we treat him with respect.

Kuligin. Well, in that case, sir, you'll never see your inheritance.

Boris. Worse than that! First he'll vent his spite on us, insult us on the slightest pretext, and then in the end he still won't give us anything except perhaps a token payment. And even then, he'll claim he gave us that out of the kindness of his heart, that we really weren't entitled to it either.

Vania. Well, that's the way the merchants are around here. And then, even if you do treat him with respect, what's to stop him saying you don't?

Boris. Yes, of course. Every so often, even now, he says: "I've my own kids—why should I give money to strangers and take it away from my own flesh and blood?"

Kuligin. So I see it's a bad business for you, sir!

Boris. If it was just me, I wouldn't care. I'd give up the whole thing and leave. But there's my sister, you see. He sent for her to come too, but our relatives on my mother's side wouldn't let her go. They wrote back that she was sick. I wouldn't even want to think what kind of a life she'd have here.

Vania. You're right there! A man like Mr. Dikoy sure don't know how to treat people decent.

Kuligin. So, what's your actual position in his house, sir?

Boris. No position whatever. "You live here," he told me, "and do what you're told to do and I'll decide what I'll pay you." That means that a year from now he'll fix whatever sum suits him.

VANIA. That's just like him! We none of us dare to say a word about our pay—he bawls our heads off if we do. "How," he says, "can you know what goes on in my mind? You think you can see right down inside me? Who knows, maybe I'll feel in the mood to pay you a whole five thousand." Just try talking to him! The trouble is, in his whole life he's never felt that way —not once.

KULIGIN. Well, what can you do, sir? You'll have to try and humor him somehow or other.

BORIS. That's just the trouble, Kuligin. It's just plain impossible. Even his own family can't humor him, so what hope do I have?

VANIA. How can anyone humor him when all he knows is abusing people? And especially when it comes to money; not one account ever gets settled without a whole lot of swearing and abuse. People'd rather give up what's their rightful due, just so he'll quiet down. And if someone steps on his toes first thing in the morning, there's hell to pay! He'll keep picking on us all for the rest of the day.

BORIS. Every morning my aunt begs us all, with tears in her eyes: "Please don't make him angry. Please try not to make him mad."

VANIA. As if you could stop him. He just has to set foot in the market and he's off. He abuses all the peasants and even if they'll settle for a loss, he still won't leave till he's sworn their heads off. And once he's started, he keeps going all day.

SHAPKIN. In fact, he's fighting mad all the time!

VANIA. And how!

BORIS. And it's terrible too, when someone he wouldn't dare tell off crosses him. Then his whole family had better watch out!

VANIA. Ah, you should have seen the time that hussar told him what he could do with himself on the Volga ferry. You should've seen the dance he did after that!

BORIS. And didn't we get it at home! For a couple of weeks afterward we had to keep ducking out of his way and hiding in the attics and storerooms.

KULIGIN. Look, are they out of evening service already? (*Several people cross backstage.*)

VANIA. Come on, Shapkin, let's go and get ourselves a drink. What's there to stand around here for?

(*They nod to the others and exit.*)

BORIS. Ah, Kuligin, it's hard for me here—I'm just not used

to it. They all give me such odd looks, as if I were out of place, as if I were in their way. I don't understand the local customs. I know it's all very Russian and should be familiar to me, but I just can't get used to it.

KULIGIN. And you never will get used to it, sir.

BORIS. Why d'you say that?

KULIGIN. It's a cruel life here in our town, sir, real brutal. Among the working people you'll find nothing but coarseness and naked poverty. And we don't have a chance to break our way out of the crust that covers us, because we can't ever earn more than enough for dry bread by honest labor. And those who do have money, they try to enslave the poor and force them to work for nothing to get more money yet. D'you know what your uncle told the mayor once? The workmen had complained because your uncle hadn't settled properly with a single one of them. So the mayor says to your uncle: "Look, Mr. Dikoy," he says, "pay your workmen properly! Every day I get complaints!" And your uncle slaps the mayor on the back and he says to him: "Why, Your Honor, should you and I waste our time on unimportant things? Why, in a year, I have a lot of workers coming and going. So, you understand, suppose I hold back one miserable kopek from each man—that makes thousands for me, which is just fine!" And that's how it goes, sir! And the way the well-off treat each other, sir! They undermine each other's trade and that not so much out of greed as out of jealousy. They keep fighting each other. Then they entice lawyers into their houses and feed them drinks. And you should see those lawyers! They don't even look human; they've had all the humanity crushed out of them. And for a small sum, they'll file fraudulent claims against those people's closest friends for them. So then there's a lawsuit between them, sir, and there's no end to the misery it causes. First they have a hearing here that goes on and on, then they go to the capital of the province and start all over. And there are plenty of people just waiting for them there, who'll lick their chops when they see them coming. So, to make a long story short, they haul them from court to court. And, what's more, they don't mind being dragged around like that at all; in fact, it's just what they want. "I'll pay if I must," they say, "as long as he has to fork out a pretty penny too." I'd like to put the whole thing into a poem.

BORIS. Why, can you write poetry?

KULIGIN. The kind of poetry they wrote in the old days, sir. I've read a lot of Lomonosov, Derzhavin . . . a wise man, that Lomonosov, believe me, sir, a student of nature, and yet, he was from the common people—just like me.

Boris. You should write that poem. It'd be very interesting to see.

Kuligin. How could I, sir? They'd eat me alive. As it is, I get it in the neck for talking too much, but I can't help it! Well, I wanted to tell you something of the family life here too, sir, but we'll have to make it another time. I'm sure you'll find it quite interesting.

(*Enter* Feklusha *and another woman.*)

Feklusha. Great, my dear, real great! My, it's so beautiful here! I'm telling you, you live in the promised land! Ah, those merchants of yours are a real, God-fearing lot, blessed with many virtues, great generosity and much almsgiving! I'm full to the gills with happiness from it all. They haven't turned us away and so, I say, their abundance will be still further increased, especially in the Kabanov household.   (*They exit.*)

Boris. The Kabanov household?

Kuligin. Ah, that hypocrite! To beggars she gives, but you should see how she treats her own people. (*Pauses.*) Ah, if only I could discover perpetual motion, sir!

Boris. Why? What would you do then?

Kuligin. What d'you mean, sir? Why, them English are offering a million to the one who finds it. Me, I'd spend all that money for the good of the community, sir. Working men should be given work. As it is, there are people with willing hands and there's nothing for them to do.

Boris. And you really hope to discover perpetual motion?

Kuligin. I sure do, sir! All I need now's a little cash to build a model. But I must be on my way now. Good-by, sir!   (*Exits.*)

Boris (*alone*). Wonderful fellow! It'd be a shame to disillusion him! He wraps himself up in a dream and he's happy. As to me, it looks as if I'm going to have to waste my youth in this hole. Ah, I'm completely done in as it is, and now I've got this new idiocy in my head! That's all I needed, really! What do I want with love, for God's sake? Here I'm shouted at and pushed around and now I have to go and fall in love like an idiot. And with whom? With a woman I'll never even get a chance to speak to. (*Silence.*) And yet I can't get her out of my head, try as I may. Oh, there she is! She's coming this way with her husband, oh, and her mother-in-law's with them too! Ah, what an idiot I am! All right I'll just steal a glance at her from round the corner and then get off home.   (*Exits.*)

(Mrs. Kabanov, *her daughter* Barbara, *her son* Tikhon *and his wife* Katerina *enter from the opposite side of the stage.*)

Mrs. Kabanov. Listen to your mother now, and when you get there, do just as I told you.

Tikhon. How could I not do as you told me, Mother?

Mrs. Kabanov. Nowadays the younger generation is not that respectful of their elders.

Barbara (aside). Just try not respecting you!

Tikhon. I don't believe, Mother, that I've ever taken a step without your consent.

Mrs. Kabanov. Perhaps I'd believe that, my boy, if I'd not seen with my own eyes and heard with my own ears how children treat their parents nowadays. I wish you'd remember at least all the suffering your mother's put up with for your sake.

Tikhon. Mother, I . . .

Mrs. Kabanov. Even if she who gave you birth does say something to hurt your pride, I think you ought to bear it—don't you agree?

Tikhon. But, Mother, when have I ever failed to bear anything from you?

Mrs. Kabanov. Your mother's old and stupid and you young people, who're so clever, shouldn't be too demanding toward us old fools.

Tikhon (sighing, aside). Oh, good Lord! (To his Mother.) Who'd even think of such a thing, Mother!

Mrs. Kabanov. Don't you realize that if your parents are stern, it's only because they love you; it's out of love that they nag you—they're trying to teach you to act right. But children don't appreciate that nowadays and they go all around the place telling people that their mother's a nag, that she won't let them breathe, that she's poisoning their lives. And if, God forbid, the mother says a word that's not quite to the daughter-in-law's liking, then everyone starts yelling that she's pushing her straight into the grave.

Tikhon. Who's ever said anything like that, Mother?

Mrs. Kabanov. Well, I must say I've never actually heard it, my boy, never. I don't want to invent things—but if I had heard something like that, I'd be talking to you quite differently now! (Sighs.) It doesn't take long to commit a sin, my boy. Just get talking on a subject that touches you and before you know it, you've lost your temper, and that's a dreadful sin. So I'd better let you say anything you like about me; anyway if I don't let you do so to my face, you'll say it behind my back.

Tikhon. May my tongue shrivel if I ever . . .

Mrs. Kabanov. Stop it, no oaths, and lying is sinful, remember. I realized long ago that you feel closer to your wife than to your mother. Since you got married, you haven't loved me the way you used to.

TIKHON. What makes you think so, Mother?

MRS. KABANOV. Everything, my boy, everything! What a mother doesn't see with her eyes, her heart tells her; a mother's heart's a weathervane. I don't know that it is, perhaps it's your wife causing the rift.

TIKHON. What are you saying, Mother? Of course she isn't!

KATERINA. But I feel toward you just as I feel toward my own mother and I know Tikhon loves you as much as he ever did.

MRS. KABANOV. Did I ask you anything? So why don't you keep quiet, my girl? You don't have to defend Tikhon, I won't hurt him—he's my son after all, something you seem to forget. And why'd you have to jump to his defense like that? To show people how much you love your husband? Why, we all know how much you love him. In public, that is.

BARBARA (aside). Couldn't she find a better place to lecture them?

KATERINA. You're wrong about me, Mother. In public or private, I'm always the same; I never try to put on a show.

MRS. KABANOV. Ah, I didn't even want to talk about you. It just happened to come up.

KATERINA. Even so, I don't see why you have to say things like that about me.

MRS. KABANOV. You're really getting too uppity; I can't say a word without your taking offense right away.

KATERINA. Who likes to be accused without reason!

MRS. KABANOV. I know, I know what I say goes against the grain, but I can't help that. I'm no stranger and my heart bleeds for you! I noticed long ago that you wanted to live your own lives. Well, why not, you'll have a chance soon enough —when I'm no longer here. Then you'll do just as you please, without your elders around. And perhaps you'll remember me then, too.

TIKHON. But we pray night and day, Mother, that God should grant you health, happiness, and success in business.

MRS. KABANOV. Enough, enough, stop it please . . . I grant you, it's possible you did love your mother as long as you were a bachelor. But when do you have time to think of me with a young wife like yours?

TIKHON. One doesn't prevent the other: a wife is a wife, but I'll always honor and respect my mother.

MRS. KABANOV. So you'd be prepared to give up your wife

for your mother? That I'll have to see to believe!

TIKHON. But what need is there to give either of you up? I love you both.

MRS. KABANOV. There you go, trying to dodge that one too! I see I'm in your way.

TIKHON. Think what you like, I can't stop you. I only know that I'm a miserable man and that whatever I do displeases you.

MRS. KABANOV. Why, you're trying to pass yourself off as a poor, stepped-on little boy! I do believe you're on the verge of tears, upon my word! What kind of a man and a husband can you be after that? Look at yourself. Do you think your wife could ever fear and respect you now?

TIKHON. Why should she fear me? She loves me and that's good enough for me.

MRS. KABANOV. What do you mean, "Why should she fear me"? Are you out of your mind or what? If your wife doesn't fear you, she certainly won't fear me either. Then what sort of order will we have in our house? Isn't she your lawful wife then? Or perhaps the law doesn't mean a thing to you? Well, and if you must talk such stuff and nonsense, at least don't do it in front of her; nor in front of your own sister, because she'll have to marry too and whoever her husband is, he won't thank you for putting such ideas into her head. You can see for yourself you don't have too much brain after all, although you keep saying that you'd like to run your own life.

TIKHON. But, Mother, I never said I wanted to run my own life. I know I couldn't manage it.

MRS. KABANOV. So you imagine you must be all kindness to your wife, never tell her off, never threaten her? Is that it?

TIKHON. But, Mother, I only . . .

MRS. KABANOV (heatedly). She could even take a lover if she takes it into her head, couldn't she? Perhaps that's nothing in your opinion either? Well, speak up!

TIKHON. But I swear, Mother . . .

MRS. KABANOV (icily). Idiot! (Sighs.) What's the good of talking to a fool this way? It just makes me irritated. (A pause.) I'm going home.

TIKHON. We'll be coming home too, Mother. We'll just take a little stroll along the avenue first.

MRS. KABANOV. Please yourselves, but don't be late. Remember, I don't like it!

TIKHON. No, Mother, God forbid.

MRS. KABANOV. You'd better see you're not! (Exit.)

TIKHON. See, you always get me in trouble with mother. Ah, what a life!

KATERINA. It's not my fault, is it?

TIKHON. I don't know whose fault it is any more.

BARBARA. Oh, you wouldn't know, of course.

TIKHON. She used to nag me all the time. "Get married," she'd say, "if only so we can see what you'll look like as a married man." And now she nags me so because of you that I can't find a place to hide. It's all your fault!

BARBARA. As if it were her fault, really! Mother keeps attacking her and you join in. And after that you dare claim you love your wife! It makes me sick just looking at you. (*Turns away.*)

TIKHON. It's easy for you to talk. What do you expect *me* to do?

BARBARA. Mind your own business and shut up if you can't do anything better. And now, why are you dancing around like that? Ah, I know what's on your mind.

TIKHON. What then?

BARBARA. You're thinking of going over to Mr. Dikoy's for a drink. Right?

TIKHON. You guessed it.

KATERINA. Take it easy and come home soon or Mother'll be angry.

BARBARA. Yes, don't be long or you know what'll happen.

TIKHON. I sure do.

BARBARA. We aren't too eager to take a lot of her ranting just because of you.

TIKHON. I won't be long. Wait for me. (*Exits.*)

KATERINA. I see you feel sorry for me, don't you, Barbara?

BARBARA (*looking away*). Of course I do.

KATERINA. That shows you're fond of me. (*Kisses her.*)

BARBARA. How could I help being fond of you?

KATERINA. I'm very happy you feel that way. You're so sweet yourself and I like you very much. (*Pauses.*) You know what's just come into my head?

BARBARA. What?

KATERINA. How come people can't fly?

BARBARA. What are you talking about?

KATERINA. I mean, why is it people can't fly? Fly like birds, you know. You know, there're times when I fancy I'm a bird. When I stand on top of a hill, I have a terrible urge to take off—to take a run, lift my arms into the air and leave the ground. Shall I try now? (*She is about to start running.*)

BARBARA. The things you think up sometimes!

KATERINA (*sighing*). Ah, I used to be full of zest once, but I've wilted in our house.

BARBARA. I know, I've noticed.

KATERINA. Yes, I used to be quite different. I lived without a care in the world, like an uncaged bird. My mother adored me, dressed me up like a doll, never made me do any work. I could do whatever came into my head. Let me tell you what my life was like before I married your brother. I'd get up early and if it was summer, I'd go out, wash myself in the stream, then bring water back with me and water all the flowers in the house. I had lots and lots of flowers. Then I'd go to church with my mother and all the pilgrim-women would come too, because our house was always full of pilgrim-women. And when we came back from church, my mother and I would sit down to some embroidery—usually gold thread on black velvet—while the pilgrim-women told us about the places they'd been to or perhaps sang psalms. And so the time would pass till dinner. Then, after the meal, the old women'd lie down for a nap and I'd go out for a walk in the garden. Then it'd be time for vespers and, later in the evening, more tales and more singing.

BARBARA. But it's very much the same in our house.

KATERINA. Yes, but in your house it's as though everything was sort of forced down your throat. Ah, I used to be crazy about going to church! I felt I was in paradise. I didn't see the people around me, and I'd forget the time and always be surprised when the service came to an end. The whole thing might've taken one second! My mother used to tell me that everyone around was staring at me, wondering what had come over me . . . And you know, on sunny days, a thick shaft of sunlight would fall from the dome with clouds of incense floating in it and I remember I sometimes fancied there were angels flying and singing in it, too. And also, when I was a girl, I'd get up during the night, kneel before an icon with a sanctuary lamp burning in front of it—ah, we had icons with lamps all over our house—and sometimes I'd stay there praying till morning. Other times, I'd run out into the garden just after sunrise, fall on my knees and pray and cry without knowing myself what I was praying and crying about, and later they'd find me there like that. And what could I have been praying for then, what could I have been asking for? Seems like I had everything I could wish. And what dreams I used to dream, Barbara, ah, what beautiful dreams! There were all kinds of gilded palaces or the most marvelous gardens and always unseen voices singing and singing, and everything around smelling of cypresses, and the mountains and the countryside beyond, not as they are in real life but just like in the icons. And at other times, I flew through the air all the time. I still have dreams sometimes, but not often and not the same.

BARBARA. Why, what sort of dreams d'you have now?

KATERINA (*after a pause*). I'll die soon.

BARBARA. What are you talking about!? What nonsense!

KATERINA. No, I know I'll die soon. Ah, Barbara, something bad is happening to me. It's as if I'd started to live again or . . . I don't know myself.

BARBARA. But what's happening to you? What is it?

KATERINA (*taking her hand*). I'm in good health. It'd be better if I were sick, because as it is there's no excuse. A wish keeps creeping into my head and I just can't get away from it. I try to think of something else but I can't keep my thoughts together; I try praying, but prayers won't keep it away. My tongue keeps mumbling the words but all the time other things are going through my head. It's as if the devil were whispering in my ear and what he whispers isn't good . . . And the things I imagine, Barbara—they're so wicked I'm ashamed. What's come over me? Something dreadful's going to happen; I know it. At night I can't sleep. I keep hearing that whisper and it coos so caressingly to me, just like a tender dove, you know. I don't dream of trees and mountains like the ones in the icons any more, Barbara, but of someone's putting his arms round me and hugging me passionately and then leading me away somewhere and I follow him on and on . . .

BARBARA. Well? Go on!

KATERINA. I shouldn't be talking to you like this, really. You aren't married.

BARBARA (*looking around*). Tell me, tell me. I'm worse than you.

KATERINA. I can't tell you. I'm ashamed.

BARBARA. You don't have to be. You can tell me.

KATERINA. I get to feeling that there's not enough air in our house and I long to run away, and I say to myself that if I had my choice, I'd be in a boat now sailing down the Volga and singing songs or driving around in a troika with his arm around me . . .

BARBARA. Not Tikhon's arm though.

KATERINA. What do you know about it?

BARBARA. How could I help knowing that?

KATERINA. Ah, Barbara, my head is so full of sinful thoughts! Believe me, I've cried and cried, and I've tried so hard but there's nothing doing, I can't get away from sin! No, there's no escape for me and it's a terrible sin. I love another man, Barbara dear. D'you understand?

BARBARA. I can't judge you. I have my own sins.

KATERINA. So what am I to do? I don't have the strength to

fight it. Where can I go? I feel I'll do away with myself in my despair.

BARBARA. What are you talking about? Wait! My brother's leaving tomorrow and we'll manage something. Maybe you'll be able to see him.

KATERINA. No, no, I don't want to! God forbid!

BARBARA. But why are you so frightened?

KATERINA. If I talk to him even once, I'll run away afterward. I'd never be able to go back home, not for anything in the world.

BARBARA. Wait, we'll see when the time comes.

KATERINA. No, no, I don't even want to hear about it.

BARBARA. Why should you let yourself dry out and fade! Even if you die of despair, they won't be sorry for you, you'll see! And why should you make things even harder for yourself?

(*Enter a* LADY *accompanied by two* FOOTMEN *in tricorns.*)

LADY. Well, my beauties, what are you doing here? Waiting for your young men? You're enjoying yourselves, are you? You're happy because you're beautiful? Well, you know where your beauty will lead you! There! (*She points to the Volga.*) Straight into the whirlpool! (BARBARA *smiles.*) Why are you laughing? You'll burn in everlasting fire and be boiled in molten pitch. That's where your beauty will get you! (*Exits.*)

KATERINA. Ah, how she scared me. I'm all ashiver. It's like a prophecy, you know.

BARBARA. She can speak for herself, the old hag!

KATERINA. What did she say? What were her words?

BARBARA. It's a lot of stupid nonsense. Why pay attention to her silly chatter? She says that to everybody. She did plenty in her youth herself—ask anyone. But now she's afraid to die and so she scares others with death. Even the streetboys duck away from her for she keeps threatening them with her cane and shouts (*Imitating the old lady.*) "You'll all burn in everlasting fire, all of you!"

KATERINA (*half-closing her eyes as if dazzled by a bright light*). Ah, stop it, be quiet. I feel dizzy.

BARBARA. There's really nothing to be afraid of. She's just an old fool.

KATERINA. But I'm scared to death. I keep seeing her before my eyes.

BARBARA (*after a pause, looking around*). What's Tikhon doing all this time? I think we're going to have a thunderstorm.

KATERINA (*sounding terrified*). A thunderstorm! Let's run home! Hurry!

BARBARA. You must really be out of your mind! How can you show yourself in the house without Tikhon?

KATERINA. No, no, I want to run home! I don't care about him!

BARBARA. But why this panic? The thunderstorm is still quite a way off.

KATERINA. Well, if it's far away, we'd better wait a little. Although I really think we should go right away. Let's go, what d'you say?

BARBARA. But you know, if something's fated to happen, hiding at home won't help.

KATERINA. Still, it's better, more reassuring, at home; and then there are the icons there and I could pray.

BARBARA. Why, I never knew you were so frightened of thunderstorms. I'm not.

KATERINA. How can you not be frightened? Everyone should fear thunderstorms. And the frightening thing about it is not that the lightning might kill you but that death might strike suddenly, when you're just as you are with all your sins and all the evil temptations. I'm not afraid to die but when I think that I might have to appear before God just as I am this minute, after all the things we've said, then I'm really scared. Ah, I'm even too frightened to name the terrible sin that's on my mind now. (*Thunder.*) Ah!

(*Enter* TIKHON.)

BARBARA. Here comes my brother. (*To* TIKHON.) Run, hurry! (*Thunder.*)

KATERINA. Oh, hurry, hurry!

CURTAIN

ACT II

*A room in the Kabanovs' house. Glasha is packing clothes.
Feklusha enters.*

FEKLUSHA. You always work so hard, dearie. What is it now?

GLASHA. Packing the master's things. He's going on a trip.

FEKLUSHA. Why, is he going away, the dear man?

GLASHA. Yes.

FEKLUSHA. For long?

GLASHA. No.

FEKLUSHA. Well, hope he has a nice, pleasant trip. And what d'you say, will his wife start wailing when he goes?

GLASHA. I wouldn't know.

FEKLUSHA. But does she wail sometimes—your mistress?

GLASHA. Don't know, I never heard her.

FEKLUSHA. Ah, I must confess, dearie, I love to hear a good wail, there's nothing like it. (*She pauses.*) And now, let me give you a piece of advice, dearie. You'd better keep your eye on that beggar-woman or she might swipe something.

GLASHA. Who can ever tell with you people? You're a funny lot, you pilgrims—you keep saying all sorts of things about each other. It'd seem you should be quite happy in this house: you get plenty to eat and drink and all that and yet you keep bickering with each other. It's a sin for sure but it looks like you aren't scared of that.

FEKLUSHA. No one can be without sin, dearie, in the world we live in. Let me tell you this, my dear: you ordinary people, you have one devil each to lure you from the path of righteousness, while we, the saintly pilgrims, we have six devils apiece working on us all the time, and some of us even have as many as twelve. And so we have to overcome the lot of them. It isn't easy, believe me, dear girl.

GLASHA. Why is it there're so many devils attached to you people?

FEKLUSHA. It's because the chief devil specially hates us for leading such a righteous life. But I personally, I don't like to quarrel—that's not a sin I can be accused of. But I do have one failing. I know it and I don't mind admitting it. I like good food. Well, and what happens? The good Lord takes pity on my weakness and sends me to houses where I can eat.

GLASHA. And have you had to go far in your travels, Feklusha?

FEKLUSHA. No, dearie, I'm not strong enough to go far but I sure have heard a lot. I heard that there are countries in this world that aren't even ruled by Christian Tsars but by sultans instead. In one country, there's a Turkish sultan called Makhnut and in another a Persian sultan called Makhnut, and they sit on their thrones and judge people and I must tell you, my dear girl, they aren't fair in their decisions, not fair at all. You see, they just can't pass the right judgment on anything because such is their fate. Our law is the righteous law and theirs is the unrighteous and whatever our law orders, theirs orders the contrary. And all the judges in those countries are unrighteous too, so that people even write to them in their petitions: "Please judge us unfairly, your honor!" And then there are lands too where all the people have dogs' heads.

GLASHA. Why dogs' heads?

FEKLUSHA. To punish them because they're infidels. Well, I must be going now, my dear. I think I'll go and knock on some merchants' doors and see whether any of them wishes to give something to a poor pilgrim. See you later, dearie.

GLASHA. Good-by. (*Exit* FEKLUSHA.) Who would've thought there were such strange lands on earth! Ah, the miracles that exist in the world! And to think we just sit here and never hear about anything. Thank God there are some decent people who'll tell you what's going on at least, otherwise we'd stay ignorant and stupid to our dying day.

(*Enter* KATERINA *and* BARBARA.)

BARBARA (*to* GLASHA). Go and put Mister Tikhon's things in the coach, the horses are ready. (GLASHA *leaves; to* KATERINA.) They married you off too young. They should have given you a chance to have some fun first. It's no wonder your heart didn't have time to settle down a bit.

KATERINA. And it never will settle down.

BARBARA. Why do you say that?

KATERINA. It's the way I was born, so full of fire. Shall I tell you what I did when I was no more than six? They scolded me unfairly at home, so I ran down to the Volga, got into a boat, untied it, and the next morning they found me ten miles or so downstream.

BARBARA. And tell me, did the boys stare at you later?

KATERINA. They sure did.

BARBARA. So why . . . didn't you like any of them?

KATERINA. No, I didn't. I just laughed.

BARBARA. You've never loved Tikhon, have you, Katerina?

KATERINA. Loved him? Well, yes, I'm so sorry for him.

BARBARA. No, of course you don't love him. If you're sorry for him you certainly can't love him. And I may as well say straight out: there's no reason why you should love him. You don't have to hide it from me. I noticed long ago that you were in love with someone else.

KATERINA (*sounding frightened*). What did you notice?

BARBARA. You're funny really! I wasn't born yesterday, you know. As soon as you see him, your whole face changes. (KATERINA *stares at her with wide-open eyes.*) Ah, there are so many ways to tell . . .

KATERINA (*looking at the floor*). Well, who?

BARBARA. You know very well yourself. No point in my telling you his name.

KATERINA. No, tell me who! Name him!

BARBARA. Boris.

KATERINA. Yes, Barbara, it's him! But please don't . . .

BARBARA. What do you take me for? You'd better watch your own tongue.

KATERINA. I'm so bad at deceit; I can never keep anything secret.

BARBARA. But it's impossible to do without it. Just remember where you live! Our entire family is held together by deception. I wasn't born a liar either, you know, but I've learned to lie when I have to. When I went out for a walk yesterday, I met him and we had a talk.

KATERINA (*after a brief silence, looking down*). Well, what did he say?

BARBARA. He asked me to give you his best . . . He said it's a shame there's nowhere he could meet you.

KATERINA (*lowering her head even further*). Yes, where? And what would be the point?

BARBARA. He looked so sad . . .

KATERINA. Don't tell me about him, please! I don't want to know anything about him! I'll always love my husband! Tikhon, darling, I won't leave you for anyone! I didn't even want to give it a thought so why do you come trying to tempt me?

BARBARA. If you don't want to give it a thought—don't; no one's forcing you.

KATERINA. Ah, you have no pity for me at all. You say "Don't think" and then you keep reminding me of him yourself. Do you think I want to think of him? I don't but what can I do, since I can't get him out of my head. Whatever I try to think about, he's always there, right before my eyes. I want to force myself to forget but I can't, however much I try. Do you know, last night the devil came to pester me again. I almost ran away from home.

BARBARA. Ah, you're so complicated, God bless you. But if you want to listen to my advice, you'll do just as you please—but just don't let anyone find out about it.

KATERINA. I don't want it that way. That's no good. I guess I'd rather try and bear things as they are as long as I can.

BARBARA. And what if you can't bear it?

KATERINA. If I can't bear it?

BARBARA. Yes, what will you do then?

KATERINA. Then I'll do just as I please.

BARBARA. Just try! They'll eat you alive here.

KATERINA. What do I care? I'll leave this place and that'll be that.

BARBARA. How can you leave? You're Tikhon's wife, remember.

KATERINA. Ah, Barbara, I see you don't know me yet. Of course, I hope it won't go so far—God forbid! But if I get to hate the whole place too much, then there'll be nothing that can hold me back, no force! I'll jump out of the window, throw myself into the Volga . . . If I don't want to live here, I won't—they can kill me if they want, that won't change a thing! (*Silence.*)

BARBARA. You know what, Katerina? While Tikhon's away, let's you and I sleep in the summerhouse in the garden.

KATERINA. Why do you want to do that, Barbara?

BARBARA. What's the difference?

KATERINA. I'm scared to sleep in an unfamiliar place.

BARBARA. What is there to be scared of? I'll have Glasha sleep there with us, too.

KATERINA. It's quite scary even with her . . . Still, if you . . .

BARBARA. I wouldn't have asked you but mother won't let me sleep there alone. And I have to do it.

KATERINA (*looking into her eyes*). And why do you have to?

BARBARA (*laughing*). We'll tell each other's fortunes there, see?

KATERINA. You're kidding!

BARBARA. Sure I am. I didn't expect you to believe that. (*A pause.*)

KATERINA. What can Tikhon be doing all this time? Where is he?

BARBARA. What do you need him for?

KATERINA. Just wondering. But it's almost time for him to leave.

BARBARA. He's sitting with mother in her room and she's nagging him; it eats him the way rust eats iron.

KATERINA. Why? What did he do?

BARBARA. Nothing special, she's just trying to teach him wisdom. He'll be out of her sight for two whole weeks—just think of that! She'll be eating her heart out at the thought that he'll be free to come and go without asking her permission all that time. So now she's giving him instructions, each sterner than the last and when she's through, she'll make him kneel before an icon and swear he'll do exactly as she's told him.

KATERINA. She has him nicely tied even when he's free and on his own.

BARBARA. Ah, you think he's tied? No sooner is he out of her sight than he begins drinking. He's there now, letting her have her say and thinking how he can manage to get away from her quickly and be on his way.

(*Enter* MRS. KABANOV *and* TIKHON.)

MRS. KABANOV. So I hope you'll remember everything I've told you. You'd better!

TIKHON. I'll remember, Mother.

MRS. KABANOV. All right, we're all set now. The horses are waiting. Say good-by and godspeed.

TIKHON. Yes, Mother, I'd better be going.

MRS. KABANOV. Well!

TIKHON. Did you wish something else, Mother?

MRS. KABANOV. Well, don't just stand there! Do you still not know the proper ways? Tell your wife what she's to do while you're away. (KATERINA *lowers her eyes.*)

TIKHON. I'm sure she knows herself.

MRS. KABANOV. Don't give me any back talk! Go on, tell her, as I said. I want to hear you give her your orders. And when you come back, you must make her account to you for how she's obeyed.

TIKHON. Obey Mother, Katerina.

MRS. KABANOV. Tell her not to be rude to me.

TIKHON. Don't be rude.

MRS. KABANOV. Tell her to honor me as she would her own mother.

TIKHON. Honor mother as you would your own mother, Katerina.

MRS. KABANOV. Tell her not to sit around not doing any work, like some duchess.

TIKHON. Do some work while I'm away.

MRS. KABANOV. She mustn't stare out of the window all the time.

TIKHON. But, Mother, when does she . . .

MRS. KABANOV. Go on, tell her.

TIKHON. Don't look out of the windows, Katerina.

MRS. KABANOV. Tell her she mustn't make eyes at young men while you're away.

TIKHON. But really, Mother!

MRS. KABANOV (*severely*). Come, stop dilly-dallying! Do as your mother says. (*Smiles.*) I know what I'm talking about.

TIKHON (*with embarrassment*). Don't make eyes at young men. (KATERINA *gives him a haughty look.*)

MRS. KABANOV. All right, now you may have a few private words if you feel like it. Come, let's go, Barbara!

(*Exit* MRS. KABANOV *and* BARBARA.)

TIKHON. Katerina! (*Silence.*) You're not angry with me, are you?

KATERINA (*after a pause, shaking her head*). No.

TIKHON. Why do you look so strange? All right, I'm sorry.

KATERINA (*looking at him absently and shaking her head*). Ah, forget it! (*Covers her face with her hands.*) That hurt, what she said!

TIKHON. If you take everything to heart like that you'll be consumptive in no time. Why pay any attention to her? You know she just has to say things like that all the time. So let her and you let it go in one ear and out the other. But I must be on my way, good-by now!

KATERINA (*flinging her arms round his neck*). Don't go, Tikhon, please! Believe me, darling, it's best if you don't go. Stay!

TIKHON. I can't, dear! How could I since it's mother who's sending me?

KATERINA. Then take me along!

TIKHON (*getting loose from her embrace*). I can't.

KATERINA. Why can't you, Tikhon?

TIKHON. Some good time I'd have dragging you along! Don't I get enough nagging from the lot of you when I'm here? I don't know how to get away from it all quick enough and here you're trying to latch on to me.

KATERINA. So you don't love me any more?

TIKHON. Oh no, I love you. It's just that, to escape my life here, I'd run away from the most beautiful wife on earth! Think for yourself: whatever else I may be, I'm still a man. And when a man is forced to live the kind of life I do, he'll run away from a wife and anything else whenever he gets a chance. Now I know that for two weeks no lightning will hit me, no thunder will roll over my head, there will be no fetters round my ankles! How can I be expected to think of my wife?

KATERINA. How can you expect me to love you when you talk like that?

TIKHON. What's wrong with the way I talk? What do you expect me to say? What are you afraid of anyway? I'm not leaving you alone, there'll be mother here to look after you.

KATERINA. Don't mention her! It breaks my heart! Ah, I'm so miserable, so miserable . . . (*Starts to cry.*) I don't know where to go. I have no one to stand up for me. Ah, I'm lost!

TIKHON. Oh, stop it, Katerina!

KATERINA (*stepping up close to* TIKHON *and putting her arms around his neck*). Ah, Tikhon, if only you'd stay here with me or take me along with you, I'd love you so, I'd be so tender, darling . . . (*She snuggles against him.*)

TIKHON. I can't understand you, Katerina: one minute I can't get a word out of you and the next you're falling all over me. I can't make you out.

KATERINA. So you're leaving me, Tikhon. I tell you there'll be trouble while you're away. Yes, there'll be trouble, trouble!

TIKHON. Well, whatever it is, I can't help it.

KATERINA. Then you know what, make me swear some terrible oath . . .

TIKHON. What oath?

KATERINA. Make me swear to you that while you're away I won't talk to any stranger whatever happens; that I won't see any man or think of any man except you.

TIKHON. But why?

KATERINA. Just to ease my mind. Do it as a favor to me, my darling.

TIKHON. How can you guarantee you won't think . . . Who knows what'll come into his head?

KATERINA (*kneeling. In a solemn tone*). May I never see my father and mother again, may I die without the sacrament if ever I . . .

TIKHON (*pulling her to her feet*). Stop it, stop it! It's a sin to say things like that. I don't even want to hear it!

(MRS. KABANOV's *voice is heard off-stage.*)

MRS. KABANOV. It's time for you to go, Tikhon!

(*Enter* MRS. KABANOV, BARBARA, *and* GLASHA.)

MRS. KABANOV. Well, off you go, Tikhon, godspeed! (*Sits down.*) But first, let's sit down for a second. (*All sit down; silence.*) All right, good-by now! (*Gets up and so do all the others.*)

TIKHON (*going up to her*). Good-by, Mother.

MRS. KABANOV (*pointing downward*). Down on your knees! (TIKHON *kneels, then gets up and kisses her.*) Now say good-by to your wife!

TIKHON. Good-by, Katerina. (KATERINA *flings her arms round his neck.*)

MRS. KABANOV. Come on, you shameless thing—hanging on his neck like that! You're not saying good-by to some lover of yours—he's your husband, your master! Or don't you know how to behave decently? Come, let go of him and bow low. (KATERINA *bows low.*)

TIKHON. Good-by, sister. (*Kisses* BARBARA.) 'Bye Glasha. Good-by, Mother. (*Bows.*)

MRS. KABANOV. Good-by, good-by, off you go now. Long partings only mean extra tears to shed.

(*Exit* TIKHON, *then* KATERINA, BARBARA *and* GLASHA.)

MRS. KABANOV (*alone*). Ah, the young! They make me laugh! If they weren't my own family, I wouldn't have been able to restrain myself, I'd have laughed till my sides split. They have no idea how things should be done. Don't even know how to say good-by. Lucky for them there's still a parent around to hold the household together while she's alive. But then, the fools want to live their own lives and whenever they try, they become the laughing-stock of decent people. Sure, some may take pity on them, but most'll just laugh. And how can they help laughing. If, for instance, they invite guests to their home, they don't know where to seat them properly and they're even liable to forget to invite some relative or other. Yes, it's funny but that's how the good old ways get lost. There are young people like that whose houses I won't put a foot in, or if I do, it makes me so sick I'm in a hurry to get out again. What will happen when we, the older generation, are gone, I hate to think. I can't imagine how the world will go on. Ah, the only good thing about it is that I won't be here to see it.

(*Enter* KATERINA *and* BARBARA.)

MRS. KABANOV. Here, you, Katerina, you kept boasting about loving your husband so much but now I see how you love him. A good wife, when she's seen her husband off, goes on wailing for, I'd say, an hour and a half, rolling around on the front steps. But look at you. It doesn't seem to touch you at all!

KATERINA. What's the point of doing that? I wouldn't even know how to do it if I tried. It'd just make people laugh.

MRS. KABANOV. It's not that hard if you put your mind to it. If you loved him truly, you'd learn soon enough. And even if you couldn't do it properly, you could at least have pretended, if only for appearances' sake. But it looks as if all your love for Tikhon is just talk. Well, I'm going to say my prayers now, so you two'd better keep quiet and not disturb me.

BARBARA. I think I'll go into town, Mother.

MRS. KABANOV (*in a friendly tone*). That's fine with me. Go on, have a good time while you can. You'll sit at home plenty once you're married! (*Exit* MRS. KABANOV *and* BARBARA.)

KATERINA (*alone; dreamily*). Ah, it's going to be quiet as the grave. And so boring, too! If only there were some children in this house! But, I have no children. If I had, I'd spend my time with them, playing and making them laugh. I love talking to children because they are like angels. (*Pause.*) It would've been better if I'd died young. I'd be looking down from the sky now and enjoying myself. Or else I could fly wherever I wished unseen. I'd fly out into the fields and flutter from cornflower to cornflower just like a butterfly. (*Sinks into reverie.*) Ah, here's what I'll do: since I promised him I'd work, I'll go to town and buy some material. Then I'll sew some clothes and give them to the poor and they'll pray for me. So Barbara and I, we'll sit down to our sewing and we won't even notice how the time passes and the next thing we know, Tikhon'll be back with us.

(*Enter* BARBARA.)

BARBARA (*putting kerchief on her head before the mirror*). I'm off to town now to have a good time. And in the meantime, Glasha will make up our beds in the summerhouse in the garden. Mother says it's all right. You know the gate in the garden, behind the raspberry bushes? Mother usually locks it and hides the key. Well, I found it and put another key in its place so she won't miss it. Here, perhaps you'll need it. (*Hands her the key.*) If I meet him, I'll tell him to come to that gate.

KATERINA (*pushing away key in dismay*). Why? Why? I don't want it! I don't need it!

BARBARA. You may not need it, but I do. Take it anyway, keys don't bite!

KATERINA. What are you trying to do, you wicked thing? You mustn't! Have you even given it a thought? What's come over you!

BARBARA. Well, I don't like to argue and anyway I haven't much time. I'm in a hurry to go out and enjoy myself. (*Exit.*)

KATERINA (*holding key in hand*). What's she doing? The things she thinks up! Ah, she's mad, mad! It would be the end of me! I must throw the key away, into the river, so that no one'll ever find it! It's burning my hand like a hot coal. (*Thinks a while.*) Yes, that's the way a woman gets lost! Who can be happy being shut up like me? All kinds of things keep cropping up in a woman's head, when she's locked up like this. And so, when she gets the chance, she throws herself at it. But how can one do anything without thinking it over, weighing what'll come of it? It doesn't take long to get into trouble and after that you'll regret it all your life and your bondage will be even more bitter than before. (*Pause.*) Ah, but it's a bitter bondage. It's bad enough as it is! People cry over being locked in, especially us women. Take me, I'm bored, I'm tormented by all sorts of things and I don't see any way out! It'll only get worse and worse with time. And now, that sinful thing . . . (*Sinks into thought.*) Ah, if it wasn't for my mother-in-law! She's made me hate this house. By now I loathe the very walls. (*Looks dreamily at the key.*) Shall I throw it away? Of course I must! Why am I holding it in my hand in the first place? It was given to tempt me, to bring about my perdition. (*Listens.*) Ah, someone's coming. Oh, that scared me! (*Hides key in her pocket.*) No, no one's coming.

Why did I have to get so frightened? Why did I hide the key?
. . . Well, all right, let it stay in my pocket. I suppose my
fate is written that way in the book. And anyway, what's wrong
if I only glance at him from a distance? Even if I talked to
him the way other people talk to each other, what'd be so bad
about that? But what about the promise I made to Tikhon? But
then, he didn't even want me to make that oath! And possibly
I'll never get another opportunity like this in my life. Then
I'll never forgive myself for having let it slip by. Well,
what's the point of lying to myself? Even if I had to die, I
would still see him if I could. For whose benefit am I putting
all this on? Throw away the key? Not on your life! It's mine
now. Whatever happens, I will see Boris! Ah, I wish it were
night!

CURTAIN

ACT III

SCENE 1. *A street. The gates of the Kabanovs' house with a
bench by them. Mrs. Kabanov and Feklusha sit on the
bench.*

FEKLUSHA. The day of judgment is approaching, Mrs. Kabanov, everything points to it. At least in our town there's peace
and quiet, but other places, it's like Sodom itself: a terrible din
and mad rushing around, people darting all over the place, one
running here, another there.

MRS. KABANOV. There's nothing for us to hurry over here,
that's why we live quietly.

FEKLUSHA. No, Ma'am, that's not the reason. It's so quiet
and peaceful here because you have so many people like you
whose virtues adorn them like flowers. That's why everything
in this town is so sober and respectable. Because what d'you
think it means, all this shouting and rushing around, even, say,
in Moscow? People there run to and fro now and no one knows
what for. That's vanity for you! People are full of vanity, Mrs.
Kabanov, and that's what makes them run. People imagine
they're hurrying about their business. They don't recognize
friends in their rush and keep imagining someone's beckoning
to them, but when they get to the place they're headed for,
there's nothing there and they see it was all their imagination.
And so they go sadly on their way. Another man may think he's
trying to catch up with someone he knows. Anyone else looking
on can see very well that there's no one ahead of him, but the

man keeps tearing along. That's because it's very much like a fog—vanity. Here in this town, very few people come out on a fine evening like this to sit by their gates, but in Moscow at this hour the noise is like thunder and people stroll around and have a good time. They don't even hesitate to harness fiery dragons to carriages, just to move around faster. That's how they are over there.

MRS. KABANOV. I've heard about it, my dear.

FEKLUSHA. But me, Ma'am, I've seen it with my own eyes. Of course, other people, looking through that fog of vanity, say it's engines pulling them along, but I've seen for myself that great, evil hairy paw with those spread-out claws pushing them. It looked like that. (*She fans out her fingers.*) And the horrible growl the devil lets out, that can be heard by people who lead a righteous life!

MRS. KABANOV. One can call anything by any name and one machine is just as good as another. People are stupid and they're ready to believe everything. As to me, I wouldn't travel in one of those unholy things for all the gold in the world!

FEKLUSHA. Ah, may God preserve you from such a calamity, Ma'am! And now let me tell you about a vision I had in Moscow once. One day, very early in the morning, as the sun was just beginning to rise, I'm walking down a street. Suddenly I look up and lo and behold, there's someone standing on top of a very tall house and his face is all black. Well, you understand, of course, who that was. Then he makes gestures with his hands as if he's scattering something, although actually there's nothing. And so I realized he was scattering some special seeds that people would pick up without knowing it, blinded as they are by the fog of their vanity. And that's why they all rush around like that and their women are so thin. Yes, it's as if they were all running and looking for something and their faces are so sad it makes you sorry for them.

MRS. KABANOV. Everything's possible, my dear. Nothing would surprise me nowadays.

FEKLUSHA. Yes, these are hard times, Ma'am, real hard. And time itself is beginning to grow shorter.

MRS. KABANOV. What do you mean "grow shorter"?

FEKLUSHA. Yes, shorter, although we, of course, don't notice it in our hustle and bustle and vanity. But wise people now, they notice that time's getting shorter. The winter or the summer used to go on and on and we'd wonder when they'd ever come to an end but now you don't even notice how they fly by. Sure, the days and the hours are the same as before but the time in them is getting shorter, to punish us for our sins. That's what clever people say.

MRS. KABANOV. And it'll get worse yet.

FEKLUSHA. I just hope I won't live long enough to see it, Ma'am.

MRS. KABANOV. Who knows, we may yet have to see it.

(*Enter* DIKOY.)

MRS. KABANOV. What are you doing out so late, dear Mr. Dikoy?

DIKOY. Any objections?

MRS. KABANOV. No, why should I object?

DIKOY. So what are you talking about? Do I have to ask permission to walk around now? What sort of damned nonsense is that?

MRS. KABANOV. You'd better take it easy with me, my good man! Go and find someone else to abuse for nothing like that, because, me, I won't let you get off lightly. Now, be on your way, back where you came from. Come, let's go home, Feklusha. (*Rises.*)

DIKOY. Wait, Mrs. Kabanov, wait a minute. You've plenty of time to get home since your home is right here, right behind your back.

MRS. KABANOV. If you're here on business don't holler the way you did just now, just state sensibly what it is.

DIKOY. I have no business, I'm just drunk, see what I mean?

MRS. KABANOV. And what do you want me to do then—congratulate you?

DIKOY. No, don't congratulate me but don't abuse me, either. I'm drunk and that's all there is to it. Until I've slept it off, there'll be no putting it right.

MRS. KABANOV. So go and sleep it off.

DIKOY. Where shall I go?

MRS. KABANOV. Home, of course, where else?

DIKOY. And what if I don't want to go home?

MRS. KABANOV. And why don't you want to go home, may I ask?

DIKOY. Because I have a war going on there.

MRS. KABANOV. Who can be at war with you? You're the only warrior there.

DIKOY. All right, I'm a warrior. So what?

MRS. KABANOV. Nothing. But I must say you don't gain much honor in your wars, because you always wage them against women only.

DIKOY. That's because they won't submit to my will. Why, you don't think I should submit to theirs, do you?

MRS. KABANOV. Well, let me tell you, I've been watching

you for a long time, marveling: there are so many people in your house and none of them can do a thing right according to you.

DIKOY. And what about you?

MRS. KABANOV. Now tell me, what do you want of me?

DIKOY. I'll tell you what: talk to me, take the load off my heart. You're the only one who can do that.

MRS. KABANOV. Go in, Feklusha, and order them to prepare a snack and something to drink. (FEKLUSHA *goes into the house.*)

MRS. KABANOV. Come in then, Mr. Dikoy.

DIKOY. No, I won't go inside. It's worse in there.

MRS. KABANOV. Tell me then, what have they done to make you so angry?

DIKOY. Ah, it's been going on since morning.

MRS. KABANOV. They must've asked you for money.

DIKOY. As if they'd agreed to drive me mad: one after the other, they kept pestering me all day long!

MRS. KABANOV. They must've wanted something very badly to pester you like that.

DIKOY. I can understand that myself, but what do you expect me to do about it with a heart like mine? Sure, I know I should pay them, but I can't make myself do it of my own free will. You're my friend, for instance, but if you came to me and claimed something I owed you, I wouldn't be able to contain myself and I'd start abusing you. I'd pay you, but I'd abuse you first! Because as soon as one mentions money in my presence, all my innards begin burning and then I start swearing at people about nothing.

MRS. KABANOV. It's because you have no one wiser than you in your house and so you go around bullying everyone.

DIKOY. No, you wait, my dear woman, you listen to me! This is the sort of thing that happened to me during Lent: As I was fasting, the devil sent me a peasant to claim the money I owed him—he had carted my logs for me. So, sure I sinned. I abused him something awful. In fact, I almost took a punch at him. That's the kind of temper I have. After that I asked for forgiveness, bowed low to him, like this, see. Yes, I tell you, I bowed to that stupid peasant! I stood in the mud in the court-yard and bowed to him! That's where my terrible temper can lead me!

MRS. KABANOV. But why are you purposely working yourself into a lather, friend. That's bad, you know!

DIKOY. Why do you say "purposely"?

MRS. KABANOV. I've seen you do it before and I know what I'm talking about. Whenever you see someone is about to ask you for something, you immediately find something to pick on and work yourself into a state because you're sure that then they won't ask you for anything. That's how you work it, my friend.

DIKOY. Well, who wants to part with what belongs to him?

(*Enter* GLASHA.)

GLASHA. The refreshments are served, Ma'am.

MRS. KABANOV. Well, what d'you say, Mr. Dikoy, come in and have something, whatever God has sent us.

DIKOY. Don't mind if I do.

MRS. KABANOV. Please come in then. (*She lets* DIKOY *into the house and follows him.* GLASHA *stands with her arms akimbo by the gate.*)

GLASHA. That looks like Mr. Boris coming. Has he come to fetch his uncle and take him home? Or is he just out for a stroll? I think he's just out for a walk.

(*Enter* BORIS.)

BORIS. Is my uncle here, by any chance?

GLASHA. He is, sir. You wish to see him?

BORIS. They sent me from home to find out where he was and since he's in your house, let him stay there. Who d'you think wants him? Everyone at home is very happy that he's out.

GLASHA. Ah, I wish my mistress was married to him—it wouldn't take her long to tame him! But what am I doing, standing here chatting with you, Mr. Boris? Good-by now.

(*Exits.*)

BORIS. Oh Lord, if only I could steal one glimpse of her! I can't just walk into the house without being invited. What a life! We live in the same town but I hardly ever see her more than once a week, in church, unless I chance to come across her in the street. In this town, when a girl gets married she really gets buried. (*Pause.*) It would be better if I never saw her at all. I only see her now and then and there are always people around and hundreds of eyes staring at you. It just breaks my heart. And then, I can't control myself: whenever I go for a walk, somehow I always find myself near this house. Why do I have to come here, since I know I can't see her anyway? It'll only make people talk and get her into trouble. Ah, what a lousy little town! (*Starts walking.* KULIGIN *approaches from the opposite side.*)

KULIGIN. Out for a walk, sir?

BORIS. Yes, the weather was so nice, I thought I'd go for a stroll.

KULIGIN. It's very nice out at this hour, sir, it's so quiet and there's not a cloud in the sky. The air is so fresh and the breeze from across the Volga carries the scent of the wild flowers over here.

A star-filled abyss black the sky does rend,
The stars are myriad—chasm without an end.

Let's go over to the square, sir, there's no one there at this hour.

BORIS. All right, let's go.

KULIGIN. That's the sort of town we have, sir: they've built a public square but no one goes there except on holidays and even then, they only pretend that they've come out for a walk or for the fresh air—really they go there to show off their clothes. The only person we're liable to meet there is some drunken clerk on his way home from a tavern. The poor haven't much time to go out, sir. They work day and night and get only about three hours sleep. You might think the rich at least would go out all the time to breathe the fresh air. But no! The gates of their houses are locked early and vicious dogs are let loose in their courtyards. Now you may think that they're busy doing something at home or saying their prayers, perhaps? Nothing of the sort, sir: all they do is bully their families and if they let their dogs loose, it's not to keep thieves out but so that people won't see or hear the tears and cries coming from their houses. I don't have to tell you, sir. You know yourself what goes on behind those locked doors—all that horrible debauchery, those drunken orgies! And it's all kept covered up and secret! But we know about those secrets that make only one person happy while the others must wail with pain. And is it really a secret? Who doesn't know it? Robbing orphans, nephews, thrashing members of their households so they won't dare to let out a squeak about what's going on in the house—that's all there is to their secrets. Ah, why bother with them! I think only girls and their young men go out in this town, to try to steal an hour or so before they go to bed. Look, here comes a couple.

(VANIA *and* BARBARA *come into sight; they stop and kiss.*)

BORIS. They're kissing.

KULIGIN. Nothing wrong with that, sir.

(*Exit* VANIA. BARBARA *walks up to the gate and beckons to* BORIS. *He goes up to her.*)

KULIGIN. I think I'll go to the square, sir. I don't want to be in your way. I'll wait for you there.

BORIS. All right, I'll join you there.   (*Exit* KULIGIN.)

BARBARA (*hiding her face in her kerchief*). Do you know the ravine behind the garden?

BORIS. I do.

BARBARA Be there later tonight.

Boris. What for?

Barbara. You're really very stupid. Come and you'll find out. Go now, your friend is waiting for you. (*Exit* Boris.) He didn't recognize me! Well, let him guess. I'm sure Katerina won't hold out—she'll rush to meet him. (*Disappears through the gate.*)

Scene 2. *Night. A bushy ravine. At the top of the bank, the fence of the Kabanovs' garden with a gate in it. A path leads down from the gate.*

Vania (*entering with guitar*). No one around. What can be keeping her? Well, never mind. I can sit here and wait. (*Sits down on a stone.*) I'll sing something just to kill time. (*Sings.*)

Oh, there was a Don Cossack led his horse out to drink,
And now here he stands at the gate, straight and still.
As he stands at the gate, a thought he does think.
He thinks as he stands there, his wife he must kill.

But his wife, yes his wife, does her husband implore,
And hastily bows to him low to the floor:
"Oh, husband, my heart's friend, my loved one, my pet,
Do not beat me now, do not kill me yet,
But wait till the darkness of midnight does fall
And sleep covers my children so dear with its pall,
My dear little children, my closest of all!"

(*Enter* Boris.)

Vania (*stopping singing*). Well, well! Everybody thought you were such a quiet one, but I see you're going in for it too, now!

Boris. Is that you, Vania?

Vania. Sure it's me, Mr. Boris.

Boris. What are you doing here?

Vania. What am I doing? Well, I suppose I have business here, for if I didn't, I wouldn't be here. And what are you doing, may I ask?

Boris (*looking around*). You know, Vania, I have to wait here and, if it's all the same to you, couldn't you go somewhere else?

Vania. Oh no, sir! You're here for the first time, but I've been coming for a long time. Why, that path was trodden by me. I like you, Mr. Boris, and I'd be glad to be of any service to you, but you'd better not cross my path here or something bad may come of it. Now that's a fair warning, sir.

BORIS. What's come over you, Vania?

VANIA. What's this, Vania? What's that, Vania? Just leave me alone and be on your way! Get yourself a girl and go wherever you wish with her and no one will interfere with you. But don't touch girls who're already taken. It's not done around here and you may find yourself with a few broken ribs. And if someone tries to fool around with my girl, I'll slash his throat for him.

BORIS. What're you talking about! I never thought of trying to take your girl away from you. Anyway, I wouldn't even be here if someone hadn't asked me to come.

VANIA. And who asked you?

BORIS. I couldn't make out who, it was dark . . . Some girl stopped me in the street and asked me to come to this very spot: the ravine, she said, behind the Kabanovs' garden gate.

VANIA. Who could it've been?

BORIS. Listen, can I talk to you openly, without your going around repeating what I say?

VANIA. You don't have to worry about that. No one'll hear a word of it from me.

BORIS. I know nothing about the ways and customs you have here but here's what's happened to me . . .

VANIA. You've fallen in love?

BORIS. Yes.

VANIA. Well, there's nothing wrong with that. We're very broad-minded about that sort of thing. Our girls go around with fellows and their parents don't want to know anything about it. Only the married women sit locked in their houses.

BORIS. That's just the trouble, Vania.

VANIA. You mean you've fallen in love with a married woman?

BORIS. Yes, Vania, I have.

VANIA. You'd better forget about it, Mr. Boris.

BORIS. That's easy to say, forget it! Perhaps you can forget one and find another to take her place but, me, once I've fallen in love . . .

VANIA. But it'll be the end of her if you ever . . .

BORIS. Oh, God forbid, no! How could I want to harm her! I'd just like to see her. I don't need more than that.

VANIA. Who can be sure of himself? And remember, the people here will get after her and they won't stop till they've nailed her coffin shut.

BORIS. Don't say that, Vania, you frighten me.

VANIA. And what about her, does she love you, too?

BORIS. I don't know.

VANIA. Have you met her? Have you spoken to her at least?

BORIS. I was in her house once with my uncle. Otherwise, I only see her in church and in the street. Ah, Vania, you should see her when she's praying! She has such a radiant smile on her face, a light seems to shine from it.

VANIA. Must be Tikhon Kabanov's wife then?

BORIS. Yes, Vania.

VANIA. Ah, congratulations!

BORIS. Why do you say that?

VANIA. Well, if you were told to come here, that must mean things are turning out fine for you.

BORIS. You mean it was she who told me . . . ?

VANIA. Who else could it've been?

BORIS. You must be joking! That's impossible! (*Seizes his head.*)

VANIA. What's the matter with you?

BORIS. I'm so happy, it's driving me crazy.

VANIA. Some reason to go crazy! You'd better watch your step. Don't get into trouble and, above all, don't get her into a mess! I know her husband's a fool, but her mother-in-law's a real dragon, so she'd better watch out!

(BARBARA *comes through the gate.*)

BARBARA (*singing by the gate*).

> Beyond the swift river I can see
> My young man walking over the lea.

VANIA (*chiming in*). He's bringing a present here for me . . . (*He whistles.*)

BARBARA (*coming down the path, her face covered with a kerchief, and approaching* BORIS). You, fellow, wait a bit. It may be worth your while. (*To* VANIA.) Let's go down to the Volga, you and I.

VANIA. Why are you so late? You know I don't like waiting. (BARBARA *puts one arm round him and they exit.*)

BORIS. It's like a dream! The night, that song he sang, this date! They walk around locked in each other's arms! This is all so new, so unknown, so marvelous! And now, I'm waiting for something myself. But I don't know what exactly. All I know is that my every vein is throbbing! I can't imagine what I'll say to her; just thinking of it takes my breath away, makes my knees shake! Ah, my foolish heart! When it starts seething, there's nothing I can do to stop it. Ah, someone's coming!

(KATERINA *walks slowly down the path draped in a large white shawl; she looks down at her feet; a silence.*)

BORIS. Is that you, Katerina? (*Silence.*) I don't even know how to thank you. (*Silence.*) If only you knew how much I'm in love with you, Katerina! (*Tries to take her hand.*)

KATERINA (*in a frightened voice, without raising her eyes*). Don't . . . don't touch me.

BORIS. Please don't be angry with me.

KATERINA. Go away, leave me alone, you evil man. Don't you know that all the prayers in the world will never wash away this terrible sin, never! It will always weigh on my heart like a heavy stone.

BORIS. Please don't chase me away!

KATERINA. Why did you come here? Do you want to cause my perdition? You know I'm married and that I'll live with him until they nail my coffin shut.

BORIS. But you asked me to come yourself . . .

KATERINA. But don't you understand, you, my enemy—I must live with him till they lay me in my coffin!

BORIS. It would've been better if I'd never set eyes on you.

KATERINA (*agitated*). But do you realize what I am doing to myself? Don't you know where my place is?

BORIS. Please, calm yourself. Sit down. (*Takes her hand.*)

KATERINA. Why do you want to ruin me?

BORIS. How could I want to ruin you when I love you more than anything in the world—more than myself!

KATERINA. But you are ruining me, as things are!

BORIS. Oh no, I'm not really a villain, I assure you . . .

KATERINA. You've ruined me, ruined me, ruined me!

BORIS. God save me from ruining you, Katerina. I'd rather die!

KATERINA. But if you haven't ruined me, why have I run away from my husband's house in the middle of the night and joined you here?

BORIS. But you did it of your own free will, Katerina.

KATERINA. I have no will—if I had, I wouldn't be here with you. (*She raises her eyes and looks at* BORIS. *A brief silence.*) I'm ruled by your will now, can't you see that? (*Throws herself on his neck.*)

BORIS (*embracing her*). You're my life!

KATERINA. You know what? I wish I could die now.

BORIS. Why die when it's so good to live?

KATERINA. No, living is not for me, I know that.

BORIS. Oh, don't say that! I can't stand it!

KATERINA. Oh, it's all right for you to talk, you're free, but I . . .

BORIS. But no one will find out about our love. Don't you trust me to keep it secret?

KATERINA. Ah, why should you? I've asked for it, so go ahead and ruin me! Let them all know, let them all see what I'm up to! (*Embraces him.*) Don't you understand that if I weren't too afraid of the sin in coming to you, I can't fear the judgment of men? They even say that it's better if you suffer for your sins on earth. It makes it easier later.

BORIS. Why think of all that now? Let's just be happy.

KATERINA. You're right, I'll have plenty of time to think of it and cry.

BORIS. You scared me at first—I thought you were going to chase me away.

KATERINA (*smiling*). Chase you away? How could I? The way I feel, I believe that if you hadn't come, I'd have gone to you myself.

BORIS. I never suspected you loved me.

KATERINA. I've loved you for a long time. It's as if you'd come here just on purpose to lead me into sin. Once I'd seen you, I was never the same again. I think if you'd beckoned to me the very first time, I'd have followed you. If you'd gone to the edge of the world, I'd have gone with you without ever looking back.

BORIS. How long is your husband going to be away?

KATERINA. Two weeks.

BORIS. Oh, we'll have a great time. It's a long time, two weeks.

KATERINA. Yes, we'll have a great time and then . . . (*Sinks into thought.*) Then they'll lock me in and it will be like death. But if I have half a chance, I'll always find a way to you!

(*Enter* VANIA *and* BARBARA.)

BARBARA. Well, how are you getting along, you two?

BORIS. We're getting along fine.

BARBARA. Why don't you go for a walk now and we'll wait here. Vania will call out if anything happens.

(*Exit* BORIS *and* KATERINA; VANIA *and* BARBARA *sit down on a stone.*)

VANIA. You sure started a big thing with that garden gate. It's very handy.

BARBARA. You see how clever I am.

VANIA. I know you're clever, but what about your mother? Won't she find out?

BARBARA. It'll never even occur to her.

VANIA. But just imagine, what if she . . .

BARBARA. She sleeps very soundly at the beginning of the night. It's only toward morning that she keeps waking up.

VANIA. But who can ever be sure? What if some evil force suddenly wakes her?

BARBARA. Well, what of it? I locked the gate behind me, so

she'll knock on it for a while and then, I guess, she'll just walk away. And in the morning we'll tell her that we were asleep and never heard a thing. And then, Glasha is looking out for us. If something goes wrong, she'll sing out. I've taken every precaution, to be sure not to get into trouble. (VANIA *strums on his guitar.* BARBARA *leans on his shoulder. He goes on playing.*)

BARBARA (*yawning*). How can we find out what time it is?

VANIA. It's just after twelve.

BARBARA. How do you know?

VANIA. I heard the night-watchman bang his gong.

BARBARA (*yawning*). It's time they came back. Give the signal. Tomorrow we'll come earlier so we'll have more time.

VANIA (*whistling and singing out loudly*).

> Home, home, all go home.
> But I want to stay and roam!

BORIS' VOICE (*off-stage*). I hear!

BARBARA (*getting up*). Good-by then! (*Yawns and gives* VANIA *a cool kiss, as to an old acquaintance.*) Mind you come a bit earlier tomorrow! (*Looks to the side on which* BORIS *and* KATERINA *went out.*) You've said good-by to each other for long enough. You aren't parting for ever, remember. You'll probably see each other tomorrow. (*Yawns and stretches herself.*)

(KATERINA *comes running in, followed by* BORIS.)

KATERINA (*to* BARBARA). Well, let's go, it's time! (*They go up the path.* KATERINA *looks back.*) Good-by!

BORIS. See you tomorrow!

KATERINA. Yes, tomorrow! Remember your dreams and tell me! (*Reaches gate.*)

BORIS. I will.

VANIA (*singing and accompanying himself on the guitar*).

> Sing, my girl, dance and play,
> Till the night replaces day . . .

BARBARA (*by the gate, singing*).

> But after the sunset red,
> A nice girl is home in bed! (*Exits.*)

VANIA (*singing*).

> When the night is black and deep,
> There my girl is, fast asleep . . .

CURTAIN

ACT IV

*Front stage, a narrow, vaulted gallery in an old building that
is falling into decay. In places, tufts of grass and bushes.
The Volga can be seen through the arches. Several people
of both sexes, out for a stroll, pass behind the arches.*

FIRST MAN. It's beginning to rain! I hope we won't get a thunderstorm.

SECOND MAN. We'll get one all right.

FIRST MAN. At least we've a shelter here.

A WOMAN. Look at all those people out for a stroll on the square, and the merchants' wives in their Sunday clothes!

FIRST MAN. They'll find some place to get out of the rain.

SECOND MAN. It'll be crowded here in no time!

FIRST MAN (*examining the walls*). Look, these walls were covered with frescoes once. One can still see them in places.

SECOND MAN. Sure they used to be covered with frescoes. The building was abandoned after the fire. They never bothered to repair it and now it's all dilapidated and grown over. Of course, you don't remember the fire. It happened forty years ago.

FIRST MAN. What'd you say this is a picture of? Difficult to make out, isn't it?

SECOND MAN. Why, it's a burning pit.

FIRST MAN. So that's what it is!

SECOND MAN. And here, you see, are all the people being thrown into it.

FIRST MAN. Oh, I see now.

SECOND MAN. And they come from all stations of life, rich and poor.

FIRST MAN. Some of them are Negroes, aren't they?

SECOND MAN. Yes, Negroes are being thrown in, too.

FIRST MAN. And what's that over there?

SECOND MAN. That's the rout of the Lithuanians. It's a battle, see. Our people are giving the Lithuanians hell.

FIRST MAN. And what did they want here, them Lithuanians?

SECOND MAN. Well, that's Lithuanians for you.

FIRST MAN. Yes, I heard they dropped on us out of the blue.

SECOND MAN. That, I can't tell you. Could be.

THE WOMAN. I can tell you for sure—that's where they dropped from and, what's more, that's why there are those funeral mounds at the place where that battle was fought.

(*Enter* DIKOY *followed by* KULIGIN, *hat in hand. All bow and assume respectful attitudes.*)

DIKOY. Ah, damn it, I'm soaked through! (*To* KULIGIN.) You leave me alone, you hear! (*Losing his temper.*) Ah, you stupid fool!

KULIGIN. But, Mr. Dikoy, please, just think—it would benefit everybody.

DIKOY. Go away! What benefit? Who needs benefits?

KULIGIN. But wouldn't you like it yourself, Mr. Dikoy? What would you think of having it put in a spot that'd been specially cleared for it? And it won't cost much either! What could it come to? A small stone pillar (*Showing with his hands the size of each item he mentions.*), a round brass plate about like that, and a style, just a straight one, like that, you know, the most ordinary kind. As for the rest, I'll fix it all up and even engrave the figures myself. After that, you, sir, when you take a stroll in the square here, as well as all the other people who come, will always know what it is. For it's such a beautiful spot here, yet somehow it always looks as if there were something missing. And then there are the travelers from out of town who come to see the sights and really, it would make the whole place more pleasing to the eye.

DIKOY. But why do you have to pester me with all this bunk? Did you ask me, in the first place, whether I wanted to talk to you at all? You should always find out first whether I'm in a mood to listen to a fool or not. Do you imagine, by any chance, that we're equals, a couple of pals or something? Ah, is that your important business that you think entitles you to push your snout into my face?!

KULIGIN. If I'd come to you with something that was just for myself, you'd be absolutely right saying that, sir. But it's for the general good, Mr. Dikoy! What can a matter of about ten rubles mean to you, if it's for the good of the whole town? It won't come to more than that, I'm sure, sir.

DIKOY. And who can guarantee you don't intend to steal the money?

KULIGIN. But since I'm offering my labor for nothing, how could I steal, sir? And everyone in this town knows me and can tell you I'd never do a thing like that.

DIKOY. So let them know you if they want. As for me, I don't wish to know you.

KULIGIN. But why do you have to be so insulting to an honest man, sir?

DIKOY. And now you imagine perhaps that I have to account to you for that, too! I don't account to people, not even if they're ten times more important than you. I think and say just what I please about people. Now if you seem honest to others, to me you're a thief and that's all there is to it. Is that what you wanted me to say? All right, so now you have it. So I say you're a crook. Perhaps you want to make something of it, you worm? Now remember: if I decide to forgive you, I'll forgive you and if I decide to step on you, I'll crush you.

KULIGIN. God forgive you, Mr. Dikoy. I know I'm a humble man and it wouldn't be too hard for you to push me around. But let me tell you this, sir: virtue is respectable even in beggar's tatters.

DIKOY. Don't you dare be rude to me! I'll show you!

KULIGIN. I certainly didn't mean to be rude, sir. I simply thought maybe you'd want to do something for our town. You're a very powerful man, sir, and you could do a great deal of good if you wanted to. Look, for instance—we have a lot of thunderstorms in this part of the country, but there are hardly any lightning rods in our town.

DIKOY (*haughtily*). Oh, they're useless!

KULIGIN. How can you say that, sir. Experiments have proved what lightning rods do.

DIKOY. What kind of lightning rods are you talking about?

KULIGIN. Steel ones.

DIKOY (*impatiently*). Well, what else is there to them?

KULIGIN. They're rods, sir, rods made of steel.

DIKOY (*working himself up into a temper*). I know what a rod is, you damned idiot, I'm asking you what else there is to them! Don't just go on repeating "rods, rods, rods."

KULIGIN. That's all there is to them, sir.

DIKOY. And what is a thunderstorm in your opinion, eh? Come on, answer me that! Speak up, man!

KULIGIN. Electricity.

DIKOY (*stamping his foot*). What are you talking about! Electricity—shmectricity! And after that, go and claim you aren't a crook! Everyone knows that thunderstorms are sent us as a punishment, to make us feel the Lord's anger, and you want to protect yourself with some sort of rods and poles! What are you, a Moslem or something? Come, admit you're a Tartar infidel—right?

KULIGIN. But Mr. Dikoy, remember, our great Russian poet Derzhavin said:

> While my body to dust will decay,
> My mind over lightning will hold sway.

DIKOY. I could hand you over to the police chief for those words and he'd throw you in jail. Hey, people, listen to what he's saying, this man!

KULIGIN. I guess there's nothing doing, so I might just as well give up. When I get my own million rubles, I'll come back to it. (*Shrugs and walks away.*)

DIKOY. Where'll you get the money? Steal it somewhere? Ah, the thief! Stop thief! You have to watch out with that kind! (*To the crowd.*) And you, you damned rotten bunch, you'd drive anyone into sin! I didn't want to lose my temper this morning, but that man made me lose it on purpose. May hell swallow him up! (*Gruffly.*) Isn't the rain over yet?

A MAN. I think it's stopped, sir.

DIKOY. You don't have to think, you fool, go and look.

THE MAN (*walking out from under the arches*). It's stopped. (*DIKOY exits, the others follow him. For a few moments the stage is empty, then BARBARA enters hurriedly and hides in a corner under an archway. She peeks out from there, apparently watching for someone.*)

BARBARA. I think that's him now! (BORIS *passes in the background.*) Psssst! (BORIS *turns his head.*) Hey, come over here! (*Beckons to him;* BORIS *approaches.*) Tell me now, what shall we do with Katerina?

BORIS. Why?

BARBARA. It's terrible, her husband's come back. We didn't expect him so soon but he's come just the same. Hadn't you heard?

BORIS. No.

BARBARA. She's simply gone out of her mind.

BORIS. It looks as if I've had my share of happiness—ten days, and now my whole life seems to be over. I won't see her again.

BARBARA. Ah, that's all you're worried about! Wait, listen to me: she's shivering as if she had a great fever. She's terribly pale and tears about the house like a wild thing, as if she were looking for something. And her eyes are like a madwoman's. This morning she started crying and she's been crying and sobbing and won't stop. Ah, my God, what am I to do with her?

BORIS. Perhaps . . . perhaps she'll get over it in time.

BARBARA. Not likely. She daren't look her husband in the face. Mother has noticed it and she keeps watching her and she looks at her with snake's eyes and that makes it even worse for poor Katerina. It breaks my heart to see her like that. And then, I'm afraid.

BORIS. What are you afraid of?

BARBARA. You don't know her—she's a strange one, she could do anything. She could cause so much trouble that . . .

BORIS. Oh, good Lord, what are we to do then? You ought to try and reason with her a bit. Won't she really listen to reason?

BARBARA. I've tried already but she won't listen. Looks as if it's better if I stay away.

BORIS. But what do you think she'll do?

BARBARA. What? She could, for instance, go down on her knees to her husband and blurt out everything to him. That's what I'm afraid she'll do.

BORIS (*frightened*). Could she really do that?

BARBARA. You can expect anything from her.

BORIS. Where is she now?

BARBARA. She's out in the square with Tikhon. Mother's with them, too. You can go and see for yourself. Although no, you'd better not. She's liable to lose her head completely if she sees you. (*Thunder in the distance.*) Looks like a thunderstorm. (*Looks outside.*) Yes, it's started raining again. Ah, and now there are people running this way for shelter. Hide yourself and I'll stand here in full view so that no one will suspect anything.

(*Enter several people of both sexes, then* KULIGIN.)

FIRST MAN. That little lady seems to be really afraid of the lightning. Look how she's running for shelter!

A WOMAN. No shelter will help her if it's written in her fate that lightning is to get her.

KATERINA (*rushing in*). Ah, Barbara! (*Catches hold of* BARBARA's *hand and holds it.*)

BARBARA. Come, take it easy. What's the matter with you?

KATERINA. I'm going to die!

BARBARA. Come, pull yourself together. Stop that nonsense!

KATERINA. No, I can't, I can't! It hurts too much!

MRS. KABANOV (*walking in, followed by* TIKHON). Well, that's why people must always live decently, so as to be ready to die at any moment. They wouldn't be afraid then.

TIKHON. But what kind of sin could she have committed? There's nothing special about her sins, they're just like anyone else's. She's just fearful by nature, that's all.

MRS. KABANOV. What do you know about her? Another person's soul is as much of a mystery to us as the blackest night.

TIKHON (*jokingly*). Unless something happened while I was away, because when I'm here, I know she's not all that sinful.

Mrs. Kabanov. Well, it could be, then, that she did something while you were away.

Tikhon (*jokingly*). All right, Katerina, my girl, you'd better confess if you've sinned, for you have no chance of keeping it a secret from me. Not on your life! I know everything about you!

Katerina (*looking straight into his eyes*). Ah, Tikhon, my dear . . .

Barbara (*to* Tikhon). Why don't you leave her alone? Can't you see it's hard enough for her as it is!

(Boris *comes out of his hiding place and bows to the* Kabanovs.)

Katerina (*suppressing a scream*). Ah!

Tikhon. What are you so frightened of? She must've thought you were a stranger. Come, we know him, Katerina. How's your uncle, Boris?

Boris. He's fine, thank you.

Katerina (*to* Barbara). What does he want of me now? Isn't it enough for him to have made me suffer so? (*Buries her face in* Barbara's *shoulder and sobs.*)

Barbara (*aloud so that* Mrs. Kabanov *will hear*). We are at our wits' end trying to think what to do with her and it's really too much when strangers come and meddle! (*She makes a sign to* Boris *and he walks off to the entrance at the farthermost end of the stage.*)

Kuligin (*stepping from the crowd into the center of the stage and addressing all*). Well, what are you afraid of? Tell me! Every blade of grass, every flower is glad, while we hide here as if the thunderstorm were a disaster. You're afraid the thunderstorm'll kill you! Why should it? Why don't you understand that it's not a calamity but a good thing? Anyway, you're afraid of everything: you're even afraid of the northern lights and you run indoors instead of looking at the sky and admiring them. "From midnight lands the dawn cometh"—and you are panicky and keep wondering whether it's a sign announcing war or pestilence. If a comet appears in the sky, one would expect a man to be reluctant to take his eye from such beauty, because while the eye becomes accustomed to the stars, a comet is something unusual and bright . . . But you, you're even afraid to look up into the sky and just stand there trembling with fear. Ah, all the bogies you folks have invented for yourselves! Me, I'm not afraid! Come, Mr. Boris, let's go out!

Boris. Yes, let's go, it's more frightening in here!

(Kuligin *and* Boris *exit.*)

Mrs. Kabanov. What speeches! Ever hear anything like it?

The times we live in! What's he trying to teach us? If he were a youngster it'd be one thing, but he's an old man! Ah, what're we coming to?

A WOMAN. Look at the sky, the clouds are so thick they cover it like a fur hat.

FIRST MAN. Look at that cloud rolling along, just like a hedgehog, and it looks as if there's a live thing inside it and it's about to come at us any moment.

SECOND MAN. Mark my word, fellow, we won't get off lightly with this thunderstorm. I know. It'll either kill someone or set a house on fire. You'll see. Look at the color of the sky!

KATERINA (*listening*). What are they saying? They said it'd kill someone.

TIKHON. They come out with the first bit of nonsense that goes through their heads.

MRS. KABANOV. Don't judge your elders. They've more experience than you have. Old people know all the signs. They don't just talk to say nothing.

KATERINA. Tikhon, I know who's to be killed.

BARBARA (*quietly to* KATERINA). Ah, keep quiet!

TIKHON. How can you know?

KATERINA. I'm going to be killed. Pray for me when I'm gone. (*Enter the* OLD LADY *with the* FOOTMAN. KATERINA *screams and hides.*)

THE LADY. Why are you hiding? It's no use. You're afraid, are you? You don't want to die? You'd like to live a little longer perhaps? I'm sure you would, pretty as you are! Ha-ha-ha! Beauty! Why, try praying to God to take away your beauty, because beauty is the cause of women's perdition. Beauty corrupts you, tempts men, and then leaves you to admire what your beauty has caused. Yes, your beauty is liable to lead many people astray. Young fools fight duels over it, slashing each other with their swords, and old fools forget to think about their impending death when they're seduced by it. And who do you think will have to answer for it all? You, you will have to. Throw your beauty into the whirlpool and hurry up about it! (KATERINA *hides herself.*) What's the point of hiding, silly thing. You can't run away from God. Yes, and all of you will burn in everlasting fire.　　　　　　　　　　　　　　(*Exits.*)

KATERINA. Ah, I'm dying!

BARBARA. Stop torturing yourself, after all. Come, step to one side and try to pray. Maybe it'll make you feel better.

KATERINA (*walking up to the wall, kneeling by it, then suddenly jumping up*). Ah, ah, the burning pit! (TIKHON, MRS.

KABANOV *and* BARBARA *crowd round her.*) Ah, my heart is all in tatters, I can't stand it any more! Mother, Tikhon, I'm guilty before God and before you! Didn't I swear to you that I wouldn't let my eyes rest on anyone while you were away! Yes, you do remember! But do you know, worthless as I am, what I did while you weren't here? The very first night I walked out of the house . . .

TIKHON (*in tears, pulling at her sleeve*). No, don't say anything, no need . . . Don't! . . . You mustn't in front of mother.

MRS. KABANOV (*sternly*). Yes, speak! Say it! Since you've begun, finish now!

KATERINA. I went out on every one of those ten nights . . . (*Sobs.* TIKHON *makes a gesture to embrace her.*)

MRS. KABANOV. Don't touch her! Who was he?

BARBARA. Don't believe her, she doesn't know what she's saying.

MRS. KABANOV. You shut up! Ah, so that's what it was. Well, what's his name?

KATERINA. Boris . . . (*A clap of thunder.*) Ah! (*Faints in* TIKHON'S *arms.*)

MRS. KABANOV. Well, son, what do you say now? I warned you what you could expect, allowing them all that freedom, but you wouldn't listen to me. So now you have it!

CURTAIN

ACT V

Same setting as Act I. Darkness is falling. Kuligin sits on a bench. Tikhon enters, walking through the park.

KULIGIN (*singing*).
> The veil of night has covered the skies,
> On earth the people have closed their eyes . . .

(*He catches sight of* TIKHON.) Ah, good-evening, sir. Are you going far?

TIKHON. I'm on my way home. I suppose you must've heard of our troubles? Our whole family is in a real turmoil.

KULIGIN. I've heard, sir.

TIKHON. And you know I went to Moscow? Before I left home, mother kept telling me how to behave but as soon as I was out of her sight, I let myself go. I was so glad to get away from it all. And so I drank all through the trip to Moscow, and I drank when I got there . . . I was trying to make up for lost time and fill myself so full it'd take me a year to sober up. I never thought about home once. And even if I had thought of it, I never would've guessed what was going on here. And have you heard what was going on?

KULIGIN. Yes, I've heard.

TIKHON. I'm a miserable, broken man! I'm lost and I don't know what I've done to deserve it.

KULIGIN. If you don't mind my saying so, sir, I think your mother's a bit rough.

TIKHON. Sure she is and, in fact, it's mostly her fault what happened. But why did it have to happen to me? What have I done to deserve it? Just now, I went over to Dikoy's and we had a few drinks. I hoped it'd make me feel better but if anything, it's made me feel worse. Ah, what my wife did to me! There can't be anything worse than that, Kuligin.

KULIGIN. It's hard to judge, sir, who's to blame for it all.

TIKHON. What are you talking about? What can be worse than what she did? I say killing her for it isn't enough! Mother says she ought to be buried alive to make her pay for it. But me, I love her, and I couldn't really hurt her. I did hit her a little but it was only because my mother made me. It breaks my heart just to look at her. Do you understand that, Kuligin? My mother keeps after her all the time, but she walks around like a dumb shadow. She does nothing but cry all the time and she's just melting away like wax. And it about kills me just to look at her.

KULIGIN. You ought to settle it all in a friendly way, I think. Perhaps you could forgive her and never mention what she did again? Why shouldn't you—I'm sure you yourself also have a few sins on your conscience, haven't you?

TIKHON. Oh, sure I have.

KULIGIN. But you should see you don't reproach her with it, even when you're drunk, and no matter how drunk. I'm sure, sir, she'd be as good a wife as you could wish for.

TIKHON. But don't you understand, Kuligin, that if it was only up to me, I'm sure I'd have forgotten the whole thing, but there's my mother, remember, and you surely don't think she'd listen to that sort of thing, do you?

KULIGIN. If I may say so, sir, I think it's high time you used your own judgment and lived your own life.

TIKHON. What d'you want me to do—tear myself in two? I'm told I haven't enough sense to live by my own judgment, so I must follow someone else's. All I'm good for is to spend my last kopek on drink, and after that I'd have to go back to my mother anyway and she'd take care of her stupid son.

KULIGIN. Ah, what a business! But tell me, what about Boris?

TIKHON. Ah, him, the rat! His uncle's sending him to Tyakhta —that's a small place on the Chinese border—to work in an office there for three years.

KULIGIN. How did he take it? Do you know?

TIKHON. Ah, he's in a state, too! He rushes all over the place, crying all the time. Just now, his uncle and I, we set on him. We abused and berated him for quite some time but he never answered back, not a word. It's as if he'd gone completely helpless all of a sudden. Do just as you please with me, he says. Just don't harm her. Because he feels terribly sorry for her too, you see.

KULIGIN. He's a nice man, Boris.

TIKHON. He's ready for his journey now and even the horses are waiting. He's miserable—something terrible! I can see that he'd give anything to say good-by to her. But why should I care? He's my enemy, after all, isn't he? He should really be tortured to death for what he's done . . .

KULIGIN. We must forgive our enemies, sir.

TIKHON. Go and tell that to mother and see what she says. So you see, friend, my family is all broken up. We're no longer like a family but like enemies to each other. My mother nagged my sister Barbara so much that finally the poor girl couldn't take any more of it and walked out on us.

KULIGIN. Where did she go?

TIKHON. Who knows? Some say she left with Vania because he's vanished, too. Now, in that, there's no doubt it was mother's fault, because she began to bully Barbara and to lock her up. Barbara said "Don't lock me in, Mother, I warn you," but mother wouldn't listen and, sure enough, Barbara ran away. So tell me, Kuligin, what am I to do now and how can I go on living? I can't bear the sight of our house. I can't look people straight in the face, and if I try to work at something, I find my hands are like wood. Now, for instance, I'm on my way home and, believe me, the mere thought of going back there sickens me.

(*Enter* GLASHA.)

GLASHA. Mr. Tikhon, sir!

TIKHON. What is it now?

GLASHA. There's trouble at home, sir.

TIKHON. Oh God, one thing after another. What is it? Tell me.

GLASHA. Your wife, sir . . .

TIKHON. Well what? Is she dead or what?

GLASHA. Oh, no sir, but she's gone. We've looked for her everywhere, but we can't find her.

TIKHON. I'd better run and look for her, Kuligin. I'm afraid she may try to kill herself, she's in such a state. Ah, she's heart-broken—I can't even tell you—and it breaks my own heart just looking at her. You sure she's not somewhere in the house, Glasha? How long ago did you miss her?

GLASHA. Not long, sir. It's our fault. We should've kept a sharper eye on her. But how could we keep track of her every second, sir. It can't be done.

TIKHON. Well, don't just stand here! Run, keep looking for her! (*Exit* GLASHA.) Come, Kuligin, let's go too. (*They exit.*)

(*For some time the stage is empty. From the opposite side,* KATERINA *enters and walks slowly across the stage.*)

KATERINA (*alone, speaking as if in a daze*). He's nowhere . . . What can he be doing now? If only I could say good-by to him, then . . . then I wouldn't mind dying. Why, why did I have to bring it all down on him? I'm worse off than before now. . . . Ah, I wish only my life had been ruined. Now, I'm ruined, he's ruined—I am dishonored and he will always be blamed for it. (*Pause.*) I wish I could remember his words. Ah, how he worried about me, how sorry he was for me. (*Clutches her head.*) I can't remember. I've forgotten every-thing . . . my nights are so painful: other people just go to sleep but for me it is like going into the grave and it's so frightening, the dark in there. I hear sounds and people singing as if they were burying someone, and all that is going on in the distance. . . . I'm so happy when daybreak comes. But I don't want to get up for I know I will only see the same faces, hear the same words, go through the same torments. Why do people look at me like that? Why don't they kill the likes of me any more these days? Why have they changed that? I hear they used to kill them. I wish they'd take me and throw me in the Volga. They say that if you're put to death, it removes the sin from you, but if you live on you must go on paying for it by suffering. But haven't I suffered enough? How much longer will I have to go on with it? What's the good of my living now? I don't want anything, nothing moves me, there's nothing for me in all God's world—but still, death won't come. I keep calling death but it won't come. All the things I see and hear can only hurt me here. (*Points to her heart.*) If I could've lived with him now, at least, I would perhaps have still found some joy in life. . . .

Yes, what difference would it make now, when I've lost my soul anyway. Ah, how I miss him! If only I could hear his voice, even without seeing him, even from afar. Oh, you wild, wild winds, carry him news of my sadness and my sorrow! I miss him so! (*Goes to the bank of the Volga and calls out loudly.*) Oh, you, my happiness! You, my life! You, my soul! I love you! Answer me! (*Starts to cry.*)

(*Enter* BORIS.)

BORIS (*not seeing her*). God, but it was her voice! Where is she? (*Looks around.*)

KATERINA (*running to him and flinging her arms around his neck*). Ah, I've found you! (*Cries on his bosom. Silence.*)

BORIS. Well, at least God has allowed us to cry a little together.

KATERINA. You haven't forgotten me!

BORIS. How could I ever forget you!

KATERINA. No, no, that's not what I meant. Are you angry with me?

BORIS. Why should I be angry?

KATERINA. Anyway, forgive me. I didn't want to harm you, but I couldn't stop myself. I said things, did things, like in a dream.

BORIS. Don't say that! How can you say such things?

KATERINA. But you, how do you feel about it all now?

BORIS. I'm going away.

KATERINA. Where?

BORIS. I'm going far away, Katerina. To Siberia.

KATERINA. Take me with you.

BORIS. I can't take you, Katerina—I'm not going of my own free will. My uncle is sending me off. I must go at once. The horses are waiting. I just got my uncle to let me go out for a little stroll before leaving because I wanted at least to see once more the place where we used to meet.

KATERINA. Then God go with you, Boris, and don't worry about me. You may miss me a little at first but later you'll get over it and forget.

BORIS. Ah, whatever happens to me, I'm free at least, Katerina, but what about you? What about your mother-in-law?

KATERINA. Well, she keeps after me, locks me in. . . . She tells everyone, Tikhon too, that they shouldn't believe a thing I say, that I am false through and through. She keeps following me around all day long and sometimes she laughs right in my face. She keeps bringing you up every minute.

BORIS. And what does Tikhon say?

KATERINA. Tikhon? Sometimes he's nice, at others—nasty, but, all the time, he keeps drinking. But I've come to loathe him now and when he tries to be tender, it's harder on me than if he beat me.

BORIS. It must be awful for you, Katerina!

KATERINA. Yes, it's awful. I wish I were dead.

BORIS. Who would've thought we'd have to pay so dearly for our love. I should have fled from here before anything happened.

KATERINA. Yes, meeting you was my undoing, my darling. I've had little happiness from you and so much sorrow! And there's much more to come still. But why think of the future? At least I've seen you now and no one can take that away from me. Now, I don't need anything else. To see you once more was all I wanted. I kept thinking that you were angry and cursing me . . .

BORIS. How could you think that? Why?

KATERINA. No, that's not really what I was trying to say. I simply missed you terribly, and now I've seen you.

BORIS. I hope they don't find us together now. That'd be the end . . .

KATERINA. Wait, wait, I wanted to tell you something else. . . . Ah, I've forgotten! I'm all mixed up. I can't remember what it was.

BORIS. I must be going now, Katerina.

KATERINA. Wait, wait!

BORIS. What was it you wanted to say?

KATERINA. I'll tell you in a second. (*Stops and thinks.*) Ah, yes, if on your way there you come across beggars, give something to each of them and ask them to pray for my sinful soul.

BORIS. If only those who are forcing us to part knew how terrible this is for me! I only wish they could feel for one day what I feel now! Good-by, Katerina! (*Embraces her and wants to go.*) Ah, you freaks, you monsters! I wish I were strong enough to show you!

KATERINA. Wait! Let me look at you once more, for the last time. (*Looks into his eyes.*) Now that's enough, God be with you! Well, go now, go quickly, hurry!

BORIS (*walks away a few steps, then stops*). I feel there's something wrong, Katerina. Perhaps you're thinking of doing something terrible? I'll worry myself to death during the journey.

KATERINA. No, no, nothing, go, good luck to you! (BORIS *wants to return to her*.) Go now, that's enough.

BORIS (*sobbing*). Well, God be with you, Katerina. (*To himself*.) I can only pray God to send her death soon, to end her suffering. (*To* KATERINA.) Good-by, Katerina!

KATERINA. Good-by, Boris!

(*Exit* BORIS. KATERINA *follows him with her eyes, remaining silent and lost in thought for some time*.)

KATERINA (*alone*). Where can I go now? Home? No, to me home is just like the grave. No, it'd be better for me in the grave. A little grave under a tree, with the sun shining on it, the rain washing it, with soft, soft grass growing around it in the spring. . . . Birds would come and sing in the tree and hatch their young . . . little flowers would grow—red ones, yellow ones, blue ones, all sorts . . . (*Dreams in silence*.) Everything's so quiet and nice. Ah, I think I feel better now. And I don't want to think any more about life. Must I really go on living? No, no, I don't want to . . . Life is bad. I don't like people, I don't like my home—I loathe it all. No, I won't go back there! No, no, no! If I went back, they'd want to talk to me, but why should I? It's all dark now and the singing has begun again. Where? What are they singing? I can't make it out. . . . It would be so nice to die now! What are they singing? What's the difference whether death comes by itself or whether I myself— All I know is I can't go on living. But it's a sin! They won't pray over me! Well, those who love me will pray anyway . . . They fold people's hands when they put them in the coffin . . . I just happened to remember that. If they catch me, they'll take me back home by force. Ah, quick, quick! (*Walks up to the bank. In a loud voice*.) My dearest! My beloved! Farewell! (*Exits*.)

(*Enter* MRS. KABANOV, TIKHON, KULIGIN *and* WORKERS *carrying lanterns*.)

KULIGIN. They say they saw her here.

TIKHON. You sure?

KULIGIN. Yes, that's what they said.

TIKHON. Well, thank God, at least they saw her alive!

MRS. KABANOV. And you were so scared and even crying already! Don't worry, we'll have to suffer her for a long time yet!

TIKHON. Who would've thought she'd try to hide in such a place! People keep coming past here all the time.

MRS. KABANOV. Can't you see what she's up to? She's still trying to have her way with you!

(*From every side people arrive with lanterns.*)

A MAN WITH A LANTERN. Found her?

MRS. KABANOV. Not yet. She seems to have vanished.

SEVERAL VOICES. Strange! Where could she have gone? There's something wrong!

A VOICE. She'll turn up!

ANOTHER VOICE. Sure, they'll find her in the end!

THIRD VOICE. I bet she'll come home by herself.

A VOICE OFFSTAGE. Hey, get a boat!

KULIGIN (*shouting in the direction of the voice*). Who's calling? What is it?

A VOICE. A woman's jumped into the river!

        (KULIGIN, *followed by several men, exits running.*)

TIKHON. Oh God, I'm sure it's her! (*Wants to run off; his mother holds him back by the arm.*) Mother, please let me go! I'll get her out of the river or . . . or I myself . . . I can't live without her!

MRS. KABANOV. No, I won't let you. You're not going to risk your life for her. She's not worth it. As if she hadn't brought enough disgrace down on our house!

TIKHON. Let me go!

MRS. KABANOV. There are plenty of people to get her out without you. I'll curse you, if you go!

TIKHON (*going down on his knees*). Let me just look at her once!

MRS. KABANOV. You'll look at her when they've fished her out.

TIKHON (*standing up, to the men*). Well, fellows, did you see anything?

A MAN. It's too dark, can't see nothing. (*Noise off-stage.*)

SECOND MAN. They're shouting something over there but I can't make out what they're saying.

FIRST MAN. They're coming this way. Yes, and I can see now. They're carrying her.

(*Some men enter.*)

ONE OF THEM. You have to hand it to Kuligin: he found her. She was very close to the bank, in a whirlpool. You can see quite far out over the water with a lantern. So he saw her dress and fished her out.

TIKHON. Is she alive?

ANOTHER MAN. Alive? How could she be? She threw herself from the steep bank and she must have hit her head against a mooring, the poor thing! But she looks as if she were alive—just a little wound on her temple and a few drops of blood.

(TIKHON *rushes forward, then stops;* KULIGIN *and some* MEN *enter carrying the dead* KATERINA.)

KULIGIN. Here's your wife. Do with her as you please. That is, you can have only her body, her soul is now facing a much more merciful Judge than you! (*Deposits body on the ground, exits running.*)

TIKHON (*falling on the body*). Katerina! Katerina!

MRS. KABANOV. Stop it! That'll do! It's sinful to cry for her.

TIKHON. Mother, it was you who killed her! It was you, you, you!

MRS. KABANOV. What! You're out of your mind! You forget you're talking to your mother!

TIKHON. You killed her! Yes, you, you!

MRS. KABANOV. Wait until we're home, we'll have a little talk about this still! (*To the* MEN, *bowing low.*) Thank you kindly, good people, for your help! (*They bow to her.*)

TIKHON. Ah, Katerina, you're all right now! But I, I must go on living and suffering. Why? . . . (*Falls on* KATERINA's *body.*)

CURTAIN

The Power of Darkness

or

When just one claw is caught
The whole bird is doomed.

by

LEO TOLSTOY

But I say unto you, That whosoever looketh on a woman to lust after her hath committed adultery with her in his heart.

And if thy right eye offend thee, pluck it out, and cast it from thee: for it is profitable for thee that one of thy members should perish, and not that thy whole body should be cast into hell.

Leo Tolstoy wrote six plays. Two of them, *The Living Corpse* and the strongly autobiographical *The Light Shines in Darkness* remained unfinished. His *First Distiller,* a one-act piece, was a dramatization of his short story, "The Imp and the Crust," and his last contribution to the stage, *The Cause of It All* (1910), was composed for amateur theatricals. Of the two remaining pieces—*The Fruits of Enlightenment,* a comedy, and *The Power of Darkness*—the latter is undoubtedly more important. Tolstoy wrote it in the fall of 1886 when he had to stay in bed because of an infected leg. Six years earlier N. Davydov, a district attorney, had told him about a case tried in the court of Tula which involved the murder of a child and the confession of the murderer at the wedding of his step-daughter. This true story served as a plot for Tolstoy's drama: he added to it, however, the poisoning of Anisia's husband. *The Power of Darkness,* initially called in one of its seven drafts "A Talon Is Caught, the Bird Is Lost," took a great deal of Tolstoy's time and energy, and he revised each act several times. He told the French scholar Paul Boyer that for the dialogue in the drama he "pillaged all his notebooks." When *The Power of Darkness* was read aloud to Tsar Alexander III he praised it highly, but the intervention of Pobedonostsev, the Procurator of the Holy Synod, reversed the situation. Pobedonostsev convinced the Tsar that the play was "an offense against taste," a "negation of ideals," and a debasing of moral feelings. The Minister of Interior was instructed to forbid the staging of such a dangerous work. Only in 1895 was the ban lifted, and the public could see *The Power of Darkness* in the best theaters in Moscow, St. Petersburg and the other big cities. It soon became a feature of the national repertory, and this situation has remained unchanged under the Soviets.

The great merit of Tolstoy's drama lay precisely in what disturbed Tsar Alexander III, who said that *The Power of Darkness* was "too realistic and frightful in its subject matter." Tolstoy showed with his usual merciless sense of reality the true conditions of peasant life in Russia. He reproduced with shattering power the backwardness, the ignorance and the elemental cruelty of "second class citizens" recently liberated from serfdom but still oppressed by poverty and evil. He showed that the law of the jungle reigned in the village and that those who made some money, such as Peter and Nikita, were corrupted by the power of money. Along with this purely realistic aspect of the play, enhanced by fully drawn characters and expressive popular idiom, Tolstoy stressed the moral meaning of what he depicted. The climax, of course, is Nikita's confession, the result of a hidden process of repentance. But the central figure of the drama is his father, the stuttering, inarticulate Akim who cannot make a complete sentence but represents the only voice of conscience in a world of crime and callousness. He possesses a natural moral sense, he condemns Nikita's lust for money and for women and he knows that the whole of existence, the whole order of things around him is sinful. Nikita is the son of Matriona, the personification of blind evil, but he is also the son of Akim, and he inherited from his humble father an unconscious yearning for the "rightful path"—and after all his crimes he comes to the side of Akim.

The Christian message of the drama is intimated rather than fully expressed—while the ethical and social themes merge organically in the movement of dramatic action—and this is what makes Tolstoy's play so successful artistically. With its immediacy of action, unity of plot, compactness of composition, terseness and almost brutal verbal directness, it is unquestionably the greatest "peasant tragedy" of Russian dramatic literature.

The Power of Darkness

CHARACTERS

PETER, 42 years old; a rich peasant in poor health
ANISIA, 32 years old; his second wife, a fancy dresser
AKULINA, 16; Peter's daughter by his first marriage, a little hard
   of hearing and a bit slow
ANUTA, 10; Peter's daughter by his second wife
NIKITA, 25; works for Peter, a sharp dresser
AKIM, 50; Nikita's father, ugly, very God-fearing
MATRIONA, 50; his wife
MARINA, 22; an orphan girl
MARTHA, Peter's sister
MITRICH, a former soldier, now a farmhand
A NEIGHBOR WOMAN
MARINA'S HUSBAND
AKULINA'S BRIDEGROOM
HIS MOTHER
HIS FATHER, a gloomy peasant
POLICE CHIEF
COACHMAN
BEST MAN, at wedding
VILLAGE ELDER
A VILLAGE WOMAN
GUESTS, men, women, girls

ACT I

*The action takes place in a large village, in the fall. A
room in Peter's spacious cottage. Peter sits on a wooden
bench, mending a horse-collar. Anisia and Akulina are spinning and singing.*

PETER (*looking out of window*). The horses have got loose
again! I'm afraid they'll end up killing that colt! Hey, you,

Nikita! Nikita! Is he deaf or what? (*Tries to listen, then shouts at women.*) Can't you shut up a minute! I can't hear a thing!

NIKITA (*from off-stage*). What is it?

PETER. Get the horses in.

NIKITA (*from off-stage*). All right, I'll do it. All in good time.

PETER (*shaking his head*). Ah, them hired hands! I'd never have one around if it wasn't for my health. They're nothing but trouble. (*Gets up, sits down again.*) Hey, Nikita! Ah, he can't hear me. Maybe one of you two, say, you Akulina, what about you going out and driving them in?

AKULINA. What, the horses?

PETER. What else?

AKULINA. All right.   (*Goes out.*)

PETER. That fellow's useless on a farm. He won't do a thing unless you push him.

ANISIA. You're a fine one to talk! When you do stir yourself, it's only to move from the stove to that there bench. But you're great at telling others what to do.

PETER. If I didn't tell you people what to do, there wouldn't be a thing left of the farm inside a year. Ah, what a bunch!

ANISIA. You give 'im ten jobs to do at the same time and then you just lie on your back and swear at him. It's easy to give orders while you're lying on a warm stove-bench, you know.

PETER (*sighing*). Ah, if it wasn't for this sickness, I wouldn't keep him a single day.

AKULINA (*off-stage*). Hey, giddup, giddup you! (*The colt neighs; the horses' hoofbeats are heard as they run through the gate; the gate creaks as it is closed.*)

PETER. He's only good with his tongue, that fellow. I'm telling you, I wouldn't keep him for a minute if . . .

ANISIA (*imitating him*). "I wouldn't keep him!" First try and move around a bit yourself, then talk!

AKULINA (*coming in*). I just managed to get 'em in. That roan . . .

PETER. Where's Nikita?

AKULINA. Nikita? He's standing in the street.

PETER. What's he standing there for?

AKULINA. What for? He's gabbing with someone on the corner.

PETER. Can't get no sense out of her! And who's he gabbing with?

AKULINA. What did you say?

(PETER *waves his hand at* AKULINA *in despair. She sits down to her spinning*).

ANUTA (*rushing in; to her* MOTHER). Nikita's parents have arrived. They're taking him back home with them!

ANISIA. You're lying?

ANUTA. It's the truth! May I die if it ain't! Nikita even said to me, he said, good-by, Anuta, don't forget to come to my wedding and you'll have a great time. I, he says, am through working here, and he laughs and laughs when he tells me that.

ANISIA (*to* PETER). See, he doesn't need you all that much. Here, he's decided to leave himself. And you kept talking about kicking him out! Isn't that something!

PETER. All right, let him go. I'll have no trouble finding another hand.

ANISIA. And what about the wages you paid him in advance? (ANUTA *walks to the door, stops, listens for a while, then goes out.*)

PETER (*frowning*). He can work off the debt next summer.

ANISIA. I know. You're pleased he's going: that makes one less mouth to feed. You don't care if I have to work like a horse all winter, do you? That daughter of yours, she isn't much of a worker, is she, and you yourself, you'll just lie on the stove-bench as usual. I know you!

PETER. Well, anyway, we don't know for sure yet. So what's the use wagging your tongue like that?

ANISIA. The yard is full of animals. You never sold that cow and you've kept all the sheep for the winter. Feeding and watering them's a full-time job by itself, and you're letting the hand go just like that! Well, I won't do a man's work to please you. I'll stretch myself out by the stove just like you and let you manage all by yourself.

PETER (*to* AKULINA). Go on, it's time to get the fodder now.

AKULINA. Get the fodder? All right. (*Puts on coat; takes a robe.*)

ANISIA. I won't work for you, I promise you I won't. Do your work yourself.

PETER. Ah, stop it. What's eating you? You're like a mad sheep or something.

ANISIA. You're the mad dog around here! What use are you to me? You don't work and what pleasure do I get out of you? Yes, a mad dog, that's all you are!

PETER (*spitting, getting up and pulling on his coat*). Ah, damn you, God forgive me! I'll go and find out what's going on.

(*Goes out.*)

ANISIA (*shouting after him*). You rotten, long-nosed devil!

AKULINA. What're you swearing at my pa for?

ANISIA. Ah, shut up, you fool.

AKULINA (*walking up to the door*). I know why you're swearing at him. It's you who's a fool and a bitch. I'm not afraid of you, you know!

ANISIA (*jumping up and looking for something to hit her with*). You'd better watch yourself or I'll give you one with the poker.

AKULINA (*opening the door*). You're a bitch, you're a devil, that's what you are! Devil, bitch, bitch, devil!   (*Runs away.*)

ANISIA (*alone; thoughtfully*). Come to the wedding, he said to her. What are they up to? Marrying him off? Watch out, Nikita, if that's what you're trying to do, I'd sure do something about it . . . I can't live without him. I won't let him.

NIKITA (*coming in, looking around and, seeing that* ANISIA *is alone, walking over to her and whispering*). Ah, I'm in trouble now! My pa has come and he wants me to go home. Come home, he says, live there and get married. He won't listen to me.

ANISIA. Well, go and get married. What's that to me?

NIKITA. So that's how it is? While I'm trying to think how best to manage it, she just tells me to go ahead and get married! How come? (*Winks at her.*) You've forgotten already?

ANISIA. Go ahead, get married! You needn't . . .

NIKITA. Why're you so prickly? Looks like you're not even going to let me love you up a bit now? What's come over you?

ANISIA. Nothing, except that if you want to get rid of me, I'd like you to know I don't need you either. So now you know.

NIKITA. Oh, enough of that stuff, Anisia. You know it isn't me who wants to leave you. What a life! So let me tell you: I definitely won't give you up. I mean, even if they marry me off, I'll come back to work here, unless they force me to stay home.

ANISIA. Much use I'll have for you once you're married!

NIKITA. But don't you understand, I can't go against my pa's will?

ANISIA. Don't try to put the blame on your pa. It's you who arranged it all this way. You've been scheming for a long time with that slut Marina. I've been watching and I know. She's put you up to it. It wasn't for nothing she came running here the other day . . .

NIKITA. Marina? Much I care about her! I have scores like her running after me.

ANISIA. Why did your father come then? You asked him to! You lied to me! (*Starts to cry.*)

NIKITA. I swear, Anisia, I never dreamt of it! I'm telling you,

I knew nothing about the whole thing. It was my old man thought it all up.

ANISIA. But if you say you don't want to go, what do you think, they'll tie you to a donkey and pull you there by force?

NIKITA. I simply say I can't go against my pa's will. But I'd still rather stay here.

ANISIA. Just say no and that's all there is to it.

NIKITA. I know a fellow who tried to refuse. They took him to the district police station and worked him over for a bit and he changed his mind. I don't think I'd like that. I understand it tickles a bit too much.

ANISIA. Stop kidding yourself, Nikita. But let me tell you—if you marry that slut, I don't know what I'll do . . . I'll kill myself, I think. I know I've sinned and broken the law but it's too late to go back now. So if you leave, I'll do away with myself.

NIKITA. Look here, Anisia, if I'd wanted to leave this house I'd have done it long ago. Just the other day Ivan Semyonich offered me a job as a coachman and I know I'd have had a fine life with him. But you know yourself I didn't accept. I guess anyone would be glad to have me and I sure wouldn't have stayed here if it hadn't been for you.

ANISIA. So just keep this in mind: my old man is bound to die any day and that'll cover up all our sins. We'll marry and you'll be master of the house.

NIKITA. Why guess what's to come? What do I care? I work now just the same as I would if it was my own place. My master likes me and so does his wife. And if women go for me, well, it's not my fault and I can't help it.

ANISIA. Will you go on loving me though?

NIKITA (putting his arms round her and hugging her tightly). Yes, this much! You'll always be in my heart.

(Enter MATRIONA; stops before icon in corner; crosses herself; NIKITA and ANISIA draw apart.)

MATRIONA. What I saw, I didn't see, what I heard, I didn't hear. There's nothing wrong in having a bit of fun with a nice, pretty woman, is there? Even calves play around and have fun and why not? But your master's in the yard and he wants you, son.

NIKITA. I came in here to get the ax, Ma.

MATRIONA. I know what ax you mean, my boy. That sort of ax's usually to be found around dames.

NIKITA (bending and picking up the ax). Well, Ma, do you really reckon to marry me off? I say there's no point to it. And then, I don't feel like getting married, you know.

MATRIONA. Why, what would I want to marry you off for, son? I don't see why you shouldn't go on living as you are and having all the fun you can. It's all your pa's idea, my boy. But now, you'd better go and find your boss. We don't need you here to settle matters.

NIKITA. It really beats me! One moment they tell me I've gotta get married, the next, I mustn't. Can't say it makes much sense to me! (*Exits.*)

ANISIA. So what is it, Matriona! Do you really intend to marry him off?

MATRIONA. Who to, dearie? What do we have to offer along with him? It's just my man—he goes around wagging his tongue about marrying off our Nikita. He's just being stupid: horses just don't run away from oats and men don't run away when they've got a good thing going for them. I'd say that goes for my Nikita, too. You don't imagine I can't see what's going on here? (*Winks.*)

ANISIA. Well, why should I hide it from you, Matriona, since you know everything anyway. So, all right, I've done wrong. I've fallen for your son.

MATRIONA. Some news, dearie! Didn't you realize that old Auntie Matriona's known it all along? I've seen plenty in my lifetime, my girl, believe me! I can see what's buried six feet underground, my little flower; and I know why young married women like you may need sleeping powders too. I've brought some with me. (*Unties her handkerchief and takes out some small papers with powders in them.*) I only see what it's my business to see and I never see what isn't any of my business and I don't know nothing about it. That's how it is with me. Auntie Matriona was young once too and she also had to get along somehow living with her own old fool. So you can be sure, I know all the seventy-seven tricks there are. I can see, my jewel, that your old man is sick and you can't have much fun living with him. He's so far gone, you could prod him with a hayfork and he still wouldn't bleed. Looks like you'll bury him before spring. So you'll have to have a man around the house and I don't see why my son Nikita shouldn't do you. He's no worse than the next fellow, is he? So why should I take him away from a good thing? Do you think I'm an enemy to my own flesh and blood?

ANISIA. I just don't want him to walk out on us now.

MATRIONA. Don't worry, he won't, dearie. It's all just a stupid idea of my old man's. He's off his head these days, and when he gets hold of a notion sometimes, you need chisel and mallet to knock it out of him.

ANISIA. How did it all start in the first place?

MATRIONA. Well, I'll tell you, love. You know yourself the way women go for my boy and no wonder, even if I do say so myself. He's handsome enough. Well, before he came to you, he used to work in a railroad yard and they had a girl working there as cook, an orphan, you know, and she latched on to him, that girl.

ANISIA. It was Marina, wasn't it?

MATRIONA. It sure was, plague take her. Well, whatever happened between them, my old man found out somehow. Either he heard people talking or the girl herself came and squealed to him.

ANISIA. Ah, the brazen hussy!

MATRIONA. And so my old man got all het up: "He must marry her at once," the stupid fool says. "He must put right the wrong he's done. So," he decides, "let's fetch the boy home and let 'em get married." I tried to reason with him, but it was just a waste of breath. All right, then, I says to myself, let's try to work it differently. So I pretend to go along with him—which, take my word, my pearl, is the best way to handle a fool— knowing that when it comes down to business, I can always switch back to my old stand and turn him around with me. A woman can change her mind seventy-seven times while she's getting down off the stove-bench, so how can he guess what's in my mind at any moment? "Well," I says to him, "you've got the right idea there. But still," I says, "we should think it over a bit more. Let's go and see Nikita's boss and talk it over with him first and see what he says." And so we came over.

ANISIA. Ah, Matriona, but what'll happen if he insists and orders him to marry the hussy?

MATRIONA. Orders? Well, he can take his orders and stick them under the dog's tail! Don't worry, love, there won't be no marriage. I'll discuss the whole business now with your old man, and when we're through taking it apart, there'll be nothing left of it. I only came along with Nikita's father to humor him. What do you expect—that I'd let my son marry a slut when he's living here in peace and happiness? Do I look like such a fool?

ANISIA. She came running after him here too, that Marina. And so when I heard his parents wanted to marry him off to her, I felt like someone had stabbed me in the chest. I imagined he had a soft spot for her in his heart.

MATRIONA. Do you think my son's such a fool then, my pet? How could he love that homeless whore? My Nikita's a clever fellow, remember! He knows who to love! And you, dearie, quit worrying! We won't take him away from you. Not on your life! And we won't marry him off, you can be sure of that. Just let us have a bit of cash to tide us over and we'll let him stay here with you.

ANISIA. If Nikita left, I think I wouldn't want to live in this world.

MATRIONA. I understand you, all right! You're a young woman full of sap and vigor, so I can see where it's no joke for you to live with an old wreck like your husband.

ANISIA. Ah, Matriona, dear, believe me, I've had my fill of that long-nosed scarecrow of mine. I wish I'd never set eyes on him again.

MATRIONA. Yes, you've got yourself into quite a mess, dearie! Here, listen though. (*Looks around; whispers.*) I went to see that old man, you know, the one who makes them powders and he gave me some of two kinds. "This is a sleeping powder," he says. "Give him one paper like that and he'll sleep so that you could walk all over him without waking him up. And that one," he says, "if you give it to someone in a drink, it has no smell at all but it's plenty strong enough. Here," he says, "give it to him a pinch at a time—seven times like that. And then," he says, "she'll soon be free."

ANISIA. Ooooh! What're you up to?

MATRIONA. Leaves no mark, the fellow swore. He charged me one ruble for it. "I can't let you have it for less," he says, "because it isn't easy to get these powders." I paid him out of my own pocket, love, because I says to myself, if Anisia don't take it, I'll sell it to Mikhailovna for sure.

ANISIA. But . . . but what if something bad came of it?

MATRIONA. What bad could come of it, dearie? I'd understand if your man was healthy, but the way he is, it's a miracle he's still alive. He's not meant to stay long with us anyway. There're plenty of cases like that.

ANISIA. Oh, my poor, poor head! I'm afraid, Auntie Matriona, this'll get us into trouble yet. Ah, what've I come to!

MATRIONA. All right, give me the powders back.

ANISIA. What do you do, dissolve them in water just like the others?

MATRIONA. He says it works better in hot tea. You just don't notice a thing—no smell, no nothing. And he's a clever man and knows what he's talking about, believe me.

ANISIA (*taking the powders*). Ah, ah, my poor head! I'd never have gone in for this if my life wasn't real hell.

MATRIONA. And don't forget that ruble. I promised the old

man, I'd give it him, and he must be worried, the poor soul.

ANISIA. Sure, sure! (*Goes to the chest and hides the powders there.*)

MATRIONA. And keep it to yourself, dearie—don't let people get wind of it. But if anything goes wrong, God forbid, say it's cockroach powder. (*Pockets the ruble* ANISIA *gives her.*) Because it does work on cockroaches too . . . (*Stops short.*)

(*Enter* PETER *and* AKIM; AKIM *crosses himself before the icon.*)

PETER (*sits down*). So, what d'you say, Akim?

AKIM. It'd be better, a bit better, that's sure . . . For it's not right somehow . . . er . . . him fooling around, I mean . . . So now, I'd like to get him down to work. And if you let him—you know what I mean—well, we could do that. It'd be better . . .

PETER. All right, all right, sit down, we'll talk about it. (AKIM *sits down.*) Well, what is it? You want to marry him off, do you?

MATRIONA. Marrying him off could wait, to be sure, Peter. You know, how hard up we are—how could we think of marriage just now? We don't have enough to fill our bellies as it is, so I guess the marriage'll just have to wait.

PETER. You're the ones to judge what's best.

MATRIONA. No hurry about the marriage, Peter: marriage isn't like raspberries, won't rot on the bush.

PETER. But there's nothing wrong with marrying him off.

AKIM. That is, I wanted to, see . . . And then I got myself a job in town and I like it fine.

MATRIONA. Eh, talk of a job! Cleaning out cesspools! When he came home the other day, I puked and puked. I almost split my guts, puking.

AKIM. Sure, at first I guess it does sort of make you feel sick but you get used to it and it isn't any worse than er . . . waste in a brewery maybe, and the likes of us can't be fussy, see. And as for the smell then, you can change your clothes sometimes too. So, see, I wanted to have my Nikita home. Let him keep things going at home while I do my job here in town and earn something for the marriage.

PETER. So you want your son to stay home? I see. But what about the money I've paid him in advance?

AKIM. That's right, Peter, very right. He hired himself out to you so let 'im work it off. I only want you to let him go for a little while, for him to get married.

PETER. Well, why not, that could be arranged.

MATRIONA. Yes, but, Peter, there's an argument there between my old man and me. I'll be frank with you like before God Himself and you'll just have to judge between us, who's right. He's got that idea into his head and now he keeps on and on: "Let's marry him off, let's marry him off!" But just ask him who he wants to marry his son to. Ah, if she was a nice, decent girl, I sure wouldn't stand in his way because, of course, I'm not my own child's enemy. But the one he's found for him is a no-good slut . . .

AKIM. That's not right . . . I say it wasn't the girl's fault. It's our Nikita was to blame, if you see what I mean.

PETER. What did he do?

AKIM. Well, see, Nikita was going with this girl and so it's him . . .

MATRIONA. Wait, let me tell it. My tongue's more soft than yours. Well, as you know, Peter, before he came to work for you, our Nikita worked on the railroad. Well, and it was there that this stupid slut latched onto him. It was that Marina, she did the cooking for the railroad workers. Well, so now the hussy's accusing our son Nikita; claims he seduced her.

PETER. Sounds like a bad business.

MATRIONA. But it's her who runs after fellows herself; she's nothing but a whore if you ask me.

AKIM. There you go again, old woman . . . I mean, it's not like you say at all. That's not the way it is.

MATRIONA. That's all I hear from my fine, God-fearing old man: I mean, you know, I mean . . . Don't take my word for it, Peter, go and ask around about the hussy. They'll all tell you she's nothing but a homeless slut.

PETER (*to* AKIM). Well, Akim, if that's so, marrying your son to her wouldn't be such a good thing after all. A daughter-in-law isn't an old sock you can just pull off and throw away.

AKIM (*with heat*). My old woman, she isn't fair, I mean, the things she says about the girl. Me, I say she's a good girl, a very fine girl and I'm sorry, I mean mighty sorry, for her!

MATRIONA. Ah, just listen to the wet rag!

> About the whole world he worries his head
> But leaves his own children home without bread!

So now he's sorry for the hussy! But he isn't a bit sorry for his own child! If you're really so sorry for her, put her round your own neck and carry her around the rest of your life instead of talking nonsense.

AKIM. It isn't nonsense.

MATRIONA. Now don't get on your high horse. Let me have my

say . . .

AKIM (*interrupting her*). No, it's not nonsense, I say. You just twist things your way. I mean, whether about the girl or yourself or anything. Because you think, the way you twist it, things'll be better for you. But God, He likes to twist things His way and that's what'll happen here, I mean.

MATRIONA. I'm just wasting breath on you.

AKIM. She's a hard worker, the girl is, a decent sort, if you know what I mean . . . And poor as we are, an extra pair of hands would be a big help and the wedding wouldn't come so high. But the main thing is that injury's been done her, and that she's an orphan and all alone, without no one to look out for her, I mean. And he done her wrong.

MATRIONA. Every hussy comes up with a story like that.

ANISIA. Don't listen to all the stories women tell you, Akim. They can make up some fine ones, you know!

AKIM. But there's God, I mean, there's God and to Him she's a human being just like the rest, don't you think so?

MATRIONA. There he goes again.

PETER. Well, let me tell you, Akim, what I think, now. It's true what they say: you can't believe everything those girls say. Now, since Nikita is alive and right here, why not send for him and ask him to tell us the truth. He won't want to destroy his soul, so he'll tell us. So call him, somebody. (ANISIA *gets up*.) Tell 'im his father wants him.

(*Exit* ANISIA.)

MATRIONA. That's the fair way, Peter. That'll settle the argument. Let's see what the lad has to say for himself. Anyway, nowadays they don't go much for forcing people into marriage and so the boy must have his say too, after all. I say he'd never want to marry her and disgrace himself to his dying day. I say let him stay here and go on working for you, Peter. And there's no need for you to let him come home in the summer either: we can hire some hands around there if you let us have, say, ten rubles now.

PETER. We'll get to that later. First let's settle this marriage business.

AKIM. What I want to say, Peter, is . . . it often happens, see . . . people try to fix things the way it suits them best and they forget about God. So you twist things the way you think it best for you but really you're only tying a load round your neck. You mean it for the best but it turns out for the worst. So, I mean, the best thing is to remember God.

PETER. Sure thing, we must remember God.

AKIM. Sometimes it looks worse, but when you do things in

God's way, it still makes you feel good, if you see what I mean. So the way I figure it, I'll have the lad marry the girl and that way he'll atone for his sin and act law-abiding like. And so he'll live home and it'll be me who'll work out in town. I don't mind my job, I say that's the way God would approve, with the girl being a lonely orphan and all that. Otherwise it'd be like when the peasants stole that firewood last winter. . . . They cheated the storekeeper but they sure didn't cheat God . . . I mean . . .

(*Enter* NIKITA *and* ANUTA.)

NIKITA. You wanted me? (*Sits down, taking out his tobacco.*)

PETER (*reproachfully*). Why, have you no manners? Your father asks for you and you sit down and take yourself a smoke. Get up and come over here! (NIKITA *stands up, leaning nonchalantly against the table and smiling.*)

AKIM. It seems there's a complaint against you, Nikita . . . a complaint, see what I mean?

NIKITA. And who's complaining?

AKIM. Who's complaining? A girl, an orphan's complaining. It's Marina's complaining against you.

NIKITA (*chuckling*). Well, that's a surprise, really. What can she be complaining about? Who told you about it, Pa? She did, I guess?

AKIM. It's me who's asking now and you must answer, see. Did you get mixed up with her? Tell me: did you or didn't you get mixed up with her, I mean?

NIKITA. I don't really understand what you're asking me.

AKIM. Did you fool around with her, I mean? Did you or didn't you fool around with Marina?

NIKITA. Fool around with her? Why, you do all sorts of things out of boredom—kid with the cook a bit, play the mouth organ while she dances, that sort of thing.

PETER. Don't try to dodge, Nikita, just answer plain what your father wants to know.

AKIM (*solemnly*). Know, Nikita, that you can hide things from men but you can't hide them from God. Remember that, Nikita, and don't lie! She's a poor orphan and it's easy to harm her, see, so you'd better tell us what really happened.

NIKITA. But what's there to say? I've told you all there is and it isn't much as you can see. (*Becomes agitated.*) But she's liable to go around telling stories as if them she's blaming were dead and couldn't talk back. Remember all the things she said about Fedka? So what it comes down to is that it's impossible even to crack a joke nowadays without getting yourself in a real mess. Why, all she has to do is say whatever comes into her head about you.

AKIM. Look out, Nikita, lies always come out. Answer now: was there something between you and her or not?

NIKITA (*aside*). I wish I could get rid of them! (*To his* FATHER.) I said, I don't know what she's talking about. I never had nothing to do with her! (*Furiously.*) I swear to Christ! May I never take a step away from here if I'm lying! (*Crosses himself.*) I say I don't know nothing about it all. (*Silence; then* NIKITA *goes on even more angrily.*) So you've decided to marry me off to her! Ah, it's a real disgrace, I'm telling you! Nowadays there's no law that says you can make people marry when they don't want to. So that's that and besides I've sworn already that I don't know nothing! What more d'you want of me?

MATRIONA (*to her* HUSBAND). So you see, you blockhead, you believe everything they tell you. I say you're pestering the lad for nothing. Better let him live here just as he did before and work for his master and Peter will let us have ten rubles to help us out. And when the time comes, we'll marry off our Nikita, all right.

PETER. Well, what do you say, Akim?

AKIM (*clicks his tongue in disapproval at his son*). Watch out, Nikita—an innocent tear never falls unavenged. I mean, it'll always fall on the head of the one who done wrong, see what I mean? So you'd better watch out.

NIKITA. Watch out yourself if you want to, there's nothing for me to watch out for. (*Sits down.*)

ANUTA. I'll go and tell ma everything. (*Rushes out of the room.*)

MATRIONA (*to* PETER). Well, you can see for yourself, dear Peter, he's a real muddlehead, this husband of mine. Once he gets some cockeyed notion into his bean, you can't beat it out even with a hammer and chisel. Looks like we've bothered you for nothing at all. So, let the boy live here with you as he's been doing; hold on to him, he's your hired hand.

PETER. And you, Akim, what do you say to that?

AKIM. Me? Well, it's up to him. I can't force him to act one way or the other. I only meant, you see . . .

MATRIONA. You don't know yourself what you're blabbering about, man. Let him go on living the way he's lived up to now. He doesn't want to quit his job and we don't really need him at home. We can manage fine without him.

PETER. One more thing, Akim: if you intend to take him home

for the summer, you might just as well take him right away. I don't need him just for the winter. If he wants to stay and work for me, it must be for the whole year round.

MATRIONA. That's right and he hired himself out for the year round in the first place. As for us, at harvest time we can get us some seasonal help if you'll let us have ten now.

PETER. So what'll it be, Akim? Shall I hire him for another year?

AKIM (*sighing*). Well, it looks as if that's the way it's gotta be, so . . . I mean, all right.

MATRIONA. So he's hired out for another year come St. Dmitri's day. And I'm sure you won't be mean about the wages and will let us have that ten rubles. It'd come in real handy right now. (*Gets up and bows.*)

(*Enter* ANISIA *and* ANUTA; ANISIA *sits down in a corner.*)

PETER. All right then, let's go to the tavern and drink to the deal. What d'you say, Akim, shall we have a glass of vodka?

AKIM. I don't drink it . . . I mean, I don't drink licker.

PETER. Well, let's go and have some tea.

AKIM. Tea? That I indulge in. All right then.

PETER. And the wives can have tea, too. And you, Nikita, go and drive the sheep in and change the straw.

NIKITA. All right.

(*All exit except* NIKITA. *It gets dark.*)

NIKITA (*alone, lighting a cigarette*). They sure pestered me about my doings with the girls. It'd have taken quite a time if I'd really wanted to tell him about all my dealing with dames. And then they wanted me to marry her! Well, if I had to marry all of them I'd have a lotta wives. And what would I gain getting married? This way, I have all the advantages of a married man. All the fellows around envy me for it. Eh, it was a real smart move of mine to go up to that icon and swear and cross myself. That made them cut out their damn nonsense. Some say its dangerous to swear to something that isn't true. But there's nothing to it really. It's simple.

(*Enter* AKULINA *wearing a long overcoat and carrying a rope. She puts down the rope, removes her coat and walks toward the storeroom.*)

AKULINA. You could at least have lighted the lamp.

NIKITA. What for? To look at you? I can see enough as it is!

AKULINA. Ah, go to hell.

(*Enter* ANUTA; *runs to* NIKITA.)

ANUTA (*whispering to him*). Come, there's a person wants to see you. I'm not tricking, cross my heart.

NIKITA. What person?

ANUTA. Marina—the one who works for the railroad. She's waiting for you around the corner.

NIKITA. You're lying.

ANUTA. Cross my heart.

NIKITA. What's she want?

ANUTA. She wants to see you. She told me she had to tell you something. I tried to talk to her but she only wanted to know if it was true you were quitting your job here. So I says to her, it isn't true, it was just his pa wanted to make him quit and get married but you wouldn't do it and are staying to work for us another year yet. And then she says to me, please, for God's sake, send him here, to see me. I have something to tell him. And she's been waiting there a long time so you'd better hurry over.

NIKITA. To hell with her. Why should I go?

ANUTA. She says, "If he don't come, I'm coming into the house and find him myself." I swear that's what she said: "I'm coming in myself."

NIKITA. I guess she'll stand there waiting for a while and then go away.

ANUTA. Then she asked me: "Is it true they want to marry him to Akulina?"

AKULINA (getting up and walking over to NIKITA). Marry Akulina to who?

ANUTA. To Nikita here.

AKULINA. Is that so? Who says so?

NIKITA. Looks like people say so. (Looks at her and laughs.) Tell me, Akulina, would you marry me if I asked you?

AKULINA. Marry you? Once, I guess I'd have accepted, but now I sure wouldn't.

NIKITA. Why wouldn't you any more?

AKULINA. Because you wouldn't love me.

NIKITA. Why wouldn't I?

AKULINA. She won't let you. (Laughs.)

NIKITA. Who won't let me?

AKULINA. Why, my stepmother, to be sure. She keeps nagging and never takes her eyes off you.

NIKITA (laughing). I see you notice things.

AKULINA. D'you think I'm blind or what? Anyone'd notice it. Today she's been nagging and nagging my pa all the time—the fat witch! (She goes into storeroom, leaving door ajar.)

ANUTA. Hey, Nikita! Look! (They look out of the window.) See her coming? I swear it's her. I'd better go! (Exits.)

(Enter MARINA.)

MARINA. What're you doing to me, Nikita?

NIKITA. What'm I doing? Well, exactly nothing.

MARINA. You want to say nothing happened?

NIKITA (*getting up; angrily*). What did you come here for?

MARINA. Oh, Nikita!

NIKITA. You dames're a funny lot. Why did you come, I asked you?

MARINA. Nikita!

NIKITA. Well, yes, I'm Nikita and you know it. Now tell me what you want of me or go away.

MARINA. I see you want to get rid of me, to forget me, Nikita.

NIKITA. And what is there to remember? You couldn't tell me that yourself. You sent Anuta to me and stood there, hiding round the corner and waiting. Well, I didn't turn up, did I? So you might've guessed I don't need you any more. It's just as plain as that. So go away now.

MARINA. You don't need me! You say that now. I trusted you when you told me you loved me and would go on loving me. And now, after you've disgraced me, you decide you don't need me no more.

NIKITA. You're just wasting your breath, woman, and what you say don't make any sense. You tried it on my father already. So please go away now.

MARINA. You know very well I never had anyone before you, never loved anyone. I don't mind whether you marry me or not, but why have you stopped loving me? What have I done wrong? Why?

NIKITA. It won't do us any good to keep talking and talking about it. Just go, please—I'm asking you! Ah, women are such a stupid bunch!

MARINA. What hurts me isn't that you lied when you promised to marry me but that you've stopped loving me. And what hurts even more is that you haven't just stopped loving me; you've fallen in love with another woman. And I know who she is.

NIKITA (*walking toward her threateningly*). It's no good trying to reason with the likes of you. You don't seem to understand what I say. So go away before I do something you won't like.

MARINA. Something I won't like? Why, would you like to beat me, perhaps? Go ahead, then! Why're you turning your snout away? Eh, you!

NIKITA. What's the good, people'll come and all that. Anyway, we've nothing to say to each other any more, so why keep on this way?

MARINA. So it's the end, you say? There was something and now it's just not there any more, and you advise me to forget it. Eh, Nikita, I treasured my maiden's honor more than anything in the world; but you disgraced me and took no pity on me, a lonely girl. (*Starts to cry.*) And now you don't want to have anything to do with me any more. You ruined me but I don't bear a grudge against you. God forgive you. If you find a better girl—you'll forget me altogether; if she's worse—you may remember sometimes. And I guess you will remember me, Nikita. Good-by, then, if that's the way you feel. Good-by for the last time. (*Wants to embrace him; clasps his head.*)

NIKITA (*pushing her away*). What's the good talking to you? All right, if you won't go, I will. Stay here by yourself.

MARINA (*screaming*). You're a beast, that's what you are! (*From the doorway.*) God won't let you be happy!

(*Exits crying.*)

AKULINA (*stepping out of the storeroom*). You're a rat, Nikita.

NIKITA. Why do you say that?

AKULINA. Ah, the way she screamed! (*Begins to cry.*)

NIKITA. And what's that to you?

AKULINA. You offended her, you did . . . you hurt her . . . You could hurt me too just like that . . . Ah, you're a dirty rat, that's what you are.   (*Exits into storeroom.*)

NIKITA (*alone; after a silence*). What a mess! I love dames better than sugar but when you let yourself go, there's always trouble.

CURTAIN

ACT II

Six months later. The village street. To the left, Peter's house with steps leading up to the entrance door. To the right, a gate and a corner of the yard where Anisia is stripping hemp.

ANISIA (*alone, putting down her work and listening*). I can hear him groaning again. He must've climbed down from the stove-bench. (*Enter AKULINA carrying two buckets on a yoke.*) He's calling. Go see what he wants. Ah, that groaning!

AKULINA. Why don't you go yourself?

ANISIA. Go, I tell you.

(AKULINA *goes into the house.*)

ANISIA (*alone*). Ah, it's awful what he's doing to me! Won't tell me where he's got the money hidden, won't tell me anything! The other day he was fiddling with something in the passage, so maybe he hid it there. But he must've moved it since and now I've no idea where it can be. A good thing he's afraid to part with his cash, though, 'cause that means it must be somewhere around the house at least. If only I could get my hands on it. He had it with him yesterday but since then he's stowed it away, I don't know where. Ah, he's got me so exhausted I'm about ready to fall off my feet.

(AKULINA *comes out of the house, tieing kerchief over her head.*)

ANISIA. Where're you off to?

AKULINA. Where? Well, he told me to go and fetch Aunt Martha. Call my sister, he says to me, I must have a talk with her before I die.

ANISIA (*aside*). So he asked for his sister. Ah, my poor, poor head! Looks as if he wants to hand the money over to her! What am I going to do? (*To* AKULINA.) Don't go! Well, where are you off to?

AKULINA. To fetch aunt.

ANISIA. Forget it. I'll go fetch her myself. You take the wash to the river or you'll never get through with it before evening.

AKULINA. But he said I was the one should go.

ANISIA. Just do as I tell you. I'll get Martha like I said. You take the shirts from the fence and be off with you to the river.

AKULINA. The shirts? But see you go to Martha's. He said he wanted her.

ANISIA. I said I'd go. Where's Anuta?

AKULINA. Anuta? She's minding the calves.

ANISIA. Send her here to me. I guess the calves won't run away.   (AKULINA *picks up the wash and exits.*)

ANISIA (*alone*). If I don't go, he'll be furious and yell at me and if I do—he'll hand the cash over to his sister. And then all my efforts will be wasted. I don't know what to do. Ah, my poor head is splitting. (*Goes back to stripping hemp.*)

(*Enter* MATRIONA *dressed for a journey with a bundle on a stick.*)

MATRIONA. May God help you, dearie.

ANISIA (*looking around, dropping her work and throwing up her hands in joy*). Oh, Matriona, I never expected you, but I guess God has sent you just in time!

MATRIONA. Why? What's the matter?

ANISIA. I'm going crazy with worry. Looks like trouble!

MATRIONA. I hear he's still alive?

ANISIA. Ah, it's terrible: he's hardly alive but he won't lie down and die just the same.

MATRIONA. He didn't hand over the money to anyone, did he?

ANISIA. Just now he was asking for his sister Martha. Must be about the money, I guess.

MATRIONA. That's for sure. But you say he hasn't handed it to anyone else?

ANISIA. No, he hasn't given it to anyone. I've been watching him like a hawk.

MATRIONA. Well, where is it then?

ANISIA. He won't tell me and so far I ain't been able to find out. He keeps changing it from one hiding place to another. And then, I can't move around freely because of his daughter Akulina. She may be an idiot but she still keeps her eye on me and watches everything. Ah, my poor, aching head, Auntie Matriona, I'm really at the end of my tether.

MATRIONA. Well, love, if that money gets out of the house, out of the reach of your hands, you'll never forgive yourself as long as you live. They'll kick you out of this house empty-handed. Then you'll have put up with a man you loathed all these years and, when finally you're a widow, you'll have to take to the road with a beggar's pouch for all your troubles.

ANISIA. Don't say that, Matriona, don't. I'm heart-broken enough and there's no one I can turn to for advice. I tried to talk to Nikita but he backs away, won't have anything to do with the business. All he did was to tell me yesterday that it was hidden under the floorboards.

MATRIONA. Well, did you look?

ANISIA. I couldn't, the old man was hanging around all the time. But I know he either keeps the money on him or stows it somewhere or other.

MATRIONA. Just remember, my dear girl, if you once make a mistake, you'll never catch up with it again. (*Whispers.*) You gave him his tea real strong, didn't you?

ANISIA. Uhuh! . . . (*Wants to go on talking but sees a* NEIGHBOR WOMAN *and stops.*)

NEIGHBOR. Anisia, Anisia! Your husband's calling you!

ANISIA. It sounds like he's calling but it's just that he coughs like that all the time. Ah, he's very sick, dear.

NEIGHBOR (*to* MATRIONA). Ah, hello, grandma, what brings you here? Where did you come from?

MATRIONA. Straight from home, dearie, I came to visit my

son and bring him some shirts. A mother's always worried about her boy, you know.

NEIGHBOR. You're so right! (*To* ANISIA.) I thought of bleaching my linen but I guess it's too soon yet. No one else has started.

ANISIA. Yes, what's the hurry?

MATRIONA. Well, have they given him the last sacrament?

ANISIA. Sure, the priest came over yesterday.

NEIGHBOR. I saw him yesterday, dear, and I say it's a miracle he's still alive. He's all wasted away. (*To* MATRIONA.) The other day it looked like it was all over already and they laid him under the icons and started wailing and even got ready to wash the body . . .

ANISIA. That's right, but he got better and now he's walking around again.

MATRIONA. What are you going to do then? Give him the sacrament again?

ANISIA. Yes, that's what people advise. If he's still alive tomorrow, we'll send for the priest.

NEIGHBOR. It must be hard for you, Anisia dear. It's just as they say: the one who's worst off isn't the sick one but the one who looks after him.

ANISIA. It's worse even than you think, dear.

NEIGHBOR. Oh, I can imagine what it's like: he's been dying like this for a whole year and you've been bound hand and foot all that time.

MATRIONA. And when he dies, it won't be no joy for her to be a widow either. Well, it's not that bad as long as a woman's young, but as she gets on, it's real rough on her and there'll be no one to be sorry for her. Ah, old age isn't any fun, believe me! I haven't come from very far but I'm so tired, I can't even feel my feet. Now tell me, where's my son, Anisia?

ANISIA. He's plowing. But why don't you come in? We'll put the samovar on. I'm sure a nice cup of tea will do you a world of good.

MATRIONA (*sitting down*). Ah, I'm so tired, dearies. As to calling the priest, you sure ought to do that. People say it's good for the soul.

ANISIA. Yes, I'll send for him tomorrow.

MATRIONA. You're right to do that. (*To* NEIGHBOR.) As to us, dearie, we're going to have a wedding in our village.

NEIGHBOR. When, in the spring?

MATRIONA. Yes, it's just like the saying goes: A poor man must make haste to marry before the night is over. It's Semyon Matveich who's marrying Marina.

ANISIA. So she got herself a husband and happiness after all.

NEIGHBOR. Must be a widower who's marrying her to look after his children.

MATRIONA. Right. He has four of them. No decent girl would've accepted, so he took her. And you should see how pleased she is! And she was right: she was like a cracked wine glass with the wine dripping out of it.

NEIGHBOR. Yes, I heard things about her. And is he well off?

MATRIONA. Enough to live on.

NEIGHBOR. Just like you said, who else could he find with all those kids. Take Mikhail, for instance, he's a fine man, I'm telling you . . .

MAN'S VOICE (*from off-stage*). Hey, Mavra, where the hell have you got to? Go drive the cow in. (*Exit* NEIGHBOR.)

MATRIONA (*while* NEIGHBOR *is still in sight, speaking in an ordinary voice*). Thank God they're marrying off that Marina now, dearie. At least my old fool will forget about her and our Nikita! (*Changes to whisper.*) Ah, she's gone at last! Well, did you give him that tea?

ANISIA. Ah, better don't mention that stuff to me! I wish we'd left him to die by himself. As it is, he still isn't dead and I've just fallen into sin for nothing. Ah, my poor little head, why did you have to come to me with those powders of yours!

MATRIONA. What's wrong with the powders, dearie? They're just regular sleeping powders and I don't see why I shouldn't have given 'em to you. They couldn't do him no harm, you know!

ANISIA. I'm not talking about the sleeping powders but that white one.

MATRIONA. That, love, is a healing powder. Nothing wrong with it either.

ANISIA (*sighing*). I know that but I'm still afraid. He's got me completely exhausted.

MATRIONA. Have you given him much of the stuff?

ANISIA. I gave it to him twice.

MATRIONA. Well, did he notice anything?

ANISIA. I tasted it myself. It's a bit bitter, I say. Him, he drank it all and after that he says to me, "Even tea makes me sick now," he says. So I says to him that to a sick man everything tastes foul and then I got scared, Matriona dear.

MATRIONA. You better try not to think about it. Thinking only makes it worse, my girl.

ANISIA. I wish you hadn't given me the stuff and pushed me into it. When I remember, it makes me shake all over. Ah, why did you have to do it?

MATRIONA. What're you saying, love? May God forgive you! Why are you trying to blame me for it all? You'd better watch out, my girl. It never pays to try blaming our sins on the innocent. Remember, if something goes wrong, I had nothing to do with it. I never gave you any powders, never heard anything about it all and I'll swear on the cross that I never even knew such powders exist in the world. You'd better use your head, my lassie. Yes, just the other day we were talking about you and saying, "Ah, the poor thing, what a terrible time she must be having with that idiot stepdaughter and a sick husband." And then someone said, "Anyone'd do anything to get away from that sort of life."

ANISIA. But I'm not trying to back out of anything. To get out of a situation like mine, I'd do anything. Either I'll hang myself or I'll strangle him. It's no life the way things are now!

MATRIONA. Well then, it's no time for blabbering. Just look for that cash and make him drink that tea.

ANISIA. Ah, my poor little head! I don't know what to do now. I'm so frightened. It'd have been so much better if he'd died by himself. I hate having this sin on my conscience.

MATRIONA (*angrily*). Why don't he tell you where the money is? You think it's a nice thing to do? What does he think, he's gonna take it with him? God forbid such a big sum should get lost! Don't you think that'd be a sin, too? What does he think he's doing? So why should you be sorry for him then?

ANISIA. I don't know any more . . . He's completely exhausted me.

MATRIONA. What is there not to know? It's quite clear, the whole thing. If you miss your chance now, you'll be sorry all the rest of your life. If he hands the money to that sister of his, you're done for.

ANISIA. Yes, and I have to go and fetch her. He's asking for her.

MATRIONA. Wait before you fetch her. Put the samovar on first. We'll give him his tea and then, the two of us, we'll search for that money. I'm sure we'll stumble on it somehow.

ANISIA. Ah, I hope nothing goes wrong.

MATRIONA. Why, can you think of something better you can do now? You haven't got this far just to get a whiff of the money and then let it slip between your fingers, have you? So you'd better get going.

ANISIA. So I'll go and light the samovar.

MATRIONA. Do that, lovie. Go on, then you won't have to be sorry later. (*As* ANISIA *walks away,* MATRIONA *calls her back.*) Wait, Anisia! Listen, you'd better not tell Nikita nothing about it all. He's silly, you know, and if he finds out about those powders, he's liable to do something real stupid. He's too soft-hearted, my lad is. When he was a boy, he hated even to cut a chicken's throat. So don't say nothing to him. He can't think straight about this sort of thing. (*Stops horrified;* PETER *appears in the doorway.*)

PETER. What's up with you, Anisia, can't you hear me? Oh, who's that here with you? (*Lets himself drop onto the bench.*)

ANISIA (*going up to him*). Why are you up? You should stay in bed, you know!

PETER. Did Akulina go to get Martha? I feel something awful! I wish I'd die quickly.

ANISIA. She was too busy. I sent her to the river. I'll go and get Martha myself as soon as I get a minute.

PETER. Why don't you send Anuta? Where is she? Ah, I feel terrible! I can't stand it any more.

ANISIA. I've sent for Anuta already.

PETER. Ooooh! Where is she?

ANISIA. That's what I'd like to know, damn her.

PETER. I can't stand it . . . It's all afire inside me. It's as if I was being pierced with an awl . . . Why do you treat me like a dog? No one even bothers to give me a drink . . . oh, send Anuta to me!

(ANUTA *comes running in.*)

ANISIA. Ah, here she comes. Go and talk to your pa, Anuta.

PETER. Anuta, girl . . . Ah, it hurts. Run over to Aunt Martha's, tell her, my pa wants you to come over right away.

ANUTA. All right, Pa.

PETER. Wait. Tell her to hurry. Tell her I'm about to die. Ouch! . . .

ANUTA. I'll just take my kerchief and run over, Pa.

(*Trots out.*)

MATRIONA (*winking*). All right, dearie, remember what you have to do now. Go and look everywhere in the house. Look for it like a dog looking for fleas, look all over the place while I search him.

ANISIA (*to* MATRIONA). All right. I feel braver with you around. (*Walks toward* PETER.) I'll put the samovar on for you. You'll have some tea with Matriona. She's come to see her son.

PETER. Good, put it on.

(ANISIA *goes into the house.* MATRIONA *approaches* PETER.)

PETER. Hello, Matriona.

MATRIONA. Good-day, Peter, my benefactor! How are you, my dear man? Why, I see you aren't feeling so good? My old man was very sorry when he heard. Go, he told me, and give him my best regards, he said, bow to him. (*Bows.*)

PETER. I guess I'm dying.

MATRIONA. I can see, Peter, that the pain's wandering all over your body like a beast in the forest. You're all wasted away, my dear. And illness sure hasn't added nothing to your looks.

PETER. I'm dying, Matriona.

MATRIONA. Well, Peter, it must be God's will then. You've taken the Last Communion, you'll receive Extreme Unction. Your wife, thank God, is a clever woman and she'll see that you get a good burial and a good funeral service and everything nice and proper as can be. And in the meantime, my son'll take care of the farm, so you have nothing much to worry about.

PETER. There's no one left to run the farm. Anisia has her head full of all sorts of stupid things . . . Why, I know everything that's going on. . . . My daughter Akulina is a fool and she's too young anyway . . . so, you see, I've built up the farm, put all that work into it and now there'll be no one left who knows how to run it; no one to give orders. I hate to think of it . . . (*Starts to whimper.*)

MATRIONA. Well, you can leave orders . . . I mean, give instructions, if it's about the money or something . . .

PETER (*to* ANISIA *off-stage*). Did Anuta go?

MATRIONA (*aside*). Ah, he's still thinking of that.

ANISIA (*from off-stage*). She just left. You come back in the house now, Peter. Come, let me help you.

PETER. Let me sit here a little longer. It's so stuffy in there. It really gets me down when I'm inside . . . Ah, my heart's so heavy! . . . I wish I was dead.

MATRIONA. God won't take your soul till he's ready, so your soul will have to stay inside you till then. It's up to God to say when we'll live and when we'll die. And so, no one can tell you just when you're going to die. You may still get well and be on your feet again, like that peasant from my village . . .

PETER. No, I feel it'll be today that I'll die. (*Leans against the wall; closes his eyes.*)

ANISIA (*coming from inside the house*). Well, Peter, are you coming in or aren't you? I can't wait for you all day! Hey, Peter!

MATRIONA (*walking off a few steps and beckoning to* ANISIA). Well, found it?

ANISIA (*coming down front steps*). No.

MATRIONA. Did you look properly? Under the floorboards, too?

ANISIA. It wasn't there either. It may be in the barn. He was pottering around there yesterday.

MATRIONA. Keep looking. Look hard. Comb through everything. I tell you he'll die today all by himself: his nails are bluish and his face is the color of earth. Is the samovar ready?

ANISIA. It's just about to boil.

NIKITA (*entering from the other side, if possible riding on horseback up to the gate; without seeing* PETER, *addressing* MATRIONA). Hello, Mother, how's everything home?

MATRIONA. Thank God, as long as there's bread to chew on, we'll stay alive.

NIKITA. And how's the master?

MATRIONA. Sh-sh-sh! He's sitting over there. (*Points to* PETER.)

NIKITA. Why're you shushing me? Let him sit there. What of it?

PETER (*opening his eyes*). Nikita, hey Nikita, come over here. (NIKITA *walks up to him.*) How come you're so early? (ANISIA *and* MATRIONA *whisper something to each other.*)

NIKITA. I finished plowing, so I came back.

PETER. Did you plow that strip behind the bridge, too?

NIKITA. Eh, that was too far out of my way.

PETER. Too far out of your way! It's much further to go there from here specially. You should've done it all at the same time. (ANISIA *surreptitiously listens in on their conversation.*)

MATRIONA (*going over to them*). Ah, son, why don't you try a bit harder to please your master? He's sick and counting on you and you must work as if you were working in your father's house. Rupture yourself if you have to, but do your duty. That's the way you were taught, remember?

PETER. So you . . . ooh! Hurts . . . You get the potatoes out . . . oooh . . . then the women will sort them . . . Ugh . . .

ANISIA (*aside*). I mustn't leave him for a second now. He's trying to get us all out of the way and I bet it's because he's got the money on him and he wants to hide it somewhere.

PETER. Otherwise . . . ugh . . . it'll be time to plant 'em and they'll be all rotted . . . Ah, I can't stand it no longer. (*Rises.*)

MATRIONA (*rushing up the front steps and supporting* PETER). Shall I help you get back in the house?

PETER. Yes, help me, please. (*Stops.*) Nikita!

NIKITA (*irritated*). What now?

PETER. I won't see you again. I'm dying . . . So forgive me, please, in the name of Christ, if I've done you wrong . . . If

I've offended you by word or deed, sometime . . . I must've many times . . . forgive me.

NIKITA. There's nothing to forgive. We're all of us sinners.

MATRIONA. You ought to be touched, son . . .

PETER. Forgive me then, in the name of Christ. (*Starts to cry.*)

NIKITA (*breathing loudly through nose*). God will forgive you, I'm sure. And me, I've nothing against you. You've never done me any wrong. It's me should ask you to forgive me, for I'm sure I'm guiltier before you than you before me. (*Also starts to cry.*)

(PETER *and* MATRIONA *exit,* PETER *sniffling and* MATRIONA *supporting him as they go into the house.* NIKITA *and* ANISIA *remain alone.*)

ANISIA. Oh, my poor aching head! I'm sure he has something up his sleeve now. (*Comes up close to* NIKITA.) Why did you tell me the money was under the floorboards? It's not there, you know.

NIKITA (*crying and answering only after a while*). I've never had anything but kindness from him . . . Ah, and now see what I've done!

ANISIA. Come on, that's enough of that! Where's the money?

NIKITA (*angrily*). Who the hell knows? Look for it yourself.

ANISIA. I suppose you're sorry for him now?

NIKITA. Yes, I'm sorry for him, terribly sorry . . . Ah, the way he cried just now.

ANISIA. Find someone else to be sorry for, can't you? He's treated you like a dog all the time. Why, only a few moments ago he was telling me I should fire you at the first opportunity. I say, if you've gotta be sorry for someone, be sorry for me rather.

NIKITA. Why should I be sorry for you?

ANISIA. He could die before I find the money and then I won't be able to get hold of it.

NIKITA. You'll get it all right.

ANISIA. But don't you know, dearest, he's sent for his sister and he wants to hand all the cash over to her. And then, they'll squeeze me out of the house and I'll find myself in the street. You should help me, Nikita. Did you tell me he went into the barn yesterday evening?

NIKITA. I saw him coming out of there, but God knows where he could've stowed the money.

ANISIA. Ah, my poor little head! I guess I'd better go and look for it in there.

(MATRIONA *emerges from the house, comes down the front steps toward* NIKITA *and* ANISIA.)

MATRIONA (*whispering*). No need to go anywhere. He's got the money on him. It's in a pouch on a string round his neck.

ANISIA. Ah, my poor little head!

MATRIONA. If you let it slip between your fingers now, you can just as well go and fish for it in the sea. Once his sister's here, you can kiss it good-by.

ANISIA. Yes, that's true. She's coming. What am I to do? Ah, my poor, aching head!

MATRIONA. What can you do? Look, the samovar's boiling. So go and make him a nice cup o' tea. (*Whispering.*) Put the whole paper in and make him drink it down. When he's drunk his cup, take the pouch off his neck and I promise you he won't tell no one about it.

ANISIA. Oh, but I'm so scared!

MATRIONA. Don't stand here talking, just get on with it and see it's done, while I stay here and keep his sister waiting if need be. Now don't mess it up: get the cash, bring it out here and Nikita'll bury it.

ANISIA. Ah, my head's splitting! How am I to do it? . . . Where shall I start? And then, I . . . I . . .

MATRIONA. Stop talking and get going. Do it the way I told you. Say, Nikita!

NIKITA. What?

MATRIONA. You wait here for a while. Sit on the step. There may be a job for you to do.

NIKITA (*waving his hand at her*). The things you women think up! I'll get in real trouble if I go on listening to you. The hell with you after all. I guess I'll go and get the potatoes out like he told me.

MATRIONA (*stopping him, catching him by the sleeve*). Stay here, wait like I told you!

(*Enter* ANUTA.)

ANISIA. Well, where's Aunt Martha?

ANUTA. She was over at her daughter's vegetable patch. She's coming, she says.

ANISIA. What'll we do when she comes?

MATRIONA. Hurry up and do what I told you.

ANISIA. Well, I don't know what I'm doing any more myself. Everything's mixed up in my head. Hey, Anuta, be a good girl and go and mind the calves—I'm afraid they'll run off all over the place. Oh, I really don't know if I can go through with it.

MATRIONA. Go, the samovar's boiling away, I'm sure.

ANISIA. Oh, my poor little head!   (*Exits*)

MATRIONA (*left alone with* NIKITA; *walking up to him*). Well, well, my boy. (*Sits down next to him.*) We should give plenty of thought to your affairs now, not just hope things'll take care of themselves somehow.

NIKITA. What are you talking about? What affairs?

MATRIONA. Well, the affairs that will pay for your life on this earth, son.

NIKITA. Other people manage to stay alive and I guess I'll manage like them.

MATRIONA. The old man won't live through the day, you know.

NIKITA. Well, if he dies, may he rest in peace. But where do I come in?

MATRIONA (*watching the house door all the time she is talking*). Eh, son, one must think of the living first and it takes quite a bit of brains, believe me! If only you knew all the trouble I've gone through for your sake. How much I've had to run around to assure your future! See that you never forget your mother and take good care of her as long as she lives.

NIKITA. What's all this trouble you've taken for me?

MATRIONA. I did it because I want you to have a good life and a safe future. You know Ivan Moseich? I went over to see him the other day and I says to him, "could you please explain a certain business to me. Suppose," I says, "there's a widower who, let's say, marries a second time. Now, suppose," I says to him, "there are only two children: one from each wife, like. Now," I asked him, "suppose that man dies, what happens if the widow marries another fellow? Could that other fellow come into the house and run the farm and when the time comes, marry off the dead man's daughters and still hold on to the farm himself?" "That can be arranged," he told me, "but it takes quite a bit of finagling and quite some money, too. Without money," he says, "it's better to forget the whole thing right away."

NIKITA (*laughing*). Yes, all he wants is for people to fork out! Everyone seems to like money nowadays!

MATRIONA. Well, so, sonny, I told him all about our business. "First of all," Ivan Moseich says, "your son must register as a peasant of that village. That'll take some money," he says, "to stand drinks to the village elders and all that, so as to make them eager to help him. Everything," he warned me, "must be done after plenty of thinking." Now look at that, Nikita. (*Produces a piece of paper from under her kerchief.*) He's written it out himself. You're literate, son, so read it for your mother. (NIKITA *reads;* MATRIONA *watches him.*)

NIKITA. It's just a document like any other. Nothing so special about it.

MATRIONA. No, you listen first to what Ivan Moseich told me: "Above all, woman," he said, "she must get hold of that money. If she don't, they won't let her marry the lad. The money," Moseich says, "is the key to everything in this business." So let's see the thing through to the end, son.

NIKITA. But what's all that to me? It's her money not mine, so let her worry about it herself.

MATRIONA. What a thing to say, my boy! You don't really think a woman like her can work it out all by herself, do you? And even if she does get hold of the money, she won't know what to do with it after that. You're a man, after all, you could tell her, put the money away for her, or whatever's best. You know yourself, you have more brains than her when it really comes down to it.

NIKITA. Ah, you women! The things you get yourselves into!

MATRIONA. The things we get ourselves into! Now, what I want is for you to hold the money. Then you'll hold her. That way, even if she does try to make things difficult one day, you can tell her where she gets off.

NIKITA. The hell with the lot of you, I don't want nothing to do with it all.

ANISIA (*very pale, rushing out of the house and around the corner toward* MATRIONA). It was on him all right, the money. Here it is. (*Shows it under her apron.*)

MATRIONA. Give it to Nikita. He'll bury it for you.

NIKITA. All right, give it me then.

ANISIA. Oh, my poor head! Well, I think I'd better do it myself. (*Walks toward the gate.*)

MATRIONA (*grabbing her by the arm*). Where are you going? They'll find out, you know! Look, his sister's coming. You'd better hand it over to Nikita. He'll know where to hide it for you. Ah, what a scatterbrain you are, my girl!

ANISIA (*stopping in hesitation*). Ah, my head!

NIKITA. So, why don't you hand it over to me? I'll stow it away for you somewhere.

ANISIA. Where?

NIKITA (*laughing*). You don't trust me then?

(*Enter* AKULINA, *carrying the washing.*)

ANISIA. Ah, my poor head is splitting. (*Gives* NIKITA *the money.*) You'd better be careful, Nikita.

NIKITA. What are you afraid of? I'll hide it so I'll never be able to find it again myself.   (*Exits.*)

ANISIA (*standing stiffly and looking frightened*). Oh! What if he . . .

MATRIONA. Is he dead?

ANISIA. Yes, he's dead all right. He didn't stir when I took it off him.

MATRIONA. You'd better go inside, Akulina's coming.

ANISIA. Well, I've committed the sin now. . . . But what'll happen to the money?

MATRIONA. Don't keep on about it. Go into the house, now Martha's coming too.

(MARTHA *approaches from one side,* AKULINA *from the other.*)

MARTHA (*to* AKULINA). I'd have come sooner but I was at my daughter's. Well, how's Peter? Is he really dying?

AKULINA (*putting down the washing*). I don't know. I was at the river.

MATRIONA. I'm Nikita's mother, my dear, I came over from Zuyevo. Ah, he's been suffering something terrible, your brother, dear. He came out himself and said, "Go get my sister because," he says . . . Wait, perhaps it's all over by now?

(ANISIA *rushes out of the house, grabs hold of a post and wails.*)

ANISIA. Ooooh! . . . oh-oh-oh! . . . Why have you left me behind, wretched widow that I am? Oooooh! . . . I'll be all alone for the rest of my life, for there's nothing left for me now he's closed his eyes, ah-ah-ah . . .

(NEIGHBOR *arrives; she and* MATRIONA *support* ANISIA *by her arms.* AKULINA *and* MARTHA *go into the house. A crowd gathers in front of the house.*)

A MAN FROM THE CROWD. We must call the old women to lay out the body.

MATRIONA (*rolling up her sleeves.*) Is there any water in the kettle? I think there must still be some in the samovar, too. I guess I'll get down to the job myself.

CURTAIN

ACT III

Nine months later. Winter. Peter's house. Anisia, shabbily dressed, sits at the loom, weaving. Anuta sits on the stove-bench. Enter Mitrich, an old farmhand.

MITRICH (*slowly removing his overcoat*). Is the master back yet?

ANISIA. What d'you want?

MITRICH. Has Nikita come back from town?

ANISIA. Uh-uh.

MITRICH. Must be having himself a wild time there. Ah, God!

ANISIA. You through at the threshing floor?

MITRICH. Sure. I cleared everything up and covered it with straw. I don't like doing a job halfway. But good God, it's time he was back, the master! (*Stands, poking at his calluses.*)

ANISIA. What's the hurry? He has money and he's having himself a time, I'm sure. I bet he's got himself some hussy, too . . .

MITRICH. Well, I don't blame him having a good time if he can pay for it. But Akulina, why did *she* go to town?

ANISIA. I don't know what came over her. You'd better ask her.

MITRICH. Well, I guess anybody can find anything in town as long as he has money.

ANUTA. I heard him say with my own ears, Ma, "I'll buy you a shawl," he said to her. Cross my heart, Ma. "You'll pick it out yourself," he even said. And you should've seen how she fixed herself up—velvet jacket, French kerchief and all that.

ANISIA. I know how it is—she loses all shame as soon as she steps out of the door, the no-good slut.

MITRICH. What is there to be ashamed of? Why shouldn't she have a good time too if she can afford it? Ah, bless my heart! Are we going to eat soon? (ANISIA *does not answer.*) All right, I'll warm myself up a bit in the meantime. (*Climbs onto the stove-bench.*) Oh Lord, Mother of God and Saint Nicholas!

(*Enter* NEIGHBOR.)

NEIGHBOR. I see your man isn't back yet?

ANISIA. No.

NEIGHBOR. He ought to be back by now. Perhaps he stopped at our inn, you know. My sister tells me there're lots of sleighs from town standing outside.

ANISIA. Hey, Anuta!

ANUTA. What is it, Ma?

ANISIA. Be a good girl and run over to the inn. See whether he's got lost there, drunk as he is.

ANUTA (*jumping down from the stove-bench and putting on her coat*). All right.

NEIGHBOR. Did he take Akulina along with him, too?

ANISIA. Sure. Otherwise he wouldn't have gone at all. It was because of her he found himself some business there. I must go to the bank, he says to me, there's some money for me there. But I know it was just because of her he went.

NEIGHBOR (*shaking her head*). Yes, looks bad all right. (*Silence.*)

ANUTA (*from the doorway*). And if I find him at the inn, what?

ANISIA. Just see whether he's there.

ANUTA. All right, won't take me a minute.   (*Exits.*)
(*Long silence.*)

MITRICH (*growling*). Ah, merciful God, ah, Saint Nicholas!

NEIGHBOR (*with a start*). Oh! He scared me! Who's that anyway, Anisia?

ANISIA. Why this is Mitrich, our farmhand.

NEIGHBOR. He gave me a real scare, you know. But tell me, Anisia, is it true what I heard—that matchmakers have been coming about Akulina?

ANISIA (*getting up from the loom and sitting down at the table*). Well, there was someone from Dedlovo village inquired once but they must've heard things 'cause they never came back. Anyway, who'd want to marry a creature like her?

NEIGHBOR. I understand there were the Lizunovs from Zuyevo, too? Is that right?

ANISIA. Yes, they did send someone but it didn't work out. He won't even let them in.

NEIGHBOR. Well, I think it'd be a good thing if she got married.

ANISIA. She sure should. You can't imagine, dear, how much I'd like to get her out of the house, but nothing seems to work. He doesn't want her to go and she doesn't want to go either. Guess he hasn't had his fill of the beauty yet.

NEIGHBOR. Ah, it's real sinful, when you think he's her step-father, after all.

ANISIA. Let me tell you, friend, they got me where they want me. They've put it over on me so cleverly that I can't say a word. I never noticed nothing when I married him, never suspected a thing, and they had it all worked out already.

NEIGHBOR. Ah, what a business!

ANISIA. And as time went by it got worse. They go away and stay together out of my sight. Yes, dear, I'm real sick and tired of my life. And the worst of it is I love him.

NEIGHBOR. Yes, I can see it must be tough.

ANISIA. And it hurts me, dear, that it's him makes me suffer like that. Yes, it hurts something terrible at times!

NEIGHBOR. I've heard too that he's getting a bit too free with his hands lately. That so?

ANISIA. He sure is rough sometimes. Before, when he got plastered, he'd be real nice; he liked me even when he was drunk. But now when he's got a few drinks in him he goes straight for me, wants to trample me underfoot. The other day, he caught me by the hair and I was lucky to get away from him. As to that hussy, she's more poisonous than any snake. I don't even understand why such vicious sluts should be allowed to live on earth at all.

NEIGHBOR. Ah, Anisia, it breaks my heart to see what you've become. It must be terrible for you. You let that beggar into your house and now he treats you like dirt. Why don't you try to pull him down a peg or two?

ANISIA. Can't, my dear. How can I fight against my own heart? My first husband was a pretty stern sort of fellow but still, I could twist him round my finger any way I wanted. But with this one, I can't do a thing. As soon as I set eyes on him, my heart goes all atremble and I haven't the courage to stand up to him. I'm like a wet hen when he's around.

NEIGHBOR. Ah, dearie, I can see they've put a spell on you. I heard Matriona goes in for that sort of business, so I suspect it must be her.

ANISIA. I've suspected something like that myself for quite a while. There're times, for instance, when I hate him so much I feel I'd like to tear him apart if I had a chance but then, when I see him, my heart just melts.

NEIGHBOR. There's no doubt then, there must be witchcraft in it, and this way, it doesn't take long to make a person waste away. When I look at you now, I can't help wondering where so much of you has gone.

ANISIA. My legs have grown thin like bean poles . . . And look at that stupid slut Akulina! She used to be untidy and ragged and dirty, but look at her now! She's puffed up like a bubble, and she's all fancy and dressed up. And she's got a notion in her head that she's mistress of the house. "The farm," she says, "the house, belong to me because my pa said it'd be mine when I got married." And you should see how mean she's become: sometimes, when she loses her temper, she tears straw from the thatching.

NEIGHBOR. Ah, what a set-up, Anisia dear! And to think there're folks who envy you: "She's rich," they say. But I say tears run just as free whether there's gold around or not.

ANISIA. I'm a fine one to envy! And even when it comes to the money—it won't last too long. It's something terrible how he squanders it right and left.

NEIGHBOR. But as to that, you don't have to let him spend it like that. It's yours after all, not his.

ANISIA. Ah, if you knew the whole story! You see, I'm paying now for a blunder I made at the start.

NEIGHBOR. If I were in your shoes, dearie, I'd go straight and make a complaint. He just has no legal right to squander your money like that.

ANISIA. People don't bother with legal rights no more these days.

NEIGHBOR. Ah, dear, when I look at you, I see how weak you've grown.

ANISIA. I sure have, dearie, I sure have. He's twisted me the way he wanted and I've got no strength left. I don't even know what I want any more myself. Ah, my poor, poor little head!

NEIGHBOR. I think someone's coming this way. (*They listen. The door opens and* AKIM *enters.*)

AKIM (*crossing himself, knocking snow from his boots and removing his overcoat*). God bless this house! How are you, Anisia? Hello, dear woman.

ANISIA. Hello, Pa. Have you come straight from home? Come in, take off your things.

AKIM. You see, what happened—I says to myself, why, I'd like to go and see my son, I says. So I ate my dinner and started out, but with this snow, it was hard going, see what I mean, and so I got here later than I thought. And where's my son? Is Nikita home? Where is he?

ANISIA. He isn't here. He went to town.

AKIM (*sitting down on a bench*). I have a little business with him . . . I mean a business matter to discuss, see. I told him the other day about the trouble . . . My horse is through, see what I mean? So, I guess I'll have to get a horse, any horse at all . . . And that's what I came about, see.

ANISIA. Yes, Nikita told me about it. You talk to him when he gets here. (*Gets up.*) Let's have some supper; he'll be back any time now. Hey, Mitrich, come, let's eat our supper.

MITRICH (*waking up and growling*). What?

ANISIA. Supper.

MITRICH. Ah, dear God, ah, Saint Nicholas, ah . . .

NEIGHBOR. I guess I'll be on my way. Good-night, folks!

(*Exits.*)

MITRICH (*getting down from stove-bench*). Ah, dear, dear God, never knew I'd dozed off. Hey, how are you, Akim?

AKIM. 'Lo, Mitrich! What're you—I mean, how come you're here?

MITRICH. I work for your son Nikita and so I live here now.

AKIM. You don't say! So you're working for Nikita now? I see.

MITRICH. Yes. You know, when I worked for that merchant in town, I drank all I had, everything went down the drain and so I had to find a place to live back here in the village. So I hired myself out as a hand. (*Yawns and stretches.*) Ah, dear, dear God, that's life, I guess.

AKIM. Well, Nikita must have his hands full, I mean, must have lots of work if he hired a hand, I mean.

ANISIA. What work? He could manage all right if he put his mind to it. But the trouble is he has his head full of other things.

MITRICH. Well, he has money, so why shouldn't he take it a bit easy?

AKIM. That, I say, is all wrong, all, all wrong, I say. A man has no business letting himself go like that.

ANISIA. That's just the trouble—he's let himself go. He's let himself go something terrible lately.

AKIM. I hoped things would get better with him, I mean, and I see it's worse than ever it was . . . Riches destroy a man, that's what I say.

MITRICH. Too much rich food spoils a dog, so how'd you want a man not to get spoiled when he has it too good. . . . Take me, for instance: I had it too easy at that merchant's. Once I stayed drunk for a whole three weeks without ever sobering up. In the end, I sold my last jacket and drank that up, too. But when I had nothing left, I stopped, and now I've sworn off it. The hell with the booze.

AKIM. And what's happened to your wife—I mean where is she?

MITRICH. My wife, she fixed herself fine: she hangs around the tavern in town and gets people to pay for her booze and her grub, too. And you should see her now! She ain't a pretty sight, I can tell you—she's lost one eye and the other's blackened and her whole mug is kind of twisted to one side. And so, that way, she has enough to eat and drink. If she was sober, she'd never get her teeth into no pies.

AKIM. But . . . but what is this? How can you, I mean . . .

MITRICH. What else is there for the wife of an old soldier? That's the right place for her.

(*Silence.*)

AKIM (*to* ANISIA). What'd Nikita go to town for? I mean, what's he doing there, selling something or what?

ANISIA (*having set the table, handing the food around*). No, he didn't take nothing to sell with him. He's gone to the bank to get some money.

AKIM (*helping himself to some food*). Why, what d'you want to do with your money? I mean, you want to put it into something or what?

ANISIA. No, it's just the interest he's gone to pick up, twenty or thirty rubles that are due us.

AKIM. Why does he pick up that money? Why don't he just leave it in the bank? If he takes money today, he'll take it again tomorrow, and another time yet, and like that he'll take out every kopek he has.

ANISIA. But that's the extra. The principal is all there, untouched.

AKIM. Untouched? What d'you mean, untouched? You're taking money out of there and you say it's still there and untouched. Why, like that, I mean, you could fill a barn with flour, keep helping yourself and it'd still be there. Well, let me tell you, it ain't untouched, see! You're being cheated, that's what I mean! So he keeps taking money out of there but all of it's still there!

ANISIA. Ah, I don't know how it works. At the time, Ivan Moseich, he advised us like this: "Put your money in the bank," he said, "and that way you'll have your money and get interest on it, too."

MITRICH (*finishing his supper*). That's right. When I lived at that merchant's it was like that: them people put their money in the bank and then just sit by the fire and rake in their interest. That's the way it works, the thing.

AKIM. It don't sound possible to me. I say, how can you just sit and get money? Who's gonna earn it for you, that money, I mean? Don't make no sense to me.

ANISIA. I told you, Pa, the bank gets you the money.

MITRICH. Wait, Akim, she can't tell it proper. Let me explain it to you. Now, say you have some money; while I don't have none, and the spring is coming and my land's idle since I've nothing to buy seed, or say, I can't pay my taxes, see? Now, suppose I come to you and say: "Lend me ten rubles, friend Akim, and when I harvest in the fall, I'll pay it back to you and besides that I'll plow an acre of your land to thank you for helping me out." But you look at what I've got and it may be a horse or a cow or something that belongs to me and you can say to me as follows: "I don't need you to plow that acre for me. All I want from you is for you to pay me three rubles for helping you." Well, since I can't do without those ten rubles, I say, "It's a deal." Then, after I've sold my crop in the fall, I pay you and you get the three rubles on top of the ten from me.

AKIM. Yes, but peasants only do those things when they forget there's a God, I mean, and it's not right, I say.

MITRICH. Wait a minute. Look at it the other way now. The way I told it, it's as if you'd squeezed those three rubles out of me. But now take Anisia here. Suppose her money is just lying idle and she don't know how to use it, being a woman and all that. So she comes to you and says, "Couldn't you do something useful with my money, too?" "Why," you says to her, "I sure could think up something." And then you just wait. Well, suppose before the summer I come to you again and ask you for ten rubles again and again promise to pay you for the loan. So you work out whether I'm still good to squeeze something out of and if you find I am, you give me Anisia's money. But if you find I've got nothing to eat even and there's nothing, but nothing, to be squeezed out of me, you say, "Sorry fellow, I can't spare nothing, go and try someone else." And you yourself, you wait for another man who you think it's safe to loan your money and Anisia's to and then to fleece him after that. Well, that's the way they work, them banks. They send the money round and round and, believe me, man, it's a clever thing, a bank.

AKIM (*excitedly*). Well, I say it isn't right. I mean, it's all wrong. So peasants do something they know themselves is a sin and, I mean, it can't be lawful, see. It's wicked and I don't see how learned people who run a bank can go on doing that . . .

MITRICH. That's the business they like best of all, Akim, my friend. Now, if you take someone who isn't too smart, or a woman say, someone who can't put his money to use himself, well all he has to do is take his money to the bank and the bank people squeeze more money out of the peasants. They have it all worked out real clever, that's for sure.

AKIM (*sighing*). Ah, I see that if there's trouble when you don't have money, there's twice as much when you do. And I still say it ain't right because God made it so we must earn our living by the sweat of our brow, but if you put money in a bank you'll be earning bread without doing nothing for it. That's bad, I say, and it isn't right by law.

MITRICH. Not right by law? Nowadays they don't worry about that no more! And you should see how they clean out the peasants! It's really something!

AKIM (*sighing again*). Well, I suppose that's the times . . .

the times we live in I mean. And it's the same thing with those public lavatories I saw in town. They look so neat and shiny and pretty, just like they was a tavern or an inn or something. But then it turns out there's no point at all to all that prettiness. No use at all, I mean. Ah, they've forgot God. Yes sirree, we've all forgot God and that's our trouble. (*To* ANISIA.) Well, thank you, dear woman, I've eaten enough and I feel fine now. (*They get up from the table.* MITRICH *climbs back onto the stove-bench.*)

ANISIA (*clearing the table as she chews some food*). I wish his father'd talk to him and make him see what a louse he's being, but I'm too ashamed even to tell his father what's going on.

AKIM. What did you say?

ANISIA. Nothing. I was just talking to myself.

(*Enter* ANUTA.)

AKIM. Hi, dear. You're a good girl, I see, busy all the time. It's cold outside, isn't it?

ANUTA. Brrr, it sure is? How are you, Grandpa?

ANISIA (*to* ANUTA). Well, did you see him in the tavern?

ANUTA. Uh-uh. But Ardrian was there and he'd come straight from town and he says he saw them there in an inn? He says pa is plastered something awful.

ANISIA. Here, have something to eat, girl.

ANUTA (*going to the stove*). Ah, I'm frozen. My hands are all stiff still. (AKIM *takes off his footwear;* ANISIA *washes the dishes.*)

ANISIA. Hey, Pa!

AKIM. What is it?

ANISIA. Tell me, Pa, how's Marina getting along?

AKIM. She's getting along all right. She's a smart, hard-working little woman, and she's doing all right, her best, I mean. She's real hard-working and quiet, see.

ANISIA. And have you heard people talking about some relative of Marina's husband from your village and our Akulina? About a marriage being arranged between them?

AKIM. You mean the Mironovs? I heard the women saying something about it but I can't remember what. My memory's getting bad, I mean. But if it's that, well, it's fine. The Mironovs are good peasants, I mean.

ANISIA. I'd like to marry her off as soon as possible.

AKIM. How so?

ANUTA (*listening*). Here, they're back!

(*Door opens;* NIKITA, *drunk and carrying a bundle under his arm and more purchases wrapped in paper in his hand, stops in doorway.*)

ANISIA. Pay no attention to them! (*She has not turned her head as the door opens and goes on washing the dishes.*)

NIKITA. Anisia! Hey, wife! Who d'you think's arrived? (ANISIA *glances at him and turns away without answering.* NIKITA *repeats threateningly.*) Who's arrived? Maybe you've forgotten who I am?

ANISIA. Stop showing off. Leave me alone.

NIKITA (*more threateningly*). Who's come?

ANISIA (*walking toward him and taking him by the arm*). All right, my husband is back. Come on, come all the way in.

NIKITA (*stubbornly refusing to move*). That's better already. But what's your husband's name? Better say it right!

ANISIA. Ah, the hell with you—it's Nikita.

NIKITA (*still in the doorway and refusing to come in*). No, that's plain ignorant. Say my full name!

ANISIA. All right—Nikita Chilikin.

NIKITA. No, no, I want my full, full name!

ANISIA (*laughing and pulling him by the arm*). Nikita Akimych Chilikin! Ah, look at the face he's making.

NIKITA (*holding onto the door jamb*). That's better, but first tell me, which foot does Nikita Akimych Chilikin step into the house with?

ANISIA. That's enough, you're letting the cold in.

NIKITA. No, tell me which foot first? You gotta tell me!

ANISIA (*aside*). Ah, he'll pester me to death this way! (*To* NIKITA.) All right, left foot first.

NIKITA. That's better.

ANISIA. Look who's here.

NIKITA. Ah, my pa. Well, I'm not ashamed of my father. I always show him respect. Hello, Pa! (*Bows, holds out his hand.*) Glad to see you, Pa.

AKIM (*ignoring the hand and looking away*). That's what liquor does to a man. Just look at him. It's disgusting, I mean.

NIKITA. Liquor? Well, I admit that, in that, I've definitely been wrong! I had a few drinks with a pal, celebrating something.

ANISIA. You'd better turn in now, I guess.

NIKITA. Tell me, wife, where is it I'm standing now?

ANISIA. All right, all right, lie down and go to sleep.

NIKITA. No, first I'll have some tea with my father. Go on, light that samovar for me! (*Enter* AKULINA, *all dressed up, carrying purchases.*) Hey, come over here, Akulina!

AKULINA (*going up to him*). Ah, look what you've done to the packages. Where's the yarn?

NIKITA. The yarn? It's there! Hey, Mitrich! Where are you? You asleep or what? Go and put the horse away.

AKIM (*not noticing* AKULINA *and looking at his son*). What's he think he's doing? The old man, he's tired, he's been threshing all day and all that while this one was just getting himself plastered in a tavern . . . And now he comes in and shouts, I mean, he says, "Put the horse away." It's a real disgrace, I say.

MITRICH (*climbing down from the stove-bench and pulling on his boots*). Ah, merciful God almighty . . . what is it? The horse's in the yard? Ah, I'm so sleepy and he's full to the gills with liquor. Ah, Saint Nicholas, ah, Mother of God! (*Puts on sheepskin coat and goes out.*)

NIKITA (*sitting down*). You must forgive me, Pa. It's true I've had a bit too much to drink but that can't be helped now. Chickens have to drink too, after all, haven't they? Forgive me this time and I'm sure Mitrich doesn't mind putting the horse away.

ANISIA. Did you really want that samovar lighted?

NIKITA. Uhuh. You can see my pa's come to see me and I want to talk to him and we'll drink tea. (*To* AKULINA.) Have you got all the purchases in?

AKULINA. The purchases? I took what was for me and left the rest in the sleigh. Here! This one isn't mine.

(*Throws a package on the table and stows away her purchases in her trunk.* ANUTA *watches her.* AKIM, *without looking at his son, picks his footwear up and puts it next to him.*)

ANISIA (*walking out with the samovar*). Her trunk is full already but he has to buy her even more stuff. (*Exits.*)

NIKITA (*trying to act sober*). Don't be angry with me, Pa. Don't think I'm drunk. I understand everything that's going on. So it's all right to drink as long as you don't lose your head. I'm ready to talk to you now and I can understand any business. Yes, and I remember you wanted some cash, Pa, because that horse of yours is no use no more. Well, I'm sure that can be arranged. Sure, if you wanted a real big sum, I might've asked you to wait a bit but otherwise, I'm sure I can help you, see!

AKIM (*fiddling with his footwear*). Eh, son, liquor thaws a man out and the thaw's a bad time for traveling, you know . . .

NIKITA. Why d'you say that? Because you think there's no point talking to a man who's had one too many? Well, you needn't worry. We'll have some tea and you'll see I can put all your affairs straight. Promise you I can.

AKIM (*shaking his head*). Eh, I mean, not this way . . .

NIKITA. You want money? Here is it. (*Takes his wallet out of his pocket, flashes a few bills, offers* AKIM *one.*) Here, take this ten rubles for your horse. I can't let my own pa down, can I? Never, 'cause you're my parent! Here, take it and that's all there is to it. I don't grudge it you! (*Gets up, pushing the bill into* AKIM's *hand.* AKIM *doesn't take it.* NIKITA *seizes him by the sleeve.*) Take it I tell you, since I'm giving it you!

AKIM. I can't take it, son, and I can't talk to you because I don't like the way you are . . . the way you act, I mean.

NIKITA. No, I won't let you . . . take it! (*Thrusts the bill into* AKIM's *hand.*)

(*Enter* ANISIA. *Stops in the middle of the room.*)

ANISIA. Ah, take it, Father, he won't leave you alone till you do.

AKIM (*taking money and shaking his head*). Ah, I mean, it's the liquor not the man who gave me that . . .

NIKITA. Now that's better. If you give it back to me some day, fine; and if you don't, fine too, and God bless you. That's the way I am. (*Catches sight of* AKULINA.) Here, Akulina, show the presents I bought for you.

AKULINA. What?

NIKITA. The presents! Let's see them. I guess Anuta'd like to have a look at them. Undo that shawl. Give it here.

AKIM. Eh, it makes me sick to the stomach just to look at it! (*Climbs on the stove-bench.*)

AKULINA (*getting the presents and putting them on the table*). Here. But what's there to look at?

ANUTA. Ah, it's real pretty! Stepanida's has nothing on it.

AKULINA. Stepanida's? Stepanida's is lousy compared with this one. (*Growing excited and unwrapping the shawl.*) Just look how fine it is. It's French, you know.

ANUTA. And this cotton is awful nice, too! Mother has a dress with a pattern like that but a bit lighter and the background's sky-blue. Yours is lovely, though!

NIKITA. So, you see! (ANISIA *walks angrily into storeroom and emerges with tablecloth and the samovar chimney. Comes up to the table.*)

ANISIA. Ah, damn you, all these things on the table! How can I set it for tea?

NIKITA. Just have a look at these presents yourself!

ANISIA. What is there to look at? I've seen enough of that as it is! Take it away! (*Sweeps the shawl on the floor with the back of her hand.*)

AKULINA. What's come over you? Throw your own things around, not mine! (*Picks up shawl.*)

NIKITA. Look, Anisia, look!

ANISIA. What d'you want me to look at?

NIKITA. Why, you thought I'd forgot you! Look at this! (*Shows her a package, then sits on it.*) That's a present for you. Only you have to earn it first. So tell me, wife, where am I sitting now?

ANISIA. Come on, stop fooling around. I'm not afraid of you. Whose money do you think you're buying yourself drinks with, and presents for your fat slut? It's my money, isn't it?

AKULINA. What do you mean, it's yours? Sure you tried to steal it but you didn't get the chance. Get out of my way now! (*Wants to go by and pushes* ANISIA.)

ANISIA. What do you mean, pushing like that? I'll show you! I'll do the pushing.

AKULINA. You'll show me? Well, go ahead! (*Advances toward her.*)

NIKITA (*stepping between them*). Come on, come on, women, stop it!

AKULINA. What's she trying to do? She'd better keep quiet! Or does she imagine no one knows nothing about her?

ANISIA. Knows what? Go on, speak up, say what you know about me!

AKULINA. I know the whole dirty business about you.

ANISIA. Why, you whore, you're going with another woman's husband, remember!

AKULINA. Why, you killed your husband, you remember that, too!

ANISIA (*throwing herself on* AKULINA). You filthy liar!

NIKITA (*holding her*). Stop it! Anisia, have you forgotten?

ANISIA. Stop threatening me. I'm not afraid!

NIKITA. Out with you! (*Turns her and tries to push her out of the room.*)

ANISIA. I won't go! (NIKITA *keeps pushing;* ANISIA *starts to cry, holding on to the door jamb.*) What now? Is he trying to push me out of my own house? Just wait, you dirty rat. I'll find a way to cope with you! Just wait!

NIKITA. Get out, I tell you, and don't you dare come back!

ANISIA. I'm going straight to the village elder, to the police!

NIKITA. I said out! (*Pushes her out of the door.*)

ANISIA (*from outside*). I'll hang myself.

NIKITA. You won't.

ANUTA. Oh, Mother, Ma, Ma, Mother . . . (*Starts to cry.*)

NIKITA. Now she knows how much I'm afraid of her. And you, what're you bawling like that for? She'll be back, you'll see. Go and see if the samovar's ready.   (*Exit* ANUTA.)

AKULINA (*picking up her shawl*). Look at that! She's messed it all up, the bitch! Wait, I'll cut her jacket to ribbons now, mark my words, I will!

NIKITA. Well, so I kicked her out, didn't I? What more can you ask?

AKULINA. She's messed up my new shawl! Ah, if she hadn't left, the bitch, I'd have gouged her eyes out for her.

NIKITA. Stop it! No reason for you to get all steamed up like that. It's not as if I loved her.

AKULINA. Loved her? Who? That fat face? If you'd ditched her to start with, nothing would've happened. You should've kicked her to hell out in the first place. The house is mine and the money's mine anyway. And she goes round saying she's the mistress here! What kind of mistress is she? She's a murderer, that's what she is and if she gets a chance, she'll murder you, too!

NIKITA. Damn that female tongue of yours! There's no way of stopping it! You go on wagging it and don't know what you're saying yourself.

AKULINA. I do know. I won't have her here no more. I'll chase her out of my house. I don't want her around. So she thinks she's mistress of this house. Oh yes? Gallow's meat, that's what she is.

NIKITA. Ah, stop it, for Christ's sake. Why d'you bother about her? Just don't look at her, look at me instead. I'm the master here and it's going to be the way I please. Well, I don't love her no more; I love you instead. I'm the master and I'm free to love who I want! I'm the boss and that's where she is as far as I'm concerned! (*Points to his feet.*) Ah, what a shame, I don't have an accordion here!

> Soup is standing on our stoves,
> In our ovens there are loaves . . .
> And so we will live,
> And enjoy without sigh
> Our life till death comes
> And then we will die . . .

(*Enter* MITRICH; *takes off his sheepskin coat; climbs onto the stove-bench.*)

MITRICH. Looks like the women had another fight, another scrap! Ah, good Lord, holy Mother of God!

AKIM (*sitting up on the edge of the stove-bench and putting on his footwear*). Go on, get back in your corner.

MITRICH (*climbing past him*). Ah, why can't they share him peacefully, them two women!

NIKITA. Get us some brandy, we'll have some with our tea. (*Enter* ANUTA.)

ANUTA (*to* AKULINA). Hey, the samovar's boiling away.

NIKITA. And where's your ma?

ANUTA. She's in the passage. She's standing there crying.

NIKITA. So tell her to bring the samovar in. And you, Akulina, put the things on the table.

AKULINA. Put 'em on the table? Sure. (*Sets the table for tea.*)

NIKITA (*getting brandy, biscuits, herring*). This is for me . . . This is the yarn for the wife . . . The kerosene is in the passage. And here's the rest of the money. Wait, let me figure it out. (*Takes an abacus and calculates.*) Wheat flour, eighty kopeks; vegetable oil . . . Ten rubles for my pa . . . Hey, Pa, come and have your tea! (*Silence.* AKIM *sits on the stove-bench, still fiddling with his footwear.*)

ANISIA (*coming in with samovar*). Where do you want me to put it?

NIKITA. Put it on the table. Ah, stop it, don't be angry now! Sit down and have some tea yourself. Here, have this! (*Pours her a glass of brandy.*) And there's a present for you. (*Gives her the package on which he has been sitting. She takes it silently, shaking her head.*)

(AKIM *gets down from stove-bench, puts on the sheepskin coat, comes up to table and puts down the ten-ruble bill.*)

AKIM. Here, put it away.

NIKITA (*without noticing the bill*). Why're you all dressed? Where're you off to?

AKIM. I'm on my way . . . I'm going, I mean. Good-by, people, God bless you. (*Takes his hat and belt.*)

NIKITA. What's going on? What business can you have in the middle of the night?

AKIM. I can't stand it in your house no longer, see, I just can't, I mean. Forgive me, people.

NIKITA. But why don't you have tea at least, first?

AKIM (*putting on his belt*). I'm leaving because it's no good here, in your house. It's not right, you know. You don't live right, Nikita, and so that's why I'm going.

NIKITA. Ah, stop it, Pa. Sit down and let's drink our tea.

ANISIA. Why, Pa, what are you angry at? We won't be able to look people straight in the face if they find you've walked out on us like this.

AKIM. I ain't angry at you. It's just I can see that my son, I mean, that he's going to lose himself, going to his ruin, I mean.

NIKITA. What ruin? You prove I'm going to my ruin, Pa.

AKIM. Sure, you're ruined and lost, son. Remember what I told you last summer?

NIKITA. You told me a lotta things.

AKIM. I told you about the orphan girl you wronged, about Marina, I mean.

NIKITA. What are you going to dig up next, Pa? What's the point bringing up all that old forgotten stuff?

AKIM (angrily). Forgotten stuff? No, man, it ain't forgotten, you know! I tell you, Nikita, one sin pulls the next one after it and that one the next yet and now I see you're all bogged down in sin. Yes, you're all bogged down to your waist, I mean.

NIKITA. Come on, sit down. Let's have tea and leave it at that.

AKIM. I can't drink tea with you because your wicked ways make me sick to my stomach. That's why I can't drink no tea with you.

NIKITA. Ah, stop that chatter, Pa. Sit down, I tell you!

AKIM. You've been caught in your money like in a net, son. Ah, Nikita, a man can't live without a soul!

NIKITA. What right have you to insult me in my own house, Pa? What do you want of me, after all? D'you think I'm still a kid or something and you can give me a thrashing for being bad? It's not done any more nowadays, you know.

AKIM. That's right, I've heard it isn't. I've even heard that sons nowadays pull their pas by the beard and I say all that's bringing them to ruin, that's what I say.

NIKITA (with irritation). Look here, Pa, we live on our own and never ask you for nothing. It was you came here for help.

AKIM. Look, see, there's that money of yours. (Points at the bill on the table.) I'd rather go begging than take your money.

NIKITA. Ah, please stop it, Pa. Don't get all angry. You're spoiling our party, Pa, and that ain't nice! (Catches him by the sleeve.)

AKIM (yelling). Let go of me! I won't stay here. I'd rather spend the night in a ditch by the road than watch these filthy ways of yours. Tfoo! (Makes a spitting sound.) Ah, God forgive me!   (Exits.)

NIKITA. That's really something!

(Door opens, AKIM's head appears in the doorway.)

AKIM. Come back to your senses, Nikita. A man needs a soul, remember that!   (Exits.)

AKULINA (taking the cups). Well, shall I pour tea then? (Silence.)

MITRICH (*growling*). Ah, God almighty, Holy Mother of God . . . Have pity on me! . . . (*All start fearfully.*)

NIKITA (*stretching himself out on the bench*). Ah, it's damn dull around here. Hey, Akulina, where's my accordion?

AKULINA. Accordion? Why, don't you remember you gave it to be fixed. Look, I've poured you your tea.

NIKITA. I don't want no tea. Turn out that light! Ah, it's so dull, so gloomy here, so dull . . . (*Starts to cry.*)

CURTAIN

ACT IV

A moonlit autumn evening. The yard of Nikita's house. In the middle, the entranceway; to the right, the winter house and the gate; to the left the summerhouse and the cellar. Loud, drunken voices can be heard inside the house. A peasant woman comes out of the door and beckons to Anisia's Neighbor.

WOMAN. Why hasn't Akulina come out?

NEIGHBOR. She couldn't, dear, I'm sure. Here they've come to see her about marrying her to their son, but she, poor thing, is lying there in the unheated summerhouse and won't show herself—the poor dear.

WOMAN. What's wrong with her?

NEIGHBOR. I heard they put the evil eye on her and her guts are all tied up in knots.

WOMAN. Really?

NEIGHBOR. Sure! (*Whispers in* WOMAN'S *ear.*)

WOMAN. Ah, that's bad! I'm sure the parents'll find out about it.

NEIGHBOR. What can they find out, drunk like they are. They're mostly after the dowry, anyway. You know what goes with the girl? Two fur coats, six dresses, a French shawl, plenty of linen and, I heard, a couple of hundred rubles in cash, too.

WOMAN. But I say even money won't put that right. It's a real disgrace.

NEIGHBOR. Quiet! . . . It's the father of the groom.

(GROOM'S FATHER *emerges from the house hiccoughing.*)

GROOM'S FATHER. My, I'm all sweaty! It's real hot there. I guess I'd better cool off a bit. (*Stands fanning himself.*) Ah, I don't know why, but I feel there's something wrong somewhere . . . Well, here's the old woman . . . (MATRIONA *emerges from the house.*)

MATRIONA. I was saying to myself, where's the father gone? And here you are, sure enough. Well, thank God, everything seems just right. I don't believe in boasting when arranging a marriage but I dare say you'll be happy with the deal and thankful too for a long time to come. And let me tell you—you won't find a bride like her in the whole district—there's not another like her.

GROOM'S FATHER. That may be so, but what about money?

MATRIONA. You mustn't worry about the money either: everything she got from her pa, she still has—three fifty-ruble bills, and that ain't nothing to spit at nowadays.

GROOM'S FATHER. Not that we're worried, but I have to look out for my son and see he gets the best bargain.

MATRIONA. I'm telling you seriously, man: if it wasn't for me, you'd never have found a bride like her! Matchmakers came for her from the Kormilins too but I insisted she be kept for you. As to the cash, I know that when Peter was dying, he ordered his widow to take Nikita into the house and give the money to Akulina. Another fellow would have tried to intercept some, but my Nikita turns it all over to her. And it's a nice tidy sum, too.

GROOM'S FATHER. People were saying there was more money than that to go with her. Nikita's a sly fellow, too.

MATRIONA. The pie looks big when it's in another's hands! Believe me, friend, they're giving her every kopek she's got coming to her. Take my word for it—quit worrying and clinch the deal. And look what a girl you're getting!—Something to look at, really!

GROOM'S FATHER. That's right, but just so, me and my woman, we were wondering how come she never got married before if she's such a gem? Is there something wrong with her health or what?

MATRIONA. Her sick? There isn't a healthier girl in the whole district, man! You'd think she was made of cast iron—just try pinching her! Anyway, you saw her the other day yourself. And what a worker! True, she's a bit hard of hearing but one little blemish like that can't spoil a nice red apple like her. And if she didn't marry before this, it's all because of that evil eye. And I know the bitch who's behind it all. They knew a spell and cast it on her. But I know how to counteract it, I do. And I promise you, she'll be on her feet tomorrow. Believe me, friend, and don't have no worries about that girl.

GROOM'S FATHER. Well, anyhow, the business is settled.

MATRIONA. Sure it is and so don't try to back out of it. I've taken a lot of trouble over it all so I'll appreciate it if you don't forget me in the end.

A WOMAN'S VOICE (*from the house*). Hey, come on, Ivan, time to go home!

GROOM'S FATHER. Coming!   (*Exits.*)

(GUESTS *crowd into the passage, then leave.* ANUTA *rushes out of the house and beckons to* ANISIA.)

ANUTA. Here! Ma!

ANISIA (*from inside the passage*). What?

ANUTA. Come here, Ma, I don't want them to hear. (*They walk across the yard toward the barn.*)

ANISIA. Well, what is it? Where's Akulina?

ANUTA. She's gone to the barn. You should see her, Ma, it's something awful. Cross my heart, Ma. "I can't stand it," she keeps shouting, "I can't, I can't, I can't . . ." Just like that, Ma, I swear.

ANISIA. I guess she'll last out a bit longer. Let's get the guests out of the way first.

ANUTA. Oh, Mother, it hurts her something horrible and she's getting mad at everyone, too. "They're wasting their time," she says, "I won't let 'em sell me. I ain't going to marry. I'd rather die." I'm frightened, Ma, I'm scared she might die, Ma!

ANISIA. Ah, I'm sure she won't die. And you, don't go in there. And be off now.

(ANISIA, ANUTA *exit;* MITRICH *comes in through the gate and starts picking up scattered hay.*)

MITRICH (*alone*). Ah, God almighty, Holy Mother! All the liquor they drank and the smell they've left behind! It even stinks out here in the yard. Ah, damn it, I'm not going to clear up after them. Look how the horses've scattered this hay around. They didn't eat, just messed it all up! Just look at this bundle —it stinks to high heaven. Ah, what the hell! (*Yawns.*) It's time for me to turn in but I don't feel like going in the house. I still have that lousy smell in my nose . . . (*Departing carts rumble off-stage.*) Good, they're gone at last, Holy Mother of God! They keep fussing around, kissing, trying to double-cross each other and all that just for nothing.

NIKITA (*coming along*). Hey, Mitrich, go and turn in. I'll clean up here myself.

MITRICH. I guess you could toss some to the sheep . . . Well, seen 'em off?

NIKITA. Yes, they've gone, but it didn't seem to turn out quite right.

MITRICH. A real stinking mess! But what else could you do? It ain't no foundling home here. In a foundling home, they pick up anything anyone happens to drop. They take as many as you want and even give you money for them if you ask. All the woman has to do is to work there as a wet nurse for a while. There's nothing to it nowadays.

NIKITA. You just watch your tongue, Mitrich, better don't talk too much.

MITRICH. Me? What do I care about it all? Just cover up your tracks the best you know how yourself. Ah, man, you sure stink of that liquor! Well, I guess I'll go and turn in. (*Walks away, yawning.*) Ah, merciful God . . .   (*Exits.*)

(NIKITA *remains silent for a long time; sits down on a sleigh.*)

NIKITA. Well, well, what a business!

ANISIA (*coming out*). Where are you?

NIKITA. Over here.

ANISIA. What are you sitting here for? We don't have any time to waste, you know. We must take it away at once.

NIKITA. What will we do?

ANISIA. I've told you already. Now just do as I said.

NIKITA. But what d'you think, perhaps the foundling home . . . It'd be better . . .

ANISIA. Well, take it there yourself if you like. Ah, you're good at making a mess but when it comes to cleaning it up, you sure aren't so smart.

NIKITA. What'll we do then?

ANISIA. I told you: go to the cellar and dig a hole.

NIKITA. But couldn't you somehow . . .

ANISIA (*imitating him*). "Couldn't you somehow." Well, it looks like it can't be done "somehow." You ought to have thought of it before. Now, go and do as you're told.

NIKITA. Ah, what a lousy business!

ANUTA (*running in*). Ma! The midwife wants you, Ma! I guess Akulina's baby must've arrived, cross my heart, Ma! I think I heard it cry even!

ANISIA. What the hell are you talking about, damn you! That's kittens in there, you fool, that're squeaking. Get back in the house and go to sleep quick.

ANUTA. But, Ma, dearie, I was telling the . . .

ANISIA (*taking a swipe at her*). I'll show you! Get in the house, I tell you, and don't let me catch sight of you again. (ANUTA *dashes off;* ANISIA *turns to* NIKITA.) Now go on where I sent you. Or else watch out for yourself.   (*She exits.*)

(NIKITA *alone; long pause.*)

NIKITA. Ah, what a business! Damn these dames! Nothing but trouble with them. You ought to have thought of that before, she says. When was it I should've thought of it? When?

When Anisia first started falling all over me? Why, am I a monk or what? Anyway, when Peter died, I made good that sin, which was the right thing to do. And I had no part of what happened to Peter. Anyhow, plenty of things like that happen. Sure, there was that story about the powders then. But was it me who put her up to it? Uh-uh. If I'd known at the time, I'd have killed the bitch with my own hands for it. Yes, I sure would've. And now, the no-good bitch, she's making out I'm her accomplice. My, I've got to loathe her since then, something terrible. As soon as my ma told me what she did, the bitch, it made me sick just to look at her. So how could I go on living with her? And then there was that business with the girl. She kept throwing herself on my neck and in the end I says to myself if it's not me so it's going to be someone else, so why not? And now, it had to turn out like this. Again, I had no part in it. Ah, what hard luck . . . (*Sits deep in thought.*) Dames are sly. See what they've thought up! But no sirree, I won't go along with that!

(*Enter* MATRIONA *with a lantern and a spade.*)

MATRIONA (*hurriedly*). What're you sitting here like a wet hen for? Didn't your woman tell you what to do? Get busy now.

NIKITA. And you, what'll you do then?

MATRIONA. We know what we'll do. You just worry about what you've been told.

NIKITA. You're just getting me in real trouble.

MATRIONA. What're you talking about? Maybe you think you can back out now? Is that it? You trying to back out on us?

NIKITA. But . . . but it's a human being, Ma. It has a soul, too . . .

MATRIONA. What're you talking about? There's hardly anything to hold onto that soul. And what are we supposed to do with it? If you take it to a foundling home, it'll die anyway and it'll just cause rumors to spread all over the place and then the girl'll be left on our hands for good.

NIKITA. And what if people find out, Ma?

MATRIONA. We're here in our house and we can do it so no one will know a thing about it all. It won't leave a whiff, I promise. Only you'll have to do exactly as you're told. We women, we can't do it all without the help of a man. So take the spade and go and dig a bit there while I hold the light for you.

NIKITA. Why dig?

MATRIONA (*whispering*). Dig a hole, son. We'll bring it out and we'll bury it here quick. There she's calling again. Go on, you, and I'll go and see what she wants.

NIKITA. What, is it dead already?

MATRIONA. Sure it is. But the main thing is to be quick about it. People are still up in the village and they're liable to get wind of it if we don't get it over with real fast. The constable has passed by once this evening already. So son, (*Hands him the spade.*) get down to the cellar and dig a little hole in the corner. The earth is soft there and you can smooth it down afterward. Mother Earth will keep the secret, she'll lick it all clean with her tongue like a cow. So go on then, my boy, hurry up, dear.

NIKITA. Ah, Ma, you're getting me all mixed up again. The hell with you, after all. I guess I'll walk out on you. Then you can just do as you please.

ANISIA (*from the doorway*). Well, has he dug that hole?

MATRIONA. Why did you leave? What have you done with it?

ANISIA. I've covered it up with rags so no one'll hear it crying. Well then, has he dug that hole?

MATRIONA. He says he won't.

ANISIA (*dashing out in a rage*). Says he won't, ha! Does he want to feed lice in jail then? I'm going straight to the police and tell 'em everything while I'm at it.

NIKITA (*horrified*). What are you going to tell?

ANISIA. What am I going to tell? Everything! Who took the money? You! (NIKITA *says nothing.*) And who gave him poison? I did! But you knew, you knew very well! We acted together, you and I!

MATRIONA. That'll do now, Anisia. And you, Nikita, why are you being so fat-headed? It can't be helped, you'll just have to work a bit now. Go on, my boy.

ANISIA. Ah, you poor innocent slob! So you won't do as you're told? Oh no, you've treated me like dirt long enough and now it's my turn! Go, do as I tell you . . . Take that spade and go or you know what I'll do! Get going!

NIKITA. Ah, stop nagging me! (*Takes the spade but draws back with it.*) I won't do it if I don't feel like it.

ANISIA. So you won't go? (*Begins to yell.*) Hey, people! Listen, hey!

MATRIONA (*putting her hand over* ANISIA'S *mouth*). What, are you crazy or something? He'll do it . . . Go on, sonny, do it, dear.

ANISIA. I'll call for help now.

NIKITA. All right, that's enough. Ah, you women! But you'd better be quick if we're gonna do it at all. (*Walks toward the cellar.*)

MATRIONA. Well, it always works out this way, sonny. You

knew how to have yourself a good time, so know how to cover up your tracks, too.

ANISIA (*still angry and excited*). Sure, he was laughing at me with his slut. But this is the end of it. Let him know how it feels to be a murderer, too. Let him have a little taste of it.

MATRIONA. Come, come, don't get all worked up this way. Don't lose your temper, girlie. Just take it easy and have patience. It'll take you much further. Go and see the slut now. He'll do his job.

(MATRIONA, *carrying lantern, crosses to the cellar, following* NIKITA; NIKITA *goes down into cellar.*)

ANISIA. I'll make him strangle his filthy whelp, too! (*Agitatedly.*) I can't get Peter out of my mind, his bones keep rattling in my ears. So let Nikita find out what it feels like, too. And, like I said, I don't care what happens to me.

NIKITA (*from cellar*). Come, give us some light.

MATRIONA (*thrusting the lantern into the cellar and turning to* ANISIA). He's digging. Go and get it now.

ANISIA. You'd better watch him or he may run away, the rat. I'll bring it out.

MATRIONA. See you remember to baptize it first, unless you want me to do it. Do you have a cross handy?

ANISIA. I'll find one and I know how to baptize it. Don't worry about that.

(MATRIONA *remains alone on stage;* NIKITA *is down in cellar.*)

MATRIONA (*to herself*). She sure got up on her hind legs, that woman. But then, she's had to put up with a lot. Well, with God's help, we'll cover up this dirty business and everything'll look smooth and neat. And then we'll marry off that Akulina like nothing's happened and my Nikita will live nice and quiet, with plenty of everything in the house, and I'm sure he won't forget me either. For where would they be now without me? They never could have used their own heads to get out of this one. (*Looks into cellar; to* NIKITA.) Is it ready, son?

NIKITA (*his head appearing from cellar*). Well, what're you waiting for? Since we're doing it, let's get it done without dilly-dallying.

(MATRIONA *goes toward the house door;* ANISIA *comes out carrying baby wrapped in rags.*)

MATRIONA. Well, have you baptized it?

ANISIA. Sure, what did you think I was doing in there? I had trouble taking it away from her though. She wouldn't let go of it. (*Comes to cellar, hands baby to* NIKITA.)

NIKITA (*refusing to take it*). Take it down yourself.

ANISIA. Take it, I'm telling you! (*Throws him the baby.*)

NIKITA (*catching it*). God! It's alive! He's moving, Ma, look! Still alive! What shall I do with it?

ANISIA (*snatching the baby from his hands and hurling it into the cellar*). Strangle him and then he won't be alive! (*Pushes* NIKITA *down.*) It's your job—finish it up!

MATRIONA (*sitting down on the doorstep*). He's so soft, my Nikita, it's hard for him to do it, the poor dear. But what else can he do? It's his fault, isn't it? (*Looks at* ANISIA *who stands by the cellar, looking down.*) Ah, he was so scared, the poor boy! Well, what can we do? It's hard but it just has to be done. What could we do with it otherwise? And to think that people often pray God to send them a child and God just won't let them have one, just sends them stillborn ones. That priest's wife, for instance . . . And here, we don't need it and it's alive . . . still alive . . . (*Looks toward cellar.*) He must have finished it off by now. (*To* ANISIA.) Well, what's happening?

ANISIA (*looking down into cellar*). He's put a board on top of it and he's sitting on it. Must be over, I guess.

MATRIONA. Ooooh! It'd be so good if we didn't have to sin this way but it just can't be helped.

NIKITA (*climbing out, trembling all over*). He's still alive! I can't do it! He's alive!

ANISIA. If it's alive where are you off to? Get back! (*Tries to stop him.*)

NIKITA (*throwing himself at her*). Get out of my way or I'll kill you! (*Grabs her by the arm; she wriggles out of his grasp and flees; he runs after her with the spade.* MATRIONA *bars her way, trying to take spade from him;* ANISIA *runs up the front steps.* NIKITA *turns on* MATRIONA.) I'll kill you too! I'll kill both of you!

MATRIONA. He's acting this way because he's scared. It'll pass. Pay no attention.

NIKITA. What have they done to me? What did they make me do? Ah, the way he squealed! . . . The way they cracked under me, his little bones . . . What did they make me do! And he's alive, still alive! (*Stops and listens in silence.*) He's squealing . . . he's still squealing. (*Runs toward cellar.*)

MATRIONA (*to* ANISIA). He's gone to the cellar. I guess he'll bury it now. Hey, Nikita, do you want the lantern?

NIKITA (*not answering her and listening by the cellar door*). I can't hear him. I must've just imagined it. (*Walks away; stops.*) Ah, the way those little bones cracked under me, krrr-krrr . . . Oh, what've they done to me? (*Listens again.*) He's squealing again, I swear he is. What's going on? Ma! Mother, Mother! (*Goes up to* MATRIONA.)

MATRIONA. What is it, my boy?

NIKITA. Ma, dear Ma, I can't take it no more, I can't! Spare me, Ma!

MATRIONA. You sure are scared, sonny. It's something terrible how scared you are! Go, get yourself a drink, that'll make you feel braver, you'll see.

NIKITA. Mother, I guess it's the end of me, Mother. What've you made of me? Ah, the way he crunched under me; the way he squealed! Ah, Ma, dear, what you two made me do, Ma! (*Moves away from her; sits down on a sleigh.*)

MATRIONA. Go and have that drink, son. It all seems worse and more scary at night, you know. It won't be this bad in the morning, you'll see, and in a day or two it'll all be forgotten, I'm sure. Just be patient. We'll marry the slut off and never think of it again. And now go and get yourself a drink and I'll manage it all in the cellar. Don't worry about it—leave it to me.

NIKITA (*trying to pull himself together*). Is there some liquor left in the house? Perhaps I'll manage to drink it off . . . (*Walks into the house. ANISIA, who is standing by the house door, silently lets him pass.*)

MATRIONA. Go ahead, go ahead, sonny. I'll see everything's done. Leave it to me. I'll bury it myself. Where's that spade now? Where did he throw it? (*Finds it, starts going down into cellar and when halfway in, calls out to ANISIA.*) Come over, here. Hold the lantern for me, will you?

ANISIA. And what about him? Can't he do it?

MATRIONA. He's too scared. You came down on him a bit too heavy, my girl. Don't worry, he'll come to his senses. Leave him alone now. I'll do the burying myself. Put the lantern down here, girl. That's fine, I can see enough now. (*Disappears into cellar.*)

ANISIA (*looking at the house door through which NIKITA has just passed*). Well, you got what you were asking for at last! You had a good time but now you'll taste what it's like to be on the other side of it. You'll lose some feathers, I'll see to that.

NIKITA (*rushing out of the house*). Ma! Ma!

MATRIONA (*sticking her head out of the cellar*). What is it now, son?

NIKITA (*listening*). Don't bury him, Ma, please! Can't you hear, he's alive, Ma! There, there he goes again! Can't you hear him squealing, Ma?

MATRIONA. What're you talking about, son? How can he squeal now? Why, you've flattened him, son. His head's just like a pancake now and it's all smashed in, too.

NIKITA. But what's that noise then? (*Stops his ears.*) He's squealing, Ma. He won't stop! I'm lost, Ma! What've they done to me? Where can I hide myself now? (*Sits down on doorstep.*)

CURTAIN

ACT V

SCENE 1. *The threshing yard. In the foreground a stack of straw; to the left, the threshing floor; to the right, a shed. The shed doors are open and around the doorway, straw is scattered. In the background, the farmyard can be seen; singing and the sound of tambourines is heard. Two peasant girls are walking toward the house along the path by the barn.*

FIRST GIRL. You see, we've managed to get across here fine without hardly dirtying our shoes. But if we'd tried to come through the village we'd be all muddy now. (*They stop, wipe their shoes against the straw; she sees something.*) Say, what's that?

SECOND GIRL. That's Mitrich, their help. He's plastered something terrible.

FIRST GIRL. But I thought he never drank?

SECOND GIRL. Never, until someone offers him a drink.

FIRST GIRL. I guess he came to get some straw. Look, there's a rope in his hand, see. And then he must've fallen asleep.

SECOND GIRL (*listening*). They're still singing the wedding songs so I don't expect they've given them the blessing yet. They say Akulina didn't even wail.

FIRST GIRL. My ma says she didn't want to marry but her stepfather threatened her; she'd never have agreed otherwise. Ah, the stories going around about that one!

(*Enter MARINA; catches up with the GIRLS.*)

MARINA. Hello, girls!

GIRLS. Hello, Marina.

MARINA. You going to the wedding, dearies?

FIRST GIRL. It must be almost over by now. Just wanted to have a look.

MARINA. Won't you call my husband then—you know Semion, don't you? Tell him I'm waiting for him.

FIRST GIRL. Sure we know him. He comes from Zuyevo and he's related to the bridegroom, right?

SECOND GIRL. But why don't you come along too, Marina? Why miss a wedding?

MARINA. I don't feel like it, my dear, and, anyway, I don't have too much time. We ought to be on our way back home, really. We weren't coming to the wedding in the first place, just carted some oats to town. We'd just stopped to feed the horses when they talked my husband into coming.

FIRST GIRL. Where did you stop in town, at Fedorych's?

MARINA. That's right. So I'll wait here, girlie, and you go in and tell my old man I'm here. Tell 'em his wife Marina says it's time we were on our way back, that the horses are being harnessed.

FIRST GIRL. All right, I'll tell him if you're sure you won't come and have a look yourself.

(*The* GIRLS *walk off along the path leading to the farmyard; the singing and the sound of tambourines grow louder.*)

MARINA (*alone; dreamily*). I wouldn't mind going but better not, I guess, since I haven't seen him since the time he threw me over. It's more than a year already. But I'd like to see, like through a keyhole, how he lives with that Anisia woman now. I hear they don't get along too well together. She's a tough, strong-headed woman. Maybe he's thought of me at times. Yes, he was lured by the easy life and dropped me to get at it. Well, I hold no grudge against him; I wish him the best of luck. But it hurt me, then. Ah, how it hurt! Today, it's all worn off and forgotten. But still, I wouldn't mind getting a glimpse of him. (*Looks toward the farmyard, sees* NIKITA.) My, but that's him coming! Why's he coming here? Perhaps the girls told him I was here? How can he leave his guests like that? Well, I guess I'd better go.

(NIKITA *walks up, his head hanging low, muttering something and gesticulating.*)

MARINA. My, but doesn't he look gloomy!

NIKITA (*catching sight of* MARINA *and recognizing her*). Marina, my dear! Hello, Marina! What're you doing here?

MARINA. I've come to fetch my old man.

NIKITA. Why didn't you come to the wedding? You could've seen me and had a good laugh at me.

MARINA. What's there to laugh at? I've come for my husband, that's all.

NIKITA. Eh, Marina, dearie! (*Tries to put his arms around her.*)

MARINA (*angrily pushing him away*). You'd better stop those tricks, Nikita. The time when you could do that to me's over and done with. Now I've come for my man, so tell me, is he at your place or isn't he?

NIKITA. So you don't want me to remember the past, uh?

MARINA. There's nothing to remember. What's gone's gone.

NIKITA. And will never come back?

MARINA. Right, never. But tell me, how come you've walked away in the middle of the wedding? You're the host, after all, and that just isn't right.

NIKITA (*sitting down on straw*). Why'd I leave? Ah, if you only knew! I'm so miserable, Marina, I wish I'd stop seeing and feeling. I just got up from the table and left the guests because I couldn't bear seeing anyone.

MARINA (*drawing closer to him*). Why, what is it, Nikita?

NIKITA. It's something I can't bury in food, drown in drink, sleep off at night. Ah, I'm so, so fed up, Marina, and then I've no one in the world to share my misery with. I'm all alone.

MARINA. No one can live without sorrow. I've been hurt too, you know, and I cried and cried, but then I got over it.

NIKITA. You're talking about something old and gone but my sorrow, Marina dearie, is here with me all the time and I can't get away from it.

MARINA. But what's the matter with you, Nikita?

NIKITA. I've had enough of life and of everything, that's what's the matter with me. I've come to loathe myself, Marina, can't stand myself no more. Eh, my girl, you didn't know how to hold me and now you've ruined both me and yourself. For it ain't no life for either of us.

MARINA (*who is standing by the shed, trying not to cry*). Me, Nikita, I can't complain. I wish everyone was as happy about his life as I am. I confessed everything to my husband and he forgave me and now he never brings it up. And my life with him is fine, Nikita: my husband's a quiet man and he treats me well and I look after his kids, wash them, dress them, and all that. Anyway, I can see he's sorry for me so there's no need for me to be sorry for myself, is there? So, it looks like God has arranged it all for the best, Nikita . . . But what's wrong with *your* life? You're rich . . .

NIKITA. Talk about a life! I don't want to spoil this wedding or otherwise I'd take this here rope (*Picks up the rope from the straw.*), throw one end over that rafter, tie myself a nice noose, put it round my neck, climb on that crossbeam and jump. That's what my life's worth to me.

MARINA. Stop such talk in the name of Christ!

NIKITA. Perhaps you think I'm just kidding or that I'm drunk?

I'm not, you know, and anyway, liquor don't help me nowadays—it's all the same whether I drink or not. It's sorrow that's eaten my heart away and there's nothing left for me to care about. Eh, Marina, the only good thing in life I had was when we were together . . . Remember those nights we spent together when we were working on the railroad?

MARINA. What's the good poking at old sores, Nikita. I'm properly married now and so are you. My sin has been forgiven me, so why stir up the past?

NIKITA. But what can I do with myself? Where am I to turn?

MARINA. But you have a wife, haven't you? So stop looking at other women and stick with the one who's yours now. You fell for Anisia, so go on loving her now.

NIKITA. Anisia? She's like bitter wormwood to me. My feet just got entangled in her like in evil weeds.

MARINA. Whatever she is, she's your wife. Anyway, what's the good talking? Better go back to your guests and send me my husband.

NIKITA. Ah, if you only knew everything . . . but, what's the use?

(MARINA'S HUSBAND, *red in the face and drunk, approaches from the farmyard with* ANUTA.)

MARINA'S HUSBAND. Marina! Hey, Marina, my old woman! Are you there?

NIKITA. There's your husband calling you, go to him.

MARINA. And what about you?

NIKITA. Me? I guess I'll lie down here on the straw for a bit.

MARINA'S HUSBAND. Where is she then?

ANUTA. There she is, Mister, near the shed, see?

MARINA'S HUSBAND. What're you standing here for? Go in and join the wedding guests! The hosts invited you to come in special. So why don't you? The wedding procession will be on its way any moment now, and then we'll be on our way, too.

MARINA (*walking toward her* HUSBAND). I didn't feel like going in.

MARINA'S HUSBAND. Come on, I'm telling you. You'll drink a glass to the bridegroom just not to offend the hosts. Anyway, we'll have enough time to get everything done. (MARINA'S HUSBAND *puts his arm around her and they walk off.*)

NIKITA (*sitting up on the straw*). Ah, now I've seen her, I feel even sicker at heart. The only time I was happy was when I was with her. Why'd I have to spoil my life like that? Why'd I have to lose my head? (*Lies down again.*) Oh, open up, damp Mother Earth, and swallow me!

ANUTA (*noticing* NIKITA *and running toward him*). Pa! Pa! They're all looking for you! All of them, even her godfather, have blessed them, cross my heart, Pa, and they're getting angry at you for leaving that way.

NIKITA (*to himself*). What am I to do with myself?

ANUTA. What did you say, Pa? What is it?

NIKITA. Nothing. Why don't you leave me in peace?

ANUTA. Pa, come along, Pa, all right? (NIKITA *doesn't answer*; ANUTA *pulls him by the arm.*) Go and bless them, Pa. I told you, they're getting angry at you.

NIKITA (*pulling his arm away*). Leave me alone!

ANUTA. Come on, Pa!

NIKITA (*threatening her with the rope*). You'd better run along!

ANUTA (*running off*). So I'll send Ma to you then.   (*Exits.*)

NIKITA (*alone*). How can I go? How can I take an icon in my hand? How can I make myself look into her eyes. (*Lies down again.*) Ah, I wish the earth would open up and I could dive into it and never be seen again. (*Sits up.*) No, I won't go. The hell with the lot of them. (*Ties a noose in the rope, puts it round his neck; starts to remove his boots.*) That's the way!

(*He catches sight of* MATRIONA, *removes the rope, stretches himself out.*)

MATRIONA (*hurrying up to him*). Nikita! Hey, Nikita! Why don't you answer? Are you completely drunk or what? Go and join the guests, Nikita. Go on, my boy, they've waited for you long enough.

NIKITA. Ah, what have you turned me into? I don't even feel I'm a man no more.

MATRIONA. What's the matter with you, dear boy? Just go join the party, give your blessing to the newlyweds like you're supposed to and everything'll be all right.

NIKITA. How can I bless them?

MATRIONA. You know very well how it goes, don't you?

NIKITA. Sure I know that, but how can I give her that blessing after what I've done to her?

MATRIONA. What did you do to her? Why do you have to dig up old memories, son? It's all neither here nor there now and, anyhow, the girl's marrying because she wants to herself.

NIKITA. What d'you mean, "she wants to herself"?

MATRIONA. Well, to be sure, she wants it because she's scared but still, she wants to marry. She should've thought of it before but now she hasn't got much choice. And his parents too feel quite satisfied: they've looked the girl over, in fact they looked her over twice. And then there's the money that goes with her, too. It's all neatly covered up, son.

NIKITA. And what's in the cellar, Ma?

MATRIONA (*laughing*). In the cellar? Cabbages, son, and mushrooms and potatoes. Why bring all that up again?

NIKITA. I wish I didn't keep remembering, but I can't help it and whenever I remember, I hear it again. Ah, what've you done to me?

MATRIONA. What is all this, after all? How long do you intend to go on playing the fool like this?

NIKITA (*turning over on his face*). Leave me alone, Ma. Don't torture me. I can't take any more of it!

MATRIONA. Still, I say you must go in to them. As it is, people are gossiping too much and now the stepfather leaves his stepdaughter's wedding without giving them his blessing. That'll start all kinds of talk. And I say they'll find out if you act scared. A good thief must always walk openly along the street. But you, you're like trying to run away from a wolf and stumbling into a bear instead. No, son, the main thing is never to show you're scared about something, because if you do, they'll get their teeth into you.

NIKITA. Ah. It's you entangled me in it!

MATRIONA. Come now, quit fooling. Just come in, give them the blessing proper and everything'll be just fine.

NIKITA (*still lying on his face*). I can't.

MATRIONA (*aside*). What's come over him? Everything seemed just fine and now he suddenly pulls this on us! It's like there's some spell on him. (*To him.*) Get up, Nikita, get up! Look, here's Anisia coming. She's left the guests too now!

ANISIA (*all dressed up, flushed, tipsy*). Isn't it all going good, Matriona? It's so nice, and everyone's pleased. But where is he?

MATRIONA. He's here, dearie, right here. He lay down in the straw and now he won't get up.

NIKITA (*looking at* ANISIA). Ah, look at her—drunk! Makes me sick just to look at her! How can I go on living with her? (*Turns on his face again.*) One day I'll kill her and then it'll be even worse.

ANISIA. So that's where he is, buried in the straw! Maybe he's had too much to drink? (*Laughs.*) If I had more time, I'd lie down here with you, but we have to go back to the guests. It's a great party going on in the house, you know, a real treat. There's this accordion and women singing beautifully and everyone's drunk. It's real nice!

NIKITA. What's so nice about it?

ANISIA. It's a nice wedding party, that's what's nice about it. Everybody's saying it's not often they've seen such a wedding. Everything's just right, so respectable. So, come on, come with me. Maybe I have had a bit too much to drink but I'm sure I'll get you back there without losing the way. (*Pulls at* NIKITA'S *hand.*)

NIKITA (*pulling his hand away with disgust*). Go by yourself, I'll come later.

ANISIA. What's the matter with you, man? Why're you acting so nasty when we've got ourselves out of trouble at last? Here we're getting rid of the slut that came between us. And everything's so neat and proper and according to law. I can't even tell you how pleased I am. It's like I'm marrying you all over again. And, my, the guests are real pleased, man, and they're ever so grateful, too! They're a great bunch, you know, and Ivan Moseich is here and so's the police chief, and they had nice things to say about us, too.

NIKITA. So why didn't you stay there with them? Why'd you come out here?

ANISIA. You're right there. We must get back to them. It's just wrong for the hosts to be away while their house is full of guests and specially such a nice bunch of guests as these are.

NIKITA (*getting up and brushing straw off his clothes.*) You go ahead, you two, and I'll follow along.

MATRIONA. The night cuckoo has outcuckooed the day cuckoo—he wouldn't listen to me but he does what his wife says straight away. (MATRIONA *and* ANISIA *begin to walk away.*) You coming?

NIKITA. Yes, I told you I'm coming. Go on, I'll be along and I'll give them that blessing . . . (*The* WOMEN *stop.*) Well, go on, go on, I'm coming! (*The* WOMEN *exit;* NIKITA *looks after them dreamily; sits down; pulls off his boots.*) You can just wait for me! Oh yeah? Perhaps you'd better have a look at the rafter first. I'll slip this noose round my neck and jump off the rafter. Lucky I found this rope here. (*Dreams.*) I guess I'd have got over it; you get over anything . . . No, but not that! It sticks deep in my heart and I can't pull it out, whatever I do. (*Looks toward farmyard.*) I think it's them coming back. (*Imitates* ANISIA.) "A nice wedding party," she says. "I'd lie down here with you if I had time!" Ah, the damn, thick-skinned bitch! You can have your fill of hugging me when they take me off that there rafter! That's the only way out. (*Takes the rope and pulls at it.*)

MITRICH (*quite drunk, sitting up, holding on to the rope*). It's mine. I won't let go. I won't let no one have that rope.

I said I'd get that straw, so I'll get it! Ah, is it you, Nikita? (*Laughs.*) Ah, hell, you come to get that straw?

NIKITA. Let go the rope.

MITRICH. No, wait, I promised to bring him the straw and I'll do it . . . (*Gets up, starts gathering straw, staggers, finally drops to the ground.*) Can't make it. It's got me.

NIKITA. Let go that rope now.

MITRICH. I said I won't give that rope to no one. Ah, Nikita, you're stupid like a pig's navel. (*Laughs.*) I like you fine but still I say you're stupid. You think perhaps I'm drunk? Think what you want, I don't give a damn about you. You think I need you? Who me, a corporal of Her Majesty's First Grenadiers? I've served Tsar and country loyal and staunch. But you think I'm a tough old soldier? Well, I ain't. I'm just a poor fellow, an orphan, a lost man. I swore off drinking and now, as you can see, I'm back on the binge. And don't get it into your head that I'm scared of you! The hell I am! I ain't afraid of no one and if I decided to get drunk, that's my private business. And now that I've started, I'll go on drinking without a let-up for a whole two weeks and I'll take the cross from my neck, sell it and buy myself more liquor and then I'll pawn my fur cap and drink that, too. Yes, I'm not afraid of anyone for, let me tell you, they flogged me in the army for drunkenness, and as they flogged me, they kept asking me, "So, will you drink again?" and I kept saying, "Sure I will," because I wasn't scared of those dung-faces. That's the way I am, see? That's the way God made me. But when one day I swore to stop drinking, I didn't drink no more. But now I've started again, I'm at it again, and I ain't afraid of no one. And that's the gospel truth. Why should I be afraid of those mugs? That's how I am. Once a priest tells me the Devil, he's the biggest bragger there is. And as soon as a fellow starts bragging, that priest says, he gets scared right away and as soon as you get scared, the evil one grabs you and carries you off wherever he wants. But me, since I'm not scared of anyone, I feel fine and easy and I can blow my nose in the face of the horned one and his mother, the filthy sow! He can't do nothing to me, so he'll just have to like it or lump it.

NIKITA (*crossing himself*). What was I thinking of doing? (*Lets go of the end of the rope.*)

MITRICH. What?

NIKITA (*getting up*). So you say you shouldn't be scared of people?

MITRICH. Why should you be scared of the filthy mugs? Why, have a look at them when they're in the bath-house. They're all kneaded of the same dough. One may be more pot-bellied than the next but that's all the difference there is between them. Ah, what a bunch to be afraid of! The hell with the lot of them!

MATRIONA (*coming from the farmyard and calling out*). Well, Nikita, are you coming?

NIKITA. Ah, it's much better this way. Yes, I'm coming! (*Walks toward the farmyard.*)

CURTAIN

SCENE 2. *Same as in Act I; now full of people, sitting at tables, standing around. In a corner front stage, Akulina and her Bridegroom sit at a table with icons and a loaf of bread on it. Among those present are Marina, her husband, Matriona, the Police Chief, the Best Man, the Bridegroom's Mother and the Coachman. Women are singing. Anisia carries drinks round and the singing stops.*)

COACHMAN. If we're going, we'd better start soon. It's a good drive to the church.

BEST MAN. Wait, man, the stepfather must give his blessing first. But where is he, after all?

ANISIÁ. He's coming, he's coming, dear friends. Here, help yourself to another glass and don't mind him being a bit late.

BRIDEGROOM'S MOTHER. Why's it taking him so long to come and give his blessing? We've been waiting for him for hours.

ANISIÁ. He'll be along, he'll be along. Don't worry, dearie. Before a short-haired girl has time to plait a braid, he'll be with us. Here, friends, drink. (*Offers drinks.*) Let's have some more music and songs, fellows, while he's on his way.

COACHMAN. They've already sung all the songs. They're waiting for him. (WOMEN *sing; enter* NIKITA *and* AKIM.)

NIKITA (*holding* AKIM *by arm and pushing him ahead of him*). Go on, Pa, I can't do it without you.

AKIM. I don't like . . . I mean, I don't like it this way . . .

NIKITA (*to the* WOMEN). Enough of your singing. (*Looks around the room searchingly.*) Are you here, Marina?

MOTHER OF THE BRIDEGROOM. Hurry up, man, take an icon and bless them!

NIKITA. Wait. All in good time. (*Looks around again.*) Are you here, Akulina?

MOTHER OF THE BRIDEGROOM. What's this, a roll call? Where else'd you expect the bride to be if not here? Ah, he's a funny one!

ANISIA. Oh mercy! But he's got no boots on!

NIKITA. Are you here, Pa? Well, look at me, Christian people! You're all here and so am I, but just look at me! (*Falls to his knees.*)

ANISIA. What are you doing, Nikita, my dearest! Ah, my poor little head . . .

MOTHER OF BRIDEGROOM. Well, I'll be blown!

MATRIONA. And me, I say he's had too much of that French stuff. Come on, snap out of it. (*People try to lift* NIKITA; *he ignores them, staring straight ahead of him.*)

NIKITA. Christian people, listen to me! I want to confess, I must . . .

MATRIONA (*pulling at his shoulder*). You gone completely mad, you? Listen, folks, he's gone clean off his bean tonight. We should get him out of here . . .

NIKITA (*shaking her off*). Leave me, you! But you, Pa, you listen to what I say! First . . . hey, Marina, look here at me! (*Bows to the ground to her and rises.*) I'm guilty before you. I promised to marry you when I led you astray but I deceived you and then abandoned you. Forgive me, Marina, forgive me for wronging you, for Christ's sake forgive me! (*Throws himself at her feet again.*)

ANISIA. What's all the big fuss about, man? That's not the proper thing to do, you know. No one asked you anything, so get up on your feet and stop this stupid fooling!

MATRIONA. Ooooh! I can see he's under a spell. Something's happened to him. Get up, man, and stop talking all that nonsense! (*Pulls at him.*)

NIKITA (*shaking his head*). Take your hands off me! So forgive me, Marina, I'm guilty before you. Forgive me for the sake of Christ! (MARINA *covers her face with her hands and is silent.*)

ANISIA. Get up, d'you hear me! Stop playing the fool! I'm real ashamed of you! Ah, my poor little head! You've gone completely berserk, man . . .

NIKITA (*pushing her away and turning toward* AKULINA). Now I want to speak to you, Akulina. Listen to me too, Christian people! I'm a damned soul, Akulina, and I'm guilty before you. Your father, Akulina, he didn't die a natural death. He was poisoned, Akulina.

ANISIA (*crying out*). Ah, ah, my little head! Why, what's he doing!

MATRIONA. Can't you see, folks, he's raving mad. Get him out of here! (*Men surround* NIKITA; *want to tie him up with their belts.*)

AKIM (*waving his arms to stop them*). Wait, fellows, wait. I mean, leave him be!

NIKITA. I poisoned him, Akulina. Forgive me, in the name of Christ!

AKULINA (*jumping up*). He's lying! He's lying! I know who did it!

MOTHER OF BRIDEGROOM. Sit down, sit down, stay out of it!

AKIM. Oh God, that's a horrible sin, a horrible sin!

POLICE CHIEF. Take hold of him and send for the Village Elder and we'll need witnesses now. We must take it all down. Get up you and come over here.

AKIM (*to* POLICE CHIEF). You wait, you with your shiny copper buttons. I mean, give the man a chance to confess his sins. Leave him, I say.

POLICE CHIEF (*to* AKIM). Don't you interfere, old man. I must take it all down in writing.

AKIM. Ah, you're a difficult fellow. Wait, I'm asking you. Don't come in now with all that writing stuff down. This is God's business, remember. A man is confessing his sins and you drag those papers of yours into it. Ah, man, it's wrong, I mean . . .

POLICE CHIEF. Get the Village Elder!

AKIM. Let him settle his account with God first, then you can do your job too, man.

NIKITA. And I sinned again before you, Akulina, sinned terribly! I seduced you and I beg you to forgive me in the name of Christ! (*Bows at her feet.*)

AKULINA (*coming from behind the table*). I won't marry no one. It was him ordered me to marry, but now I won't.

POLICE CHIEF. Repeat what you said!

NIKITA. Wait, Chief, let me say everything there is first.

AKIM (*in rapture*). Talk, boy, say everything. You'll feel better afterward. Confess to God and don't be afraid of men! Because God, you see, God, I mean . . .

NIKITA. And so I poisoned a man and then I ruined his daughter, dog that I am. She was in my power then and so I ruined her and I killed her little baby.

AKULINA. Yes, that's the truth.

NIKITA. I dug a hole in the cellar and then I smothered the child—I put a board on him and sat on it and crushed him and his little bones cracked . . . (*Starts to cry.*) And then I buried him in a hole and covered it with earth. I did it, I did it all on my own!

AKULINA. He's lying, it was me asked him to.

NIKITA. Don't try to help me, Akulina. I'm afraid of no one now. Forgive me, Christian people! (*Bows to the ground.*)

(*A silence.*)

POLICE CHIEF. Tie him up, men. I guess the wedding is off anyway.

(*Men approach with belts.*)

NIKITA. Wait, you'll have plenty of time for that . . . (*Bows deeply to his* FATHER.) Forgive me, Pa, forgive me, damned as I am! You told me from the start, when I first went astray. You warned me that when just one claw is caught, the whole bird is doomed. But, dog that I am, I didn't listen to you then and now I see things have turned out just like you said they would. So forgive me, Pa, in the name of Christ.

AKIM (*rapturously*). God will forgive you, my boy. He will forgive you, dear boy. (*Embraces him.*) You had no mercy on yourself, so He will show you mercy. Because, God, you know . . . You know, son! . . .

VILLAGE ELDER (*coming in*). I see there are plenty of witnesses here.

POLICE CHIEF. We'll take down his confession then.

(*Men bind* NIKITA.)

AKULINA (*walking up and standing next to him*). I speak the truth, ask me too.

NIKITA (*bound*). No need to question her. I did it all by myself. I planned it all and did it. Take me away wherever you want, I've nothing more to tell you.

CURTAIN

NOTE: Tolstoy wrote an alternative version of the ending of Act IV in which, instead of making the audience attend this grim scene, he conveys it through a dialogue between Anuta and Mitrich.

The woodcuts on the cover of this Bantam Classic are reproduced through the courtesy of the picture collection of the New York Public Library.

BANTAM CLASSICS

are chosen from the whole span of living literature. They comprise a balanced selection of the best novels, poems, plays and stories by writers whose works and thoughts have made an indelible impact on Western culture.

BANTAM CLA

BRAVE NEW WORLD Aldous Huxley...............FC189 50¢

THE IDIOT Fyodor Dostoevsky.......................SC179 75¢

SISTER CARRIE Theodore Dreiser.....................FC6 50¢

LORD JIM Joseph Conrad..............................FC7 50¢

OF MICE AND MEN John Steinbeck..................JC143 40¢

HERMAN MELVILLE FOUR SHORT NOVELS......FC16 50¢

CANNERY ROW John Steinbeck......................JC163 40¢

ANNA KARENINA Leo Tolstoy.......................NC180 95¢
  (Translated by Joel Carmichael. Introduction by Malcolm Cowley)

ARMS AND THE MAN George Bernard Shaw...........AC68 35¢
  (Introduction by Louis Kronenberger)

CRIME AND PUNISHMENT Fyodor Dostoevsky.......HC140 60¢

ALL THE KING'S MEN Robert Penn Warren..........SC167 75¢

WASHINGTON SQUARE Henry James................JC185 40¢

THE RED AND THE BLACK Marie-Henri Beyle de Stendhal SC40 75¢
  (Translated by Lowell Bair—Introduction by Clifton Fadiman)

THE DARING YOUNG MAN ON THE FLYING
  TRAPEZE William Saroyan........................FC105 50¢

THE AENEID Vergil..................................HC108 60¢
  (Edited and with an Introduction by Moses Hadas)

EYELESS IN GAZA Aldous Huxley....................SC93 75¢

HENRY ESMOND William Makepeace Thackeray..........FC90 50¢
  (Introduction by Lionel Stevenson)

SWEET THURSDAY John Steinbeck...................FC103 50¢

FIVE SHORT NOVELS Ivan Turgenev...............SC92 75¢
  (Translated and with an Introduction by Franklin Reeve)

THE HEART IS A LONELY HUNTER Carson McCullers SC102 75¢

REFLECTIONS IN A GOLDEN EYE Carson McCullers.FC100 50¢

THE MEMBER OF THE WEDDING Carson McCullers.FC139 50¢

FOR A COMPLETE LISTING OF BANTAM CLASSICS WRITE TO: Sales
Department; Bantam Books, Inc.; 271 Madison Avenue; New York 16, N. Y.